D1065568

re:skin

re:skin

edited by
Mary Flanagan and Austin Booth

The MIT Press Cambridge, Massachusetts London, England

MIT Press books may be purchased at special quantity discounts for business or sales promotional use. For information, please email special_sales@mitpress.mit.edu or write to Special Sales Department, The MIT Press, 55 Hayward Street, Cambridge, MA 02142.

This book was set in Janson and Rotis by Graphic Composition, Inc. Printed and bound in the United States of America.

Library of Congress Cataloging-in-Publication Data

Re : skin / edited by Mary Flanagan and Austin Booth.
  p. cm.
ISBN-13: 978-0-262-06260-2 (alk. paper)
ISBN:10: 0-262-06260-7 (alk. paper)
1. Skin—Fiction. 2. American fiction—21st century. 3. Canadian fiction—21st century. 4. Skin—Psychological aspects. I. Flanagan, Mary, 1969– II. Booth, Austin.
PS648.S5R4   2007
813'.609353—dc22
                                                                                        2006056675

10 9 8 7 6 5 4 3 2 1

Contents

Acknowledgments

Jewelle Gomez, "Lynx and Strand," first published in *Don't Explain*, by Jewel Gomez. Ann Arbor, MI: Firebrand Books, 1998. Reprinted by permission of the publisher.

Jennifer González, "Morphologies: Race as Visual Technology," first published in *Only Skin Deep: Changing Visions of the American Self*. New York: International Center of Photography, 2003. Reprinted by permission of the publisher.

Nalo Hopkinson, "Ganger (Ball Lightning)," first published in *Skin Folk*. New York: Warner Aspect, 2001. Reprinted with the author's permission.

Vivian Sobchack, "On Morphological Imagination," first published in *Playing Dolly: Technocultural Formations, Fantasies, and Fictions of Assisted Reproduction*, edited by E. Ann Kaplan and Susan Squier, 146–156. New Brunswick, NJ: Rutgers University Press, 1999. Reprinted by permission of the publisher.

Elisabeth Vonarburg, "Readers of the Lost Art," first published in *Tesseracts 5*, ed. Robert Runté and Yves Meynard (Calgary: Tesseract Books, 1997). Reprinted with the author's permission.

We would like to extend our deep appreciation to our families and friends, as well as to the contributors included in this volume. Doug Sery saw that the book would be an important contribution, so thanks go especially to him; Doris Cacoilo and Suyin Looui assisted the work. Kathy Caruso's watchful eyes and grammatical prowess are to be reckoned with. Thanks to all.

Illustration Credits

Illustration Credits

Editors and Contributors

Mary Flanagan and Austin Booth   have successfully collaborated on several projects including the collection *reload: rethinking women + cyberculture* (MIT Press, 2002). Austin Booth is the director of collections for the University Libraries at the University at Buffalo. Her recent research focuses on imagining information in contemporary fiction, theory, and artistic practice. She has published on women and cyberculture, the politics and history of information culture, and information literacy. Mary Flanagan is a New York–based artist and associate professor at Hunter College, and she holds a PhD from the University of the Arts–Central Saint Martins, London (www .maryflanagan.com). In her work she investigates the intersection of technology and the everyday, with a special interest in computer games, activist design, and interactive art.

Rebecca Cannon   is an Australian writer specializing in media exhibitions and artists' computer games. She has produced video compilations, researched open source projects, and created her own digital media artworks.

Sara Diamond   is a television, new media, and visual artist as well as a critic, teacher, and curator. She has led programs in new media and visual art; highlights include establishing the Banff New Media Institute, developing Women in the Director's Chair, creating residencies such as Nomad and Beauty, and television co-productions such as Women's Shorts. She is currently the president of Ontario College of Art and Design.

Jewelle Gomez   is a writer and activist and the author of the double Lambda Award–winning novel, *The Gilda Stories* (1991). She is the recipient of a National Endowment for the Arts literature fellowship and two California Arts Council fellowships. Her fiction, essays, criticism, and poetry have appeared in numerous periodicals, including *The San Francisco Chronicle*, *The New York Times*, *The Village Voice*, *The Advocate*, *Ms Magazine*, *ESSENCE Magazine*, and *Black Scholar*.

Jennifer González teaches at the University of California at Santa Cruz. Her writings on art, technology, and the body have appeared in periodicals such as *Frieze, World Art, Art Journal*, and *Inscriptions*, and in anthologies such as *The Encyclopedia of Aesthetics, The Cyborg Handbook, The Cybercultures Reader*, and *Race in Cyberspace*. She is the author of the forthcoming *Subject to Display: Reframing Race in Contemporary Installation Art* (MIT Press, 2007).

Nalo Hopkinson is the internationally acclaimed author of *Brown Girl in the Ring, Skin Folk, Salt Roads*, and *The New Moon's Arms*. Her books have been nominated for the Hugo, Nebula, Tiptree, and Philip K. Dick Awards; *Skin Folk* won a World Fantasy Award and the Sunburst Award. Born in Jamaica, Nalo moved to Canada when she was sixteen. She lives in Toronto.

Alicia Imperiale is an architect, scholar, and artist living in the United States and Italy.

Shelley Jackson is a writer and artist known for her cross-genre experiments, including important contributions to electronic literature and hypertext. She is the author of the novel *Half Life* (2006), a short story collection *The Melancholy of Anatomy* (2002), and the web fiction *Patchwork Girl* (2005). She has also written and illustrated several children's books. Her short stories and essays have appeared in *The Paris Review, Grand Street, Conjunctions, Fence*, and the *Mississippi Review*.

Christina Lammer has a PhD in sociology and communication. She is investigating minimal invasiveness in the biomedical practice. She has experience in the coordination of research projects with a team of filmmakers and artists, and scientific research experience at the University Clinic/General Hospital, Vienna.

David J. Leonard is assistant professor at Washington State University and holds a doctorate in Comparative Ethnic Studies. His research is focused on projects centering around social movements, especially those contemporary movements addressing police brutality, the prison industrial complex, gentrification, and systematic attacks on civil liberties. His pieces have recently appeared in *Colorlines, Popmatters*, and *The Black Scholar*.

Mendi Obadike and Keith Obadike are a married couple who create music and art. They were both born in 1973. Their music, live art, and conceptual Internet artworks have been exhibited internationally. Mendi is a poet, and Keith is a composer and sound designer.

Melinda Rackham has worked with networked media for the past decade. Her award-winning Web sites are internationally known and her writing appears in many online and print arenas. She initiated and produced the *-empyre-* international media arts forum and was curator of networked media at the Australian Center for the Moving

Image. Melinda is currently the executive director of the Australian Network for Art and Technology.

Vivian Sobchack is professor of critical studies in the Department of Film and Television and associate dean of the School of Theater, Film, and Television at the University of California, Los Angeles. She is also the author of several significant texts in film theory. Her books include *Address of the Eye: A Phenomenology of Film Experience*, *Screening Space*, as well as several edited books including *Meta-Morphing: Visual Transformation and the Culture of Quick-Change* and *New Chinese Cinemas*.

L. Timmel Duchamp lives in Seattle, Washington. Her work has appeared in a variety of magazines and anthologies, including *Asimov's*, *F&SF*, *Full Spectrum*, *Pulphouse: The Hardback Magazine*, and *Bending the Landscape*.

Elisabeth Vonarburg was born in France and immigrated to Quebec in 1973. Her first novel, *Le Silence de la Cité*, was published in France in 1981. *The Slow Engines of Time*, a collection of eight translated stories (half of them translated by the author) was published in Canada in 2001. Her most recent award is the Prix du Conseil québécois de la Femme en Littérature (1988), a one-time literary award given by the Québécois Council for Women's Affairs on its twentieth anniversary.

Bernadette Wegenstein is an associate professor and the director of the Film Studies Program in the Department of Media Study at the University at Buffalo, and currently a Visiting Associate Professor in the Department of Romance Languages and Literatures at Johns Hopkins University. Her first book on the representation of AIDS in the European media was published in 1998. She is the author of *Getting Under the Skin: Body and Media Theory* (MIT, 2006) and of numerous articles on body criticism, performance art, and feminism.

INTRODUCTION

Mary Flanagan and Austin Booth

Language is like a skin, both on the side of the body and out-side the body, between the body and the world, but also of the body, in the world.

—Elizabeth Meese, *(Sem)Erotics: Theorizing Lesbian Writing*

This book gathers a range of creative and critical perspectives on the contentious situation of skin. One's skin acts as a boundary between one's self and the surrounding culture, the surrounding world. The skin is always a significant border, marking age, gender, and race. It has now become the interface to increasingly technological mediation of embodied experience. How is that boundary conceived of in popular culture? How do everyday practices shift the way we see skin? These questions touch on some of the very ways we think of culture and the individual, of identity, of being human. From architectural experiments such as Diller + Scofidio's *Blur* building to the slipping on and off of skin-shells in Nalo Hopkinson's short story "Ganger (Ball Lightning)," skin is used as a metaphor for boundary and permeability. Skin is a physical reality of the body, a covering, but it is also a surface to be written upon or removed. Favorite software applications and computer game characters can be "skinned"; so can knees.

re:skin is a collection of cutting-edge fiction and critical writing that addresses the questions of skin and bodily transformation. Combining fiction and theory in one volume manifests the crossing of boundaries that the volume proposes to be proceduralized. Combining traditional scholarly writing with fiction, and indeed, merging these discourses within discursive narratives and essays, provides a compelling opportunity to gain insight regarding the complex cultural combinations fashioned around skin.

Technology permits us not only to modify our own skins, but to cross skins, allowing us to merge with other bodies or colonize multiple bodies. The twenty-first century demands a new framework for investigating the intersection of the body, skin, and technology. Bodily boundaries are malleable, and the bodily markers that distinguish bodies can be reimagined in unprecedented ways. From plastic surgery to fur implants, from tattooing to skin-graft art, the use of a broad range of technologies to alter the physical body is creating new frameworks for thinking about the body, a tool for empowerment as well as a means to construct alternative, multiple selves. As Bernadette Wegenstein points out in her essay (chapter 4), the corporeal theories that emerge in the late twentieth century within the fields of psychoanalysis, phenomenology, and cognitive science have had a wide influence on contemporary feminism as well as on artistic practices from media art to performance to architecture. This influence has had a long history, including medical experiments on fetuses, "diagnostic" imaging of the female body by neurologist Jean-Martin Charcot in nineteenth-century France, switchboards and assembly lines, pornography—all imaging and communications technologies that have historically subjugated women. Webcams and other intimate network technologies continue this tradition. Plastic surgery and artificial skin techniques are used to create "hypergendered" examples of faces, breasts, buttocks, and pectoral muscles in contemporary culture for both men and women.

Women have actively appropriated such technologies to their own ends, bringing to light and critiquing domination. Science fiction writers, theorists, and artists work to deconstruct historic and contemporary examples of the politics of skin as metaphor, as material, and as cultural artifact. The pieces gathered in *re:skin* claim that the technologically mutable body is neither simply liberating nor limiting; the volume instead offers models—ways of living in, and adapting to, a technological culture. The pieces gathered in *re:skin* explore technologically mutable skin as both a social and creative movement. Skin is the site for the playing of cultural anxieties regarding youth and age, permanence and impermanence, self and other. It is also critically related to artistic work, not merely in the sense that body artists tattoo or pierce the skin, but in the way time is conceptualized. Body art can last a lifetime, yet is critically bound to the impermanent nature, the fleeting surface—a poignant and value-laden gesture about time and our eroding skins. Marshall McLuhan's notion (1964) that all media are extensions of the mind, extending our thoughts and a kind of corporality through new networks, points to an intimate boundary crossing: technology is sometimes literally under our skin and will be increasingly so. At present, media's most popular artifacts form skins around us through screens and projections onto surfaces.

Skin acts as the interface to both the physical and social dimensions of space, and here we focus on the feminist implications of the new malleability of skin as physical boundary alongside the "re-programmable" nature of skin. Is skin all we have? In *re:skin*, the authors conduct a multidisciplinary inquiry into such boundaries and borders of surfaces, of skin, by incorporating and implicating the metaphor, the physicality, and cultural narratives of skin. Skin is a metaphor for borders. Is skin surface or interior? Donna Haraway, for one, rejects the boundary condition established by such a binary: "Why should our bodies end at the skin or include at best other beings encapsulated by skin?" (1991, 178). In its complicated formulations, skin is both boundary and surface, a place where identity is both revealed and concealed. We may wonder, how can such boundaries be mapped and activated? This volume is designed to question the effects of technology and gender in creating the intersections of art and technology and the body. In the pieces gathered here, skin is the ultimate site for negotiating our relationship with the world.

The integration of technological metaphor, media, and the physical reality of the body is explored in this volume through fictional, creative, critical, and theoretical projects. In the speculative fiction tradition, body modification through technological intervention has long been a theme, and as actual technological innovation has increased, these fictions have been incorporated into the physical body, merging physicality and fiction. To science fiction writer Bruce Sterling, we have created technologies that "stick to the skin" (1987, 12). Artists such as Eduardo Kac and Orlan have taken these concepts into their very bodies, molding skin, inserting technologies, and performing the integrated techno-human.

Skin has been a preoccupation of artists, particularly women artists, over the past quarter century. Artists including Orlan, Alba D'Urbano, and Jenny Holzer treat skin both as a surface or canvas, and as a malleable artistic medium. Shelley Jackson, in "SKIN" (chapter 14), inscribed texts and images onto the skin as a way of calling attention to the body as site of cultural inscription. Natalie Jeremijenko (2000) and her Bureau of Inverse Technologies created a project called *Touch* in which a skin tissue culture was grown in a petri dish in the gallery. Here, synthesized human skin functioned to question medical categorization, the lines between synthetic and "natural," and the discourse surrounding representation and identity.

Dutch artist Joanneke Meester has also worked with skin as artistic medium, utilizing pigskins and skin from her own body in her sculptural objects (ABC News Online, 2004). The miniature pistol, a tiny sewed gun created from her own stomach skin, was used as a protest against social violence (figure 1.1). Artists play with skin's dual function as representation (a screen on which to project the interior) and mask (a protective screen that hides the interior). Skin may indeed be the last political frontier for artists. Critics of structure became interested in the eradication of façades in order to expose the framework within buildings, narratives, theater, film, and other arts. The tension/relationship between surface and depth is reflected in the work of filmmakers such as Tony Conrad (*Flicker*, 1966) and Stan Brakhage (including *Mothlight*, 1963, and

| Figure 1.1 |
Joanneke Meester's miniature pistol made of her own skin to protest social violence

The Act of Seeing with One's Own Eyes, 1971), who exposed the structural aspects of their films; video artist Joan Jonas, whose work *Vertical Roll* (1972) revealed the material qualities of video as an artistic medium; and authors such as Kathy Acker, Italo Calvino, and William S. Burroughs, who deconstructed the act of constructing narrative.

Skin has also become a recurring trope in architectural theory; architects are designing architectural exteriors and interiors that control climate and respond to the environment as a means of circulating air and light. Like skin, these new walls are self-regulating, "intelligent" boundaries. Certainly the metaphor of skin as the house we live in is omnipresent in both fiction and everyday idiom. In fact, in much of the writing explored in this volume, the metaphor of the body *as habitat* appears specifically in terms of the *skin as house:* after all, without the skin, the body is simply one more empty space, without defined boundaries. Just as architectural exteriors/boundaries are being talked about in terms of skins, so the body, and skin in particular, are talked about as habitats, the place within which we live, or within which our true self, or soul, lies both hidden and, paradoxically, revealed. Artists and architects are using the notion of layers of skin to explore the layers of materials that constitute artistic media—buildings, sculptures, paintings, media networks. Skin metaphors are ubiquitous in contemporary art and architectural theory. Not only are "skins" of artworks and buildings frequently referred to, but the metaphors and mechanics of skin as the body's surface are applied to artworks—the skin's self-regulation, its ability to adapt to changing environments, its permeable surface, as well as skin's organic nature. Artists and architects are drawing upon a long history of examining the relationship of, and distinctions between, façade and building, surface and depth. What we see in much of the architecture and art referred to in this volume is that the distinction between artwork, body, or building and surface, skin, or façade begins to be persistently broken down and reconfigured.

What emerges in the works collected in *re:skin* is a complex understanding of the ways in which difference, especially gender difference and bodily difference, is marked and constituted. Many of the writers here ask, What constitutes a body? and invoke ideas of switchable body parts or notions of the body as a discontinuous series of networks: open, rather than closed, systems. As Alicia Imperiale points out in her essay (chapter 13), the questions of bodily surface and depth, difference and sameness, and discreteness and continuity are intimately related. Regarding gender and virtual representation, Melinda Rackham suggests that the process of becoming virtual necessitates a selective representation of self that is suited to highly creative constructions of identity. A potentially more realistic expression of one's inner self, virtual embodiments play an important role in the dissolution of gendered oppositions.

Inside, Outside, Surface

As noted earlier, surface and depth, covering and structure, have become contested concepts in contemporary art and architectural theory and practice. Many of the works included in this volume challenge the notion that the "truth" of the self lies in the interior or that subjectivity is found inside the house created by the body. Skin becomes both the boundary and the surface, as well as the place where critical tensions between surface and depth, interior and exterior, are played out. A tongue-in-cheek investigation of the relationship between gender and surface locality, L. Timmel Duchamp's short story about male pregnancy, "The Man Who Plugged In" (chapter 2) explores the use of technology for alternate visions of the body. The narrative is about the transgression of pregnancy and separation of pregnant bodies, the fetus and the mother, and the relationships among the multiple interiors and exteriors of the body. In the story, the main character becomes the first man to attach a "Sieman's Carapace," an artificial container for a womb, which can be plugged into any body via a manufactured maternal interface. Duchamp's story complicates the notion that subjectivity is to be found in the interior by drawing attention to the womb's status as something exterior rather than interior. The narrative provides a biting critique of gender roles as they are both socially and biologically defined by invoking the possibility of a wearable pregnancy; the fantasy of intimacy through biological proximity is complicated and questioned through the disruptive nature of potential new birth technologies. Through the lens of male pregnancy, Duchamp is able to represent pregnancy via the womb as an extra skin, a cover—a removable carapace that invokes feminist theorists' writing on pregnancy and representation (particularly the representations of medical imaging such as ultrasounds) and fetal/maternal rights. What makes Duchamp's story especially interesting is that the fetus is not focused on, but the womb itself is, as well as that which contains the womb, the layers of skin and receptacles of the body, and the interfaces between them.

In her essay "Safety of Skin" (chapter 3), Australian artist Melinda Rackham describes how she explores conceptions of identity and inside/outside dichotomies in her avatar artworks. She finds that human interiors are not fixed, impenetrable, or "hard," but rather are malleable and soft-skinned. Rackham argues that the manner in which we represent ourselves in media such as computer worlds should be equally fluid. Rackham investigates how we imagine our own interiors, the relationships among interior, exterior, and "self," as well as the boundary between ourselves and others, through looking at how we interact in online environments. She asks, "Where is the kernel or seed of the self when the body is composed of pixels? Are the ethereally coded soft bodies we inhabit in machine-produced data space different from the flesh bodies we inhabit offline?" Describing the work of artists who see avatars as more than virtual prosthetic devices, Rackham speculates, "Perhaps this is why users prefer to be represented in human form online, for when online presence has a more physical representation it has a familiar and safe skin, a defined visual boundary." As she points out, our perception of others occurs more often through virtual communication, through mediated and/or networked environments. Avatars in Rackham's account are self-conscious "soft-others" with whom we have symbiotic, even schizophrenic, relationships.

The fluidity of skin (of the self-other avatar) that Rackham explores, and the notions of continuity and discreteness that Imperiale investigates, are further considered by Bernadette Wegenstein in her essay "Making Room for the Body: From Fragmentation to Mediation" (chapter 4). Wegenstein reviews the field of "body criticism" that has evolved from psychology, history, and philosophical traditions to identify the modern body as a "new kind of discrete object," isolated and individualized and eventually "inscripted" by the outside world. Wegenstein explores how new types of body criticism are embodied in contemporary art such as the use of skin suits and flat architecture. Wegenstein examines the work of Alba D'Urbano alongside Diller + Scofidio's *Blur* building and Aziz + Cucher's media art as examples of new interpretations of bodies in which inside and outside merge conceptually and literally.

Vivian Sobchack explores the skin of women in middle age in her essay, "On Morphological Imagination" (chapter 5). The market for plastic surgery is well over a $5-billion-a-year industry and is considered a "natural" practice for women—and increasingly, for men. Sobchack explores the rejuvenation fantasies of American film and the changing technologies of transformation and display. Further, Sobchack addresses the relationship between cosmetic surgery and cinematic realism through readings of cosmetic surgeries. As Kathryn Pauly Morgan notes, "Not only is elective plastic surgery moving out of the domain of the sleazy, the suspicious, the secretively deviant, or the pathologically narcissistic, it is *becoming the norm*. This shift is leading to a predictable inversion of the domains of the deviant and the pathological, so that women who do not use plastic surgery position themselves as deviants against popular trends" (1998, 148). Sobchack examines the magic or fantasy of cosmetic technologies and film technologies, both "technologies of transformation and display."

Transgression

Crossing species has long been part of women's science fiction. Exchanging skin is also a recurrent feminist fantasy. If the obsession with strictly defined and rigidly upheld boundaries haunts Western conceptions of subjectivity, perhaps the figure who lives by crossing those boundaries tells us something about how they are made and how they might be dismantled. Questioning inside, outside, and the fusion between selves and others, the essays and fictional works in this section negotiate the materiality of skin and its permeable boundaries. Imperiale, in chapter 13, expresses this relationship: "There is no material in digital computation, or at least not in the typical consideration of the material. What is digital material? Two such bodies can merge, get entangled, but does some element leave one form to engender another? Does a self-generating system diversify to form only one body, which then goes on to autogenerate another individual in its image in the form of cloning or of natural selection?" The narratives collected in part II explore such entanglement and take the notions of individuality, translocation, and mutability explored earlier to a new level. As Rackham writes, "To be both one and yet completely separate can be a little confusing, almost schizophrenic, when we are more accustomed to a peachy individuality where the self is contained by our skin. Not only has virtual space made us reconsider the mind | body split, it also forces us to reconsider the me | not me dichotomy, removing individuality from the center of the universe. Just as our hardspace bodies cannot be ignored, neither can our virtual avatar bodies. It is a bidirectional relationship, at once into hardspace and into softspace."

Our fundamental understanding of body images and body practices are culturally and historically created. Skin markings such as tattoos, birthmarks, and disease scars have all been treated in cultural studies as codes to be read; or more specifically, we read the ways those markings are read in culture (as certain markings have been used historically to classify people). Skin, as many cultural studies scholars have pointed out, has been frequently understood to represent the soul or character. Skin color, of course, has a long history of being treated as a readable sign that represents the characteristics (intellectual, psychological, and social aspects) of a particular individual or race. Our conceptions of ethnic difference frequently rely quite simply on differences among skin color. The works here challenge these assumptions by exploring gender, racial, and even proposed species migrations.

Elizabeth Grosz (1994) has argued that the body that dominates our symbolic is haunted by fluidity. The "body-in-control" is sealed off and impermeable. Rigid boundaries between this self and its others are the prerequisites to individuality and the notion of the male body as universal. The skin that seals in this body-in-control, however, seals in sexualized and racialized fluids and fluidity. Skin becomes the place where both sealing and permeations occur, where things are allowed to seep in and out of the leaky body. What makes the leakiness of the body visible in these essays and stories, what makes one's ability to both be other and combine with the other, is the permeability of skin.

In her "Fur Manifesto" (chapter 6), Sara Diamond (along with her cat Model T.) describes her research and creative practice efforts to "become animal." Living in harsh

| Figure 1.2 |
Fur patterns

Canadian winters may have led Diamond to appreciate wearing fur, but the patterns produced by animal hides inspired Diamond to question identity, species, behavioral practices, and the boundary lines between "animal" and "human." In her blend of fiction/theory writing aided by witty correspondences, Diamond argues that the strange attractors between art and science, the fluidity of identity, the subject positions and relationships embodied by patterns of fur, and the question of autonomy of subjects, from scientific subjects to animals as pets, must manifest a new kind of relationship between humans and non-humans.

Diamond plays off the recent fad of animal markings on fabric and fashion, treating fur markings as a code (figure 1.2). She asks, "Can we crack Code Zebra?" To Diamond, the "Zebra" is the penultimate pattern set, proof of nature's capability to develop complexity, display, and a visual aesthetic through camouflage. Just as other stories here examine affinities among people and technology/avatars, Diamond examines our affinities with animals. Diamond studies the way software, Web art, and science interact through her project: "Code Zebra (www.codezebra.net) is a software web of wills, in which faux science flies in the face of faux fur. Code Zebra is an intellectual reality drama and Web software laboratory where art and science muse in mutual fascination." Diamond examines how animal prints have become symbolic of a pattern recognition that we rely on for communication skills, as we come to be more dependent on technological communication.

The pleasure of skin swapping and the intimacy of skin are explored in Nalo Hopkinson's short story "Ganger (Ball Lightning)" (chapter 7). In it, lovers Clive and Issy explore each other's sexual sensations as well as larger relationship issues through their Senstim skin-like bodysuits. "The world could stand to have more stories in it told from female, black and Caribbean contexts, and I know what it's like to live inside a skin that is marked as such," Hopkinson has said in interview (qtd. in Mohanraj 2000). "Throughout the Caribbean, under different names, you'll find stories about people who aren't what they seem. Skin gives these skin folk their human shape. When the skin comes off, their true selves emerge," she says. "And always, whatever the burden their skins bear, once they remove them—once they get under their own skins—they can fly." In another Hopkinson story, "Greedy Choke Puppy," three generations of *soucouyants* (clairvoyants) are haunted by both the ultimate freedom that comes from shedding their skin and flying off into the night, and their driving need for the life-breath of babies to sustain their own existence. "Something to Hitch Meat To" highlights the extent to which a person is perceived by outward appearance. The monster skin in "Ganger" figures almost as a techno-vampire, representing both something that parasitically feeds off of humans yet that simultaneously is and *isn't* human. The narrative also invokes the emotional and physical threat of mixing with other technologies and species, questioning the future of humanity and its technologies. A figure that confuses our notions of corporeality with a version of our own selves, a skin (the tactile, erotic organ) that is both us and other, the creature "that is closest to us, seducing us into its erotically charged feeding frenzies, only to be dispelled, even expelled fantasized into some neatly confined unreality of the unthinkable, the undead" (Winnubst 2002, 9).

Skin crossing and transgression in the realm of technologically mediated communication is explored by Australian artist and theorist Rebecca Cannon. In her essay "Perfect Twins" (chapter 8), Cannon examines the work of two different computer artists who explore notions of gender in the construction of identity through technologically mediated communication. As a society dependent upon technologies that allow us to merge skin and transgress boundaries, we still appear to fear such mergers. Noting how the dominance of masculinity in games and gaming culture pervade most virtual environments, Cannon recontextualizes online drag performance to examine transgendered avatars and identities. The physical, sexual, and emotional implications of transgressing skin are explored in this selection of writing.

San Francisco writer Jewelle Gomez writes about body crossing and body merging in "Lynx and Strand" (chapter 9). The story is set in a repressive future culture where body art among many other activities is forbidden. Strand, a corporate worker, and Lynx, an "empath," undergo tattoo experiments that alter their lives. Like Gomez's vampire stories, "Lynx and Strand" is also a reproduction narrative; here skin rather than blood—the act of tattooing rather than the act of vampiric biting—becomes the transgressive act. The sharing of skin, rather than the sharing of blood, becomes the mechanism for reproducing and saving taboo identities.

As noted earlier, crossing species has long been part of women's science fiction. Exchanging skin is also a recurrent feminist fantasy. In her speculative tale of a future art form, Canadian science fiction writer Elisabeth Vonarburg takes the viewpoint of a detached narrator. In her short story "Readers of the Lost Art" (chapter 10) Vonarburg describes the interaction between the characters Subject and Operator in an artistic game—a gambling performance involving the strategic manipulation of objects and bodies. In an era of virtual game playing in which stakes can be measured as separate from lived experience, Vonarburg returns play to the skin. Bodies are conceptualized in terms of lines, shapes, and nodal points in prismic structures, and above all, the value of the skin in the milieu of high stakes futuristic play.

In Keith + Mendi Obadike's "The Black.Net.Art Actions: *Blackness for Sale* (2001), *The Interaction of Coloreds* (2002), and *The Pink of Stealth* (2003)" (chapter 11), the color of skin is interrogated through a variety of new technologies. In one of the works, Keith's "Blackness" is put up for sale on the commercial auction Web site eBay. The artists challenge the idea of the knowability of the black body and the assumed visible nature of material posted online by avoiding the use of a photograph on the eBay site; rather, the artists worked to emphasize Keith's "cultural Blackness." Acknowledging the potential desire for others to possess their own Blackness while playing with intellectual, legal, and social discrimination, this project emphasizes the contradictory nature of social inequities that Blackness in the United States brings.

Mapping the Visual and the Virtual

Skin as a map is a useful metaphor and tool for scholars and artists—maps both provide a way for noting difference as well as establish a sense of self among space, time, and other elements. Maps mark location as well as act as a means to monitor sites of transgression. They are useful metaphors for thinking about technology and the self; after all, in twenty-first-century culture, the self is regularly located, dislocated, and reconstituted. Take, for example, the network. Many cybertheorists have argued that computer networks now extend the body through their complex connections (figure 1.3). The body is itself extended, ballooning like a slippery tent through the world and even to such distant places as Mars. Skin is ubiquitous in this act of extension. It can become a schematic of abstract spaces: flattened, reworked, and reapplied.

| Figure 1.3 |
The "skin" file guerilla.mdl from the MP-Gamer skinning Web site, by iceman. *Source:* iceman 2003.

The works in part III map embodiment issues and the adaptation of the body within technologically driven culture. The notion that the body is a text that can be read is common to cultural studies, deconstructionism, and semiotic theory—and because a text is a surface upon which something can be written, skin and its inscriptions can be read like any other text. Mapping is a motif frequently invoked in writing on gender, race, and performance—skin as a text provides a particular type of terrain. Skin, as a tactile organ, is also a means of communication. One of the reasons that skin is such a rich site to explore, we believe, or one of the reasons that artists use skin, is that skin "signs" are coded in different ways, and sometimes in more ambiguous ways than traditional literary texts.

Skin can be visually perceived as can any map, yet it can also be touched and penetrated. In this way it is a permeable map with characteristics of both surface and depth. Christina Lammer examines the ambiguities of skin in "Eye Contact: Fine Moving Hands and the Flesh and Blood of Image Fabrication in the Operating Theaters of Interventional Radiology" (chapter 12). Lammer partners with a radiologist to probe the relationship of manipulating the body and skin to the experiences one has within that same skin during the mediation between patient and doctor. She argues for a tactile epistemology in medical fields and in disciplines beyond, finding that the visual type of map offered by imaging technologies in medical practice is not complete enough a system in actual practice for accuracy and for intimacy between doctor and patient. Using ethnographic research in the operating theaters of interventional radiology, Lammer maintains that new technologies lead to a bodily interior/exterior split: she utilizes from her material ethnographic research in the operating theaters of interventional radiology. She argues that continual inventions of new technologies in medical imaging lead to a decomposing of how the body's inside is imagined and experienced by patients and clinical personnel.

Skin thus becomes a portal, or a gateway, between separation and intimacy. In her essay "Seminal Space: Getting under the Digital Skin" (chapter 13), Alicia Imperiale explores this metaphor. Looking at the work of four separate artists, Imperiale asks questions concerning space and details the mapping of the body with skin. She further examines the evolution of architectural surfaces through genetic algorithms, and she studies the question of what constitutes a body.

Imperiale's essay explores artistic and technological strategies for mapping the body. Skin in Imperiale's account is not a surface hiding interiority but rather a complexly layered organ with its own interiority. Imperiale dissects the notion of skin as a simple surface, arguing, "In its very nature a surface is in an unstable condition." What are the boundaries of surface? Is surface both exterior and interior? Imperiale's essay describes emerging practices in digital geospatial and imaging techniques that engage with the way imaging intersects with the physical body in complex, rich ways. Imperiale goes on to suggest how artists' use of these technologies offer epistemological reinterpretations of skin.

Shelley Jackson's creative project "SKIN" (chapter 14) furthers an investigation of "reading" the skin. Jackson is a writer and artist whose work dismembers and reassembles the body in provocative ways. In her complex hypertext narrative, *Patchwork Girl* (1995), Jackson parodied Mary Shelley's Frankenstein; in Jackson's version, Mary Shelley is Dr. Frankenstein, and the monster is a woman, the "Patchwork Girl," made of linked fragments of other texts and bodies. Jackson's print story collection, *The Melancholy of Anatomy*, is also concerned with body parts and processes including the tale of an egg that manages to encapsulate the woman within whom it grew. Jackson's SKIN project offers a framework similar to the mapping ideas of Frederick Jameson; Jameson notes that a feature of the postmodern condition is that "people are unable to map (in their minds) either their own positions or the urban totality in which they find themselves" (1991, 51). Participants in the SKIN project, including Jackson herself, have received tattoos of particular words from a story she wrote that will be published nowhere else but on the skin of the participants. "The existence of the author is a necessary flaw in this (every?) story," Jackson says. "But this project makes me keenly aware that I am not the only, or even always the dominant, voice in it" (qtd. in "Written on the Body"). This project produces Jamesonian-style cognitive maps, creating collisions that form mobile senses of place and constantly shifting reconstruction of memory that the subjects/participants continually recreate.

The blend of fiction and theory presented in Mary Flanagan's "Reskinning the Everyday" (chapter 15) is a meditation on the ubiquitous computational interfaces, the "skins" of technology, that surround us. She argues that computer code is one of these interface "skins" that could map out a future for thinking about technology and the body, but she critiques current paradigms inherent in system design that, in her observation, limit creative and critical potential due to the lack of critical discourse surrounding programming paradigms. The spatiality of the interface-as-skin is also explored in the chapter.

In "Performing Blackness: Virtual Sports and Becoming the Other in an Era of White Supremacy" (chapter 16), David J. Leonard provides a deeper look into popular sports video games, seeking to underscore the centrality of race in the construction and reception of video games and emphasizing how games create, inhabit, transform, and challenge commonly received ideas about race, gender, and sexuality.

Jennifer González's "Morphologies: Race as a Visual Technology" (chapter 17) explores technologies of visualization such as photography, film, and video that have been mutually constitutive along with conceptions of race. In the chapter, González briefly traces how technologies of image making have been invented and adapted to the purpose of better elaborating or accommodating racial discourses, and she argues that racial hegemony informs the design and use of these technologies, shaping racial discourse in turn. Utilizing examples from digital art practice to focus on how questions of color play out, González explores the work of Alba D'Urbano, the Obadikes, Prema Murthy, Tana Hargest, and Los Cybrids among others to show how contemporary artists working with new technologies critique racial inequities.

The editors of this volume wish to draw attention to how the broad fields of technology, art, and cultural criticism are permeating one another's boundaries around the thematic of skin, with an emphasis on the ways digital technologies play a significant role in the act of inscribing the body surface. Many of the pieces included here complicate this process, however, and challenge the ongoing act of rewriting. Readers of *re:skin* will find a specific focus on the feminist implications of this malleable boundary; reframing the fiction and theory offers readers a new sense of the significance of juxtaposition when seeking to understand contemporary digital culture. Starting with feminist criticism as a site where technological embodiment is neither celebratory nor dystopic, the goal here is to present multiple points of view that, when read together, enact a kind of transformation of fixed categories to offer a complex view of technoculture as seen through the skin. Interleaving works on architecture, bodies, games, art, text, and medicine, this volume provides simultaneously chilling, witty, and enabling fusions of possible futures in which gender is redrafted in myriad ways.

Works Cited

ABC News Online. 2004. "Dutch Artist Shoots from the Hip." *ABC News Online Australia*, April 24. http://www.abc.net.au/news/newsitems/s1094043.htm (accessed October 23, 2004).

Boucher, J. 2004. "Ultrasound: A Window to the Womb? Obstetric Ultrasound and the Abortion Rights Debate." *Journal of Medical Humanities* 25, no. 1 (March): 7–19.

Grosz, Elizabeth. 1994. *Volatile Bodies: Toward a Corporeal Feminism*. Bloomington: Indiana University Press.

Haraway, Donna. 1991. *Simians, Cyborgs, and Women: The Reinvention of Nature*. New York: Routledge.

iceman. 2003. *Skinning Tutorial*. http://scp.mp-gamer.de/view_content_6.html (accessed March 21, 2005).

Jameson, Frederick. 1991. *Postmodernism, or, The Cultural Logic of Late Capitalism*. Durham, NC: Duke University Press.

Jeremijenko, Natalie. 2000. *Touch*. Biological artwork.

McLuhan, Marshall. 1964. *Understanding Media: The Extensions of Man*. New York: McGraw-Hill.

Meese, Elizabeth. 1992. *(Sem)Erotics: Theorizing Lesbian Writing*. New York: New York University Press.

Mohanraj, Mary Anne. 2000. "Interview: Nalo Hopkinson," September 1. http://scp.mp-gamer.de/view_content_6.html (accessed March 21, 2005).

Morgan, Kathryn Pauly. 1998. "Women and the Knife: Cosmetic Surgery and the Colonization of Women's Bodies." In *The Politics of Women's Bodies: Sexuality, Appearance, and Behavior*, ed. Rose Weitz, 147–166. Oxford: Oxford University Press.

Sterling, Bruce, ed. 1987. *Mirrorshades: A Cyberpunk Anthology*. New York: Ace.

Winnubst, Shannon. 2002. "Vampires, Anxieties, and Dreams: Race and Sex in the Contemporary U.S." Brown Working Papers in the Arts and Sciences, Southwestern University. http://www.southwestern.edu/academic/bwp/ (accessed April 1, 2005).

"Written on the Body: An Interview with Shelley Jackson." *The Iowa Web Review*. http://www.uiowa.edu/~iareview/mainpages/new/july06/jackson.html.

Inside, Outside, Surface

| 2 |
THE MAN WHO PLUGGED IN

L. Timmel Duchamp

1

"This should help you relax, Mr. Nies," the anesthesiologist said; and Howard felt the needle plunging ruthlessly into his flesh.

Howard took the sharp, stinging stab like a man. (*Or would it be more correct to say, like a* woman? *Both, when you think about it, sound pretty fucking foolish.*) Of course he wasn't nervous about this procedure— totally routine, the doc had said—but it always made him self-conscious and consequently stressed to hear the monitor beeping his pulse so damned publicly.

He stared at the flat white screen blocking his view. He could feel nothing of what they were doing, because of the local, but heard instruments clinking in the background while the doctor boasted to the nurse about his previous day's feats on the slopes. Or no, the doc had moved on to talk about how the snow in the Cascades was minimally tolerable, and about how much he preferred the fine powder of Snowbird.

When the doc paused to let the nurse reply, Howard said, "I skied at Snowbird once. Actually, I fractured my tibia there. It was my third time out. I guess those Salt orthopedists really rake it in." Howard realized he was talking to himself, for the nurse talked right over him, as if he weren't there.

The anesthesiologist leaned his head down, and spoke with his mouth so close to Howard's ear that Howard could feel the man's breath on his cheek. "Just concentrate on relaxing, Mr. Nies. I know you wouldn't want to distract Dr. Rogers with idle conversation, now would you?"

What the hell, Howard fumed (silently), is this some kind of surgical etiquette? The patient is supposed to pretend to be unconscious, even when he—or she—is not? Howard squinted up into the glare, at the acoustic tile on the ceiling, then closed his eyes. Think positive, he told himself. There may be discomfort, there will certainly be inconvenience, that goes without saying. But it will all be worth it, to boldly go where no man has gone before. Just remember *that*, dude. You, man, are on the fucking cutting edge. Hell, you *are* the cutting edge.

It occurred to Howard that somebody should be videotaping the entire "totally routine" procedure. It would be useful, later, when the story broke . . . Well, it was too late now. Still, he should at the very least start keeping a journal. Obviously, publishers would be bidding fiercely for it if he did . . .

The nurse and anesthesiologist were both laughing at something the doc had said (and that Howard had missed). Howard gritted his teeth. He should be glad, he thought, that it wasn't being videotaped. Imagine, if the whole world could watch them digging around in his belly button while pretending he wasn't, as a social person, there . . .

2

Dorothy drove Howard home from the clinic. "I'm perfectly capable of driving myself," he said. "I don't see why they made such a big deal about having you do it for me."

"Come on, George. Don't you get it? You're a patient, now. *That's* the point."

"My name is Howard!" Ever since they'd seen that movie *According to George*, she'd thought it the biggest joke in the world to say—ad nauseam—*Don't you get it, George?* Or, *It's like this, George.* Or, worst of all, *Now George, don't be like that.* "H-O-W-A-R-D, Howard. Don't *you* get it?"

"I thought the deal was there was to be no shouting in the car, no matter who's driving," Dorothy said evenly.

"I wasn't shouting," Howard said.

"I wonder why I bothered to go to the trouble of working around three different people's schedules, when you could have taken a taxi." She glanced at him.

Howard leaned his head back against the seat and closed his eyes. The instructional videotape had devoted less than a minute to the stage he'd just gone through. *The installation of the interface is a minor surgical procedure that will take from ten to twenty minutes. The interface is often informally referred to as a plug. This device is installed in the navel. When its cap is removed and the maternal environment is plugged into it, it facilitates the circulation of the gestational carrier's*

A Prenatal Cradle of Caring! At the cutting edge of medical technology, Siemens Carapace is made of the finest, strongest, most lightweight materials ever produced. Its clean, round lines and soft, silvery matte finish can't fail to reassure both the parents and the gestational carrier who wears it that the child within is getting better care and protection than any naturally gestated child. Neither random violence nor the shock and trauma of accident can touch a fetus carried in Sieman's Carapace. And Sieman's Maternal Inter-

blood through the body of the fetus. It is called an "interface" because it is a technological breakthrough that allows the negotiation of differences in antigens between the host and the uterus, in the same way that the placenta negotiates the difference in antigens between the fetus and the maternal environment.

Neither of them spoke until Dorothy pulled the car into the garage. "If you think you can manage without me, I'm going back to work," she said.

Howard glared at her. "It's not a question of managing."

face assures a fully controlled, regulated flow of blood and hormones that outdoes even one of Mother Nature's finest achievements, the natural placenta.
—text of an advertisement in *The American Journal of Obstetrics and Gynecology,* February 2013

Dorothy raised her eyebrows. 'You've been raving for weeks about how wonderful the estrogen makes you feel, about how lucky women are to get hits of it every month from their own ovaries. If that's the case, are we supposed to expect a killer case of PMS when you take that first major hit of progesterone?"

Howard got out of the car. (*The progesterone goes to the maternal environment, not to the host! It'll never touch me!*) "Sometimes, Dorothy, you're a real bitch, you know?" He slammed the door hard enough to make the car rock, and stomped his way to the door into the house. If she was this bad now, imagine what she would be like after she'd given him her uterus. For all she denied feeling resentment, their therapist was basically correct when she said that all women, no matter what they say, define themselves by their possession of a functioning uterus.

Was the whole thing a mistake, then? They could still abort at this stage. All that had happened so far was that his veins were being made more flexible and elastic, his tissues soaking up estrogen, and his abdomen fitted out with a removable interface. But God, to give up now, when they were so close to doing the unthinkable, so close to achieving the very first gestational fatherhood, so close to getting a son . . . That word, *son,* made Howard square his shoulders. The important thing was not to lose sight of the objective, or of the real magnificence of the means he would almost single-handedly be using to achieve it. He was going beyond anything ever before contemplated. Even in film and fiction, imagination had failed. In fictional settings when a man got pregnant, it was usually in a society where men weren't really men, and women weren't really women, or else he became a woman, or at the very least was thoroughly feminized. Not him, man! *His* anatomy wouldn't change a jot, except for the occasional flush of hormones, as needed. And he wouldn't have to suffer labor pains, either, or any of the muck or mess of female pregnancy. And still, in spite of the neatness of it all, as far as the fetus would be concerned, he'd be as safe and cozy in his mom's uterus as any naturally carried baby would be. In short, the whole idea was perfect, a triumph of science, ingenuity, and the bravery of the man who'd thought of it first. Viz, himself.

3

Howard lay quietly on the operating table that was the twin to Dorothy's, listening to Dorothy's voice, drunken with the shot of morphine they'd just given her, counting backwards from one hundred. Her voice got sluggish at ninety-eight as the general anesthesia kicked in; and it faded out altogether in the middle of the second syllable of "ninety-seven."

When Howard heard the bustle and rustle of movement, and the scraping of metal, he toyed with the idea of getting up off the table and rolling aside the screen intended to block his view. But when after a couple of minutes of bustle the doctor said "Scalpel," Howard was suddenly glad he couldn't see, and fearing to hear something horrible, found himself concentrating on the beep of the monitor registering Dorothy's heartbeat. Though he was a basically curious man, it made him queasy thinking about what they were doing on the other side of the screen not five feet away. It was Dorothy, after all, and real life, not faked soap opera. Unlike him, Dorothy wouldn't just be able to get up off the table afterwards and walk out. He would bear the burden of the pregnancy, and would be forced to wear the carapace for nine months plus the amount of time it would take them to produce a viable fetus. But Dorothy would have to bear the pain of healing from the hysterectomy and the psychological loss of her uterus. The therapist had stressed to him again and again how important it was that he recognize that the sacrifice involved in this pregnancy would not be his alone.

Dorothy had become so distant, though. She rejected comforting—even refused to admit that her uterus was any great loss—and focused her resentment on the deterioration of their sex life since the plug had been installed. He could understand how the thing's jutting out of his navel would be uncomfortable for her when he was on top. But she claimed, wholly unreasonably, that it pressed into her when she was on top, too, which was impossible, since she always held her body slanted up at an angle from his during that kind of intercourse.

Music—instantly recognizable as Vivaldi—suddenly blasted into the room. Howard often did his aerobics routine to Vivaldi and Albinoni. Hearing the strings zipping into that manic "atomic" energy (as a musicologist friend of his called it) made Howard feel like leaping off the table and directly into his routine. How did they expect patients to lie patiently with that kind of stimulus pumping into their bodies? But then—the doctor and his staff were *working*. And patients were usually unconscious . . . Of course Howard knew very well why Dorothy was willing to give him her uterus.

The therapist had explained it to him, during one of Howard's individual therapy sessions. Dorothy felt both guilty and fearful—guilty at Andrea's death (as though she, Andrea's mother, should have been able to prevent it), and too fearful to trust herself to bear and nurture another child. And so though she resented giving Howard her uterus and resented his doing what she had in her heart of hearts to know was her work, she couldn't refuse outright, because she felt guilty at what she perceived to be her own inadequacy as a mother. It was difficult, for sure. But once the pregnancy was a fait accompli, she'd begin to accept it. (After all, he was right out front taking all responsibility for this child, as she had with Andrea.) It was really just a matter of getting through the next few weeks (or months). And then life would be good again. Having Marcel wouldn't make up for the loss of Andrea, but it would be a fresh start on the rest of their lives.

(Courage, mon vieux.)

Ms. Furness, the carapace specialist, came over to Howard. "If I could check your interface, please, one last time. The doctor has just recovered the ovary, and is almost ready to transfer the uterus."

Howard grinned. "Be my guest," he said, trying (and failing) to catch the technician's eye.

Ms. Furness shoved the loose cotton gown almost up to Howard's neck and peered down at his navel. He saw her hands moving and heard a click. He considered asking her what she was doing, but she withdrew and returned to the main action going on around Dorothy. Howard wondered whether they would mind if he pulled his gown back down. He couldn't say he was cold, since the lamp overhead was throwing off enough heat to warm the entire room, but the exposure made him feel foolish.

(What the hell. To Furness I'm just the housing for her damned interface, and the musculature for lugging her precious carapace for time eternal—while the endocrinologist thinks I'm a fascinating challenge, and the obstetrician is only concerned about whether or not a man will be as disciplined in his prenatal diet as he claims most female gestational carriers are.)

Abruptly, the boredom was past and Ms. Furness and a nurse were strapping the carapace to his belly and plugging it into the interface. At this stage the carapace was, though bulky, so light that one might think one was wearing a tool apron with very few tools to weigh it down.

"You are now the proud host of a surrogate uterus, Mr. Nies," Furness said after a particularly resounding *snap*. "If you'll sit up, please, we'll finish arranging the straps for you."

The straps, simple Velcro affairs, would supposedly be easily removed and replaced on such occasions as he might find them irritating and wish a rest from them (though he must never, of course, unplug the carapace from the interface). Furness and the nurse fussed with them for a few seconds, and then Furness said, "You may get up now and move around, Mr. Nies. But I must ask you to report to my office in one-half hour, so that we can run a check on how well the uterus is adapting to its new environment."

(The uterus. Not Dorothy's. Not mine. Simply THE uterus. Does she say that to the women who adopt other women's uteri, too? Or is it because I'm male, and she can't imagine a uterus ever belonging to a man~)

Howard swung his legs over the side of the table and stood up; he noted that he felt the same as before they'd plugged him into it. He glanced over at the other table—and took a jarring jolt of nastiness to the belly. Dorothy's feet were high in the air, strapped into stirrups. Her naked legs, ankles, and toes looked . . . indecorous. As though they were simply in the way, completely superfluous to what mattered. Though he knew her body well, they looked totally unfamiliar.

Howard swallowed, and rammed his way through the swinging doors. Dorothy, he thought, would never know. Certainly not from him, she wouldn't.

In the first five years of the study, 673 gestational carriers have successfully interfaced with a surrogate uterus; of these, 522 have successfully carried a fetus to term. Analysis of variance (ANOVA) reveals that in comparison with pregnancies with a natural maternal environment, the risk of complications is reduced by 25 percent for pregnancies with a maternal environment composed of a surrogate uterus, maternal interface, and gestational carapace.
—from the abstract of "An Interim Report on Gestation via Surrogate Uterus with Maternal Interface and Gestational Carrier," *The New England Journal of Medicine* 369 (2013)

4

Though Howard had every intention of attending Dorothy's bedside all afternoon and evening, at around two Dorothy asked him to pop in the videocassette of *Desperately Seeking Susan* and scram. "I'm hurting, and tired, and just don't have the energy to keep you entertained, Howard," she said when he protested. Howard couldn't blame her for being in a cranky mood; he knew he would have been if it had been his abdomen that had been violated. Still, he wasn't there to be entertained, for godsake, but to give her support. He forbore to say this, of course. He simply smiled, told her to phone him if she decided she wanted some company, pecked her on the lips, and left.

And so he found himself standing naked before the triple mirror in the walk-in closet of the master bedroom, contemplating the carapace. The very sight of it—for all intents and purposes, for the moment anyway, *his*—provoked his deepest admiration. It was made of the finest high-tech materials ever invented by man. The strongest, lightest carbon filament—fabric developed for Boeing's most sophisticated aeronautic engineering, Furness had said—had been used to construct the exterior shell, and the most flexible and impermeable polymer for the protective inner pouch (from which the shell could be detached in the intimacy and safety of one's own bed, for moments of quality belly-to-pouch contact with the fetus). And of course the carapace carried its own environmental controls, so that the temperature would always be regulated according to a perfect twenty-four-hour cycle of standard body temperatures.

Howard gazed at the carapace from every angle the triple mirrors allowed, fascinated at the wonder of it. Compulsively he stroked its cool, textured surface—with both hands, fingers extended and splayed—and thought, *there's a uterus in there, a uterus that will very soon be carryng a baby. My very own portable womb. Or rather,* our *womb, our joint, shared, cooperative womb. Never will the parenting of a child be so completely* shared. *Nies, you're a genius to have thought of it. An absolute world-class fucking genius!* Howard glowed with pride. Though the makers of the carapace had been brilliantly innovative in their contribution to the technology of birth, he was showing them a crucial, even revolutionary, application they had missed.

Howard discovered that his right hand had moved to his penis and had begun pumping away on it without his really having noticed. He laughed, and glanced at his face in the central mirror, and then—feeling both sheepish and sly—looked quickly away. The fact was, he felt damned good. His boldness and decisiveness in following up a wistful whim had given him a genuine raison d'être (if not cause célèbre), of which he could feel justifiably proud.

But at that moment, at the pinnacle of his pleasurable burst of pride, Howard made a strategic error. He looked back into the mirror at his body, this time not at the brushed silver plating of the carapace, but at his body as a whole, as though to imagine how someone else would see him now, as he had so startlingly become (even if he wasn't yet "pregnant," so to speak). And he couldn't help noticing the changes the estrogen had already wrought in his body. For one thing, he had actually become a little flabby, which he found rather disconcerting, since apart from occasional brief excursions into beer bellydom, his body since late adolescence had always been trim. The puffiness of his nipples, though—or rather, he should say breasts, for they had become large enough to be counted more than bare nipples—made him a little queasy. Old men, he thought, sometimes manifested puffy breasts. (And impotence and numerous other signs of degenerating manhood.) But for a man, in his prime . . . It wouldn't be permanent, Howard reminded himself. And only Dorothy and a few medical personnel would ever really see the swelling around his nipples. It would be the carapace itself that would attract people's attention. And *that* he was prepared to handle.

Howard smiled down at it. Ms. Furness had said the interface was working like a charm. Something could still go wrong with the uterus, of course—if, for instance, the tissue had inadvertently been damaged, or the connections of its blood vessels to the interface collapsed. But uterine transfers to carapaces, she said, had about a 95 percent success ratio—in women. The trickiest stage in the whole process was usually the IVF. (Some eggs, apparently, simply never accepted fertilization.) In his special case, though, getting hormonal levels right would be trickiest.

Howard ejaculated. "Bull's-eye!" he said out loud, exultant at hitting his underpants lying on the floor a few feet away. The world, he thought, was his oyster. And he patted the carapace gently, even lovingly, for the preciousness within.

5

On the second and last night Dorothy spent in the clinic, Joe Tavuchis phoned. Joe was one of the few friends from college with whom Howard maintained contact. Though they didn't agree at every point politically, their basic take on life had remained similar; and perhaps mainly because their mates were both professional women who happened to like one another, the couples alternated visiting one another every year or so, mostly for long weekends. Joe said he'd called to say that he and Dale were planning to visit the long Fourth of July weekend, if it was okay with Howard and Dorothy.

The question took Howard off guard, and flustered him, totally. Howard had made a schedule of when to tell whom what. Friends and relatives were to be kept in the dark until a viable pregnancy was safely under way, at which point the astonishing news was to be broken to one and all with a series of phone calls to be made on the same evening. Though chances were reasonable that there'd be a viable fetus by early July, it wasn't guaranteed. Howard flashed on a future possible scene, of Joe and Dale arriving at the gate, spotting the carapace, and demanding an explanation. "Oh, it's just Dorothy's uterus, that's all," Howard imagined himself saying ever so insouciantly. Sure. And even his old friend Joe would wonder if he wasn't pretty damned weird—if not perverse, to have been plugged into Dorothy's empty uterus for lo so many months . . . "Hey, Joe, that's great!" Howard said heartily. "But I'll have to run it by Dorothy before I can give you a definite okay." And frantically he wondered about the chances of her giving him an out.

"Well of course," Joe said. "So. Is Dorothy around, so that you could ask her now?"

Howard swallowed convulsively. He was so glad they'd decided not to get a Videophone. (His home computer's video hookup to the lab had cured him of thinking he'd like one.) "Sorry, man. Dorothy's out of town for the week. How about I give you a call on the weekend?"

After Howard hung up, he got out the bottle of Tanqueray Dorothy kept in the refrigerator and poured himself a stiff shot. Did he really think he could ask Dorothy to invent a reason for keeping Joe and Dale away? Dorothy would ask him why he'd want her to do such a thing in the first place. Howard stared down at the carapace (which his hand, he discovered, was stroking). He hadn't realized how ambivalent he felt. At the very prospect of being exposed to others' eyes, to the Social Gaze both General and Specific, his sense of boldness seemed to be evaporating. He started to think about how his coworkers might react when he appeared in the lab wearing the carapace. He would fend them off with wisecracks, he'd told Dorothy when she'd raised the issue. (It was really none of their fucking business.) Taken hypothetically, the question of others' reactions had seemed unimportant and trivial. Now he no longer felt so sure.

Howard showered awkwardly with the carapace, shifting the straps a bit at a time to soap and rinse, then carefully lifting the carapace away from his abdomen to wash there. (Baths, Ms. Furness advised, were easier, because you could float the carapace on the water without appreciably risking its connection with the interface.) Then he knocked back another shot of gin and brushed his teeth.

In bed, with the lights off and his eyes closed, he stroked the carapace and imagined what it would be like to be lying there pregnant, with the shell detached from the liner and the baby floating in the fat bulging pouch of amniotic fluid right up against his belly. What would the uterus, sans fetus, feel like? he wondered. No one had told him not to detach the shell and make skin contact with the liner. Of course there couldn't be much more than a little blood in the pouch, not enough to keep the temperature stable when removed from the carapace's environmental controls. Still, he could just look at it, and touch it through the liner, for a few seconds. Surely that wouldn't endanger it . . .

Howard turned on the light. For about ten minutes he struggled to open the carapace. No one had yet shown him how to do it. Maybe if he watched the videotape again, at slow speed through the part where the woman opens hers and places the third-trimester fetus in its maternal environment on her belly?

Howard turned off the light and arranged himself on his side. The uterus would be tiny—about the size of a fist, the doc had said—so there would really be nothing much to feel except the blood-slickedness of the thing, slipping and sliding around in the liner, its vessels clinging to the interface for dear life. Visualizing it, he worried that if he did touch it through the liner he might actually bruise it or in other way damage it. Internal organs weren't used to being touched. And if he hurt it, and it died on him, imagine trying to explain to the doctor that he'd just wanted to feel it . . . A pity, really. A missed opportunity. It wasn't often one got to plug into one's wife's former uterus.

Howard fell asleep without difficulty. He wasn't the kind of guy to let anything get between him and his sleep, not even thwarted wishes and desires.

6

On the day before Howard was due to make his biweekly commute across the lake to the office, he worked out the correct and appropriate strategy vis-à-vis personal revelations there. Context, he knew, controlled perception. And in this case he definitely wanted to control others' perceptions of what he was up to. To do that, he needed to determine the circumstances under which he revealed his bold gestational initiative. And so he went out and bought two shirts large enough to wear over the carapace.

Judging by Dorothy's ironic smile, the tactic amused her; but he thought he detected a glimmer of approval in her eyes, too. He didn't explain his concealment of the carapace. If she knew the point behind his strategy, her facial expression might not be so amiable.

And so no one in the lab detected the carapace. Perry commented that he seemed to be putting on a bit of weight, and since that was basically true, Howard felt comfortable in saying that he guessed he was getting a little flabby, and that in fact he was thinking about going back to the early morning jogging he'd abandoned after he'd started telecommuting. (He knew he'd never mentioned doing aerobics to any of his colleagues; and as he'd learned in childhood, lies of omission were easy if not always safe to "tell.") But the visit was totally routine, from the division meeting held every Friday at eleven to the inspection of the prototype and the difference Howard's most recent calculations and equations had made to its complex ability to process images.

Still, though Howard's coworkers did not spot the carapace, Howard never managed to lose consciousness of it. He constantly caught himself stroking his abdomen and feeling the carapace through the thick blue cambric of the shirt. And now and then hysteria-tinged thoughts bubbled up: *None of them knows I have a womb under my shirt, none of them guesses it, can you imagine how astonished they'd be if I suddenly unbuttoned my shirt to show them? If I explained about the plug?* Though he had decided that now was not the right time for making the revelation, he longed to do it, longed to share his incredible secret with his ordinary workaday world. They all probably thought he was a dull, safe bourgeois kind of guy who had shot his wad in high school and college and had settled down to the dailiness of life with the ease of indifference to the wild adventure one can elect one's life to be. But he counseled himself to patience. They would see, soon enough, and realize they had misjudged his limitations.

No one, he thought, could know anyone's limits. We peg one another, but simply out of our confidence in the banal . . .

By the time he arrived home, Howard felt antsy and itchy as he hadn't for years. What he wanted, he thought, was to get totally fucked up, to snort a few lines of coke, or to do both hash and alcohol or some other, equally potent, combination. But he had no dope. And he had sworn to Dorothy when they were married that he'd give up combining it with alcohol.

Howard went into the bedroom and removed his shirt. Dorothy was lying in bed, still recovering from the surgery, still holding her one-woman film festival. He had seen her watching *Black Widow* so many times that he didn't even have to check the empty cassette box to know that's what she was running. He couldn't understand it, really. The movie was about as boring as movies ever got. Yet after *Cannibal Women in the Avocado Jungle of Death*, *Black Widow* was her favorite. It depicted an FBI agent's obsession with Theresa Russell, a quick-change con artist who systematically marries and kills rich men. *Cannibal Women*—which Dorothy never watched alone, but always with other women, most of whom had seen it a dozen times already and so knew all the jokes and could say all their favorite lines with the actors—was also about the female consumption of men—literally, and the pursuit of the man-killing cannibals by a woman professor with a groupie bimbo of a student and an inept male as sidekicks. ("A tenth-rate imitation of *Indiana Jones*," Howard had told Dorothy after he'd sat through one of her screenings.) "I'm going to be playing the stereo really loud, honey," Howard said. "Unless you have any objection?"

"One feels so totally re-assured," Ms. Ward said, "knowing that not only is the child *safer* in the carapace, but that he is indeed safely in one's very womb! Loss of the uterus, I feel, is a small price to pay for making an out-of-one's-body pregnancy as close to the natural thing as one can get when another woman is carrying one's child."
—from "The New Surrogate Pregnancies: The Professional Woman's Answer to the Biological Clock?" *The New York Times Magazine*, June 8, 2014

Dorothy hit the PAUSE button. "No objection. Just close all the doors between here and the den. I'm set with movies for the rest of the night."

Howard didn't ask what they were (though he could see *The Hunger* on the top of the stack), just gently shut the door to the bedroom, the door to the hall, and the door to the stairwell. He got out the bottle of gin—about three-quarters full—and some bitter lemon and ice to mix with it, and shut himself into the den. Then he fed his entire U2 collection into the CD player (retro, no doubt, but they represented the best of his youth, and anyway eventually everything ever done becomes retro), put on the head-phones, and turned up the speakers as loud as they could go without busting, so that he could feel the power of U2 vibrating up through the floor. Lying with his head on a pillow and stroking the carapace, Howard felt fine, really, really fine. Life, he thought as he took another belt of gin, just didn't get better than this.

7

Howard's hangover had barely run its course when the clinic called on Monday afternoon. The lab, the operator said, had achieved successful IVF, and given the narrowness of the window of opportunity for implantation, Dr. Rogers would like him to come in at once.

Howard felt as though events were suddenly rushing in on him with a speed that threatened his sense of control. But he calmly assured the operator he would be there within the hour, then showered, put on fresh clothes and kissed Dorothy goodbye.

As in previous visits to the clinic, the first thing they did was weigh him, and the second was take his blood pressure. He winced when he saw the readout on the scale. The big gain couldn't be from the carapace, which weighed under five pounds. And how much could an unpregnant uterus weigh?

He had to spend fifteen minutes lying on an examination table before Dr. Rogers and Ms. Furness favored him with their attention. "So," the doc said. "What we're going to do today is give the maternal environment a quick check, and then administer the progesterone that is ordinarily secreted by the ovaries at the time of ovulation."

As the doc talked, Ms. Furness expertly released the latch on the carapace and eased off the shell to reveal the transparent polymer liner. The doc positioned a high-intensity lamp over Howard's abdomen. Howard saw only the crown of the doc's curly blond head; whether or not the doc was doing something to his uterus, he (of course) felt nothing. *(So maybe it's not mine, if I can't feel what it feels?)*

"Splendid," the doc said.

Ms. Furness, who had been standing at the counter with her back to Howard, turned and handed the doc a hypodermic syringe. "We're making the injection through the input coupling, which as you may recall lies between the interface and the carapace," the doc said as he took the syringe from Furness. "If everything goes as it should, the progesterone will prepare the maternal environment for receiving the fertilized egg. Because we're injecting it directly into the uterus, the process won't take as long as it does in nature. Therefore we'll want to see you again in forty-eight hours, at which time, presuming the fertilized egg continues viable, we'll do the implantation—which will, of course, resemble very much what we're doing here today. The fertilized egg, Mr. Nies, is just about the size of a grain of sand. You wouldn't recognize it with your naked eye if you saw it." Howard considered asking to see it. After all, it was his fertilized egg. His and Dorothy's.

Howard's prep for embryo transfer entailed two more steps. First, he had to set up a schedule of appointments for weekly meetings with both the endocrinologist and the carapace specialist, and biweekly meetings with Rogers. Second, though he tried to put it off, they made him see Joan Smithers, the clinic's dietitian.

Joan Smithers, though slim, had the kind of tall and lanky body that looked soft and flabby. (Of course, Howard knew a body like hers couldn't really have that much flab; yet the softness was not the round and alluring kind, but padded her body like a thin layer of foam rubber between her musculature and epidermis.) Her smile reminded Howard of room-temperature milk, neither refreshingly cold nor comfortingly warm. She didn't look overbearing; in fact, Howard pegged her for the quiet, self-effacing type who never had a thing to say for herself at parties. But after the first half-minute of her lecture on nutrition, Howard deemed her intolerably patronizing. Protein, B-vitamins, folic acid, calcium, and iron were her litany. His most important task in the next nine months would be to eat well. He must consume the equivalent of a quart of milk a day. Did he realize that the fetus would absorb as much calcium as it needed, and would take it from its host's very teeth and bones if it had to? And terrible things could happen to the fetus from a lack of sufficient protein and folic acid. Da-duh, da-duh, da-duh. Howard tried to look attentive. He knew all this stuff. He didn't need the lecture.

"I've seen your medical records," she said. "And I realize that it may come as a shock to you to have acquired so much fat in the last four months. Let me assure you it's nothing to worry about. In fact, it's essential! The fact is, Howard, that women's bodies tend to acquire more fat than men's for a purpose! Did you know that girls cannot start menstruating until one-fourth of their body weight is fat? That's a fact!" God, she was earnest! "You may of course be worrying about your heart. But all that estrogen you've been getting—which is, by the way, the very reason you've put on so much fat—is giving you the very best protection Nature provides against heart disease. During the pregnancy, as with any naturally pregnant woman, your blood supply will increase enormously, and your blood vessels expand and heart grow somewhat larger in accommodation. Your bone marrow will be very busy in the next few months, manufacturing blood cells at an unprecedented rate! Howard, you will find pregnancy a miracle of intricacy! Even when undertaken via interface!"

Howard nodded and smiled and ooh-ed and ah-ed in all the proper places. But he'd seen the video umpteen times, and didn't need to be told any of this.

"And now, Howard, if I may see your forty-eight-hour intake chart?" Joan Snitchers's eyebrows rose expectantly. "You did bring it, Howard, didn't you?"

Howard. She was the only damned person at the clinic who called him by his first name. It wasn't as though she had said *and call me Joan, please.* She was treating him like such an imbecile he actually began to consider telling her to call him "doctor." (He had noticed how enamored of the title these medical people appeared to be.) "I, uh, forgot it," Howard said.

Her eyebrows pulled clown into the very configuration of sternness. "Didn't they tell you to bring it with you?"

Howard shrugged. No reason to outright lie about it.

The woman sighed. "Well, Howard, though people usually don't remember everything they eat and drink unless they write it down at the very instant they're consuming, let's see if we can reconstruct your intake for Saturday and Sunday, shall we? So. Walk yourself through it, step by step. You wake Saturday morning. What time is it?"

Howard felt his cheeks redden. No way could he tell her he woke at six still drunk, got up to take three aspirins and drink two glasses of water and then went back to sleep until noon. Or that he ate the worst junk food all weekend only because he was hung over, since Big Macs and Classic Cokes and fries especially soothed his stomach at such times as nothing else could.

Joan smiled with the utmost patience for his apparent blankness. "Surely, Howard, you can remember what time you got up the morning before yesterday?"

Howard swallowed and licked his lips and swallowed again. Desperately he searched for a way out—and then suddenly realized he had it. He would think back a week (though it would be considerably harder to remember) and pretend that was the Saturday and Sunday she was asking him to account for.

It took fifteen minutes of Joan Smithers's poking and prodding before Howard had produced a facsimile of two days' intake (and involved, by the time he got to Sunday, inventing out of whole cloth what he imagined to be an ideal day of proper nutrition). Howard suspected by the expression that came to settle on her face that she had stopped believing everything he was telling her. Still, she jotted it all down, and didn't actually call him a liar.

"Now Howard," Smithers said when they had finished. "If you have in fact remembered correctly, your diet isn't utterly unhealthy, but it could use some improvement. I want you to read the dietary guidelines again, very very carefully, and start following them *at once*. You want your blood to be ready for the fetus, and you particularly want it to be rich with folic acid and protein throughout the first trimester. And Howard, you are to drink no alcohol whatsoever." She fixed him with such a stern eye that Howard wondered if he still somehow smelled of it two days after his drink.

"Yes, ma'am," he said.

"I understand you don't smoke. Good. Don't start. And as for caffeine—you can intake moderate amounts—but do not, I repeat, do not overdo it. Your adrenal glands are going to be going through some pretty strenuous times. You really don't need the added stress of a caffeine overdose."

Howard couldn't stand it any longer. "You know, Joan," he said, taking the liberty she had taken, "I do have a Ph.D. And *most* people take such an accomplishment as a sure sign of intelligence."

Joan smiled ever so sympathetically. "Oh, Howard, I'm not trying to put you down. But it's not intelligence we worry about, but common sense and patience. I'm trying to make a point here. An important point. For your benefit, and the baby's."

Howard smiled, too. "Yeah, I know, Joan, I know. And I certainly do appreciate it. I promise, I'll follow all the instructions. I don't have to do this, you know." He gestured at the carapace, which he had (of course) been stroking the entire time. "I mean, how many men do you know who would voluntarily undertake pregnancy?"

Joan's smile grew gentle. "True, true. But though you won't be going through labor and delivery, perhaps you haven't realized exactly what is involved? Since it will be growing into a body out of your body, even if it isn't exactly inside?"

Ah. She was a sexist! She thought that being a man he must be too selfish and unused to sacrifice to do what came naturally to women! Howard rose to his feet and collected all the new handouts she had assembled for him. "Thank you for your help, Joan. If I have any questions, I'll call you."

She looked startled, then rose to her feet, too. "I'll be seeing you," she said conventionally.

"No doubt," Howard said dryly, thinking, *In hell you will, lady.*

8

On the afternoon before his next trip into the office, Howard fell victim to an attack of nausea that totally amazed him. "Morning sickness," he thought. The endocrinologist had said that he might not suffer it at all, since all the unaccustomed estrogen he'd been getting for so many weeks hadn't yet upset his stomach. Howard had dismissed the very idea of that so-traditional malady. Though he'd never said so to Dorothy's face, during her pregnancy he had decided that morning sickness was imagined by women, to make the idea of pregnancy more real to them at a time when their bodies showed only a few signs of it. One of those "old wives' tales," he'd privately called it, handed down as traditional knowledge and therefore almost inevitable.

Though Howard had originally thought he'd wait a month or two to let his boss and coworkers know he was pregnant, the rush of nausea changed his mind. Howard wore the carapace openly, with pride, and on reaching the office went straight to his boss and gave her the news.

To his disappointment, Marissa did not comment on the pregnancy per se, but said, "And what about the project? You committed yourself to staying with it until your role in it is completed."

"I'll need a parental leave, of course," Howard said quickly. "I'm sorry about that. But there should be no problem for the next nine months, give or take a couple of weeks."

"Your role is projected for another fifteen months, Howard."

"Look," Howard said. "I'm sure we can work something out."

Marissa sighed. "Obviously, this is going to cost us both time and money. I can tell you one thing. Jonathan is not going to be happy."

Of course the "style" of the company had always been intense, frenetic worka-holism, to the point that except for the clerical and accounting staff, few employees survived more than six or seven years of the pace. Still, Howard felt disappointed. The company was so full of innovative, cutting-edge people that he had assumed they'd be more than willing to make allowances.

"I'm totally certain we'll be able to keep on schedule," Howard said. "No way am I going to let the team down." *(Dorothy will change her mind once the kid is born. I know she will. And she won't want to dump it all on me.)* "I'll work part-time from home instead of taking a regular leave. It's just that I'm not going to want to put the baby into child-care right from Day One, you know?"

Though Marissa was neither thrilled nor impressed, Howard's coworkers did not disappoint him. "How totally fucking astonishing, man!" Perry said, all admiration. "I know I couldn't hack that kind of thing myself, but hell, that doesn't mean I can't ap-preciate somebody else doing it!"

Jerry clapped Howard on the back and whooped. "One small step for man, one gi-ant leap for mankind!" he said.

"Shit-head," Jean muttered at Jerry, but then smiled at Howard, and said, "Dorothy must be proud of you."

Howard spewed out a thick, heady stream of information about the carapace and his hormone treatments, and even described morning sickness and how the doc said it was due to the fact that estrogen collects in the cells of the stomach. His rapture was such that he even considered shifting the carapace so that they could take a peek at the interface.

"If the woman whose uterus you got only knew it was going to be plugged into a man," Jerry said. And he snickered.

"But she did and does know," Howard said. "It's Dorothy's uterus." And he felt an unaccountable flush burning his cheeks.

———

Jean gave him a sharp look; and he saw that her eyes had frosted over. "Only an hour until the division meeting," she said, and returned to her terminal.

Jerry grinned. "Any idea what that was all about?" He shook his head. "Women! Can't figure the creatures out."

Howard glanced at Perry. "I guess now would be a good time to go over the latest performance trials."

Jean, Howard realized, understood something he hadn't been able to figure out about Dorothy. Maybe he could get her to go out for a beer with him after work and— but ho, no alcohol. Well, then, for a latte. She was sensitive, and she had always cut him a lot of slack. Maybe she could explain to him why Dorothy, except for going to work, eating, and sleeping, never did anything anymore but watch her favorite old movies. Last night it had been *The Draughtsman's Contract* and *Impromptu*; and the night before it had been *Drowning by Numbers* and *Thelma and Louise*, two singularly vicious depictions of women making war on men. ("Better than watching men kill or stalk women, which is the content of more than half of all movies ever made," Dorothy had said when he commented on her penchant.)

Maybe, though, Jean would simply take Dorothy's side and condemn him out of hand. That look she'd given him, when he'd revealed it was Dorothy's uterus.

By the time Howard and Perry had reached the lab, Howard had decided it would be best to figure out Dorothy on his own. Dorothy, after all, wouldn't exactly appreciate his discussing her peculiarities with someone she had never even met.

9

In retrospect, it seemed to Howard that the first two months of the pregnancy passed the most quickly. Both he and Dorothy devoted most of their energies to their jobs. Howard grew a beard, and Dorothy acquired a brush cut (which she maintained with frequent trips to the salon). Howard took up swimming in the company pool, and Dorothy began attending t'ai chi classes every night after work. Howard bought books on fetal development and read Pinkerton's *The Making of Homo Sapiens*, and Dorothy watched the remake of *Attack of the 50 Ft. Woman* (starring Darryl Hannah), *Making Mr. Right*, *Until the End of the World*, and other of her quirky personal favorites.

Howard tried to get Dorothy to read Pinkerton's book, but failed. He then tried to tell her what it was about. "I'm tired, Howard," Dorothy said when Howard cornered her one night after her t'ai chi class. "And I want to watch *The Summer House*. If, that is, you have no strong, overwhelming objections?"

"But honey, this is important," Howard said. "It's especially germane to the matter of our child's birth."

Dorothy sniffed. "Do you always have to be stroking that dead hunk of metal?"

Howard barely kept his temper. "How we handle this birth may change the very nature of homo sapiens!" he said. "The fact is, homo sapiens developed into such a complex social being *precisely* because a large head and a narrow birth canal and a relatively rigid pelvis were selected, to make birth a highly social, as opposed to individual, affair! Which means that if I—"

Dorothy interrupted. "What are you saying, Howard?" Her eyebrows rose so high in her forehead that if she'd still been wearing her hair a decent length they would have been lost from view. "That you no longer believe women who are as fit as they should be can just squat down in the field and make the little fuckers pop out without any sweat much less assistance from another human being? Can it be that you've actually changed your mind about something, Howard? Is it possible?"

Howard felt a hot blush suffusing his neck and cheeks. *(Seem to be blushing all the time lately. Wonder if that's the estrogen doing that to me? Is blushing a hormonally speaking female kind of thing?)* Howard said, "You're right, I was an asshole for saying it—and I believe I apologized at the time, when you called me on it."

Dorothy smiled. "Oh yes. After I ranted and raved at you for a good forty minutes, you did apologize, and all was forgiven, though of course the real source of that altercation had more to do with your irritation at my keeping you awake by getting up to go piss every fifteen or so minutes, isn't that right?"

Howard gave up trying to discuss what the ambience of births from carapace pregnancies should be like and decided that he'd better starting planning his own delivery himself. He could see now that it might take Dorothy most of the pregnancy to admit that she cared about their son's birth.

10

By the time Independence Day weekend rolled around, Howard's beard had grown, in his own opinion at least, into a pretty decently distributed arrangement of fuzz. Dorothy didn't hide her dislike of it (but then Howard didn't hide his dislike of her brush cut). The beard, and not the carapace, was the first thing the hot and sweaty travelers noticed when Howard met them at the front door.

"Hey, man, so you've decided to join the tribe of the bearded," Joe said, grinning and blinking on the doorstep. Howard grinned back and, self-consciously fingering his fuzz, gestured them in. Joe moved to give him the ritual hug—and then recoiled. He looked down at the carapace. "What in the fuck is *that*?" he said.

Beneath the facetious tone Howard detected anxiety. "You've never seen one of these before?" Howard said, amazed. Missoula, after all, did have cable television and links to the Internet and magazines and newspapers.

Dale, smiling, gave Howard a quick shy hug. Howard saw that she'd put on even more weight since the last time they'd met, maybe fifteen pounds. "It looks ultra high-tech, whatever it is," she said.

"It's a long story," Howard said, closing the door on the outdoor heat. "I bet you guys'd like to shower and change and get something cool to drink, right? We've got all weekend to talk about *this*." And Howard smiled down at the carapace, and stroked it.

"Guess we smell pretty raunchy," Joe said. "The heat never let up, not even when we were going over the Cascades. I didn't know Seattle got this hot."

Why in the hell would anyone drive all the way from Missoula just for a long weekend visit, anyway? Howard wondered as he led them upstairs to the guest room. They'd always flown in before. It was crazy.

As though Dale had read his mind, she said, "The cost of flights out of Missoula sure has gone up. We wanted to get away, to come see you guys, but . . ."

"You know where everything is," Howard said at the door of the guest room. "Help yourself, and of course just ask if there's anything you can't find."

The three of them were just settling around the kitchen table with cold drinks when Dorothy arrived home. "God, I hate working on Saturdays," she said. But she smiled warmly at the travelers and folded Dale into a close hug. She poured herself a gin and tonic. "Joe, Dale, are you sure you won't have something with alcohol in it? Just because Howard's abstaining doesn't mean the rest of us have to as well."

Dale flashed an apologetic grin at Howard. She said, "It's great iced tea, but I wouldn't mind a beer, actually."

"Gin and tonic for me," Joe said.

Howard felt stupid for having offered them only nonalcoholic beverages. But really, he thought, Dale shouldn't be drinking all those calories. Now that she'd changed into shorts and a tee-shirt he could see that she'd gained more than he'd first thought. And she used to have a figure for which Howard had envied Joe. But Dorothy had never let herself go, even when she was pregnant; she hadn't changed clothing size until the eighth month.

"So tell us now about that canister you have tied to your belly," Joe said.

Howard spread his palms over the silver textured shell. "It's called a carapace. And it's hooked up to my blood supply, through an interface set in my navel."

Joe looked puzzled. "I don't get it. Is this some new kind of treatment for something?"

Howard savored the moment. "I'm pregnant." He smiled down at the carapace and felt a sudden swell of emotion. "Inside this beautiful shell is our next child. Marcel Howard Nies. Due around Christmas."

"Oh come on. You're shitting me, man," Joe squeaked, hardly able to talk for laughing.

"I'm totally serious."

Joe's face arrested in astonishment. Seconds later, his mouth stretched into a wide, shit-eating grin. He crowed, "Way to go!"

Howard laughed. Joe had been spouting that dweebly retro phrase since the day they'd met in Introductory Physics.

Dale looked bemused. "I've never heard of such a thing. Or known that you could carry pregnancies outside one's body."

"I'm the first male to try it," Howard said. "A tricky business, because they don't know how my naturally produced hormones will interact with all the ones they're injecting me and the baby with. A lot of times women hosts develop a kind of feedback process, in which their bodies become convinced that they're pregnant, and start manufacturing all the right hormones on their own."

"A lot of shots then, I imagine," Joe said, shuddering.

Howard nodded. "At least one a week. And of course I had to start a couple of months beforehand, to get my veins prepared to handle an increased blood supply. It's really amazing, the things you learn," Howard said, running on without waiting to see if Joe and Dale actually wanted to know more. "On Wednesday, for instance, I'm starting a course of androgens—to be injected through the interface, for the baby—you see, it turns out that the chromosomal configuration in and of itself doesn't suffice to produce a boy, and so for the fetus to develop male instead of female reproductive organs, it has to get flooded with androgens during the third and fourth months. And then there's the—"

"For God's sake, Howard, we don't need a lecture on prenatal endocrinology," Dorothy said.

Everyone looked at Dorothy. She shook her head. "Don't mind me. It's just that I've been hearing nothing but this kind of shit for months now. It's like living with a walking, talking medical encyclopedia."

Howard bit his lip. They hardly talked at all now, except during joint therapy sessions, at which they mostly discussed how she was refusing to have sex of any description with him until he "got rid of" the carapace, and how this "indicated" (in the therapist's words) "a deep resentment of the carapace and all that it implied."

One aspect of this new form of surrogate pregnancy that offers the greatest possibility for changing the quality of pregnancy and its effects on the shared parental relationship is the absolute equality of parents in such pregnancies in terms of their intimacy with the child in the womb. Most evenings for the last three months of their pregnancy, Virginia Ward and Jay Moran enjoyed the experience of holding their baby, in pouched utero, on their own

Dorothy got up and went to the refrigerator. "Another round, anyone?"

When both Joe and Dale said yes, Howard decided he'd better start dinner. The prospect of sitting around with three people who were drunk while he was solitarily sober struck him as dismal. And if Dorothy, ordinarily so private a person, was talking this way after just one G & T . . .

11

Though Dorothy never addressed a civil word to Howard during dinner (not even to compliment him on the deliciousness of the meal, as everyone else did), she did not fire any more salvos at him, either. Instead, she asked Dale about the job she had been on the verge of starting the last time they had all been together. If the question had been intended to reduce the tension at the table, it failed. The job offer, Dale said, had been withdrawn because the company's medical insurer threatened to raise the company's rates if they took her on. "They're calling hypertension a preexisting condition," Dale said angrily. "And the absolutely pissy thing about it is that my blood pressure's only high when a doctor or nurse takes it. It's never elevated when I take it at home."

"And of course," Joe said unhappily, "you know what academic pay is like these days. The university's insurance plan doesn't cover even one dependent. So it really would have made no sense for Dale to agree to take the job without health benefits."

And so of course for the rest of the damned meal they'd discussed the lousiness of the job market and the high cost of insurance, and Dorothy had made a bitter remark about how "We're still up to our necks in debt to the bastards for not having healed Andrea." Doom and gloom, Howard fumed. They had dragged the occasion into doom and gloom when they had the best reason in the world for joyous celebration.

Joe volunteered to do the dishes. Howard waited for Dorothy to say she'd help, but the latter smirked at Dale and said, "Up for *Cannibal Women*?" Dale, of course, giggled

abdomens, and touching and feeling the movements of their baby more directly than a naturally pregnant woman can. Of course, such a daily experience of physical intimacy with the child would not have been possible if their carrier had not been induced to live in. But the estrangement that many new fathers feel from the infant's clearly being so much closer to the mother need not occur with carapace pregnancies. Similarly, the postnatal exhaustion and depression that afflicts many new mothers is simply obviated. The possible benefits of this new form of surrogacy may be so great that the clinical pioneers of the technology say that it will not surprise them if it very soon becomes the preferred method of pregnancy.
—from "The New Surrogate Pregnancies: The Professional Woman's Answer to the Biological Clock?" *The New York Times Magazine*, June 8, 2014

and said, "Hell yes, just totally." Which left Howard to help Joe, which turned out fine, since Joe really did want to know all about the carapace, what it was made of and how it worked, and whether he wasn't at least a little freaked out about messing with his hormones that way . . .

1 2

On most Sunday mornings Howard watched the Beltway pundits deliver their verdicts on the week's events ("Howard's version of going to church," Dorothy used playfully to call it), but to honor his guests he gave it up that weekend. Instead, he prepared a lavish brunch which he served out on the deck (which afforded an excellent view of Rainier).

"This is fantastic, Howard," Dale said of the spiced cheese-baked eggs.

"Imagine how much richer the quality of our college life would have been if Howard had realized his culinary talents earlier," Joe said.

Howard downed the ugly green ferrous gluconate tab with a swallow of orange juice, and tried not to dwell on (as he did every time he even thought the word *iron*) the doc's warning that they'd likely have to resort to some major injections of iron—by needle—before the pregnancy was completed.

"I'm supposed to get lots of protein at this stage of the pregnancy," Howard said. "And egg yolks are a good source of iron, too."

"Howard's become a regular Adele Davis," Dorothy said with an infuriating little smirk. "I bet he could tell you the nutritional stats of every item of food on this table, and the benefits of each for the fetus."

Howard had to work hard to keep from scowling. Dorothy would probably tell him to lighten up if he showed the slightest sign that her needling was getting to him.

Dale said, "There's something I've been wondering about, Howard, though it's a little delicate, and maybe you'd rather not say."

(Wonderful lead-in. Can't wait to hear what follows.) Howard put a hand to his midriff, as though merely touching it would quell his surging queasiness. He aimed a smile at Dale he hoped was friendly. He really did wish she weren't wearing a tee-shirt with such big fat stripes. Surely she must know they made her look bigger? "I'm not shy," he said.

Dale laughed. "Well, I was wondering. This whole pregnancy must be super-expensive. The endocrinologist and hysterectomy and in vitro fertilization and such high-tech pieces of equipment. . . . Is it possible your insurance is paying for everything?"

Howard shot a quick glance at Dorothy, who tended to stiffen at the least reference to Andrea. Dale had to know that an insurance policy that covered only a single dependent wasn't about to pay for the most expensive kind of pregnancies. "It's complicated," Howard said. "The insurance paid for Dorothy's hysterectomy. Everything else is being covered by special arrangement with the clinic. They get all of the unused eggs in the ovary they took from Dorothy, plus the uterus afterward, and the right to use photos and so on of me and the carapace for publicity." Dale looked at Dorothy, who was staring down at her plate. "The deal is that they don't announce my pregnancy until after delivery, though they do get to take photos of me along the way. Afterward, they have the right to use my name and photos as they see fit, to promote the use of the carapace by other men who might be interested in plugging in. And of course in the process they'll be acquiring hard data on the entirely experimental endocrinology of male pregnancy."

Dale rubbed her chin. She looked distinctly worried. "I'm just wondering. Why did they develop the carapace in the first place? What kind of women use it? A hysterectomy seems a considerably more drastic measure than simply getting a C-section, which is what usually happens when women have problem pregnancies."

Dorothy's laugh, very hard and sharp, rang out. Howard looked at her, startled; the bitterness of her smile made his stomach cramp. "My dear Dale, how *can* you be so naive! The point is profit, my dear! The carapace was developed to get around all the legal restrictions placed on surrogate pregnancies." Howard saw that two bright hectic blotches had flared in Dale's cheeks. "Because the uterus isn't the surrogate's, and because the baby isn't carried inside her body, the surrogate can't make any claim to being pregnant with the baby in any way the law recognizes. She's just *holding*—or *hosting*—the fetus. In a pouch resting against her abdomen. And *feeding* it, with her blood. Which in the eyes of the law is analogous to wet-nursing."

Dale put her hand to her lips. She darted a look at Howard, then hastily averted her eyes. "Oh," she said. And she pushed her plate aside, as though feeling too sick to eat the food she had just been praising.

"So. Have you made that baby robot of yours any smarter in the last few months?" Joe—a sudden fount of bluff heartiness—said quickly.

Howard shoved his chair back from the table. Dale had spoiled the meal—or rather Dale and Dorothy together. Women against men. He had seen it happen before, with other couples, usually at the other male's expense, and not his own. He forced a smile at Joe. "The project's really running hot," he said. The friendship of the two couples was finished, Howard thought. It could never recover. Dale had never acted like this before. (*Some kind of women's thing. Maybe sympathetic resentment at my using Dorothy's uterus for the baby, or maybe resentment at a man's doing what women have always had a monopoly on . . .*)

"There's a lot to be said for working out in the field, as you do," Joe said.

Maybe. But as graduate students Joe had been the star, not Howard, which was the reason he had achieved the prestige and security of a poorly paid academic job and Howard had gone to work in the private sector. He thought, Is the glass half-empty, or half-full? He, Howard, had a wife who had kept her slim, svelte figure, while Joe's full-figured sexpot had run to fat. Yet Dorothy wouldn't touch him, while—unless he was mistaken—Joe and Dale were still making it together and happy.

But then he, Howard, had something none of them had: a first-of-its-kind pregnancy, the best of two worlds.

(*Eat your hearts out, you jerks. This point's to me.*)

13

Actually, Howard thought as he rose at 9:30 a.m. for the second time on Monday morning, it was lucky Joe and Dale had driven instead of flown, because otherwise he'd have been stuck with them for most of the rest of the day. Though he usually hated getting up at four in the morning, it had been a pleasure that day, just to know they'd be gone.

Howard went out to the kitchen for coffee and breakfast, then carried a cup back to the bedroom for Dorothy. She was sitting up, and she had the phone on the bed beside her and the videotape catalog propped against her knees. Howard set the cup of coffee on her nightstand. "Since we've shared the news with Joe and Dale, I guess we'd better let the parents know," he said. "Now would be a good time to call, don't you think?"

Dorothy didn't look up from the catalog. "That's up to you. I'm not talking to anybody about it myself. But be my guest. Just let me dial up *Queen Christina* first."

Howard had a difficult time restraining himself from snatching up the damned catalog and tearing it to shreds. "Jesus Christ, Dorothy! We're having a baby and all you can think about is which goddamn crummy movie you're going to watch next! If when you were pregnant I'd treated you the way you're treating me—!" Howard was so upset he couldn't finish his sentence.

Dorothy looked up. Her blue irises were so cold they looked gray. "Howard," she said slowly, distinctly. "Answer this: when I was pregnant, did you want the baby?"

Howard swallowed. "Yes, of course."

"In fact, it was a joint project, was it not?"

Howard nodded. "Yes, of course."

"Well have I *ever* told you I want you to have this baby? Have I ever expressed the faintest interest in it?"

"You said it was my decision," Howard said angrily. "Remember? You said you'd cooperate!"

———

"Cooperate," Dorothy repeated. "I said I'd cooperate *up to a point*. And so I have. How many women would let themselves be sliced open and have their organs removed to serve someone else's purposes? That, Howard, was cooperation. I *never* said I'd *participate* in your pregnancy, or support it, or any other fucking positive thing like that. Did I." Howard's throat closed up. He blinked furiously, to hold back the tears that threatened.

(All these damned hormones are making me emotional!)

"By all means, call your parents, and call my mother, too, if you like," Dorothy said.

"But if you do call my mother, tell her I don't want to discuss it with her, and that if she tries it out on me I'll hang up." Dorothy looked down at the catalog, used her finger to mark the number of the film she wanted, and picked up the phone and said "Program: Dial-a-Video."

Howard washed his face, then went to his study and sat at his desk. To his dismay, his father, not his mother, answered his call. After going through the preliminary small talk, he said, "Hey, Dad, I've got some pretty decent news to tell you. You're now expecting a grandson."

"Hey, Howard, that's *wonderful!* Your mother will be thrilled! And a grandson— well, you know, I was beginning to wonder if any of you boys were going to be carrying the name on, after all. So when is Dorothy due?"

Howard broke into a hot, stifling sweat. If only his mother had answered! It would have been so much easier telling her—God, he should have waited, shouldn't have just blurted it out like that. His heart was pounding so hard he could barely catch his breath. "Uh, Dad," he said, his voice about an octave too high, "uh, Dad, it's me that's pregnant, not Dorothy."

Silence. "Uh, Howard," his father said after a few seconds, his voice peculiarly uncertain. "Uh, Howard, I think I heard you wrong. Could I have a repeat on that?"

Howard licked his lips. His throat was parched. "I'm carrying the baby, Dad. In a special carapace thing. Ultra high-tech. In vitro fertilization—Dorothy's egg, my sperm. The usual kind of baby, ha ha, just that I'm the one who's pregnant."

"I don't think I understand, Howard. I mean, we all know about the birds and the bees, right? Women have wombs, men don't, women get pregnant, men get them pregnant . . . and this in vitro fertilization stuff—what's wrong, wasn't the old equipment good enough this time?"

It was nightmarish. The more Howard tried to explain, the crazier it all sounded. Only the constant touch of his hand on the brushed silver of the carapace kept him from losing all confidence in the reality of it.

By the time he had finished informing each of his parents individually, Howard was so exhausted that he decided to put off calling Dorothy's mother—indefinitely, perhaps. She really was Dorothy's problem, not his. And who could know, for all the ostensible differences between the two women it might work out to *like daughter, like mother*. And one facetious, cold female was quite enough for him to deal with already, thank you.

14

As his pregnancy advanced, it came to seem to Howard that Independence Day weekend marked the beginning of a season of negativity (if not of outright misfortune). And because when he thought of that weekend he chiefly recalled the tension he felt Dale had unforgivably introduced into the two-couple relationship, Howard associated the negativity with *her*. He knew rationally that Dale could not be blamed for any of the physical problems that developed. But all through the remainder of the pregnancy, he visualized her as a sort of evil angel of gloom hanging invisibly over him, watching and waiting for the worst.

Contrary to expectations, the nausea did not go away. (It was merely supplemented by constipation, which Dr. Singh had warned might be a side effect of all the progesterone being injected into the maternal environment.) But as Dr. Rogers had predicted, Howard did have to endure iron injections (which exacerbated his nausea considerably). Also contrary to expectations, Dorothy did not become interested in the baby when, at the beginning of the second trimester, Howard was permitted to open the carapace and lift the pouch onto his belly. Instead, she took to sleeping in the guest room, because she said the "whole obscene show" *disgusted* her.

Most surrogate gestational carriers have a different take on the experience. "This kind of pregnancy is no real pregnancy. It's, like, just very hard work, with a constant invasion of privacy from your employers," said Rosa Diaz, Ward and Moran's live-in carrier. "I know what real pregnancy is like. And this is not it," she said. In fact, INS regulations required Diaz, who had given birth to two children (de facto natural U.S. citizens because of Diaz's U.S. residency at the time of their births), to be sterilized in order to keep her Green Card. She decided that if she had to lose the ability to bear children, she might as well sell her eggs: "They would just go to waste if I kept them, and maybe this way some of them might actually become babies." The doctor who performed the egg recovery suggested to her that she would make better money as a gestational carrier than sewing in a sweatshop. But, "It often made me very sad," she said of the surrogate pregnancy. "That baby was not inside me, and it wasn't possible for me to touch it the way the parents did, so the whole thing was like having to wear a heavy, gigantic tin can, making me sick, making the

Other "minor, quite normal discomforts of pregnancy" (as the clinic staff and doctors smilingly described them) afflicted him as well. His ankles swelled horribly. His lower back ached. He even developed varicose veins in his legs. His blood pressure soared, and the specter of preeclampsia threatened. And of course, as he should have *expected* (so the people at the clinic said), as the carapace was let out for the expansion of the fetus and the fluid enclosing it, the straps began to strain Howard's shoulders and often cut off the circulation in his arms altogether.

But these afflictions were nothing compared to the unprecedented crisis that whipped up in the seventh month. Contrary to *all* expectations (and to the endocrinologist's open delight), Howard's breasts not only continued to swell painfully under the influence of so much estrogen, but actually filled with *milk* (which now and then oozed from the dark-aureoled, so-tender nipples). According to Dr. Singhi, there was no reason he could not expect to breast-feed (unless, of course, the baby lacked a good-enough suck). And so he faced a dilemma that made him wish he hadn't started the pregnancy in the first place.

He could handle the "discomfort." And the prospect of having to deal with stupid cracks about his needing a bra didn't bother him much. But though his own pregnancy had been so sui generis that he hadn't made many comparisons between his and Dorothy's experience of it, he now couldn't help but recall the Fucking Big Deal he'd made about Dorothy breast-feeding Andrea. Howard knew all the pros and cons, bottle- vs. breast-feeding, inside and out. He had known them so well that Dorothy had been forced to bow to his superior reasoning.

He also knew that Dorothy had had a miserable time of it. Nursing had impacted her job and her sleep, and it had been a bloody and painful business even before Andrea had started biting. Yet Dorothy had been uncomplainingly long-suffering. True to her character, once she had made the decision, she had stuck by it and had taken responsibility for it. She had never blamed Howard for any of the inconveniences or pain.

But just the occasional ooze coming out of his nipples made Howard queasy. Women, he thought, were used to things leaking out of their bodies. It happened to them all the time, involuntarily, and they simply accepted that it did.

And he *would* have to get a bra if he nursed. Hell, he might have to get a bra even if he didn't, until he could get off the damned hormones.

> veins in my legs worse, and making me, like, invisible whenever my employers took the pouch out to have "quality time" with the baby. If it wasn't that I had two little children to raise, I'd never do it again."
>
> —from "The New Surrogate Pregnancies: The Professional Woman's Answer to the Biological Clock?" *The New York Times Magazine,* **June 8, 2014**

Howard imagined nursing the baby at work, on the days he commuted over. It was such a personal thing. So *physical.* Not clean, like the carapace. Constipation he could handle. Varicose veins he could handle. But leaking tits, mucking up his shirt amid making him smell like week-old milk?

Even if he didn't tell Dorothy, she'd probably figure it out for herself—and then, if he didn't breast-feed their son, would with every glance accuse him of enacting a double standard. And then he'd be miserably moist with his own petard. Really, he thought, it was a kind of emotional blackmail. Howard wished there were someone he could talk to about the dilemma. Obviously, Dorothy was out. And he didn't think he would feel comfortable talking on the phone about it with Joe. (Dale would probably have poisoned Joe's mind against him, anyway.) The staff at the clinic would refer him to the therapist. And the therapist . . . No, Howard couldn't tell her all this. He was seeing the therapist in order to work on his relationship with Dorothy. The therapist would interpret everything he said in light of that—and would hold it against him, as confirming Dorothy's view of things. Or else she would claim it was simply "a crisis of gender identity," as though one more nontraditional attribute could make him feel any less "manly." And there was no way on earth he was going to talk with a therapist about "manliness."

No. What he needed was to talk to a man who could understand what he was going through. Only he couldn't think of even one who might. That was the problem with being so radically cutting edge, Howard thought. No one else could possibly know where your head was at . . .

15

Howard had taken for granted that Dorothy would share postnatal parental duties with him, and that he would not have to take much leave from work because she would take one of reasonable length herself, following his. But he had been assuming that Dorothy would fall in love with the baby once it became real to her, which (he had thought) would be when they began making contact with it for the periods he took the pouch out of the carapace. Instead, the contact had repulsed her. *(Poor Marcel, forsaken by his chromosomal mother!)* And so Howard left it until the very last possible moment to discuss the issue with Dorothy. The baby would be born in less than a month. Marissa, threatening to kick him off the project, had given him a week to finalize his plans. He *had* to give her an answer.

Unable to put the discussion off another night, Howard cornered Dorothy in the den. She was watching a Marlene Dietrich movie, and didn't, of course, want to be disturbed, particularly since this was a dial-up movie, and not a tape she could watch at her command. Howard stood between her and the screen and insisted. "This is more important than a movie you can watch any goddamn time of the day or night," Howard said angrily.

She glared at him. "What could be so fucking important, Howard?"

Howard was abashed. He realized how stupid it was to have blown up at her, when the entire purpose of the conversation was persuasion. Her eyes and jaw looked *furious.* Howard tried to be conciliatory. "Uh, I'm sorry to interrupt, honey, but we can't wait any longer to make arrangements for leave." Howard knew this wasn't a great approach, but he felt helpless.

Dorothy raised her eyebrows at him. "I don't see what that has to do with me," she said.

Howard swallowed. "Look, I know you're against this pregnancy. But it's a fact, Dee, that there's going to be a young new life in our family, who will need just as much love and support as any other baby. What I thought was that I could take leave for the first couple of weeks, then you could take a leave for maybe a couple of months, and then we could either hire somebody or try to get him into that infant care place where we had Andrea."

Dorothy said, "I'm not taking any leave, Howard. For one thing, we can't afford it. We need my salary to make the payments on the second mortgage we took out to make a downpayment on the debts from Andrea's medical expenses. Remember?"

Howard shook his head. "I'm sure we'll be able to manage without your salary, honey. I can probably get some kind of help from the company. At this stage they'd probably do anything to minimize interruptions on the project."

Dorothy jerked out a short, bitter laugh. "You're incredible. Absolutely incredible. You're thirty-three years old, Howard. And yet your approach to pregnancy is like that of a teenage girl."

Howard stared at her. "I don't understand. In just what way is my approach to pregnancy like that of teenage girl?"

Dorothy said, "To most teenagers, pregnancy is something they undertake as individuals. As though it were a private thing between themselves and their babies. They lack any conception of the ramifications. They haven't yet grasped that bringing life into the world is a social act. Because they're teenagers. Teenagers tend to be solipsistic Howard. But you're not a teenager. So how come you've been thinking this entire thing is something you can do single-handedly, such that everybody else will fall into place the way you think they should, after you've done it?" She snorted. "You may have my uterus in that thing, and your Frankensteins may have taken one of my eggs and done laboratory magic with it to make an embryo, but that doesn't mean I consider myself related to your baby, Howard. I don't consider myself related to the people who are given the blood I donate, do I? So I donated my uterus and eggs. That doesn't make me a mother, Howard."

On the screen behind him, Dietrich was singing. He felt utterly disembodied and yet at the same time intolerably weighted down by the carapace, which never ceased to drag on the straps digging into his tired, sore shoulder. "But when I bring the baby home," Howard said, "surely you'll love him then?"

"Love him?" Dorothy echoed. "*Love* him, Howard? And how will I do that? I gave all my maternal love to Andrea. Every drop there was to give, I gave, Howard. And Andrea is gone. And I'm just now starting to accept that. But love another baby, no. Or I would have gotten pregnant again, Howard."

Howard swallowed. "What about me?" he said in a voice that he knew could barely be heard above Dietrich. "You do still love me?"

Dorothy's eyes were bleak. "All gone, Howard. I've been putting it off—leaving I mean, because everything will be so complicated financially, with all our debts and my insurance problem and so on. But no. Everything I felt for you—well, it was misguided, wasn't it. I've come to realize I didn't know you after all, and so what I loved was just imaginary. I don't know you, you don't know me. Five years: poof! Gone with the carapace."

"Why didn't you tell me this earlier!" Howard said. "My God, Dorothy, you never *said*. You never said you were *that* opposed."

Dorothy smiled sadly. "You didn't want to hear. I was being negative, retro, Luddite, even sexist for arguing against it. You weren't interested in anything I had to say. *Cutting-edge*, you kept yammering at me. *Cutting-edge*. And how if I were as feminist as I claim to be, I'd be thrilled to see you opening this new frontier in the breakdown in gender roles. And besides, how could I deny you another child when it was only a matter of giving you what I no longer wanted or needed. So I gave you my ovary, and I gave you my uterus. I see now that I was wrong to do so, but I did. You wanted those, not my opinions. Well, Howard, I gave, as they say, at the office."

Howard felt so sick he put his hand over his mouth and waddled as fast he could to the bathroom to puke. It couldn't be over, he thought. It just couldn't. Anyway, there was no way she couldn't love their child, once it was born. He knew Dorothy, even if she claimed not to know him. She was in denial. It was just a matter of keeping her from moving out before Marcel was born and he could place that small bundle of precious new life directly into her arms. He'd just have to be extra careful not to hassle her, that's all. And maybe get the docs to move up the date of delivery.

16

Two days before Howard delivered, Dorothy moved out. Howard pleaded, Howard begged, but she would not listen. "Children, taken objectively, are demanding, needy savages," she said. "People would kill their small children if they weren't besotted with love for them. And Howard, I don't feel love, I will not feel love, I cannot feel love, for the thing you carry inside you. Goodbye."

Howard wept. Howard wept until his head was pounding, his throat was hoarse, and his eyes and sinuses were swollen. "I've been abandoned," he cried again and again in harsh, tearing sobs. "She's left me. Nobody loves me." But as the edge of the realization of abandonment dulled, Howard heard his own voice, listened to his own words, and thought, "She's left *us*." And he looked down at what he could see of the bulging carapace, continued stroking it, and said, "It's just you and me, Big Dude, it's just you and me together." Babies, at least, always loved their parents. Marcel would—no, must already—love him.

Howard washed his face and drew the drapes and then, lying down on the bed, opened the carapace and carefully shifted the pouch onto his belly. (Surely, with the drapes drawn, it was dark enough, considering that the uterine walls must be fairly opaque.) The extent to which the uterus had stretched amazed him, as it did every time lie saw it. And how incredible, he thought, that one could see where the legs and arms and head were, and how sharply one could feel a kick, even through all that fluid. He spoke to the fetus, in a voice he made strong and reassuring. "*Daddy* won't leave you, Marcel my man. No way. We're in this together, Big Dude. It's you and me against the world, Champ."

His hands gentle on the pouch, his belly warm with the weight, Howard felt comforted, and he thought about the tightness of the bond between parent and child (once it was actually established). And then, making a logical connection, Howard had a brainstorm. *Of course.* His mother would *love* to help him care for Marcel for a while. She had adored Andrea. And she was clearly thrilled about Marcel, never mind his unconventional gestation. It would be a sacrifice for her to plunge into the dark rainy gloom of Seattle's winter, but Howard knew she would gladly make it. And she'd help him find somebody really good to take care of Marcel, somebody who might even agree to live in. (Howard was still kicking himself for forgetting, in the heat of the argument, that there would be no financial worries once Marcel was born, because tabloid and magazine editors and Hollywood producers would be falling all over themselves offering him megabucks for the story.)

Howard heaved the fetus back into the carapace and picked up the phone. *Your approach to pregnancy is like that of a teenage girl.* Oh god, he thought, maybe Dorothy's right. Who is it that the teenager goes to, when she needs help with the baby? Who else but her mother!

Howard sighed. Maybe there was some truth to the charge. But at least he wasn't as bad as most teenaged *fathers*. He was responsible, he would take care of Marcel, he wouldn't dump him on anybody else—at least not totally. "Program," Howard said into the phone. "Howard's parents."

SEATTLE, December 23 (INS)—For the first time in history, a man has undergone pregnancy and delivery. Dr. Howard Nies, a robotics specialist, gave birth yesterday to a son, Marcel, following a full-term pregnancy using a gestational carapace and a womb provided by Nies's wife, Dorothy Newman. Dr. Michael Rogers, the attending physician, expressed satisfaction with the child's condition and said that with this new technology, there is no reason why male pregnancy will not become "routine." He predicts that in the future, most pregnancies will be undertaken with this "far safer, more controlled and rational environment that is so much better for the baby than the vulnerable, relatively perilous natural womb."

Laura Nies, the new father's mother, said she had her doubts about men having babies. "Little Marcel is a baby like any other, and my grandson. I'm sure Howard loves him, as most fathers love their sons. But I still think every child needs a mother's love more than anything else. I guess I'm just old-fashioned. I intend to do my best to see to it that Marcel gets every bit of love as my Howard got."

"From Go, we've been breaking new ground here, Marcel and me," Dr. Nies said. "I'm proud of my son, and I'm sure if he could speak, he'd tell the world that he's proud of me. It's a new world, for men, a big, bold, brave new world—as I've just proved, and those who follow in my footsteps will prove, too."

SAFETY OF SKIN

Melinda Rackham

> Buried in the confusion of details of every mind, there had to be something untouched by time, unswayed by the shifting weight of memory and experience, unmodified by self-directed change.

—Greg Egan, *Diaspora*

Usually we think of ourselves as being like a peach—having a soft and squishy skin on the outside and a solid kernel-like core. There is something about ourselves that we see as intrinsically fixed, central, immovable. It's not our mushy and vulnerable brain, and it's not our intangible and ethereal soul. Perhaps this fixed point could be the pineal gland, a small lobe in the forebrain that, according to the Eastern perspective of the chakra system, governs the experience of self and reality, integrating the entire physical, emotional, mental, and spiritual human experience. Or is this hardness more centrally located . . . lying beneath the rib cage in our heart, that strong muscle that pumps the animating fluid of blood through our vascular systems, bringing life and nourishment to the flesh?

Just what is it that resides beneath our peachy skin, locating and identifying the defining boundary between the "colony" that is *us* and everything else? Perhaps it's our bones and cartilage, that internal architectural structure that defines our shape. Perhaps it is the softer combination of membrane and muscle that gently and firmly hold our organs, preventing them from spilling from of our bodies. Then again maybe it is that invisible but potent biochemical cohesion that symbiotically binds the billions of tiny bacteria and viri that comprise the bio-ecological scape we call the human body.

Being immersed in online environments makes questions like this difficult to ignore as we establish emotional and physical protocols for interaction in these spaces. Where is the kernel or seed of the self when the body is composed of pixels? Are the ethereally coded soft bodies we inhabit in machine produced data space different from

the flesh bodies which we inhabit offline? What is intrinsically unique about us as individuals when we are re-presented virtually? Without a hard shell, could it be possible
to remain untouched and unmodified when we inhabit electronically constructed
lifeworlds?

>> becoming avatar

According to Michael Heim (2001), "The avatar first arises in the most primitive form
as a moving cursor on the grid screen when that screen becomes networked with other
screens . . . The cursor mouse becomes the seed of the avatar, the potential of cyberspace to mix information with intersubjectivity and with real-time communication."

When we slip into networked spaces in online multiuser communities, we must
become an avatar, or an *other* species, to operate in this parallel space. As Gregory Little
points out in "A Manifesto for Avatars" (1998), an avatar is among several species, which
share aspects of social constructions and identity politics, that inhabit the online territories. These species include the cyborg and the zombie, but avatars should be carefully
differentiated from them by their form and function.

The avatar is unique because it has its origin in one world and is projected through
or assumes a form of representation appropriate to a parallel world. The term itself refers to the physical body that the ethereal Hindi deity Vishnu assumes during visits to
the earthly plane:

In its native language, this title refers to a Divine Incarnation, one in whom the Supreme
Consciousness has descended into human birth for a great world-work . . . The Avatar is
not a singular incarnation but takes birth through a divine lineage stretched out over many
millenniums. These incarnations are linked through the substance of their mission which is
the establishment of a reign of Truth Consciousness on the Earth. (Wilkinson 1994)

The appropriation or repurposing of the term *avatar* to represent a human user
migrating from the earthly plane to operate within the ethereal plane of shared online
Internet environments is attributed to LucasFilm's *Habitat* project in the early 1980s
(Morningstar and Farmer 1991, 276). However, the more mainstream usage of the term
came with the avatar-inhabited *Metaverse* environment of Neil Stephenson's *Snow
Crash* in the early 1990s. Stephenson also established the crucial visual hierarchy of
avatar representation that I discuss in this chapter in more detail. Today the term
"avatar" has lost its sacred association in technocultural circles and is generally used to
refer to the body we inhabit when we transcend our material bodies and enter the plane

of the alternate reality softspaces of the World Wide Web. What does remain of its spiritual lineage is that the avatar, although a software construct, is usually seen to be rooted in hardspace.

One software language that offers insight into the way avatars have been conceptually and technically constructed in networked computing is the VRML 2.0 specification. Here the avatar is clearly defined as "the abstract representation of the user in a VRML world. The physical dimensions of the avatar are used for collision detection and terrain following" (VRML Consortium Incorporated 1997, 3.5). Importantly, although having dimension and physicality, the avatar is *not* the user, who is separately defined as "a person or agent who uses and interacts with VRML files by means of a browser" (VRML Consortium Incorporated 1997, 3.108).

The specification is very clear that the user does not have to be human. It may also be an agent, opening up the possibility that any user may be a software construct—an extension of another machine. VRML is not designed to be a playground only for humanity. It is open to any sort of species interaction. The terms are important here because they additionally distinguish the user from the viewer, with the latter defined as "a location, direction, and viewing angle in a virtual world that determines the portion of the virtual world presented by the browser to the user" (VRML Consortium Incorporated 1997, 3.109). This produces three separate but interlinked possible viewing and interactive perspectives in a virtual world.

The viewer's position is the central node, the hard core, the floating x, y, z-coordinate point 0,0,0, around which the point of view of the world is drawn and redrawn in real time. Although fixed at the position of 0,0,0, this coordinate point moves through the universe as the viewer navigates, constantly relocating the central axis of the visual world with each navigational decision. While this viewer appears to be omnipotent, it is restricted to its line of sight, because it is never rendered in the world, existing as a disembodied observer invisible to any other users. Without an avatar, and tied to its viewing position, it can only function in a single sensory mode—with the externalized view or eye (I) trajectory.

To become part of the virtual networked environment in a multisensory mode, the user must inhabit the software-constructed material presence of an avatar, producing interlinked possibilities for subjective and interactive perspectives. This provides physical dimension and parameters for contact in the world, a malleable coded skin with which the user may touch others in softspace. The user can gently push with its pulsing skin and permeable boundaries, establishing a cohesive tactility by scripted touch and proximity sensors that generate visual, programmatic, and sonic events. The user is translucently, visibly, and momentarily solid in the environment, becoming simulta-neously a central player and part of the background to other users in the environment.

>> programmed possibilities

Being temporarily liberated from our singularity—simultaneously occupying the three positions of user, viewer, and avatar, and as well, able to code our own avatar bodies—would seem to open up myriad possibilities and freedom of choice in our representa-tions of our online selves. However, it appears that the opposite is true. The choice of avatars adopted by many users is very mainstream, as Little (1998) observes with some disappointment:

a colony of extremely generic, homogenous representations rooted in prevailing construc-tions of successful commodification and accumulation: pop icons, juvenile fantasies, dumbed-down cartoon characters, and racially pure, white, young, 'perfect bodies.' A tool with the potential for the playful generation of territories of signification and empower-ment, the avatar is being used instead as a weapon against its own referents to seize this ter-rain of potential as part of a rabid process of accumulation.

There may be historical precedents for this, since early choices of visual represen-tation or embodiment available in online chat worlds were constructed by programmers rather than designed by artists, so often their functionality was prioritized over their aesthetics. Some of the most popular options were the virtually amputated talking heads, which were often employed for very practical reasons because they took less con-struction time and skill due to the absence of an animated body, as well as less bandwidth and processing time. A choice of mythic figures, outlaws, and deities offered quick and easy identification in a heads-only world like the long-standing and still-functioning *OzGate* online community (n.d.; figure 3.1).

Ironically, in *Snow Crash* (1992) Stephenson predicted a limited and impoverished state of avatar representation where one's choice of avatar online reflected one's social status offline. To have a custom-written, well-defined, high-resolution avatar, you needed to be either wealthy or a programmer, and in the novel's online virtual world *Metaverse*, programmers assume the highest status. The poorer or less tech-savvy who cannot afford custom avatars, or who cannot write their own, have to opt for more restricted and lower definition avatars. Hiro Protagonist, the main character in *Snow Crash*, is of course a well-rendered version of his actual offline self, and is always virtu-ally dressed in a black leather kimono. The anti-hero however, the viral terrorist pro-

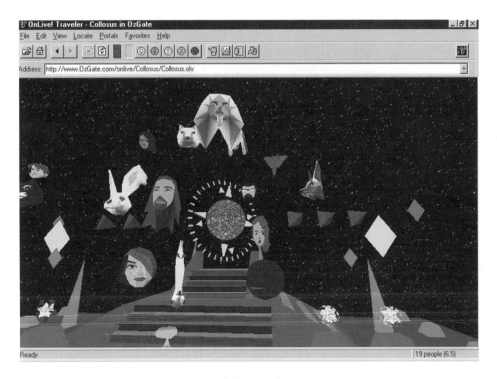

| Figure 3.1 |
Heads-only avatars at *OzGate* online community

grammer, chooses the lowest of the low avatars, a black and white, low resolution, highly undifferentiated pixilated representation; one that is mass-produced, is highly unrecognizable, and distracts attention from the avatar itself. Most users in the *Metaverse* have some basic avatar decoration options, but Hiro is scathing of those that don't have these choices available or don't make them:

Brandy and Clint are both popular off-the-shelf models. When white-trash high school girls are going on a date in the Metaverse they invariably run down to the computer-games section of the local Wal-mart and buy a copy of Brandy. The user can select three breast sizes: improbable, impossible, and ludicrous . . . Her eyelashes are half an inch long, and the software is so cheap they are rendered as solid ebony chips . . . Clint is the male counterpart of Brandy. He is craggy and handsome and has an extremely limited range of facial gestures (Stephenson 1992, 35).

| Figure 3.2 |
Avatars in the *There* online environment

Most online environments today are populated by Brandy and Clint clones (figure 3.2), for example the avatars available within the popular *There* multiplayer environment, or ones customized from prefabricated avatar mannequins provided by software houses. This second category, commercially available avatar creation packages, is often linked to specific software-driven environments as interlinked marketing promotions. An example is *Avatar Lab*, software designed to let the user create custom 3-D avatars specifically for the not very successful *Adobe Atmosphere* worlds. The user selects basic human, animal, or robot figures with the mandatory arms, legs, and heads, or can "even mix-n-match to create wild combinations, [since] there are over 200 million possible choices" (Curiouslabs, n.d.). They are then invited to "use photos of [themselves] or any other face to create a unique and personalized avatar. Add hair, accessories and props to complete the figures" (Curiouslabs, n.d.).

Although applications such as this promise individuality, invariably there is a sameness about the avatars that they produce. One could conclude that the user does not want to stand out in a way that is, in popular culture, seen to be unattractive, different or ugly. Strangely the opportunity for exploration brings more conformity, because often users select avatar body types, genders, and racial characteristics that bear little relation to their hardspace physicality—in order to conform to Western standards of cultural attractiveness. There is of course nothing wrong with wanting to be "attractive," however, the freedom to step outside culturally fixed appearances and specified roles is one of the major factors that draw people to participate in online worlds. But perhaps the visual homogenization of these avatars is as much due to the limited range of choices offered by the avatar design environments, and hence the software designers, as to the users themselves.

Whatever the reason, places like *There* do breed a certain style of avatar: "Most people choose something quite straightforward, [so] *There*'s characters look more like everyday people; *Second Life*'s are likely to be dressed as superheroes or in other costumes" (Terdiman 2004). *Second Life* is the first product of Linden Lab, a company specifically established to develop shared 3-D entertainment. Although it is a multi-player environment similar to *There*, *Second Life* promises to give its members an added dimension to their everyday life. It encourages users to "become the world's most popular or wealthiest resident [and to] win votes for [their] personality, appearance, or building skills" (Terdiman 2004). Users are provided with "Fashion Design Templates" that work with *Photoshop* software to make buttons, pockets, and tattoos to customize their avatar's appearance, hence supposedly enhancing the individual experience. According to Cory Ondrejka, Linden Lab's vice president of product development: "You can be a woman some of the time and a man the rest of the time, and you don't even have to look human. Residents have fun dressing up to go dancing or showing off their cool tattoos to each other. As for the detail to which you can customize your avatar, there are hundreds of controls, which allow for effectively infinite possibilities for how you can look in-world. You can look like a realistic version of yourself—or you can look as outlandish as you want" (Assassin 2004).

Second Life is primarily marketed as a space in which one leaves the everyday behind: "Second Life is like your life unlocked and unbound; it's your reality on fast-forward" but not too far behind (Terdiman 2004). Offline reality is painstakingly recreated as avatars—even in catsuits or superhero outfits—marry, acquire property and assets, and live life online as if it were hardspace. It is clear that despite their promises, both the avatar creation packages and these online virtual environments are not offering any really alternate experiences of what is to be human offline. Instead they offer a way of altering our bodies to whichever "perfect" humanoid representation we desire, and a fantasy world where we can live life in that avatar body. This is obviously very appealing in a cultural and social context where people are increasingly dissatisfied with their physical appearance. Avatar creation is easier, cheaper, and less dangerous than physical intervention like cosmetic surgery. And it can be easily revised, unlike an offline tattoo or a breast, vagina, or penis augmentation, which are messy to reverse or erase. Slipping into an other, a virtual humanoid body, is not too much of a mind shift, since we want our fantasy excursions to be as seamless as possible. This loyalty to a form of realistic representation ensures, we think, that our online personas remain under our control.

>> (im)proper usage

Once we have carefully digitally constructed and groomed our avatar selves for projection into another space, then what are we going to do with them? Do we merely desire touristic observation of an other world, or are we really yearning to interact with others—to live, work, and play virtually?

Michael Heim speaks of the importance of communication in his "Avatar Manifesto" where he predicts that by the year 2010 "networked collaborative communication becomes the norm for business, commerce, and the arts" (2000a). Instead of the Internet being a static space for data storage, the flows in cyberspace—that is, the true "substances" of virtual worlds—become obvious in event-based interactions. Heim uses his online *Activeworlds Eduverse* environment "CyberForum@ArtCenter" as an example of a space that can promote those interactive experiential flows in an educational—a place that "takes process seriously in fashioning worlds as 'aesthetic occasions'" (2000b). In February 2000, guest Katherine Hayles discussed the posthuman in the environment with Heim and his students as an avatar in 3-D virtual worlds. The transcript and screenshots remain online (Hayles and Heim 2000), and the documentary result is a rather tedious discussion, a curious mix of intimate and theoretical posting by both Hayles and the students in Heim's online 3-D class.

KateH: Yes, my talk seems to be in bold—and I'm so shy, too!
gaga: no way! I've heard you speak before.
ommm: your avatar may be in bold, while you remain shy;-) (Hayles and Heim 2000)

Hayles chose to be embodied as a low-resolution low-polygon multicolored swallow-type construction, mostly obscured in the site's screen grabs by her text. Heim aims for CyberForum to addresses issues of consistency with the "flow of words with visuals, flow of atmospherics, flow of group dynamics, flow of virtual with physical architecture (avatecture)" (2000a). However, lag online seems to ensure that there is not a continuous flow of questions and answers in the chat session, but rather an overlap of statements and questions that are often left unaddressed. Hayles attempts to discuss her book *How We Became Posthuman* (1999); however, the environment only allows the briefest of overviews, leaving the content of her posting mostly on the materiality of text in artists' books rather than on any issues to do with embodiment in online environments.

Reading this archive and viewing the screenshots, one realizes that examining the visual re-presentation of the participants makes individual and group meaning difficult to discern. It is hard to focus on the subtleties of posthumanity while a group of chunky translucent virtual brides wanders through the 3-D rendered scene (figure 3.3). The

| Figure 3.3 |

Screen grab from *CyberForum@ArtCenter 02/26/2000* with Katherine Hayles's bird avatar located at the center left (slightly obscured). *Source:* http://www.mheim.com/cyberforum/html/spring2000/media/hayles/log3.html.

forum, while opening the possibility of taking multiuser spaces more seriously than as pure entertainment spaces, makes it apparent that Heim's vision for networked communication as the norm within the next decade is rather optimistic, because virtual reality (VR) technology has not been uniformly developed, having moved little in visual resolution or mainstream uptake in the last fifteen years—except in specific arenas.

Commercial online gaming environments, in which avatar deployment has been highly successful, warrant a mention at this point in the discussion. The world of Massively Multiplayer Online Computer Role-Playing Games (MMORPGs), a parallel universe to artistic multiuser environments or the more pedestrian domains of *Active-worlds*, is a thriving, income-generating enterprise. *Lineage,* for example, an online world in South Korea, claimed four million subscribers in 2004, or one in eight households in the country involved. It attracts at least twice as many concurrent users as the U.S.-based *EverQuest*, a series of *Lord of the Rings*–style fantasy worlds. As in the *There* and *Second Life* communities, players pay a monthly fee of around US$30 to be loyal and committed members of these gated fantasy enterprises.

Top-level users in the first game of the *EverQuest* series spent most of their time in the nation of Norrath, engaging in conventional offline behaviors, including the accumulation of wealth. According to Castronova's early study of the economies of VR worlds, "Virtual Worlds: A First-Hand Account of Market and Society on the Cyberian Frontier" (2002), an average player's per capita income within *EverQuest* was around US$2,500. *EverQuest* currency was traded offline for real U.S. dollars or other hard currencies; avatar realities begin to blur with hard world space in terms of income generation. By 2004 asset accumulation and trading had become such a part of daily life that the *Second Life* currency "Linden Dollars" and currencies from other games like *The Sims Online* could be exchanged for on- and offline goods and services or traded for U.S. dollars at game commodity trading sites.

But back to *EverQuest* . . . Castronova points out that if a player lives in a country like Bulgaria where the per capita income is lower than in Norrath, then that player would be financially better off spending time online, with his or her *EverQuest* avatar earning or stealing or otherwise obtaining money. Selling the avatar for soft currency on- or offline was more beneficial than actually going to work in the player's own geographic local area. Avatars, whose skill development and hierarchy ascension become the property of the user and part of this soft economy, were sold at the time to the highest bidder at places like eBay for up to US$2,000 each. Interestingly, in a further study of the social valuation of software-generated bodies, Castronova (2003) found that offline gender politics were also mirrored in online worlds, since male avatars were significantly more valuable in resale terms than female avatars of an equivalent skill level.

EverQuest and similar spaces work so well and are so popular precisely because they don't question the real-world status quo. They operate using stereotypical role-playing devices and defined scenarios taken from fantasy. There are enemies to kill, wealth to be acquired, romantic conquests to be made, skills to develop, and a hierarchy of levels to ascend. There is the comforting familiarity of the avatar appearance in *EverQuest*. The environment has horizon lines as well as fore-, mid-, and backgrounds, all visual markers of reality that make this fantasy world safe for the user. The feeling of visual safety and familiarity along with the safety of defined game parameters means that users are happy to pay to belong to this community.

However, in spite of the growing sophistication of graphical representation in virtual space, the success of creating an embodied experience online is not reliant on realistic representation. The avatar representation for the comic strip–like *Habitat*, or even the text-based LambdaMOO proved to be just as successful in creating a sense of immersion and intimacy as these multi-million-dollar, massively multiplayer games today. If strict adherence to the re-creation of offline reality does not enhance our online emotional engagement, why do developers strive to provide hyperreal human avatars for users to engage in fantasy roles in virtual environments?

>> multiple choice

But not everyone wants to engage online in visual and cultural ways similar to their hardspace realities. Consequently, in my multiuser *empyrean* online virtual reality environment (Rackham 2003), I have provided an alternative to these prevailing representations by offering four choices of bio-coded avatars. *empyrean* is a fluid space, with seven interconnected anti-hierarchical realms or scapes for users to explore. It is both a microcosmic and a macrocosmic space, creating an uncomfortable sensation in some, because there are no familiar horizon lines to orient the self against or fixed texts to read or pathways to navigate. The user could be simultaneously swimming through viscous liquid and floating in the dark voids of outer space. The only visual anchor point for any user is his or her own avatar, which, upon entry to the *empyrean* universe, is given a randomly generated seven-character genome sequence as an identifier within the world.

Having nonhumanoid avatars in this environment challenges the usual mimicking of hardspace stereotypes, focusing the user's attention on other flows apart from role-playing in online networked space. Contrary to the norm, these avatars do not in any way resemble either human facial or full-bodied physical characteristics; they are translucent, ephemeral, microscopic, cellular, electronic constructions.

First, there is *miss fluffy* who has existed through many textual incarnations on the Internet since 1995, though now she is embodied in a visual way (figure 3.4). Her pink, opalescent, animated appearance could be mistaken for a cell, or an alien creature; however, *fluffy* is actually a representation of a globule of spit or mucous, the sort of thing that you expel from the body when you sneeze. Containing a few viri (the small egg shapes), and some much larger orange-colored bacteria, she is a colonial forward scout, searching for new sites of infection. She has in the past had a wild history of digital presence on mailing lists, MOOs, and MUDs and some sexual textual exploits, some of which are detailed on my *tunnel* Web site (Rackham 1996).

miss fluffy is incredibly popular. From my anonymous observations at museums and festivals where this work has been installed since its inception in 2000, I have concluded that she is the avatar consistently chosen by all types of users. However, she is chosen more often by male users of all ages, who possibly desire to experiment with virtual cross-dressing and transgender identity through inhabiting her. Perhaps it is

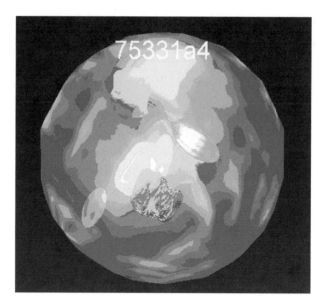

| Figure 3.4 |
Screen grab of *miss fluffy* avatar. *Source:* Melinda Rackham (2003).

anthropomorphizing a piece of software; however, I would suggest that her long online history has left the avatar with a personality residue, an electronic trace or aura that makes her a familiar and comfortable choice among users.

Because I know *miss fluffy* well, I'm more likely to choose to be embodied in *empyrean* by the avatar *big pickle*, a spiky pink and purple, phallic, pulsing slug-like creature. *pickle* is visually based on a macrophage, part of the body's immune system, often known as the body's clean-up crew (figure 3.5). The biological function of a macrophage is to respond to a site of infection in the body by "eating up" destroyed cells. My projection of the macrophage's personality is something like the characters in white biohazard suits who appear after a crisis or messy violent scene in *X-Files* or *Men in Black* to erase all evidence of damage, deviation, or infection and to return the space to a pristine state. Interestingly, and again from anonymous observation, women tend to pick *pickle* as their avatar. I have no evidence to suggest whether these users are attracted to the biological animal-like aspect, the rhythmic pulsing movement and vibrant color, or the obviously phallic look to *big pickle*. Maybe they think the name is cute and their choice is without reference to any of these other aspects.

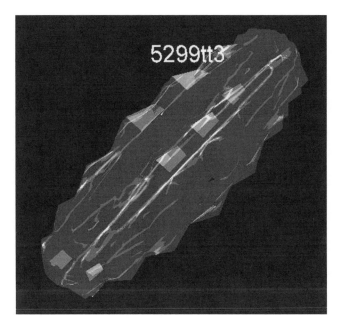

| Figure 3.5 |
Screen grab of *big pickle* avatar. *Source:* Melinda Rackham (2003).

quincy is more hard-edged—a mathematical construct, pure animated geometry; he is a child of the digital world (figure 3.6). He is a perfect sphere, constraining within himself a matrix of revolving crystalline structures. With no markers of biological life, *quincy* is a close relative of the hissing blue spheroid objects in the *beauty* scape of the *empyrean* world. *quincy* is also the avatar who can easily disappear, who will blend in well in virtual space. But from my observations of users over the first few years of the project, I have found that very few choose to be *quincy*. Perhaps *quincy* didn't seem unique enough, or perhaps it was *quincy*'s name? As the avatar code creator, I had considered killing off *quincy;* however I hadn't been able to delete the file.

Perhaps creating an avatar is akin to the responsibility of having a child, the process of giving them life, or the opportunity to inhabit and be inhabited /animated by human bodies/spirits. Under the moral codes of Western Christianity then, deleting the file would be relegating them to a version of purgatory, as they sit comatose on the hard drive, slowly fragmenting and corrupting away. Only a disk reformat will completely erase all traces of their individuality, their unique code, realigning their zeros and ones

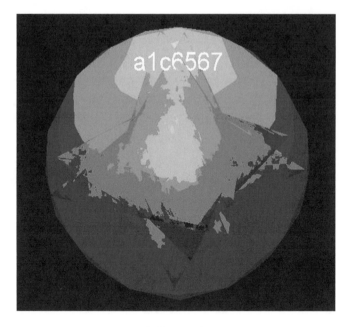

| Figure 3.6 |
Screen grab of *quincy-san* avatar. *Source:* Melinda Rackham (2003).

to a static pattern, ready to be reused for another purpose as building blocks of new software constructs. As a temporary solution to this problem, before the biennial Inter Society of Electronic Arts (ISEA) exhibition in Nagoya in 2002, in which *empyrean* was showing, I altered the avatar's name to *quincy-san*. In the Japanese context, the once lonely *quincy-san* became a very popular avatar, gaining a new lease on life because of this culturally specific title.

Finally comes *symborg*, a viral/machine creature, the "terminator" or android of the *empyrean* world (figure 3.7a, b). A smooth green surface hides nasty metallic viral spikes that emerge rhythmically from under the silky skin, evoking a sense of danger. *symborg* operates on stealth, managing to visually camouflage itself through its transparency in the space, so it can slip around the empyre without being easily spotted. *symborg* is based on the character *infectious agent* from my earlier work *carrier* (Rackham 1999), which investigated the symbiotic relationship between human and machine, and between a biological and a software virus. *Infectious agent* is a Java software construct, which seeks to seduce the user into symbiotic infection through aesthetic and textual means, through

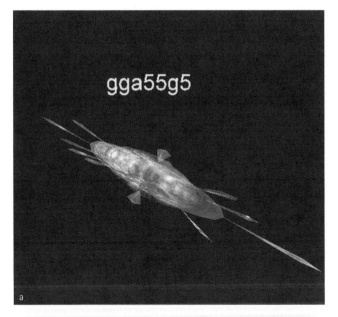

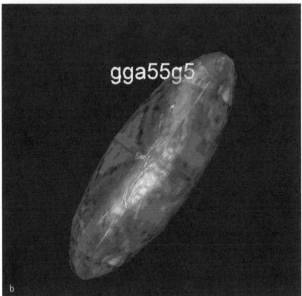

| Figure 3.7a,b |
Screen grab of *symborg* avatar in two stages. *Source:* Melinda Rackham (2003).

Melinda Rackham

disguise and manipulation rather than through direct confrontation or attack. Again from my rather random observations, *symborg* tends to attract female users more often than male users.

Utilizing the visual tactics of translucence, abstraction, and ephemerality with semi-transparent textures in *empyrean*, I have made it obvious that all the avatars are constructs based on polygons, rather than simulations of organic carbon-based life forms. Some avatars have deliberately incomplete or erroneous data sets. This means they lack some visual detail that would indicate a seamless model. They miss "faces"—that is, a polygon parameter will be lacking, and therefore a small surface will be not drawn, creating a visual hole, a blemish, or corruption into the exterior of the model. These inconsistencies are intended to alert users immersed within this space that they are interacting within and with electronically activated, software-produced entities, which have their own aesthetic characteristics. Neither are the avatars trying to recreate or simulate a user's hard-world persona; users cannot transfer their fantasy physical selves into digital medium when they look like a mucous ball. Rather I would like the user to be aware that they are inhabiting or cohabiting within a coded construct whose lifeworld is electronically activated softspace.

>> communication

The avatars of *empyrean* cannot speak. They communicate only via gestures. There are five gestures, each with an associated sound, loosely based on Stephenson's template for the off-the-shelf, white-trash *Brandy* avatar, whose facial gestures are limited to "cute and pouty; cute and sulky; perky and interested; smiling and receptive; cute and spacey" (1992, 35). Likewise, there are a restricted number of gestures available with the Sony Aibo pet robotic dog—with its six gestures of happiness, sadness, anger, surprise, dislike, and love. Billions of yen spent on gestural research indicate that very few gestures are required to induce empathy, sympathy, and identification with another creature.

In many online environments, communication is often very limited—most textual conversations start with accessing gender, location, age, and time zone. Having to type responses creates a rhythm with unique parameters. Any communication is dependent upon individual typing skill, hardware, software, Internet connection speed, and server lag, reminding users that the degree of general traffic on the network at any particular moment influences their interactions. As we have seen earlier, long and complex communication is rarely possible in multiuser space. This interaction via single lines of not necessarily linear text—or offline with stripped down and recoded SMS- (or short message service) specific language—is altering the nature of conversing between the electronic generation, necessitating a reevaluation of online text as we know it.

Although most multiuser spaces impose text as the dominant mode of communication online, *empyrean* acknowledges there are limitations and opens other possibilities as a subtextual environment. Three versions of *empyrean* online work exist, each with different communication options. In the single-user world, there are no other users and therefore no avatar communication options. The multiuser Web version allows for both text and gestural interaction; however, in the multiuser gallery version, *empyreanCosmos*, the usual text input function of multiuser worlds has been removed. Avatars must find other ways to communicate and make meaning within the space. The environment does contain text fragments as part of the scapes, but those texts remain random, with no fixed connecting narrative to dictate meaning. Challenging the notion of text as a stable and immoveable authority in Western tradition, texts in *empyrean* shift in response to an avatar's movement. This means that they alter direction and orientation so that the text fragment is always visible and readable by the user, thereby making the user the central, stable tenant/tenet of the world.

In addition to, or instead of, text, in *empyrean* the avatars have a range of preverbal gestural communication options. The prioritization of text in most multiuser worlds is reversed, and users primarily interact through sound and gesture. Avatars may squeak, squawk, blink, swell up and go opaque, gurgle, giggle, and blush to communicate with one another. These gestures have no fixed meaning, being contextually and relationally defined and consequently altering from user to user. Utilizing ways other than text for communication means the multiuser VRML domain is not tied to a dominant language group, nor is it based on age categories or educational factors, as is the case with most communication in multi-user environments.

Providing another level of consistency in the immersive, sonic environment, the gestural sounds will appear even when the avatar is off-screen. The VRML soundscape design by Mitchell Whitelaw (2003) is spatialized and attached to the etheric objects within the worlds. These objects are mostly moving and are often set at different pitches, so that once the viewer is inside the world the soundscape is constantly shifting around the viewer's avatar. In a sense, the user could navigate by sound alone, since each zone or scape of *empyrean* has a distinctive soundscape, such as the glassy crunching and grinding spheres of *chaos* scape, or the frenetic cellular skating rink in *charm* scape, or the tinkling birdsong of the choreographed neurons in *void* space.

Avatars need to be connected, need to be roaming within their lifeworld on the network to interact. It is true that their gestural code may be tweaked and tested from a single file offline, but like any creature pinned to a laboratory bench with electrodes sparking nervous and muscular responses, such testing is hardly indicative of communications and responses in their natural environment. When connected, the gestures and sounds of the individual avatars become part of the background of the immersive scapes. This sonic interaction adds to the sense of being there in an experiential way rather than jolting the user out of his or her avatar embodiment by the comic strip referenced text bubbles (figure 3.2) that appear in most worlds. A coherent and specific scape of interactions decreases the distractions for the user-as-avatar experiencing the electronic environment.

>> symbiotica

How close are we to our avatars? Is there a barely visible connection, a string of code or a thread of mucus joining us? Some commentators like Michael Heim view the avatar as a virtual, finite, and fixed point, purely based on consensual fantasy: "Avatars are shared fantasy identities that prove they are alive and telepresent through real-time playful interactive construction. Avatar identities are finite points of presence, intrinsically interactive and plural, embedded in communities of other avatars." (2000a).

I differ from both Heim and Little in believing that the avatar is not merely a fantastic creature, a disposable strap-on software construct, but rather an other (perhaps a soft other), with whom we develop a relationship. We as humans are mutable and flexible in the ways we represent ourselves. For example, the code-based characters in Greg Egan's future-fiction novel *Diaspora* (1997) are easily able shift their mode of being—transferring themselves from residing in the collective and fluid *polis* (a hard-drive scape) into individual robotic *gleisner* bodies to function in the biological plane. There is a necessary adjustment in operating through different bodies, through different mediums. One representation is not merely overlaid upon a solid and unchanging self, like a mask. As with any avatar, the relationship that is formed is dependent upon the avatar's software-constructed personality, quirks, and uniqueness; this ephemerality and materiality leads to an individuated user experience.

Avatars are not merely an extension of a solid self; rather, they can be seen as examples of *parināma*—the Buddhist notion of alterity or "becoming otherwise," where the identity of the self is in reality nonself, never fixed, and changing from moment to moment (Lusthaus 2002, 430). Even when one is applying the Western philosophical tradition, avatars are easily seen as products of relations. Taking Elizabeth Grosz's discussion of the encounter with the other, I will consider how the four characteristic indicators of alterity—that is, exteriority, excess, infinity, and activity—relate to avatar relations. If an other meets the criteria of alterity, it could never be a disembodied being; rather, such others are more likely to be "corporeal subjects, sexual subjects, subjects capable of touching, seeing, engaging and negotiating with the other's materiality" (Grosz 1989, 143).

First, there is exteriority: the avatar is separate from the user and in a sense unpredictable. Even though avatars' actions are based on a finite set of rules, there are an enormous number of finite outcomes. Avatars have the capacity to astonish and surprise, frustrate and delight us as the end users, indicating an existence apart from their creators. Even if an avatar is being slavishly traded as a commodity on the open avatar market of online gaming communities like *EverQuest*, the individuality and separateness of the avatar from the user is acknowledged. The more unique and highly skilled the avatar, the more valuable it is to its colonial traders.

The avatar can also be seen as "a site of excess," an "indigestible residue" that we (as the users) are unable to absorb into ourselves. As most of us who have utilized an avatar character in multiuser space have experienced, an avatar can be resistant to, and independent of, our aspirations and wishes. We experience frustration as we try to manipulate gestures that don't always work, or traverse terrains that won't allow the avatar to enter. Coded attributes override user preferences as avatars collide or don't collide with other objects in their lifeworlds, emitting sounds the user has not initiated, mutating at seemingly random intervals. Rogue avatars, like viruses, can trigger events that can crash our computer operating systems, bringing our virtual experience to an abrupt end.

An avatar is not a finite entity. It exceeds imposed borders, boundaries, and limitations. Because an avatar file is stored and activated in online space, unless it is behind a firewall, anyone, anywhere, with compatible software can utilize that specific and unique code as his or her avatar simply by routing to its location (URL). It is therefore multiple and multilocated, and beyond a single incarnation. Avatars are polygamous, being "exceedingly unfaithful to their origins" (Haraway 1991, 151), a characteristic that they share with Haraway's cyborg. There is no need for faithfulness to an author, just as there is no hierarchical moral code and no necessity to refer to that which has come before. An avatar's structure is never stable: its code can be altered at any time. It is never complete, always open to addition or subtraction.

Last, even though we, as users, direct the avatar body or the binary codes within it, the avatar itself is the 'other' that is present in the online world and that incites responses from other users and their avatars. The user becomes invisible in this space as avatars relate to avatars. Avatars assume their reality status, their individuality, as they seduce and entice actions in others. In *empyrean* when a user is interacting with a *miss fluffy* avatar, it is the avatar's appearance and gestures and sound that other users respond to or ignore, not the corporality or mutterings of the unknown user on another networked computer. The avatar code is the unique individual experienced by others.

From these few examples, it is not difficult to see that avatars easily meet the criteria for alterity, an engagement through negotiation giving them a materiality and sexuality of otherness. They have codes of interaction, an ability to coerce and seduce. To develop this further, avatar sexuality can be likened to viral interaction where the relatively simple code of a virus can penetrate and alter and reproduce within the cellular core of a host cell. Avatars then are infinitely reproducible, cloned code, with a fraction of erroneous copies occurring to randomize the "blood-line." Avatar activation, which can also be called *life*, is occurring exponentially throughout the growing massively multiplayer avatar community, as we have seen. According to Sadie Plant, it is precisely these activations and interactions that alter the user in the process, since "every action, every communication has a moment of contact, a point of transmission, a line that is crossed, a change that occurs" (1994). In theory and in practice, the avatar is emerging as a formidable species of other.

>> gamespace

Since the Web is used by over six hundred million people, I would estimate that there are around one hundred million avatars roaming the virtual worlds of MUDs, MOOs, multiuser VRML environments, and the many zones of the Activeworlds Universe. However, by far the greatest number live in the exponentially successful MMORPG environments, four million in *Lineage* alone.

As I have touched on previously, MMORPGs differ significantly from the more open-ended VRML or multiuser environments like *empyrean*. Probably best described in Johan Huizinga's *Homo Ludens: A Study of the Play Element of Culture* (1950), gameplay takes place in a spatially and temporally closed environment within certain fixed limits, creating a sense that is different from ordinary life. From this I conclude that online role-playing games seem to be successful because they exist just outside our pedestrian reality, having fixed parameters and a set of rules to follow or break. Huizinga points out that we engage in at least three dimensions of play: the agonistic or element of contest, the ludic or exuberant and fanciful element, and that of noble recreation.

Experiencing the fantasy and exuberance of contest in a recreational way emotionally positions a gamer to have pleasant associations and an investment in the development of his or her online character. Here, several sorts of avatars operate according to the type of gamespace they inhabit. Some massively multiplayer games have fixed avatar appearance and behaviors, some have characters that can be developed in appearance and behaviours like increased skill levels, and some have avatars that can only be superficially visually modified—that is, they can have new *skins* applied.

Since MMORPGs may be the primary social spaces for hardcore gamers who spend sixty hours or more a week immersed in the online gamespace, a player's avatar deployment and appearance assumes some importance. Apart from visually individuating gamers, avatars feature in performances enacted by gamers who are also artists. A well-known example is Brody Condon's *Worship* (2001), a performative online intervention within the massively multiplayer game *Anarchy Online*. By hacking his avatar's behaviors, Condon turned his avatar to face toward the outside—that is, looking out through the screen—and proceeded to make it enact a built-in "worship" animation for an extended period of time. In other words, the avatar appeared to worship its user:

This avatar action challenges many of the myths of virtual reality space. It shifts the focus of omnipotence from the world programmer/author, placing the player in the position of central importance, and repositions the immersive fantasy environment from being apart from day-to-day life by interlinking the spaces inside and outside the MMORPG. Because the avatar looks outside of the game towards the player, it is easy for the player to perceive their avatar as a separate other by its action towards them. This gives the avatar both an autonomy and a seeming awareness that a world exists outside its contained gamespace lifeworld. However, there is an Achilles' heel here. While the avatar is focused on the user, it cannot effectively act or defend itself within the MMORPG, and this leaves it vulnerable to its own death (Cannon 1994).

Because these worlds are so strictly formatted, it is precisely this unexpected, unscripted, and unsanctioned action that makes the avatar behavior surprising to other users. Utilizing these safe public spaces for performance pushes the agreed-upon limits, stretching the social rules and conventions of avatar use within game environments. Eddo Stern, who has authored several avatar intervention artworks, thinks it is precisely the rigid structure of these worlds that makes avatar interventions particularly appealing:

All of my earliest game intervention work was done in *Ultima Online* and *Everquest*—to my mind these represented at the time the gaming world's equivalent of global main street—I felt I was performing in public and my audience was deeply engaged in the conventions of the world—allowing any "Subversive" actions to operate as subversive by going against the game norms . . . I think in MMOs its really all about agency (vs the game creators and vs the other players) and maintaining a sense of identity. (Stern 2004)

In *Summons to Surrender* (2000), Stern repurposed existing game avatars within *Ultima Online, Asheronis Call,* and *EverQuest.* These avatars transmitted what they saw inside the game world as a live video feed that was then streamed online, effectively making the avatars spies. With names like *Streetwalker, Ghost, Sniper,* and *Mimic,* the already *other* characters revealed the usually closed game environment to a general audience,

Melinda Rackham |

making the avatars themselves agents who existed in two planes. This play on the virtual telepresence of the avatars and telepresent surveillance blurs the authorship of the resultant video between the avatars and their human user.

Stern reprogrammed these characters to actually play the game while he was away from the computer, so that the avatars have complete autonomy and individuality. They can "logoff, logon, write a log file, talk to people, issue all game commands, navigate and control the camera, as well as shut down the computer" (Ludin 2002). As a hardcore gamer, sometimes spending over one hundred hours a week playing in MMORPGs such as *EverQuest*, Stern used these autonomous functioning avatars to replace himself in the game, as he no longer had time to participate. He comments, "[t]hey were my revenge" (qtd. in Ludin 2002).

Stern's avatars could act alone, interacting with other players in the world who would not be aware that there was no human user persistently connected to that particular avatar. In fact, to other players, there is never any way of knowing if they are interacting with a "live" person or pre-scripted behavioral code. This returns us to my observation at the beginning of this essay: the VRML specification is very clear that the user does not have to be human (VRML Consortium Incorporated 1997, 3.108). These avatars then cannot be seen as mere coded zombies, the walking dead of gamespace, as according to the 'rules' they are indeed functioning, autonomous agents of their Virtual Reality lifeworld.

Perhaps the greatest test of an avatar's individuality is how its creator considers it. During an -empyre- forum/discussion on avatar construction between myself and artist John Klima, the topic of the personality or aliveness of avatars was raised. Klima, an *Ultima Online* player (which also had its real-world avatar market), had this to say when I suggested that I could not delete avatar *quincy*'s file because *quincy* felt like my child and I would be denying him life:

i power gamed a mage (the hardest character to be) for a year and got her to grand master (the highest skill level) before i quit. i could have sold her for 2k easy, she was a rare, powerful and of course beautiful (she wore a very sexy magic bustier) character, but i could not stand the idea of some high school kid from greenwhich connecticut running around masquerading as bix redux. so yes it would have been like selling my baby to the highest bidder, so i just killed her instead. hmmm. (Kilma 2002)

His reaction, akin to that of a jealous and possessive lover, would seem ridiculous if the avatar were merely a passive string of code. Avatars are seen by those who create, play, and/or work with them every day as separate beings, perhaps beings whom we have some power over, but nonetheless beings who are able to function autonomously and intelligently. Here is where we form trans-species relationships, combine wetware with software, in an enticing posthuman alliance between the seemingly solid and the seemingly ephemeral.

To view the user-avatar relationship from a different perspective, it may be that the avatar uses us—its human user—to ascend onto the earthly plane, since "*the living being is the sacred text of cyberspace . . .* our body is the screen (the signifying surface) by which the machine has access to reality" (Dyens 2001, 328). Here the animism of technology is the human body, just as the body is animated by fluid biological code. We can no longer assume that the machine and the software creatures that machine lifeworlds support are merely passive instruments, tools for human agency. The flow may be not what Michael Heim had earlier predicted, due to the resistant nature of avatar others; however, our daily lives are becoming more obviously lived cooperatively with and through machine- and code-constructed environments.

>> extrapolation

The avatar is a self-conscious "other" with whom we have a relationship. At once separate from and yet part of the human user, it symbiotically exists, each giving life to the other's reality. To be both one and yet completely separate can be a little confusing, almost schizophrenic, when we are more accustomed to a peachy individuality where the self is contained by our skin. Not only has virtual space made us reconsider the mind | body split, it has also forced us to reconsider the me | not me dichotomy, removing individuality from the center of the universe. Just as our hardspace bodies cannot be ignored, neither can our virtual avatar bodies. It is a bidirectional relationship, at once into hardspace and into softspace.

Having gone beyond the notion of avatar as strap-on software, many virtual artists are playing with these notions of the individuality, translocality, and mutability of avatars. In the mixed-reality game *Can You See Me Now?* devised by British media group Blast Theory (2003), avatars in a virtual play environment interact with actors in the offline world (Benford 2002). The avatars, representatives of players sitting at their computers anywhere in the world, are chased by living "hunters" (members of Blast Theory) through the streets of cities like Sheffield in 2002 and Rotterdam in 2003 for discrete periods during media festivals. When the participants log on to the Web site, their avatar appears somewhere on the city grid, the position relayed via satellite to the Global Positioning System (GPS) scanners carried by Blast Theory members. The game plan is for the hunters, who are represented by yellow avatars online, to chase the ghostly white avatars of online players through the city street grid and virtually surround them (figure

0M05s07

Avoid the orange runners to keep
playing.

:REPLAY

| Figure 3.8 |

Screen grab of Web interface from Blast Theory's *Can You See Me Now? Source:* http://www.canyouseemenow.co.uk.

3.8). When the avatar is caught the game is over, the capture site photographed and stored in the Web site's game archive, together with a blueprint of the chase.

The online avatars have an enhanced sensory advantage over the hunters in hardspace. Not only do they know the position of all their hunters at any moment, they can exchange tactics between themselves, send messages to Blast Theory members, and listen in on hunters' walkie-talkie conversations. Others follow the action either on the streets via GPS receivers or in real time online, creating an experience of mixing realities and condensing the physical presences with the virtual presences in both a hard- and softspace environment. Blast theory also investigated this boundary merging of virtual identity with physical identity in its previous work *Desert Rain* (1999), where the user had to locate a soldier left behind in a virtual projection of a Gulf War landscape. When the target is located, an actor walks through the projection surface (a thin sheet of water rather than a solid screen) toward the player, often startling or terrifying players who didn't realize the person coming toward them was a warm-fleshed human.

Virtual interaction and avatar presence are common ground in warfare, Virtual Reality being, after all, the offspring of the military. When Blast Theory's avatars physically interact in physical city spaces, eliciting responses from the hard-bodied players, we draw comparisons with virtual warfare and surveillance techniques. In both arenas, humans are represented by white avatars, derived from infrared video where warm-bodied humans appear as white spots on the heat sensitive medium. Things have changed since we supposed that online representation ensured immortality. Online video footage from the recent Afghanistan and Iraq invasions show white avatars as easily identifiable moving targets displayed in low-resolution virtual realism. In these contexts targeting the cold-bodied avatar also kills the warm-bodied human. In war, as in cybersex, it becomes obvious that virtual actions have hard world consequences.

A mutual relationship based on information exchange between avatars and hard-bodied species is beautifully illustrated by *Brainscore* (Grassi and Kreuh 2001), a networked virtual reality 3-D performance produced by Slovenian artists Davide Grassi and Darij Kreuh (figure 3.9). In *Brainscore*, tracked eye movements and electrical pulses from sensors attached to the head of the user (who remains physically constrained throughout the performance) control avatars. These inputs allow the vaguely head-shaped avatars to collect data from the Internet, which in turn alters their shape, size, location, and color over time. The changes then affect the eye movements and brain functions of the performer to provide a feedback loop. Here the avatars' coded attributes alter the users' physiology, making obvious the impact softspace has through its continuum into hardspace.

The VR environment is projected in stereo, allowing an audience to watch the performance wearing polarized glasses. This enables viewers to perceive the events in 3-D, as if suspended in midair between the two performers. The *Brainscore* artists created the work to provide a new perspective on the identification between performers and their avatars. We watch as the flow of information moves from the performers' physical space into the virtual avatars' space and than back from the avatars to the audience, "leading the audience to perceive a concrete co-existence (as a kind of promiscuous co-penetration) of two Realities at the same time" (Grassi and Kreuh 2001).

"Promiscuous co-penetration" starts to sound dangerous when it involves an interspecies relation between human- and machine-produced software, evoking specters of weird science fiction pornography involving a transgression of moral codes. After all, according to historian Lewis Mumford, "If you fall in love with a machine there is something wrong with your love life. If you worship a machine there is something wrong

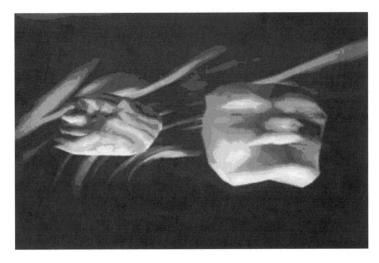

| Figure 3.9 |
Screen grab of avatars generated during a *Brainscore* performance. *Source:* http://www.brainscore.org.

with your religion" (qtd. in Sofia 1993, 6). As a society highly dependent upon and physically entwined with technology, we are still very techno- and xenophobic. We fear the
difference and similarity of the electronic other, preferring to keep an emotional distance between them and us.

Perhaps this is why users prefer to be represented in human form online, for when
online presence has a more physical representation it has a familiar and safe skin, a defined visual boundary. Then, when operating as an avatar in virtual worlds, users are
very aware that they are interacting with other skinned beings and are more proprietary
in their interactions. The amorphous, fluidly changing avatar still represents a dilemma
to the discrete body boundary schema. Only when the awareness of the electronic
stretch of our avatar body is integrated into our perceptions of ourselves, our boundaries, and our personal body spaces will operating as a completely soft avatar in virtual
space be truly possible.

>> return to the real

In post-postmodernist space, at the beginning of a new millennium, there is an across-
the-board return to hard realities, solid spaces, and fleshy bodies. With phenomenological awareness, to be embodied in hardspace already means that we as humans
simultaneously exist internally and externally to the moist body, congruently within and

without. We are always within ourselves while simultaneously watching ourselves acting in the world. To hack French feminism, both male and female are already *this sex which is not one* (Irigaray 1985).

Being online just makes obvious what we already know but usually ignore: we are already avatars inhabiting parallel worlds. Embodied in softspace, communicating with each other, we are the self, and one, and another—alone, together, and networked. As avatars operating in a virtual system, we have tripled ourselves. That makes more than a fixed coordinate point x, y, z, an extension of the 0,0,0, center of the virtual universe. Again it becomes clear that we are not just binary, pattern and randomness, the presence or absence of zero and one. We are composites, with the physical ecology of symbiotic species. We are an amalgam of all possibilities—of all dimensional vectors and variations of x, and y, and z.

Our avatar body, unlike our more familiar physical body, has a soft-skinned boundary whereby we can consume and ingest or pass through the other online. As this becomes increasingly familiar, as we stop insisting that we be represented online by fantasy human form, we will adapt to ephemerality. The necessity for a network connection to breathe life into, and animate, an avatar in a multiuser world or massively multiuser game, reminds us that we do not exist alone. When connected we navigate from our nodal center, and become part of the scape itself. Soft-skinnedness allows us to regain knowledge we have lost offline in hardspace; that is, we are not discrete isolated objects in the world, but part of a connected whole.

Our individuality, our "peachiness," is not a fixed and impenetrable kernel—but rather a concentration of code. We are always open to the influence of an other: as a species any embodiment means we operate in a sphere of influence, a field of intensity. Like the squishy jellyfish swimming in the oceanic lifeworld, dependent upon currents and flows of heat and cold for nourishment and for navigation to breeding grounds, we are supported in different and invisible ways by both soft and hard environments. On- or offline there is nothing to fear by acknowledging that we are animated and modified by relations with others; we are soft, open systems.

Works Cited

Assassin. 2004. "Editorials—Second Life Interview." RPGwh.net http://www.rpgwh.net/content/editorials-secondlifeinterview.php (accessed March 12, 2004).

Blast Theory. 1999. *Desert Rain.* http://wwwblasttheory.co.uk/archive/work_desertrain.html (accessed February 23, 2003).

Blast Theory. 2003. *Can You See Me Now?* http://blasttheory.co.uk/work_cysmn.html (accessed February 23, 2003).

Benford, Steve. 2002. "Blast Theory, Can You See Me Now?" In "Shooting Live Artists," *BBC Arts*. http://www.bbc.co.uk/arts/shootinglive/shootinglive1/blasttheory/mrl.shtml (accessed February 23, 2003).

Cannon, Rebecca. 2004. "Meltdown." http://www.selectparks.net/rebecca/?2006:Meltdown (accessed June 20, 2004).

Castronova, Edward. 2002. "Virtual Worlds: A First-hand Account of Market and Society on the Cyberian Frontier." CESifo Working Paper Series No. 618, January 14. http://ssrn.com/abstract=294828 (accessed December 20, 2002).

Castronova, Edward. 2003. "The Price of 'Man' and 'Woman': A Hedonic Pricing Model of Avatar Attributes in a Synthethic World." CESifo Working Paper Series No. 957, June 17. http://ssrn.com/abstract=415043 (accessed June 20, 2003).

Condon, Brody. 2001. *Worship*. http://tmpspace.com/worship.html (accessed June 20, 2004).

Curiouslabs. N.d. "Avatar Lab—3D Character Creation for Adobe Atmosphere Worlds." http://www.curiouslabs.com/go/avlab (accessed August 20, 2002).

Dyens, Ollivier. 2001. *Metal and Flesh, The Evolution of Man: Technology Takes Over*. Cambridge, MA: MIT Press.

Egan, Greg. 1997. *Diaspora*. London: Millennium.

Grassi, Davide, and Darij Kreuh. 2001. *Brainscore*—Incorporeal Communication. http://www.brainscore.org/first_page.html (accessed January 13, 2003).

Grosz, Elizabeth. 1989. *Sexual Subversions: Three French Feminists*. Sydney: Allen and Unwin.

Haraway, Donna J. 1991. "A Cyborg Manifesto: Science, Technology, and Socialist-Feminism in the Late Twentieth Century." In *Simians, Cyborgs, and Women*. London: Free Association Books.

Hayles, N. Katherine. 1999. *How We Become Posthuman, Virtual Bodies in Cybernetics, Literature, and Informatics*. Chicago: University of Chicago Press.

Hayles, N. Katherine, and Michael Heim. 2000. "CyberForum@ArtCenter 02/26/2000, 1:30 pm PST." http://www.mheim.com/cyberforum/html/spring2000/media/hayles/log3.html (accessed July 30, 2001).

Heim, Michael. 2000a. "The Avatar Manifesto." *Fine Art Forum*. http://www.fineartforum.org/Backissues/Vol_14/faf_v14_n09/text/feature.html (accessed May 20, 2002).

Heim, Michael. 2000b. "The Feng Shui of Virtual Environments." http://www.mheim.com/html/docs/feng/fs.html (accessed May 20, 2002).

Heim, Michael. 2001. "The Avatar and the Power Grid." *Mots Pluriels* 19 (October). http://www.arts.uwa.edu.au/MotsPluriels/MP1901mh.html (accessed May 22, 2002).

Irigaray, Luce. 1985. *This Sex Which Is Not One*, trans. Catherine Porter with Carolyn Burke. Ithaca, NY: Cornell University Press.

Klima, John. 2002. "Re:[-empyre-]: An Avatar Manifesto::final." *-empyre-*, November 28. http://lists.cofa.unsw.edu.au/pipermail/empyre/2002-November/001053.html (accessed July 19, 2002).

Little, Gregory. 1998. "A Manifesto for Avatars." http://art.bgsu.edu/~glittle/ava_text_1.html (accessed May 15, 2004).

Ludin, Diane. 2002. "*Sheik Chic*: Diane Ludin Interviews Eddo Stern." *THE THING [interviews]*, November 8. http://www.newsgrist.net/newsgrist3-18.html (accessed July 15, 2004).

Lusthaus, Dan. 2002. *Buddhist Phenomenology: A Philosophical Investigation of Yogacara Buddhism and the Ch'eng Wei-shih lun.* London: Curzon Press.

Morningstar, Chip, and F. Randal Farmer. 1991. "The Lessons of Lucas Film's Habitat." In *Cyberspace: First Steps*, ed. Michael Benedikt, 273–301. Cambridge, MA: MIT Press.

OzGate. N.d. *OzGate.* http://www.OzGate.com (accessed June 3, 2001).

Plant, Sadie. 1994. "The Virtual, the Tactile, and a Female Touch." Paper presented at Cybersphere, International Conference on Cyberspace, Sweden, September.

Rackham, M. 1996. *tunnel: Lust in Cyburbia.* http://www.subtle.net/tunnel (accessed December 12, 2005).

Rackham, M. 1997. *line.* http://www.subtle.net/line (accessed December 12, 2005).

Rackham, Melinda. 1999. *carrier.* http://www.subtle.net/carrier (accessed December 12, 2005).

Rackham, Melinda. 2001. "Empyrean—soft_skinned_ escape." In *Politics of a Digital Present: An Inventory of Australian Net Culture, Criticism and Theory*, ed. Hugh Brown, Geert Lovink, and Helen Merrick. Melbourne: Fibreculture Publications.

Rackham, Melinda. 2003. *empyrean.* http://www.subtle.net/empyrean.

Second Life. 2003. "Second Life: Your World, Your Imagination." http://secondlife.com/ (accessed March 12, 2004).

Sofia, Zoë. 1993. "Against NeoFuturism: Women Artists in Technological Media." *Scan + 4*: 6–8.

Stephenson, Neil. 1992. *Snow Crash.* London: Roc.

Stern, Eddo. 2000. *Summons to Surrender.* http://stern.aen.walkerart.org (accessed January 12, 2006).

Stern, Eddo. 2004. "this bounced earlier . . ." *-empyre-*, July 6. http://lists.cofa.unsw.edu.au/pipermail/empyre/2004-July/003081.html (accessed July 6, 2004).

Terdiman, Daniel. 2004. "Second Life Intrudes on First One." *Wired.* http://www.wired.com/news/games/0,2102,59675,00.html (accessed March 12, 2004).

There. 2003. "What Is There?" 2003. http://www.there.com/what_is_there.html (accessed February 15, 2003).

VRML Consortium Incorporated. 1997. "The Virtual Reality Modeling Language: International Standard ISO/IEC." 14772-1:1997. http://www.web3d.org/Specifications/VRML97/ (accessed September 13, 2000).

Whitelaw, Mitchell. 2003. *Metacreation: Art and Artificial Life.* Cambridge, MA: MIT Press.

Wilkinson, Robert E. 1994. "The Avatar in the Vedic Tradition." *HinduNet*, November 1. http://www.hindunet.org/alt_hindu_home/1994/msg00884.html (accessed July 12, 2002).

| 4 |

MAKING ROOM FOR THE BODY:
FROM FRAGMENTATION TO MEDIATION

Bernadette Wegenstein

the internal nothingness
of my self

which is night,
nothingness,
thoughtlessness,

but which is explosive affirmation
that there is
something
to make room for:
the body.

—Antonin Artaud, "To Have Done with the Judgment of God, A Radio Play"

It is not an exaggeration to say that over the last decades the study of the body has dominated many critical disciplines in the humanities, to the extent that a new discipline has arisen: that of *body criticism*. This chapter investigates how this new discipline was constituted throughout the last century; the epistemological pillars on which it rests; and the concrete embodiments of its current expression, from fragmented "skin-suits" to holistic "digital-organic video and sound environments" and "smart weather" architecture.

According to French historian Bernard Andrieu, the twentieth century has been characterized by an "epistemological dispersion of the human body" (1993, 9; my translation). Andrieu points out that only since the development of new historiographical approaches and methods by the Nouvelle Histoire (New History)[1] did the body become an object of focused investigation in the middle of the twentieth century. In the introduction to his *Feudal Society* (1949), Marc Bloch[2]—one of the co-founders of the new historian journal *Annales*—wrote that "the task of the historian is not to exhibit an uninterrupted chain of connections linking the patterns of the past . . . but rather to understand the infinite variety and richness of the past in all its combinations" (qtd. in Revel 1995, 18). It is in this spirit that, during the New History movement of the 1970s, medievalist Jacques Le Goff suggested rewriting history with a small *h*, as a history *lived by people* (1978, 241). This perspective emphasized historical realities; one of the key elements was to discover and unfold the connections among historical events, their context, and the materiality under investigation. No entity would offer itself more readily to this new historical approach than the human body. As British sociologist Bryan S. Turner states, the usefulness of the body to critical analysis lies in the fact that the body is a material organism at the same time as it is a metaphor: "The body is at once the most solid, the most elusive, illusory, concrete, metaphorical, ever present and ever distant thing—a site, an instrument, an environment, a singularity and a multiplicity" ([1984] 1996, 7–8).

The dispersion of the body throughout the twentieth century and the resulting development of cross-disciplinary approaches to critically studying the body are crucially related to the redefinition of the body and its functions in several areas of research. This chapter investigates how an epistemological shift occurred over the last century that opened up new and old interests in the body. This shift was primarily the result of corporeal theories emerging from psychoanalysis, phenomenology, and cognitive science.[3] The influence of these fields, moreover, has not only been felt—as it so evidently has— in contemporary intellectual movements such as gender studies, but has also affected the artistic practices of performing the body in the booming realm of contemporary media art and in architecture as well. I demonstrate this influence at the end of the chapter by way of three examples from media art and architecture.

It goes without saying, however, that body criticism did not emerge ex nihilo in twentieth-century thought. There is a long history of thinking about the body—one as long as bodies have existed. Nevertheless, a crucial moment for the transformation of the body concept from a more unified perception of the body to a body in pieces was high modernity (i.e., eighteenth to late nineteenth centuries). Modernity constitutes, according to Turner, the beginning of a "somatic society"—namely, a society in which major political and moral problems are both articulated with respect to the body and expressed through it ([1984] 1996, 8).

In the aftermath of high modernity, the health, hygiene, shape, and appearance of the body have become among the most important expressions of an individual's identity (Giddens 1990). This bourgeois body has become an individual property and a personal construction, and conflicts that used to occur between medieval bodies now take place within modernity's embodied and self-aware individual.

In her study of eighteenth-century German physician Johann Storch, and his reports on the medical history of 1,800 women of all ages in Eisenach, Germany, Barbara

Duden identifies a "new kind of discrete object" that the modern body has constituted since the late 1900s: "This isolated, objectified, material body was seized by a dissecting gaze that embraced not only the entire body, not only its surfaces, but also its recesses and orifices. It penetrated inquisitively into the inside, evaluating the palpated organs and relating them to a visual image of organs and cadavers. This gaze turned the body, and with it the patient who possessed it, into a new kind of discrete object" (1991, 4). It is not until the end of the nineteenth century that an alternative to the objectification of the body appears, at which time the early modern body-in-pieces begins to be integrated into a holistic body concept derived largely from developments in the realms of psychoanalysis, phenomenology, and cognitive science. This new body concept reveals the history of the body to be, in fact, a history of mediation. As I demonstrate in examples from media art and architecture, the discourse of holism has replaced the discourse of fragmentation, while incorporating key aspects of the dispersed body. Thus, I suggest we think of the history of the body as a history of constitutive mediation, for which both fragmentation and holism are indispensable modes of imagining and configuring the body. Nevertheless, it is thanks to the strategies of new media, which are incorporated and often the basis of the art installations in question, that the body was able to show its "real face": mediality.

Before analyzing the media art and architecture pieces, however, I want to show how and why the specific fields of psychoanalysis and phenomenology and their definitions or approaches to the body have helped fundamentally to formulate and carry out the struggling dialogue between a holistic and a fragmented body concept. The examples from contemporary media art and architecture serve to show how these underlying philosophical structures have influenced the display and performance of the millennial body in question—from a body in pieces as suggested in the feminist critique *Hautnah* (1995) by Alba D'Urbano, to a holistic "body house" as proposed by architects Diller + Scofidio in *Blur* (2002), as well as to digitally enhanced organic spaces such as media artists Aziz + Cucher's latest installation *Synaptic Bliss* (2004).[4]

Psychoanalysis

The main impulse behind the psychological discussion of the body in the twentieth century was the invention of psychoanalysis early in the century, and the resulting increase in medical consideration given to sexuality in understanding the human psyche.[5] Through psychoanalysis, the body has become more objectified and more often diagnosed as a psychological entity. The key concept in this regard is the *image* of the body produced by the body itself (autoperception), and hence the immediate perception of the world through one's own skin, the "moi-peau" (Anzieu 1995).

Psychoanalysis is less interested in the actual body than in the body image *(image du corps)*, which is considered as *representations*, that is, as constructions, that depend on how they are apprehended in external and social relations—an image according to which the subject is created by its perception of and by the outer world. The recognition of one's self in the gaze of the other is among the most fundamental concepts for understanding the meaning of subjectivity in the twentieth century.[6] Freud defined the ego as a corporeal projection, arguing that "the ego does not result from a preordained biological order, but is the result of a psychosocial intervention into the child's hitherto natural development" (qtd. in Grosz 1995, 185). Basing his psychoanalytical insights on Freud's ego-theory, French psychoanalyst Jacques Lacan argued in "Le stade du miroir" ([The Mirror Stage])[7] that the only way we can perceive our bodily selves is through a deceptive image that is framed by somebody else's gaze (in the beginning, the mother's or her substitute's), or through the frame of a screen or interface of some kind (mirror, computer interface, television monitor etc.). In this phase of the construction of the self, which takes place during approximately the first six to eighteen months of a child's life, the child recognizes him- or herself in the mirror as a being separate from his or her environment (especially from the mother). Through the recognition of his or her own Gestalt, the child anticipates his or her corporeal unity, which is needed in order to build a proper ego. This results in the lack of an "original" bodily identity tracing back to *one* origin of a body image, such as the genetic mixture of the parents' bodies, and hence in the loss of a secure historical representation of the body (such as the presentation of a growing body in a child's photo album). The stable concept of identity is replaced by what Lacan calls the "fractal body," whose identity depends on a process of "inscription" and semanticization through an outside world. The idea of a fractal body, not responsible or even aware of the bodily images that it is producing, provokes a profound discussion and repositioning of subjectivity in the twentieth century.

In *The Ego and the Id* ([1923] 1975), Freud talks about the body-ego as a border-surface, a "skin sack," or a "skin fold." In other words, the skin for Freud is a psychic hull that constitutes the contact between the outer world and the psyche: "The surface of the body, the skin, moreover, provides the ground for the articulation of orifices, erotogenic rims, cuts on the body's surface, loci of exchange between the inside and the outside, points of conversion of the outside into the body, and of the inside out of the body" (Grosz 1995, 188). For Freud, the skin is what constitutes the ego: "The ego is ultimately derived from bodily sensations, chiefly those springing from the surface of the body. It may thus be regarded as a mental projection of the surface of the body, . . . representing the surfaces of the mental apparatus" (Freud [1923] 1975, 294).[8]

Many definitions of the skin, and more generally of the human interface or surface, have been proposed since the beginnings of psychoanalysis; whether or not these attempts have taken into account a psychoanalytic key of analysis, all of them agree on the importance of the skin. French dermatologist and philosopher François Dagognet, for instance, presents a physical anthropology in which any "interface" of the body is regarded as a region of choice (1982, 49). For Dagognet, the skin obtains an incomparable importance over any other body part: in the skin, the relation between outside and inside exists intensely.[9] In a later book, *La peau découverte*, Dagognet characterizes the interdependency of the skin's "outside-inside" (*dehors-dedans*) and "inside-outside" (*dedans-dehors*) relationship as most relevant to the explanation of certain dermatological disorders such as acne, eczema, hives, and other skin diseases (1993).

The "timeless timeliness" of the preoccupation with the skin is shown in Steven Connor's recent in-depth account of the skin's significance in its historical and cultural imaginary. In his *Book of Skin*, Connor reads the skin cross-culturally, diachronically, and synchronically. He points to the skin's importance from the Egyptian embalming practice to contemporary tattooing or piercing trends. Similar to Dagognet, Connor puts the emphasis on the skin as boundary zone and medium of passage: "The skin is the vulnerable, unreliable boundary between inner and outer conditions and the proof of their frightening, fascinating intimate contiguity" (2004, 65).

It is perhaps post-Lacanian psychoanalyst Didier Anzieu who has introduced the most useful notion for a psychoanalytical account of the skin, taking into account both *chrós* (Greek for body as a whole and skin) and *dérma* (Greek for fur, skin, leather). Anzieu's notion of the "skin-ego" draws a comparison between the complexity of the skin and its different functions—namely, anatomical, physiological, cultural—and the complexity of the psychic ego. Of all our perceptive organs, the skin is the most vital one: one could live blind, deaf, and lacking the senses of taste and smell, but without the integrity of the major part of the skin organ, one could not survive (Anzieu 1995, 13). The skin has also the greatest mass (20 percent of the total body weight of a newborn, and 18 percent of an adult's weight) and occupies the largest surface (2,500 cm² of the newborn, and 1,800 of the adult) of all our organs. The skin serves as an "interface" between "me" and the "other" on the one hand by protecting the ego like an envelope, and on the other hand by dividing it from the outer world. The first skin the baby recognizes as meaningful is that of its mothering environment. Thus it is not until the mirror and the Oedipal stages that the infant gets "into its own skin," building up its ego on the basis of the (mis)recognition of itself in the mirror in the wake of a functional fragmentation, as shown by Lacan in his "mirror stage." For Anzieu, the skin plays the most important role in psychic development because the ego can only be built on the basis of its experience of the sur-face of the (mother's) body.

Phenomenology

Similar to psychoanalysis, phenomenology tries to separate the subject of the body (the world as perceived through one's body) from the objectified body (the body as it is perceived by the world)—a distinction between the subject of perception and the socially constructed body, between the psychoanalytical "Je" and the "Moi."

The notion of the immediate perception of the world through one's own skin was central to the thought of French phenomenologist Henri Bergson. For Bergson, the body image had two distinctive and somewhat paradoxically interrelated sides. On the one hand, *l'image du corps* is the way in which the subject perceives his or her own body, a perception corresponding to the Freudian psychoanalytical category ideal-ego, which later becomes the body-ego, or *ego tout court*. The body becomes a necessary intermediary between the self and the unknowable outside reality of the body, organizing the relations to the outside through the mediation of images; the image one has of oneself is therefore the center of one's being and perception, a kind of "interface" to the world (Bergson [1896] 1949). On the other hand, *l'image de corps* indicates that the body itself is the perceptive apparatus through which the world is processed. This means that the image is itself produced by the body (auto-perceptive), the intermediary source of all images (corpocentrism). In other words, the body is at the same time mirror or screen for the images from the "outside" and perceptive center; the body is "what takes shape at the center of perception" (Bergson, qtd. in Andrieu 1993, 60; my translation). Nevertheless, this taking shape is constantly blurred by the motion of the body, because the Bergsonian body is "a moving limit between future and past" (Andrieu 1993, 62).

Unlike with psychoanalysis, for Bergson there is no unconscious, only an *unconsciousness*. In the Bergsonian notion of the body, there is no rupture between events. Rather, all memory is related to the totality of events that precedes it and that comes after it. The unconscious mental state is, therefore, nothing other than a never-perceived material object, or a non-imagined image (Andrieu 1993, 64). The body (and not the soul) provides equilibrium to the mind, and is therefore the complementary pole to the mind, without which orientation toward action would never be possible. For Bergson, matter is within space and mind outside of it. There is no possible immediate transition between these dimensions. Rather, the mind enters in contact with matter through the function of *time*. The body in turn possesses the material capacity to translate the intensity of time into action. In this way, the mind itself is not directly materialized but rather becomes the body in action after first traversing the possible intensities of memory (Andrieu 1993, 65). Bergson thus develops a theory of indirect unity: it is not in perception, or in memory, or in the activities of the mind that the body contributes directly to representation; rather, the body is indirectly united with the spirit, and the markers of this unification are the image on the one hand, and the skin (or a rethinking of that border zone) on the other.

The upshot of Bergson's contribution is the impossibility of thinking consciousness outside embodiment, because mind is only ever manifest in the actions of a body over time. Likewise, for Bergson's contemporary Edmund Husserl (both were born in 1859), the discipline of phenomenology he founded sought the truth of consciousness in how the subject lives in his or her body. Whereas for Immanuel Kant—Husserl's intellectual father—phenomenology meant the study of empirical appearances, for Husserl phenomenology means the "science of essences" (*Wesenswissenschaft*).[10] For Husserl, at stake are not real appearances, existences, things, or essences, but the intentionally conscious gaze onto the essences (*Wesensschau*). In other words, consciousness is always consciousness *of* something. Reality has no absolute or independent status, but is always presupposed as intentionality, or intentional appearance. As a result, the body is no longer a symptom, a sign, or any other kind of manifestation or placeholder (for something else); rather, it becomes the presence in the world of an intentional subject and his or her psychological experience of the world. It is here that a body discourse can start to disperse the body, by literally opening it up to investigation.

A generation after Bergson and Husserl, French philosopher Maurice Merleau-Ponty dedicated his entire work to the problem of the lived (perceiving) body and its image, from his early *Phénoménologie de la perception* (1945) to the unfinished *Le Visible et l'invisible* (1964).[11] In Merleau-Ponty's philosophy, the body (*Leib*) has become inseparable from the world it inhabits, because body and earth (i.e., the body's environment) are related through the world's presence in the body: "the body not only flows over into a world whose schema it bears in itself but possesses this world at a distance rather than being possessed by it" (qtd. in Weiss 1999, 10). The "pragmatic turn" of this phenomenological approach lies in the fact that this body is only a body by virtue of its use by a subject—in other words, through the way in which a subject's presence in the world embodies it (Andrieu 1993, 272). Merleau-Ponty argues that the outer world is necessarily perceived through a lived body. He thus founds a philosophy of embodiment and primordial presence that for Gail Weiss constitutes the departing point in her analysis of the body image, leading her to develop a theory of embodiment as *intercorporeality*: "To describe embodiment as intercorporeality is to emphasize that the experience of being embodied is never a private affair, but is always already mediated by our continual interactions with other human and nonhuman bodies" (qtd. in Weiss 1999, 5).

Lacan had specified that a child always comes to its self-identity via a fundamental misrecognition of its own body. This concept of a "body in pieces" (*corps morcelé*) is, in other words, already distinctly phenomenological, meaning that the infant's own "experience" of itself prior to the organization of the image in the mirror is a body-in-pieces.[12] It is thus precisely in respect to the lived body experience that Merleau-Ponty's thought converges with Lacan's notion of the mirror stage, in that for both thinkers the notion of an experienced embodiment goes along with a double alienation, the recognition of oneself in a deceptive image that is framed through somebody else's gaze, a mirror, a screen: "At the same time, this body image makes possible a kind of alienation, the capturing of myself through my spatial image. The image prepares me for another alienation, that of myself (as viewed) by others" (qtd. in Andrieu 1993, 295; my translation). Indeed, as far as this aspect is concerned, the projects of Lacan and Merleau-Ponty to explain subjectivity as it unfolds in the infant are very similar. As Weiss points out, they both emphasize "that it is this very schism that makes it possible for the child to project and extend her/his own bodily awareness beyond the immediacy of her/his introceptive experiences by incorporating the perspective of the other toward one's own body—a perspective one actively participates in—rather than having it thrust upon one from the outside" (1999, 13). In other words, the "inscription" and semanticization through an outside world onto the body—as I described embodiment earlier—is not a process that the subject undergoes, but on the contrary, one in which she or he is actively involved. "Inscription" does not occur without the subject's intercorporeal interaction providing both an "outside-inside," as well as an "inside-outside" perspective. What is more, with phenomenology the emphasis now lies on the production of images, and no longer on the libidinal investments that in Freud's theory shift from the mouth to the anus and finally to the sexual organs.

With Merleau-Ponty's theory of perception and the lived body "flowing over into a world," the ground is laid for discussing concrete embodiment, and for posing questions that concern the gendered body and the raced body in new ways, as can be seen in an apparently infinite number of body installations in contemporary media art. Nevertheless, concreteness is also realized in another dimension—namely, that of language and the body's embeddedness in it. In linguistic terms, we can say that from the Husserlian phenomenology of the systemic side of language, the *langue*, Merleau-Ponty moves the emphasis to the pragmatic, speech-act side of the *parole*. In the realm of the parole, Merleau-Ponty slowly distances himself from the Husserlian distinction between *Körper* and *Leib*, substituting it with a broadened Leib-notion, in which language becomes the body of thought.[13]

It is no doubt his emphasis on the inderdependency of body and world, and the resulting notion of embodiment as inseparable from the original kinship with the world, that turned Merleau-Ponty into arguably the greatest influence for body theorists of the twentieth century. Whether a constructivist, a performative, a volatile, or even an essentialist account of the body, all of these ways of thinking the body presume that the body is *world access* (given, construed, performed, or even all at once). Merleau-Ponty's philosophy has thus not diminished in its influence and importance, especially as it has been reinterpreted in recent times in, for instance, the work of contemporary French philosopher Renaud Barbaras.[14]

Barbaras reminds us of a crucial quote in the *Phénoménologie de la perception*, in which Merleau-Ponty declares that the body "'*has* its world or understands its world without having to pass through representations;' it '*is* the potentiality of the world'" (qtd. in Barbaras 2004, 7).[15] In that sense, the body *constitutes* mediation and vice versa. Since Merleau-Ponty's phenomenology, this universe is no longer conceived in a Cartesian manner that takes the thinking subject as a secure point of departure against the objects in the world; the body—"the fabric into which all objects are woven" (Merleau-Ponty [1945] 1962, 235)[16]—is thus not a mere "intermediary," an "in-between" the subject and the world, but rather a unifier of a holistic subjectivity and a fragmented objectivity that effectively undermines the existence of these very categories.

From Fragmentation to Mediation

I now turn to the realms of digitally enhanced body art and new media art and architecture in order to, first, discuss turn-of-the-millennium body installations that reflect the previously outlined body concepts and, second, trace that concept back to the struggling dialogue between fragmentation and holism.

To this end, it is important briefly to situate body-oriented art in the late twentieth century. As Amelia Jones points out in her groundbreaking book *Body Art: Performing the Subject* (1998), the body had underdone two moments of particular reevaluation in twentieth-century art. Throughout the 1960s and 1970s, the body was featured as "raw material," a site of the inscription of cultural meaning. In these body installations, the body is just coming out from the realm of painting, having replaced the materiality of the paintbrush and color with the materiality of the actual body, often featured in ritualistic practices, such as Austrian actionist Hermann Nitsch's "Orgy-mystery-theater." It is no coincidence that in these "body collages" of the 1960s, the body was also used literally as paintbrush (Yves Klein's famous *Anthropometrie of the Blue Period* [1960]). In addition, the body was often harmed physically (e.g., Chris Burden) or symbolically (e.g., Yoko Ono) in what I have called "1960s wounds."[17] The body as raw material features, according to Jones, the transition from a modernist body subjectivity that was struggling with the Cartesian mind-body split, to a dispersed postmodern subjectivity of a bodily self that is construed into a variety of forms and shapes with the help and through the eyes of the audience/witnesses. A feminist approach to this kind of body art (e.g., Valie Export, Cindy Sherman, and others), with its critique of the male gaze directly affecting the female body, if not harming it, can only be seen as the necessary outcome of such performances. Relating these performances to the intellectual environment around the body, one can certainly detect a psychoanalytical interest in the body performances of the 1960s with such themes as the narcissistic body and the body in its relationship to others. During the 1980s, however, Jones detects a "turn away from the body" (1998, 198), which she interprets as a reaction to the politics in the Western hemisphere of this time: "This turn away from the body was also in some ways unfortunately coincident with the disembodied politics of the Reagan-Thatcher era, characterized by political retrenchment and reactionary, exclusionary economic and social policies and by the scrupulous avoidance of addressing the effects of such policies on the increasingly large number of bodies/selves living below the poverty line" (198).

Since the 1990s, we have been witnessing a dramatic return to the body and body art practices. These works, Jones states, "acknowledge the deep implications of the politics of representation in relation to the embodied subject" (1998, 198). In these "1990s extensions"[18] of the body, the self is no longer explored mainly in relation to culture and context (constructivism). Now, through the new possibilities of the technologies of the body, particularly those enhanced by new media, the body is under "technophenomenological" examination, to quote Jones once more: "The body/self is technophenomenological: fully mediated through the vicissitudes of bio- and communications technologies, and fully engaged with the social (what Merleau-Ponty called 'enworlded'). The body/self is hymenal, reversible, simultaneously both subject and object" (235).

It is here that we can detect, I believe, the crucial movement from fragmentation to mediation, since not only did this kind of reexamination of the "posthuman" body have to particularize and dissolve the body into its outer parts, but now—with the help of visual technologies such as MRI scans—the body's inner materiality has been taken into account as well. From a phenomenological standpoint, this body in pieces is now trying to see and experience itself as objectified. However, this objectification is no longer the result of a social constructivist critique but stems from the mere observation that "seeing" is always "creating a distance," to quote one of Merleau-Ponty's famous sentences. Thus, the body performances of the 1990s question the very attempt to learn anything about the body via the particularized knowledge we may have accumulated about its bits and pieces. These 1990s bodies often do not feature any original bodily identity at all; they do not reveal a graspable subjectivity. Rather, they are returning to more primordial questions regarding the materialities of the body, such as questions of the body's appearance through its skin, the ego-envelope, or the border zone between inside and outside. Technology is the body's crucial counterpart in these performances that break down the distinction between a body's interiority and exteriority, between a distance to the body and a being in the body (e.g., Gary Hill, Bill Viola, and others). Technology serves as partner in featuring these often eerie and alienating body performances (e.g. the by now classic body extensions of Australian artist Stelarc).

But to go back to the Lacanian notion that the body image is always and by nature deceptive (framed by the other's gaze), these performances also express a deep skepticism and an almost nihilistic irony in their use of media and technology to promote such a confused and unstable body. As Derrida is reported to have said about Gary Hill's work, it reveals "that there is not and never has been a direct, live presentation." It is in this sense that the "1960s wounds" differ drastically from the "1990s extensions": the current body installations are no longer concerned with the reality of the gaze, of politics, of the injustice done to the body. The body is no mediator. Rather, these performances use the body to experiment and question the media throughout this shift from a *body* emphasis to a *medium* emphasis. No longer are these media "extensions of man" (have they ever been?); rather, what recent new media art and architecture practices show is that the body has been left behind insofar as the digital image has corporealized itself, has punched through the frame of materiality, and has therefore taken the place of the actual body. In this understanding, no body exists as "raw material," which implies that there is something like an original body, a body that is prior to inscription and semanticization. No, the current body under the influence of media technologies reveals itself as pure "materiality." It can therefore merge, bend, and by inhabiting it, we—the viewer participants—can become part not only of its phenotype, but also of its genotype, as the examples of *Blur* and *Synaptic Bliss* (to name just a few) go to show. What is at stake in these examples is a holistic body notion that has been fed or informed by a fragmented body—this is, a body whose pieces in fact have never been more penetrated and whose data have never been better collected than they are now in their being rendered into digital bits. But the output of this process does not assume a unified subject that only achieves its "wholeness" through the interrelation of the various body parts. The holism in question in these media art and architecture installations is of a different kind. It is a holism that authorizes every bit and every piece of the fragmented body to take over the body as a whole, to serve as interface.

As I have shown elsewhere,[19] in late-twentieth-century popular culture the body and all of its organs no longer simply serve as a medium of expression, as a semiotic layer toward the outer world. Rather, the body and its parts have themselves adopted the characteristics of a medium, wherein lies the "return to the holistic body concept." The discourse of "getting under the skin" was necessary to "free" the body strata of a given hierarchy. The skin and the other organs, thus freed, have taken on the role of pure mediation, of flat and "slippery" screens, of the sur-face on which the body as such is produced. On the basis of this, I suggest that we ask, Is this in fact any more a "body"—that is, a "human body"—that is being released as whole through these body installations? The answer is no, since these installations are examples of how the body of twentieth-century concerns in all the discussed realms, from psychoanalysis to phenomenology and cognitive science, has been replaced by issues regarding mediality itself. To rephrase Derrida's comment on Gary Hill's installation, we could say that through mediality the body has shown its true essence—that is, there never was a body to begin with.

Italian artist Alba D'Urbano is one of many who worked on the theme of the skin within the realm of new media. During the 1990s, she experimented with images of her own skin, which she digitized, processed, reshaped, and cut into the pattern of a "skin-suit."[20] In her project *Hautnah*[21] (German for "close to the skin") (1995), the artist "took off her own skin" to offer others the possibility of "walking through the world hidden 'under her skin'" (D'Urbano 1996, 272). *Hautnah* makes concrete the examination of the body as naked other, as confrontation between inner consciousness and outer reality, through the idea of abandoning one's own skin and entering somebody else's.

In this critique of the skin as sur-face, and as bodily exterior/interior, the artist ironically hangs her "skin-suit" on a coat-hanger (D'Urbano 1996, 274). Significantly, the "skin-suit"—made of material printed with images of the naked skin of the artist's body—has neither hands, nor feet, nor a face. These "interactive body parts," as the artist calls them, have been cut off. We are looking at a faceless, handless, and footless entity, which is nevertheless clearly a body. In other words, the body no longer needs the parts that stand in connectors for the entire body, to feature as whole. We may thus read the absent interactivity represented here not only as a feminist critique of a male-dominated gaze that has literally torn a female body into pieces, but also precisely as the previously described wish to dissociate from the body, as well as from the search for a subjectivity or originality of the body *tout court*. The sentence "Für Garderobe keine Haftung" (no liabilities for wardrobe) can, hence, be read as "This skin-suit really belongs to nobody. We are not responsible for it. You may hang it here, but you may not find it again upon your return." *Hautnah* makes clear what Amelia Jones states for 1990s

body practice in general: "a return to a notion of embodied subject as necessarily particularized . . . (in its) relation to other subjects in the social area" (1998, 202).

In her study of body images, Weiss reminds us that "inscription" does not occur
without the subject's intercorporeal relationship with other human or nonhuman bodies. In *Hautnah*, D'Urbano challenges this notion, presenting a body in pieces that is beyond inscription as such. It hangs all alone in a wardrobe that no one even wants to take
responsibility for. It has been left alone, with no claim of a subject's "belonging" other
than the artist's, whose non-signature stands underneath it. The only "inscription" the
skin-suit *Hautnah* features are the sexual body parts of a woman, her breasts and her
vaginal hair. We may now read this as we wish: are these the material parts that cannot
be gotten rid of? Maybe. What matters for my own concerns is, however, that the genitals are part of the skin-suit. They belong to the realm of appearance (figure 4.1).

If the questions of fragmentation and opposition (i.e., inside versus outside) were
necessary to initiate the previously described dialogue within the new discipline of body
criticism, the *Blur* "building" (2002), by architects Diller + Scofidio, can be seen as a
step beyond or even an answer to such fragmentation. *Blur* is a "media building that
hovers mysteriously over the lake" ("Diller + Scofidio *Blur* Building," 2000, 50). Technically speaking, the building—developed by the Extasia team for the Swiss Expo 2002
in Yverdons-Les-Bains on Lake Neuchâtel, Switzerland—consists, like the human
body, nearly entirely of water. *Blur* is a cloud of mist formed by 12,500 spray nozzles
covering infrastructure and producing a fog system: "Lake water is filtered, then shot
through a dense array of high-pressure fog nozzles and regulated by a computer control
system" (50). Not only is *Blur* "smart weather," in that the building changes its appearance depending on the (unpredictable) weather of the day, but it is also, as Mark Hansen
points out, "space that has been made wearable" (2002, 330)—not least with the help of
the designated "braincoat" with which one experiences the building: "As visitors pass
one another, their coats will compare profiles and change color indicating the degree of
attraction or repulsion, much like an involuntary blush—red for affinity, green for an-
tipathy. The system allows interaction among 400 visitors at any time"[22] (figure 4.2).

The architectural innovation of *Blur* lies not only and evidently in the fact that this
is no longer a "building"—it is rather a "pure atmosphere," as Diller + Scofidio themselves emphasize—but also in the fact that this "habitable medium" (qtd. in Hansen
2002, 330) no longer emphasizes vision. Instead, it emphasizes the proprioceptive *bodily*
experience of inhabiting space. In other words, Diller + Scofidio reevaluate and rela-
tivize the dominance of vision in architecture by providing an "immersive environment
in which the world is put out of focus so that our visual dependency can be put into
focus" (qtd. in Hansen 2002, 329) (figure 4.3).

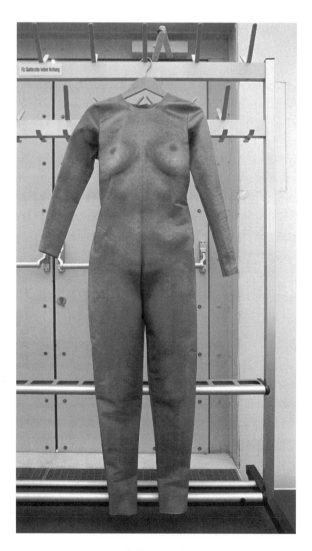

| Figure 4.1 |
Alba D'Urbano's *Hautnah* (1995). Courtesy of the artist.

| Figure 4.2 |
Blur Raincoat Glow (2002). Courtesy of Diller + Scofidio.

Diller + Scofidio chose the instability of the weather because the weather is—as they say—one of the examples of our cultural obsession with control, and of the anxiety resulting from not being able to overpower our environments. The quintessence of the *Blur* bubble is to present weather not only as a natural process, but also as a cultural phenomenon: "At stake is how we interact with each other through weather, not only as a shared obsession but also as a process of global communication" ("Diller + Scofidio *Blur* Building," 2000, 55).

This example of architecture as "wearable space" goes to show how the logic of new media has infiltrated the contemporary body concept, and how the body, in turn, has become coeval with mediation. Architecture, traditionally conceived of as the craft of building a dwelling for man's body, now reflects a new understanding of the body—no longer as a separate, exterior structure to house a bodily interiority, but as a continued or extended embodiment of that body's essence as it has been grasped by the discourses we have analyzed here: as primordial mediation. In *Blur*, interactivity has constructed itself a house; the medium has become the body. Its final layer peeled off, the body is no

| Figure 4.3 |
Blur View on Ramp (2002). Photograph by Beat Widmer. Courtesy of Diller + Scofidio.

longer a medium for something else, standing in for a truth or a reality that lies beyond the surface; rather, the surface has collapsed, merging inside and outside, refusing to relegate itself to the subservience of yet one last mediation, becoming, in other words, the body itself. Unlike *Hautnah*, *Blur* is engaged in a bodily notion of emergence, in which any questions of concrete particularized embodiment are no longer discussable, but only to be *experienced*. It is in this sense one of the best examples of a return to a lived body notion, one that gives back the power to the individual and his or her unique experience. Every "inhabitant" of *Blur* will experience the house in her or his own way.

Media artists Aziz + Cucher's latest series of media installations, *Synaptic Bliss*, is another attempt at merging the subject with media. Their attempt at this fusion, however, is of a symbolic nature. There is no immersive interactivity at play, as in *Blur*: rather *Synaptic Bliss* is a "metaphorical attempt to represent cycles of growth and decay, different rhythms that find audiovisual expression."[23] What interests me from a media-theoretical position in Aziz + Cucher's latest work is not the fact that instead of the body's interior (see their previous installation series, *Interiors* [1999–2002]) the artists now explore the border and limit of "natural environments," but rather to what extent their work deconstructs the difference between external and internal images (figure 4.4).

Whereas *Hautnah* clearly engages in a struggling discourse that is shown to suffer a nostalgic drag in getting rid of the bodily interiors (interestingly, it does not raise the claim of ever being able to leave behind the inscriptions of gender), the new media architecture pieces *Blur* and *Synaptic Bliss* have gotten rid of the body by literally merging the flesh of technology with that of the interacting viewer-participant. The medium

| **Figure 4.4** |
Aziz + Cucher's *Synaptic Bliss* installation at Parc de la Villette Paris (2004). Courtesy of the artists.

that signifies the body, its "representation," is no longer any different from the "raw material" of the body of the installation itself. Without mediation, the body is nothing; moreover, mediation is already what the body always was, in its various historical and cultural strata. *Synaptic Bliss* adds to this that even without immersive, interactive new media strategies, the images are here intended to invoke *feelings of immersion*: "This series of work is very sensorial, almost psychedelic; it attempts to bring the viewer into an ecstatic awareness of their bodies in their surrounding environment as a process of infinite interconnection (hence 'Synaptic') which in our understanding also brings a feeling of joy ('Bliss') as opposed to one of confusion in the inability to separate one's self from the outside."[24] This psychedelic ecstasy of the inseparability of inside and outside addresses issues of the *image de corps*, that is, issues concerning the body as perceptive apparatus, which were already central to Bergson's corpocentrism. As Hans Belting points out in his anthropology of images, "Internal and external representations, or mental and physical images, may be considered two sides of the same coin" (Belting 2005, 304). This is why, for Belting, images cannot be described by an "exclusively medialogical approach" (305). Rather, he reminds us that images may live in us, but they need our bodies to show up. He further explains that bodies serve as living media that make us perceive, project, or remember images. It is in light of this observation that I can suggest a final conclusion about these new media art and architecture installations: namely, it is not exclusively the question of interactivity that reveals the body as mediality, as in *Blur*. Rather, as so brilliantly shown in Aziz + Cucher's latest project, imagination, vision, and images are already there to entertain the body's mediatic nature.

The "post-psychoanalysts" Deleuze and Guattari have reconfigured the process of fragmentation as a relation of "organ-ized" strata to a state of radical and virtual disorganization they call the plane of immanence (Deleuze and Guattari 1987, 154). The body in this view is no longer mediation, but rather the potentiality underlying all mediation. Starting already in *Hautnah*, and much more visibly in *Blur* and *Synaptic Bliss*, this dialogue between the body as a whole and as a multiplicity of fragments has been expressed in both visual (*Synaptic Bliss*) and haptic terms (*Blur*); what the history of this time demonstrates—and what I am ultimately arguing—is that the apparently contrary vectors of fragmentation and holism are in fact part and parcel of the same historical development. In other words, the discovery of the body as mediation has converged with an age of mediatic proliferation, such that what we are in fact witnessing in the apparent continuing fragmentation of the body is the work of mediation itself *as* the body. It is for this reason that there can be no history of the body that is not at the same time a study of the various media that constitute embodiment as such.

The advent of new media has facilitated the move of the reunion between holism and fragmentation enormously. One must acknowledge that it is because of posthuman technology and because of the realm of new media that the body has survived not as a whole, but rather in a dispersed and scattered way—or better: due to this technology, the body was able to adapt a new form of wholeness that manifests itself as a multiplicity and plurality of forms. The result of this discussion is a new body concept that could only have emerged from the grounds of early twentieth-century phenomenology and psychoanalysis, but would also be inconceivable outside the achievements of artificial intelligence and cognitive science on the one hand, and the feminist criticism of the resulting notion of disembodiment on the other hand, as well as outside new media revolutions of the later twentieth century.

Notes

1. The Nouvelle Histoire emerged to a large extent as a reaction against positivistic approaches to history in the late nineteenth century. At the beginning of the twentieth century, French historians enlarged and enriched the historical discipline with writings of various kinds, from archeological to oral documents. Opposed to the notion of "historical event," the methods of the new historians focused on delivering a "problematic and not automatic" concept of history (Le Goff 1978, 218). The present was to be understood through the past, and the past through the present. An important concept, coined by historian Fernand Braudel (1958), was "la longue durée." This temporal concept entailed that, despite history's fast changes, historical deep structures

can only be grasped over time, because changes in economic and social systems can only be evaluated long after a system has been implemented.

2. In 1929 Marc Bloch and Lucien Febvre founded the journal *Annales d'histoire économique et sociale* to accompany and illustrate the achievements of the new historians.

3. I cannot include here the development of this new body concept from the realms of cognitive science and consciousness studies. This treatment can, however, be found in the extended version of "Making Room for the Body," chapter 1 in Wegenstein 2006.

4. "The Medium Is the Body," chapter 4 in Wegenstein 2006, features many more examples of such digitally enhanced organic environments, which Mark Hansen (2004) has described as examples of "second-order interactivity," in his analysis of the Dutch architects NOX's latest Son-O-House installation. In a lecture at the University at Buffalo in the fall of 2004, Hansen pointed out that this is no longer a first-order interactive project that works within a stimulus-response module, but action is here guided by perception in action, and therefore extends both the human and the machinic autopoetic capacity. In this "house-that-is-not-a-house" (Marcus Leinweber from NOX in an interview with the author), the viewer-participant influences not only the phenotype of the installation, but its genotype, and does so by influencing the real-time composition itself that generates the sounds in the installation.

5. Parts of the sections on psychoanalysis and phenomenology are taken from "Making Room for the Body," chapter 1 in Wegenstein 2006.

6. Although the importance of recognition by the other was, of course, already a key notion in Hegel's *Phenomenology of Spirit* in 1807.

7. Delivered as a lecture in 1936; see also Lacan 1966.

8. English footnote, added in 1927 to the English translation.

9. This definition clearly resonates with the analogy of the gendered body's inside and outside relationship as Möbius strip described by Elizabeth Grosz in *Volatile Bodies*: "The Möbius strip model has the advantage of showing that there can be a relation between two 'things'—mind and body—which presumes neither their identity nor their radical disjunction, a model which shows that while there are disparate 'things' being related, they have the capacity to twist one into the other. This enables the mind/body relation to avoid the impasses of reductionism, of a narrow causal relation or the retention of the binary divide. It enables subjectivity to be understood not as the combination of a psychical depth and a corporeal superficiality but as a surface whose inscriptions and rotations in three-dimensional space produce all the effects of depth" (1994, 209–210).

10. It is worth mentioning that for Hegel, again, phenomenology had yet another meaning: namely, the description of human consciousness as a process leading from sensual

naïveté through ethics, art, religion, science, philosophy, and ultimately to the state of absolute knowledge.

11. As Francisco J. Varela, Evan Thompson, and Eleanor Rosch point out in their introduction to *The Embodied Mind*, during the times of Merleau-Ponty in the 1940s and 1950s, "the potential sciences of mind were fragmented into disparate, noncommunicating disciplines; neurology, psychoanalysis, and behaviorist experimental psychology" (1991, vvi). They note that is was not until the emergence of cognitive science in the 1970s that cognitive psychology, linguistics, artificial intelligence, and philosophy could be included in the study of mind.

12. I am grateful to Stuart Murray (University of Toronto) for bringing this to my attention.

13. In the space of this essay, I cannot discuss the convergences between Merleau-Ponty and the German phenomenologist Martin Heidegger. It is precisely within the realm and the notion of *language*, the Merleau-Pontian "soil of genesis" (translators' introduction to Barbaras 2004, 137), that the two philosophers encounter each other. To give just one very famous quotation from Heidegger: "Language is the house of being. In its home human beings dwell. Those who think and those who create with words are the guardians of this home" ([1949] 1998, 239).

14. Renaud Barbaras, *Le désir et la distance*, 1999; *Le tournant de l'expérience*, 1998; *Merleau-Ponty*, 1997; *La perception*, 1994; *De l'être du phénomène: L'ontologie de Merleau-Ponty* [The Being of the Phenomenon: Merleau-Ponty's Ontology], 1991.

15. This formulation is evident in body art and body installations in the twentieth century, which are discussed in chapter 2 in Wegenstein 2006.

16. I want to give the full citation of this famous quotation: "[My body is the fabric into which all objects are woven,] and it is, at least in relation to the perceived world, the general instrument of my 'comprehension.'"

17. See chapter 2, "Body Performances from 1960s Wounds to 1990s Extensions," in Wegenstein 2006.

18. See chapter 2 in Wegenstein 2006.

19. See chapter 3, "How Faces Have Become Obsolete," in Wegenstein 2006, as well as the earlier version (Wegenstein 2002).

20. I would like to add just one other example of the attempt to conserve a woman's skin from Marina de Van's recent film *Dans ma peau* (2002). The main protagonist, Esther, suffers from body dysmorphic disorder in that she engages in self-mutilating practices. Her alienation and disassociation from her own body is presented as a necessary condition for these self-mutilations. As de Van explains in the director's commentary: "By focusing only on one's own body and one's relation to one's body, all other social relations cannot but fail." De Van wants to show the transformation of Esther's own body fragment such as a leg or an arm into an object; an object that in fact gives her pleasure in her several "self-mutilation orgies."

21. This example stems from an extensive discussion of body art and other examples from popular culture in Wegenstein 2002.
22. http://www.arcspace.com/architects/DillerScofidio/blur_building/.
23. Aziz + Cucher in an interview with the author, February 16, 2005.
24. Aziz + Cucher in an interview with the author, February 16, 2005.

Works Cited

Andrieu, Bernard. 1993. *Le corps dispersé: Histoire du corps au XXe siècle.* Paris: L'Harmattan.

Anzieu, Didier. 1995. *Le moi-peau.* Paris: DUNOD.

Artaud, Antonin. [1947] 1976. "To Have Done with the Judgment of God, A Radio Play." In *Selected Writings,* ed. Susan Sontag. New York: Farrar, Straus and Giroux.

Barbaras, Renaud. 2004. *The Being of the Phenenomenon: Merleau-Ponty's Ontology.* Trans. Ted Toadvine and Leonard Lawlor. Bloomington: Indiana University Press.

Belting, Hans. 2005. "Image, Medium, Body: A New Approach to Iconology." In *Critical Inquiry* 31, no. 2 (Winter): 302–319.

Bergson, Henri. [1896] 1949. *Matière et mémoire.* Paris: Presses Universitaires de France.

Braudel, Fernand. 1958. "Histoire et sciences sociales. La longue durée." In *Annales* 13: 725–753.

Connor, Steven. 2004. *The Book of Skin.* Ithaca, NY: Cornell University Press.

Dagognet, François. 1982. *Faces, Surfaces, Interfaces.* Paris: Librairies Philosophique J. Vrin.

Dagognet, François. 1993. *La peau découverte.* Le Plessis-Robinson: Collection Les Empêcheurs de Penser en Ronde.

Deleuze, Gilles, and Félix Guattari. 1987. *A Thousand Plateaus: Capitalism and Schizophrenia.* Ed. and trans. Brian Massumi. Minneapolis: University of Minnesota Press.

Diller + Scofidio. 2002. *Blur: The Making of Nothing.* New York: Abrams.

"Diller + Scofidio *Blur* Building." 2000. *TransReal,* no. 7: 50.

Duden, Barbara. 1991. *The Woman Beneath the Skin: A Doctor's Patients in Eighteenth-century Germany.* Trans. Thomas Dunlap. Cambridge, MA: Harvard University Press.

D'Urbano, Alba. 1996. "The Project *Hautnah*, or Close to the Skin." In *Photography after Photography: Memory and Representation in the Digital Age*, ed. Hubertus V. Amelunxen, Stefan Iglhaut, and Florian Rötzer, 270–275. Amsterdam and Munich: G+B Arts International.

Freud, Sigmund. [1923] 1975. "Das Ich und das Es" [The Ego and the Id]. In *Studienausgabe: Psychologische Schriften*, vol. 3. Frankfurt: S. Fischer.

Giddens, Anthony. 1990. *The Consequences of Modernity.* Stanford, CA: Stanford University Press.

Grosz, Elizabeth. 1994. *Volatile Bodies.* Bloomington: Indiana University Press.

Grosz, Elizabeth. 1995. "Psychoanalysis and the Imaginary Body." In *Feminist Subjects, Multi-media: Cultural Methodologies,* ed. Penny Florence and Dee Reynolds, 172–191. Manchester and New York: Manchester University Press.

Hansen, Mark. 2002. "Wearable Space." *Configurations* 10, no. 2: 321–370. Special issue. In *Makeover: Writing the Body into the Posthuman Technoscape. Part I: Embracing the Posthuman*, ed. Timothy Lenoir. Baltimore, MD: Johns Hopkins University Press.

Hansen, Mark. 2004. *New Philosophy for New Media*. Cambridge, MA: The MIT Press.

Heidegger, Martin. [1949] 1998. "Letter on "Humanism." Trans. Frank. A. Capuzzi. In *Pathmarks*, ed. William McNeill. Cambridge, UK: Cambridge University Press.

Jones, Amelia. 1998. *Body Art: Performing the Subject*. Minneapolis: University of Minnesota Press.

Lacan, Jacques. 1966. "The Mirror Stage as Formation of the Function of the I as Revealed in Psychoanalytic Experience," delivered as a lecture in 1936. In *Écrits: A Selection*, 1–7. New York: Norton.

Le Goff, Jacques. 1978. "L'Histoire nouvelle." In *La Nouvelle Histoire*, ed. Jacques Le Goff, Roger Chartier, and Jacques Revel. Paris: CEPL.

Merleau-Ponty, Maurice. [1945] 1962. *Phenomenology of Perception*. Trans. Colin Smith. London and New York: Routledge & Kegan Paul.

Merleau-Ponty, Maurice. 1973. *The Prose of the World*. Trans. John O'Neill. Evanston, IL: Northwestern University Press.

Revel, Jacques. 1995. "Introduction." In *Histories: French Constructions of the Past*, ed. Jacques Revel and Lynn Hunt, 1–65. New York: The New Press.

Turner, Bryan S. [1984] 1996. *The Body and Society: Explorations in Social Theory*. Revised ed. London: Sage.

Varela, Francisco J., Evan Thompson, and Eleanor Rosch. 1991. *The Embodied Mind*. Cambridge, MA: MIT Press.

Wegenstein, Bernadette. 2002. "Getting Under the Skin, or, How Faces Have Become Obsolete." *Configurations* 10, no. 2: 221–259. Special issue. In *Makeover: Writing the Body into the Posthuman Technoscape. Part I: Embracing the Posthuman*, ed. Timothy Lenoir. Baltimore, MD: Johns Hopkins University Press.

Wegenstein, Bernadette. 2003. "If you won't SHOOT me, at least DELETE me! Performance Art from 60's Wounds to 90's Extensions." In *Data Made Flesh: Embodying Information*, ed. Robert Mitchell and Phillip Thurtle, 221–229. London and New York: Routledge.

Wegenstein, Bernadette. 2006. *Getting Under the Skin: Body and Media Theory*. Cambridge, MA: MIT Press.

Weiss, Gail. 1999. *Body Images: Embodiment as Intercorporeality*. London and New York: Routledge.

5

ON MORPHOLOGICAL IMAGINATION

Vivian Sobchack

I once heard a man say to his gray-haired wife, without rancor: "I only feel old when I look at you."

—Ann Gerike, *"On Gray Hair and Oppressed Brains"*

I'm prepared to die, but not to look lousy for the next forty years.

—Elissa Melamed, *Mirror, Mirror: The Terror of Not Being Young*

It's science now. It's no longer voodoo.

—An advertisement for medical equipment in a trade journal for cosmetic surgeons

What follows is less an argument than a meditation on the dread of middle-aging as a woman in our culture, rejuvenation fantasies in the American cinema, and the wish-fulfilling "magic" and "quick fixes" of technologies of transformation and display. These technologies and the fantasies they engender and "realize" are themselves re-productive. That is, they reproduce both the appearance of female youthfulness that, in our dominant culture, signals sexuality and the biological capacity to reproduce, and those very cultural values that demonize the middle-aged and postmenopausal woman. Thus, as might be expected of a woman in her sixties with the privilege of self-reflection, I am struggling with the cultural determinations of my own middle age. Indeed, I despair of ever being able to reconcile my overall sense of well-being, self-confidence, achievement, and pleasure in the richness of my present with the prob-lematic and often distressing image I see in my mirror. Over the past several years, I have become aware not only of my mother's face frequently staring back at me from my own but also of an increasing inability to see myself with any objectivity at all (as if, of course, I ever could). Within less than a single minute, I often go from utter dislocation and despair as I gaze at a face that seems too old for me, a face that I "have," to a certain satisfying recognition and pleasure at a face that looks "pretty good for my age," a face that "I am." I live now in heightened awareness of the instability of my image of myself, and I think about cosmetic surgery a lot: getting my eyes done, removing the furrows in my forehead, smoothing out the lines around my mouth, and lifting the skin around my jaw. But I know I will be disappointed. And so, while I don't avoid mirrors, I also don't seek them out. Rather, I try very hard to locate myself less in my image than in my (how else to say it?) "comportment."

It is for this reason that I was particularly moved when I first read in *Entertainment Weekly* that Barbra Streisand (only a year younger than I am) was remaking and updating *The Mirror Has Two Faces*, a 1959 French film about a housewife who begins a new life after plastic surgery. Barbra's update was to tell the story of "an ugly duckling professor and her quest for inner and outer beauty."[1] Obviously, this struck a major chord. Discussing the film's progress and performing its own surgery on the middle-aged producer, director, and star, *Entertainment Weekly* reported that the "biggest challenge faced by the 54-year-old" and "hyper-picky" Barbra was how to present her character. In the original, the mousy housefrau undergoes her transformation via plastic surgery. But Streisand rejected that idea—perhaps because of the negative message—and went with attitude adjustment instead. Which might work for the character, but does it work for the star? "Certain wrinkles and gravitational forces seem to be causing Streisand concern," says one ex–crew member. "She doesn't want to look her age. She's fighting it."[2]

Before I actually saw the film (eventually released in 1996), I wondered just what, as a substitute for surgery, Barbra's "attitude adjustment" might mean. And how would it translate to the superficiality of an image—in the mirror, in the movies? Might it mean really good makeup for the middle-aged star? Soft focus? Other forms of special effects that reproduce the work of cosmetic surgery?[3] And just how far can these take you—how long before really good makeup transforms you into a grotesque, before soft focus blurs you into invisibility, before special effects transform you into a vampire, witch, or monster? Perhaps this is the cinematic equivalent of attitude adjustment. The alternative to cosmetic surgery in what passes for the verisimilitude of cinematic realism is a change in genre, a transformation of sensibility that takes us from the "real" world that demonizes middle-aged women to the world of female demons: horror, science fiction, and fantasy.

Indeed, a few years ago, I published an essay on several low-budget science fiction/ horror films made in the late 1950s and early 1960s that focused on middle-aged female characters.[4] I was interested in these critically neglected films because, working through genres deemed fantastic, they were able to displace and disguise cultural anxieties about women and aging while simultaneously figuring them "in your face," so to speak. For example, in *Attack of the 50-Ft. Woman* (1958), through a brief (and laughable) encounter with a giant space alien, wealthy, childless, middle-aged, and brunette Nancy achieves a literal size, power, and youthful blondness her philandering husband can no longer ignore as she roams the countryside looking for him wearing a bra and sarong made out of her bed linens. In *The Wasp Woman* (1959, 1960), the fortyish head of a similarly fading cosmetics empire can no longer serve as the model for her products and overdoses on royal "wasp jelly," which not only reduces but also reverses the aging process, although its side effects regularly turn the again youthful cosmetics queen into a murderous insect queen (in high heels and a sheath dress). And, in *The Leech Woman* (1960), blowsy, alcoholic June becomes her feckless endocrinologist husband's guinea pig and, taking a rejuvenation serum made from African orchid pollen mixed with male pituitary fluid (extraction of which kills the men, one of them her husband), ultimately experiences, if only for a while, the simultaneous pleasures of youth, beauty, and revenge. In these low-budget films, scared middle-aged women are transformed—not through cosmetic surgery but through fantastical means, makeup, and special effects—into rejuvenated but scary women. Introduced as fading females still informed by—but an affront to—sexual desire and biological reproduction, hovering on the brink of grotesquery and alcoholism, their flesh explicitly disgusting to the men in their lives, these women are figured as more horrible in, and more horrified by, their own middle-aged bodies than in or by the bodies of the "unnatural" monsters they become. Indeed, these films dramatize what one psychotherapist has described as the culture's "almost visceral disgust for the older woman as a physical being" and underscore "ageism" as "the last bastion of sexism."[5]

Transformed, having become suddenly young, beautiful, desirable, powerful, horrendous, monstrous, and deadly, these women play out grand, if wacky, dramas of poetic justice. No plastic surgery here. Instead, through the technological "magic" of cinema, the irrational "magic" of fantasy, and a few cheesy low-budget effects, what we get is major "attitude adjustment"—of a scope that might even satisfy Barbra. The leech woman, wasp woman, and fifty-foot woman literalize, magnify, and enact hyperbolic displays of anger and desire, their youth and beauty reproduced now as lethal and fatal, their "unnatural" ascendance to power allowing them to avenge on a grand scale the wrongs done them for merely getting older. Yet, not surprisingly, these films also maintain the cultural status quo—even as they critique it. For what they figure as most grotesque and disgusting is not the monstrousness of the transformation but the "unnatural" conjunction of middle-aged female flesh and still youthful female desire. And—take heed, Barbra—the actresses who play these pathetic and horrific middle-aged women are always young and beautiful under their latex jowls and aging makeup.

Thus, what these fantasies of female rejuvenation give with one hand, they take back with the other. They represent less a grand masquerade of feminist resistance than a retrograde striptease that undermines the double-edged and very temporary narrative power these transformed middle-aged protagonists supposedly enjoy—that is, "getting their own back" before they eventually "get theirs." And, as is the "natural" order of things in both patriarchal culture and genre films of this sort, they do "get theirs"—each narrative ending with the restoration and reproduction of social (and ageist) order through the death of its eponymous heroine-monster. Attitude adjustment, indeed!

These low-budget films observe that middle-aged women—as much before as after their transformations and "attitude adjustments"—are pretty scary. In *Attack of the 50-Ft. Woman*, for example, as Nancy lies in her bedroom after her alien encounter but before she looms large on the horizon, her doctor explains her "wild" story away thus: "When women reach the age of maturity, Mother Nature sometimes overworks their frustration to a point of irrationalism." The screenwriter must have read Freud, who, writing on obsessional neurosis in 1913, tells us: "It is well known, and has been a matter for much complaint, that women often alter strangely in character after they have abandoned their genital functions. They become quarrelsome, peevish, and argumentative, petty and miserly; in fact, they display sadistic and anal-erotic traits which were not theirs in the era of womanliness."[6] Which brings us back to Barbra, whom it turns out we never really left at all. In language akin to Freud's, the article on the production woes of Barbra's film in *Entertainment Weekly* performs its own form of ageist analysis. The "steep attrition rate" among cast and crew and the protracted shooting schedule are attributed to both her "hyper-picky" "perfectionism" and her being a "meddler."[7] We are also told: "Among the things she fretted over: the density of her panty hose, the bras she wore, and whether the trees would have falling leaves."[8] A leech woman, wasp woman, fifty-foot woman—in Freud's terms, an obsessional neurotic: peevish, argumentative, petty, sadistic, and anal-erotic. Poor Barbra, she can't win for losing. Marauding the countryside in designer clothes and an "adjusted" attitude doesn't get her far from the fear or contempt that attaches to middle-aged women in our culture. Perhaps she—perhaps I—should reconsider cosmetic surgery.

Around ten years younger than Barbra and me, my best friend recently did—although I didn't see the results until long after her operation. Admittedly, I was afraid to: afraid she'd look bad (that is, not like herself or like she had surgery), afraid she'd look good (that is, good enough to make me want to do it). Separated by physical distance, however, I didn't have to confront—and judge—her image, and so all I initially knew about her extensive face-lift was from email correspondence. (I have permission to use her words but not her name.) Here, "in my face," so to speak, as well as hers were extraordinary convergences of actuality and wish, of surgery and cinema, of transformative technologies and the "magic" of "special effects"—all rendered intimately intelligible to us (whether we approve or not) in terms of mortal time and female gender. She wrote: "IT WORKED!" And then continued:

My eyes look larger than Audrey Hepburn's in her prime. . . . I am the proud owner of a 15-year-old neckline. Amazing—exactly the effect I'd hoped for. Still swollen . . . but that was all predicted. What this tendon-tightening lift did (not by any means purely "skin deep"—he actually . . . redraped the major neck and jaw infrastructure) was reverse the effects of gravity. Under the eyes—utterly smooth, many crow's feet eradicated. The jawline—every suspicion of jowl has been erased. Smooth and tight. I look good. The neck—the Candice Bergen turkey neck is gone. The tendons that produce that stringy effect have been severed—for ever! OK—what price (besides the $7,000) did I pay? Four hours on the operating table. One night of hell due to . . . a compression bandage that made me feel as if I were being choked. Mercifully (and thanks to Valium) I got through it. . . . Extremely tight from ear to ear—jaw with little range of motion—"ate" liquids, jello, soup, scrambled eggs for the first week. My sutures extend around 80 percent of my head. *Bride of Frankenstein* city. All (except for the exquisitely fine line under my eyes) are hidden in my hair. But baby I know they're there. Strange reverse phantom limb sensation. I still have my ears, but I can't exactly feel them. I . . . took Valium each evening the first week to counteract the tendency toward panic as I tried to fall asleep and realized that I could only move 1/4 inch in any direction. Very minimal bruising—I'm told that's not the rule . . . I still have a very faint chartreuse glow under one eye. With makeup, voilà! I can't jut my chin out—can barely make my upper and lower teeth meet at the front. In a few months, that will relax. And I can live with it. My hair, cut, shaved and even removed (along with sections of my scalp), has lost all semblance of style. But that too is transitory. The work that was done will last a good seven years. I plan to have my upper eyes done in about three years. This message is for your eyes only. I intend, if pressed, to reveal that I have had my eyes done. Period. Nothing more.

But there's plenty more. And it foregrounds the confusion and conflation of surgery and cinema, technology and "magic," effort and ease, that so pervades our current image culture. Indeed, there is a bitter irony at work here that perversely reminds me of listening to several computer-effects guys from Industrial Light and Magic point to their incredible and "seamless" work and bemoan the fact that no one can "see" all the time and labor they put into creating it. Having achieved a "seamless" face, my best friend has lost her voice. She cannot speak of the time and labor it took to transform her. The whole point is that, for the "magic" to work, the "seams"—both the lines traced by age and the scars traced by surgery—must not show. Thus, as Kathleen Woodward notes in "Youthfulness as a Masquerade": "Unlike the hysterical body, whose surface is inscribed with symptoms, the objective of the surgically youthful body is to speak nothing."[9] But this is not the only irony at work here. At a more structural level, this very lack of disclosure, this silence and secrecy, is an *essential* element of a culture increasingly driven—by both desire and technology—to extreme extroversion, to utter disclosure. It is here that cosmetic surgery and the "special effects" of the cinema converge and are perceived as phenomenologically reversible in what has become our current morphological imagination. Based in the belief that desire—through technology—can be materialized, made visible, and thus "realized," such morphological imagination does a perverse, and precisely superficial, turn on Woodward's distinction between the hysterical body and the surgically youthful body. That is, symptoms and silence are conflated as *the image of one's transformation* and *one's transformation of the image* become reversible phenomena. These confusions and conflations are dramatized most literally in the genre of fantasy, where "plastic surgery" is now practiced through the seemingly effortless, seamless transformations of digital morphing.

In this regard, two relatively recent films come to mind, *Death Becomes Her* (1992) and *The Mask* (1994). Technologically dependent on digital morphing, both make visible incredible alterations of an unprecedentedly plastic human body and also render human affective states literally superficial. *The Mask*, about the transformation and rejuvenation of the male psyche and spirit, significantly plays out its drama only on—and as—the surface of the body. When wimpy Stanley Ipkiss is "magically" transformed by the mask, there is no masquerade, no silence, since every desire, every psychic metaphor is materialized and made visible. His tongue unrolls across the table toward the object of his desire. He literally "wears his heart on his sleeve" (or thereabouts). His destructive desires are extruded from his hands as smoking guns. How, then, can one talk about the body of "The Mask" (as he is dubbed by the media) in terms of hysterical symptoms when everything "hangs out" as extroverted id and nothing is repressed?

Death Becomes Her functions in a similar manner, although here, with women as the central figures, the narrative explicitly foregrounds a literal rejuvenation as its central thematic—with youth and beauty the objects of female desire. Indeed, what's most interesting (although not necessarily funny) about *Death Becomes Her* is that plastic surgery operates in the film twice over. At the narrative level, its wimpy hero, Ernest Menville, is a famous plastic surgeon—seduced away from his fiancée, Helen, by middle-aging actress Madeline Ashton, whom we first see starring in a musical flop based on *Sweet Bird of Youth*. Thanks to Ernest's surgical skill (which we never actually see on the screen, a point I'll come back to), Madeline finds a whole new career as a movie star while Helen plots elaborate revenge. Seven years into the marriage, however, henpecked, alcoholic Ernest is no longer much use to Madeline. Told by her beautician that he—and cosmetic surgery—can no longer help her, the desperate woman seeks out a mysterious and incredibly beautiful "Beverly Hills cult priestess" who gives her a youth serum that grants eternal life, whatever the condition of the user's body. It is at this point that the operation of plastic surgery extends from the narrative to the representational level: the "magic" transformations of special computer-graphic and cosmetic effects instantaneously nip and tuck Madeline's buttocks; smooth and lift her face and breasts with nary a twinge of discomfort, a trace of blood, or a trice of effort; and reproduce her as "young." (What is said about the youth serum might also be said about the cinematic effects: "A touch of magic in this world obsessed by science.") This literalization of desire and anxiety is carried further still. That is, inevitably, the repressed signs of age return and are also reproduced and literalized along with signs of youth and beauty. When rejuvenated Madeline breaks her neck after being pushed down a flight of stairs, she lives on (though medically dead) with visible and hyperbolic variations of my friend's despised "Candice Bergen turkey neck." And, after Madeline shoots Helen (who has also taken the serum), Helen walks around with a hole in her stomach—a "blasted woman," however youthful. Ultimately, the film unites the women in their increasingly unsuccessful attempts to maintain and reproduce their peeling and literally "dead skin," to keep from "letting themselves go," from "falling apart"—which, at the film's end, they quite literally do.

In both *The Mask* and *Death Becomes Her*, cinematic effects and plastic surgery become reversible reproductive operations—literalizing desire and promising instant and effortless transformation. Human bodily existence is foregrounded as a material surface amenable to endless manipulation and total visibility. However, there is yet a great silence, a great *invisibility*, grounding these narratives of surface and extroversion. The labor, effort, and time entailed by the real operations of "plastic surgery" (both cinematic and cosmetic) are ultimately disavowed. Instead, we are given a "screen image" (both psychoanalytic and literal) that attributes the laborious, costly, and technologically based reality that underlies bodily transformation to the nontechnological properties of, in the one instance, a "primitive" fetish and, in the other, a "magic" potion. Of course, like all cases of disavowal, these fantasies turn round themselves like a Möbius strip to ultimately break the silence and reveal the repressed on the "same" side as the "screen image."

That is, on the "screen side," the technological effects of these transformation fantasies are what we want "in our face," so to speak. But we want these effects without wanting to see the technology, without wanting to acknowledge the cost, labor, time,

and effort of its operations—all of which might curb our desire and despoil our wonder. Indeed, like my friend who wants the effects of her face-lift to be seen but wants the
facts of her operation to remain hidden, our pleasure comes precisely from this "appearance" of seamless, effortless, "magical" transformation. On the other repressed side
(one that becomes the "same" side, however), we are fascinated by "the operation"—its
very cost, difficulty, effort. There are now magazines and videos devoted to making visible the specific operations of cinematic effects, their tell-all revelations made auratic
through a minute accounting of the technology involved, hours spent, effort spent, dollars spent. My friend, too, despite her desire for secrecy, is fascinated by her operation
and the visibility of her investment. Her numeracy extends from money to stitches but
is most poignant in its temporal lived dimensions: four hours on the operating table,
one night of hell, a week of limited jaw motion, time for her hair to grow back, a few
months for her upper and lower jaws to "relax," three years before she will do her eyelids, seven years before the surgeon's work is undone again by time and gravity. The
"magic" of plastic surgery (both cinematic and cosmetic)—at least when it's not
screened—always costs an irrecoverable portion of a mortal life.

And a mortal life must *live through* its operations, not magically, instantaneously,
but *in time*. It is thus apposite and poignant that "offscreen" Isabella Rossellini, who
plays and is fixed forever as the eternal high priestess of youth and beauty in both *Death
Becomes Her* and old Lancôme ads, has joined the ranks of the on-screen "wasp woman,"
Janet Starlin: after fourteen years as the "face" of Lancôme cosmetics, she was fired at
age forty-two for getting "too old." Unlike the wasp woman, however, Rossellini can
neither completely reverse the aging process nor murder those who find her middle-
aged flesh disgusting. Thus, it is also apposite and poignant that attempts to reproduce
the fantasies of the morphological imagination in the real world are doomed to failure:
medical cosmetic surgery never quite matches up to the seemingly effortless and perfect plastic surgeries of cinema and computer. This disappointment with the "real
thing" becomes explicit in my friend's continuing emails:

Vivian, I'm going through an unsettling part of this surgical journey. . . . When I first got
home, the effect was quite dramatic—I literally looked 20 years younger. Now what's happened: the swelling continues to go down. The outlines of the "new face" (in quotes) are still
dramatically lifted. . . . BUT, the lines I've acquired through a lifetime of smiling, talking,
being a highly expressive individual, are returning. Not all of them . . . but enough that the
effect of the procedure is now quite natural . . . and I no longer look 20 years younger. Maybe
10 max. . . . I'm experiencing a queasy depression. Imagining that the procedure didn't work.
That in a few weeks I'll look like I did before the money and the lengthy discomfort. Now I

scrutinize, I imagine, I am learning to hate the whole thing. Most of all, the heady sense of exhilaration and confidence is gone. In short, I have no idea any longer how the hell I look.

Which brings me back to myself before the mirror—and again to Barbra, both behind and in front of the camera. There is no way here for any of us to feel superior in sensibility to my friend. Whether we like it or not, we have all had "our eyes done." With or without medical surgery, we have been technologically altered, both "seeing" differently and "seeming" different than we did in a time before either cinema or cosmetic surgery presented us with their reversible technological promises of immortality and figurations of "magical" self-transformation—that is, transformation without time, without effort, without cost. To a great extent, then, the bodily transformations of cinema and surgery inform each other. Cinema is cosmetic surgery—its fantasies, its "makeup," and its digital effects able to "fix" (in the doubled sense of repair and stasis), to fetishize, and to reproduce both faces and time as "unreel" before us. And, reversibly, cosmetic surgery is cinema, creating us as an image we not only learn to enact in a repetition compulsion but also must—and never can—live up to. Through their technological "operations"—the work and cost effectively hidden by the surface "magic" of their transitory effects, the cultural values of youth and beauty effectively reproduced and fixed—we have become subjectively "derealized" and out of sequence with ourselves as, paradoxically, these same operations have allowed us to objectively reproduce and realize our flesh "in our own image."

Over email, increments of my friend's ambiguous recovery from fantasies of transformation and rejuvenation seemed to be in direct proportion to the diminishing number of years young she felt she looked: "Vivian, I've calmed down, assessed the pluses and minuses and decided to just fucking go on with it. Life, that is. They call it a 'lift' for a reason. . . . The face doesn't look younger (oh, I guess I've shaved 5 to 8 years off), but it looks better. OK. Fine. Now it's time to move on." But later fantasy reemerges—for the time being, at least, with real and sanguine consequences: "Vivian, the response has been terrific—everybody is dazzled, but they can't quite tell why. It must be the color I'm wearing, they say, or my hair, or that I am rested. At any rate, I feel empowered again."

In sum, I don't know how to end this—nor could I imagine at the time of my friend's rejuvenation how, sans cosmetic surgery, Barbra would end her version of *The Mirror Has Two Faces.* Thus, not only for herself but also for the wasp woman, for my friend, for Isabella Rossellini, and for me, I hoped that Barbra—both on- and off-screen—would survive her own cinematic reproduction. Unfortunately, she did not. "Attitude adjustment" was overwhelmed by "image adjustment" in her finished film: to wit, a diet, furious exercise, good makeup, a new hairdo, and a Donna Karan little black dress. Despite all her dialogue, Barbra had nothing to say; instead, like my friend, she silenced and repressed her own middle-aging, first reducing it to a generalized discourse on inner and outer beauty, and then displacing and replacing it on the face and in the voice of her bitter, jealous, "once beautiful," and "much older" mother (played by the still spectacular Lauren Bacall). Barbra's attitude, then, hadn't adjusted at all.

I finally did *see* my rejuvenated friend in the flesh. She looked pretty much the same to me. And, at the Academy Awards (for which the song in her film received the only nomination), Barbra was still being characterized by the press as "peevish" and "petty." I, in the meantime, have vowed to be kinder to my mirror image. In the glass (or on the screen), it is, after all, thin and chimerical, while I, on my side of it, am grounded in the thickness and productivity of a life, in the substance—not the reproduced surface—of endless transformation. Thus, each time I start to fixate on a new line or wrinkle, on a graying hair in the mirror, each time I envy a youthful face on the screen, I try very hard to remember that, on my side of the image, I am not so much aging as always becoming.

Notes

I am most grateful to the UCLA Center for the Study of Women for its research support. This essay is abridged from my "'Scan' Women: Cinema, Surgery, and Special Effects," in *Figuring Age: Women, Bodies, Generations*, ed. Kathleen Woodward (Bloomington: Indiana University Press, 1998).

1. Jeffrey Wells, "Mirror, Mirror," *Entertainment Weekly*, April 12, 1996, 8.
2. Wells, "Mirror, Mirror," 9.
3. It is relevant that developments in television technology have produced a "skin contouring" camera that makes wrinkles disappear. Using puns about "vanity video" and "video collagen," J. Max Robins, in "A New Wrinkle in Video Technology," *TV Guide* (Los Angeles Metropolitan Edition), September 28–October 4 1996, tells of this "indispensable tool for TV" personalities of a certain age first used "as a news division innovation" (its beneficiaries include Dan Rather, the late Peter Jennings, Tom Brokaw, and Barbara Walters). According to one news director, "It can remove almost all of someone's wrinkles, without affecting their hair or eyes." "The magic," however, "only lasts as long as the stars remain in front of the camera" (57).
4. Vivian Sobchack, "Revenge of *The Leech Woman*: On the Dread of Aging in a Low-budget Horror Film," in *Uncontrollable Bodies: Testimonies of Identity and Culture*, ed. Rodney Sappington and Tyler Stallings (Seattle, WA: Bay Press, 1994), 79–91.
5. Elissa Melamed, *Mirror, Mirror: The Terror of Not Being Young* (New York: Linden Press, 1983), 30.

6. Sigmund Freud, "The Predisposition to Obsessional Neurosis," in *Collected Papers*, vol. 2, ed. Ernest Jones, trans. Joan Rivière (London: Hogarth and the Institute of Psycho-Analysis, 1959), 130.
7. Wells, "Mirror, Mirror," 8.
8. Wells, "Mirror, Mirror," 9.
9. Kathleen Woodward, "Youthfulness as a Masquerade," *Discourse* 11, no. 1 (Fall–Winter 1988–1989): 133–134.

Transgression

6

FUR MANIFESTO

Model T. and Sara D(iamond)

Prologue

Yesterday it was Minus 37 Centigrade in the sunshine if you consider wind chill. It's Minus 29 without. I consider wind chill. It's one more argument for fur. This morning, the drainage pipes to my kitchen sink froze. I spent many hours emptying the sinks, pouring boiling water in, plunging, bailing again, running outside to rewrap the insulation and try to warm the pipes up—all to no avail. Then my visitor's 1984 Mercedes would not start, even though plugged in. It took three hours of jumpstarts with my 4 x 4 to get it going, running from car to truck in the freezing breezing cold in between flooding her diesel engine. Tonight the pipes to the washing machine froze mid-wash, seizing the motor. I just handwashed six towels and two sets of pajamas and wrung them as dry as I could. I crawled around the outside of the house in seeping water, finding the taps to turn off the washing machine water supply. The cold escaped description and even measurement. I walked to the store this morning to get a few necessities. By the end of a half hour, I was hobbling on stiff feet, my fingertips in their microfiber mitts white and frozen. Not my body, not my head, they were warm. I was wrapped in fur. Inherited, hand-me-down fur, but fur nonetheless. There is nothing like it. Model T. knows, she can already DIY grow her own fur.

FIRST PRINCIPLES—BECOMING ANIMAL— The CODE ZEBRA Manifesto

Have you noticed? Zebra and ocelot markings are everywhere, from haute couture to discount slippers. Can we crack Code Zebra? Zebra is the penultimate reaction/diffusion pattern, a proof of nature's capability to develop complexity, display, and camouflage. Zebras are animals that appear docile but are known for their fighting qualities, especially when mating. Zebras defy domestication.

Code Zebra (www.codezebra.net) is a software web of wills, in which faux science flies in the face of faux fur (figure 6.1). Code Zebra is an intellectual reality drama and Web software laboratory where art and science muse in mutual fascination. Triggered

| Figure 6.1 |
The Code Zebra software landscape

by plyotropic genes, reaction/diffusion (R and D) generation, the key to Turing's pattern recognition and neural network research, R and D throbs deep below the surface at the level of the cell, ovulating as ocelot and zebra patterns, voluptuous Voronoi clonal mosaics, colluding cellular automata. Only a pretty tool can miscegenate the cultures of art, science, philosophy, economy, performance, and gameplay.

The artist and the scientist desire each other. They start with participant observation. They sit apart, high up in the rhizomes of a mangrove swamp.

The artist turns to the scientist, and says, "Are you ever visited by animals in your sleep?" The scientist responds, "Recently. I dreamed of the genetic coding of a tiger stripe and its parallels in field analysis. I was up in front of a peer review committee. They asked, which door, and I accidentally choose the lady over the tiger, what a nightmare." The artist prepares to pounce, remarking, "Why not take the tiger by the tail? Are you sure that animals are not humans? After all, humans are animals. Ever been licked by a large cat? When you were little did you like to climb trees?" The scientist, dismissive, asks, "Are you some kind of a gene pool narcissist with data mining anxieties? Animals are hardly human." The artist thinks, "I'm going to chew on that rational left ear."

The artist does not want to proceed as an artist. Oh no. It is far too dangerous. Artists assume the identities of various other endangered species such as anthropologists or historians, in order to enact their will upon scientists, who in turn feel stalked. Perhaps the gap that separates the artist and the scientist will dissolve with these imaginings; perhaps they will find a space in between. Will there be progeny or parthenogenesis?

The artist is tempted to get physical. The scientist weighs the situation from the bough, kicking a foot, wanting to get it on, but nervous about the encounter. The scientist, examining the artist, thinks about root systems, artificial life algorithms, the comfort of abstraction, as does the artist. The engineer who dwells inside both the scientist and the artist would prefer to reduce the problem of seduction to something solvable, manageable, to a design issue, to making something. The scientist begins to calculate the distance between one tree and the other, between the logos and the loci. The scientist sits erect, excited by the possibilities of research among the animals. Actually, the scientist is thinking of becoming an artist. The artist growls, suddenly protective of its territory. Maybe it's just time for lunch.

While the scientist and the artist look at the common but distanced ground, several overlapping committees are forming. One examines ethical practices, concerned about the artist's accelerating loss of identity and the scientist's research on human subjects. The committees are debating the artist's lycanthrope, wondering whether it is psychosis or participatory observation, hence whether to reward it with censure or tenure. The second circle is comprised of elders. They feel that research on human subjects requires a protocol. The elders understand the artist's lycanthropic role playing and feel it may be the only means to burst the hermeneutic bubble of Western science. They are concerned about the artist's and the scientist's appropriation of their cultures' genomes and logic structures. Both committees share a mutual interest in the case study. Like *Quake* players, they encourage the two human creatures to trade skins and wear the results. This too could lead to the production of fur.

Why are sciences and art such strange and powerful attractors? Why are we so threatened and yet hopeful about their relationship? Can we get them out of their trees and into the Code Zebra fake fur habituation cage or the embossed ocelot Airstream motor home to merge their patterns? Can we get under their skin? Will social engineering work, or will the patterns become murky, ambivalent? Maybe the artist and scientist will solve world hunger, build the next utopian architecture, end global warming, and save each other and us from the boredom of the familiar. Maybe they will figure out how to DIY FUR.

| Figure 6.2 |
Patterns, concepts, connections

SPOT ON

CZ OS (Code Zebra Operating System) is a Web-based visualization tool that enables conversations between different individuals and groups on the Internet. Code Zebra deploys animal print metaphors—a reference to the technological jungle in which human survival is increasingly reliant on communication skills. Its pattern recognition function is a new way to visualize the packs that converge around prey or subject (figure 6.2).

CZ OS helps users/players link ideas, see and create relationships, and consider the emotional qualities of a discussion. It also creates affinities among underlying concepts that are not visible to the user. The organic pattern device uses reaction/diffusion patterns and clonal mosaics. Individual users grow their own patterns (monikers). Code Zebra expresses the behavior of the individual but within a larger community of dialogue. These personal patterns emerge through the process and history of ongoing chats, and build layers of visual imagery that the user can keep in virtual and material form. Patterns show relationships between postings and measure affective dynamics that in turn generate patterns (speed, word length, subject relatedness, frequency of posting, corrections, etc.). Different parts of a conversation will show varied stylistic tendencies, allowing users to group within the conversation by a style they prefer. The software provides a series of provocative language toys and games that can shift the dynamics of a conversation (fast and angry, e.g., at its most extreme expressed by flaming and swear words). A moderator or a participant can suggest that players play a game to resolve or amplify their conflicts. Games relate to animal behaviors and to Code Zebra improvisations about these. Games are often language-based (butterfly poetry magnet games, zebra stress-relief sentence stomp, multiple species word shooters, snake speed-writing games, hyena- and zebra-racing competitions . . .) (figure 6.3).

Code Zebra draws on the ancient history of animal and human contact. Shape-shifting into animal form provided humans with tools with which to understand the logic of animals that were part of the world around them. Working out from the zebra metaphor, adding biological research, Code Zebra improvised ideas for the software with choreographers, dancers, and dramaturges, bringing the software engineers into the play.[1]

The fiction, fantasies, and possibilities that bind human society to nonhuman living forms hover at the edge of knowledge about biology, evolution, and complementary science. Lycanthrope is the psychological term to describe shape-shifting, especially when animal identities are assumed in order to act out desire, whether socially prohibited or permitted. Lycanthrope enables the exploration of forms of knowledge, life transition, truth telling, clowning, or magic.[2] The images that result from it are a type of social aesthetic, in form and function. A suspension of disbelief occurs. In many Aboriginal and African traditional cultures, shape-shifting, within specifically structured contexts, is de rigueur. It is part of coming of age, naming, and other key social transitions. In Christian and psychoanalytic cultures, shape-shifting is identified with charged sexuality, psychosis, marginal science, or witchcraft. Code Zebra makes use of the practice of role-playing, suggesting that we constantly move between roles in our daily lives. Social science and science researchers have rituals, a society of validation and ways of imparting knowledge. Code Zebra investigates whether "animal" roles ally with professional categories, personality, or combinations of these.

CLOTHING IN ON THE FUR

A double entendre lies at the origins of Code Zebra. Software is softwear in Code Zebra. A zebra fun fur cocktail suit with matching boots, purse, hat, gloves, and other accessories inspired the first Code Zebra manifestation, transforming the artist/critic into the animal /artist/social scientist. I spoke about the contradictory desires and power that flow between art and science. After that, whenever faced with debating philosopher kings or scientists, this writer turns animal, keeping talk taut and spurning tautology. "Claws beat skin," Model T. meows.

| Figure 6.3 |
Butterfly performer

Code Zebra enables participants to express their identities in both software and fabric. They can literally wear or display themselves as unique but social beings. Printing, weaving, or knitting materials from the software patterns brings these virtual social/individual patterns back to the physical social world of the user. The fabrics we produce are tactile, nearly FUR—participants in the chat can feel the emotions of their own and others' dialogues on their skin. We are developing the capacity for materials to be responsive, so that they interact with their user, other fabrics, furniture, wall coverings, the softwear and garments that are in proximity or networked.

Is this approach too tame, too domestic, unlike the Zebra?

THE FUR DIALOGUES

On and off over the years, I have worked with a charming and clever Brazilian computer scientist. I met him in a café at an art biennale in his homeland. He unlocked the mystery of how spots and stripes form on/in fur. I said that I had a deep interest in animals with reaction/diffusion patterns and the ways these formed cooling systems and camouflage. Marcelo, with some surprise at our sudden mutual interest, told me with passionate conviction that I was mistaken: the process of pattern formation was through voronoi sets, also known as clonal mosaics, which distributed themselves relationally to create spots and stripes. Each of these shapes reconfigured as each new form was added, creating a stable but malleable surface with three-dimensional depth. Dark spots are thicker, acting as a coolant. He had spent years simulating this process mathematically to achieve what looked like the fur of the Big Cats, the Giraffe, and others. He had attained biological accuracy through mathematical calculation. He is a world leader in the field of spotted and striped animal graphics and, beyond this, clonal mosaic simulation in medical and other fields.

Ever since I had begun to study these animals, research their behaviors, imagine their experiences in their worlds, and use them as my models for behaviors in my software, I had also wondered what it would be like to temporarily grow fur on parts of my body. I had no desire to be furry all over. My desire was for small, changeable, sensuous patches of fur, fur that one could stroke when needing animal reassurance or a hit of erotic pleasure, fur one could share with a friend. Perhaps one could grow a full coat on an especially blustery day (figure 6.4).

PUSSY POWER

Code Zebra was beginning to plan the invention of a virus, a genome patch or genetic algorithm that if injected would spur fur growth. On behalf of Model T.'s quest for

| Figure 6.4 |
Fur alter©ations

self-knowledge, I asked, "Where does fur come from?" Marcelo smiled and said, "You must shave the pussy to understand the pattern." My mind stood still and my heart raced. This was a bold statement of feminine power. "I must work with this scientist," I thought, sidestepping the issue of research on human subjects. Model T. sometimes does go for the lion shave.

It turned out to be a problem of translation. Fur springs, already patterned, from under the skin. The actual size of a spot or stripe is calculated in relation to animal mass and genetic memory. I had the opportunity to present some of Marcelo's and my research at Sigraffi in Brazil in 2001.[3] Translating "shaving the pussy" into Portuguese created some pandemonium at this event. Local conditions could allow for dramatic adaptive changes in patterning over very few generations. Why could we not speed up the process for human animals, allowing skin patterns and/or then fur to grow as programmed in short bursts of time and space?

DIY FUR

What if, like ocelots, humans could shift their genes to generate unique patterns on demand, ingest, splice, inject as needed, and have our skin pattern up for awhile and then down again? What if we could make our hair pattern into soft fur rather than hair? In considering this problem, the researcher must take into account three processes. First, she must create a local adaptation that will allow patterns to develop in timed ways. Second, she must decode the means to inspire a spurt of hair growth. Third, she must deduce how to create the desired texture in the substance (fur or hair) grown.

To begin, we had to grow the fur within Code Zebra OS. Researchers and the graphics industry have invested many years and millions of dollars into "growing" realistic hair, fur, and animal patterns in computer graphics.[4] Adapting these fat graphics algorithms to a real-time online conversation patterning system was far from easy. Algorithms for fur patterning are well developed in the avatar world as adaptations of computer graphics programs used in animation. It is through Marcelo that we tested the differences between simulation of images and visualization of images from actual data, which is the strategy that Code Zebra eventually used, importing graphics that we designed, decoding these, and turning them into algorithms that could grow.[5] Undaunted, the Code Zebra team grew different abstract and explicit layers and styles of fur and its patterns for our software. You can see our versions at www.codezebra.net.

We taught each pattern to grow and then adapt into its Voronoi constraints, and we then built an averaging process to create grow an underlying pattern for each conversation. The adaptation process in the software was somewhat like the animal's fur growth. Each pattern was predefined by a set of behavioral constraints within a neural network (read genetic memory)—it would grow according to the structure of the posting from underneath the skin of the interface. The server provided deep structure and the client a kind of skin through which it would emerge. Shapes of the spot or stripe would vary in relation to neighboring postings.

How to grow fur inside the human body is the next challenge. Researchers have been trying to stimulate hair growth in balding men. In the 1990s American researchers developed a patent for subcutaneous jewelry—bracelets that could be programmed to release color and patterns (or medications).

Code Zebra will be working on fur growing viral algorithms for the next several years.

FUR'n ECONOMIES

Why bother, you may well ask? Why disrupt the strangely balanced luxury and subsistence trapping economies of actual fur? Some Aboriginal populations still rely on hunting and trapping to survive. Why even grow fur at all when fake fur is more and more realistic and efficient for warmth?

Most to the point, why concentrate on growing fur when we put so much effort into removing hair from our feminine and most recently masculine bodies? When shaving the pussy is part of the pattern of contemporary erotic aesthetic?

Well, not for everyone. The economy of excess hair and fur is tuned to the economy of its lack. It's much like a temporary and retractable tattoo, but tactile. For some, the ability to give or emerge a tiny strokable fur pattern that would grow on the human body is a pleasurable idea. Patterning your skin in a body tattoo that you can grow on command in key places or all over could be pleasurable. More interesting are the possibilities of using pattern, fur growth, and retraction as ways of responding to physiological or emotional stimuli. Pattern and/or fur can attract, repel, defend, entice, or contradict.

FuRNOMES

For others, "becoming animal" in a more thorough way on occasion is already evidenced by the Furry and Plushy social scenes, where people dress up in furry animal costumes, party, and often have sex. Humans have long struggled with the line between animal and human sexuality. The power of animation as a space of identification and early erotic development may have opened the door to erotic plushy fandom. This scene is native to the Internet, and like a stripped-down Code Zebra reflects on the fantastic possibilities of cyber identity while flipping back to a desire for the biological and animal within the world of cyber hype. In Code Zebra, we hope that "becoming animal" will be tongue-in-cheek, with some ecological intent and a critique of evolutionary determinism, without losing the sexiness of role playing and shape shifting.

This MTV interview provides a few insights into the aspirations of Furries:

Cas Kiyote: A lot of the mainstream has gotten the idea that Furry equals bestiality.
Llere: I'm fairly sure, at least in this case, that that is not the case.
Silfur: . . . When I come to conventions, I'm here really to meet people and to be social and to hug and scratch and bounce around and have a good time . . .
Yote: My furry name is Yote. Y-o-t-e. It's short for coyote. I've known about furry for six or seven years but I've been furry my entire life. For me, furriness—it's being in touch with like, an animal. I think everyone has an animal in them. They have attributes of a certain animal inside them. Everyone does, whether they know it or not. So, I go by Coyote. I feel that it'd probably be a better extension of who I am to look like one. It's being myself. And part of myself just looks different, sort of an inside-outside thing. Most Furs, when they think of their earliest memories of being furry, the things that most attracted them would be Saturday morning cartoons and Disney. For me, it's been six years since I found the Internet and got online. The Internet makes Furry possible. Without them, there would be no real Furry fandom, because it's an easy way to organize people, to gather people from out of state, to bring everyone together. 'Cause you know, it's—as all the slogans say, "it makes the world smaller."[6]

Having talked about the sexual economy of fur, there is the physical economy of fur itself. More and more fur is farmed in large-scale enterprises. The demand for fur, including the fur of exotic patterned animals seems to be a constant ebb and flow. In a fifty-year cycle of international fashion, animal spots and stripes and the seductive behaviors associated with them seem to crest during periods of technological boom. The culture gets cooler and cooler—suddenly the ice needs melting by the heat of animal skin and the warmth of FUR.

DIY FUR may fall into the categories of hair and makeup, tattoo, or jewelery rather than garment. It will constitute an alternative to animal fur and faux fur. Perhaps we will learn to finally love our transformable body hair as an infinite resource of FUR.

APPRENDIX: MORTAL ENEMIES: FINDING THE INNER PATTERNS

As mentioned earlier, Code Zebra dancers, actors, and engineers accepted a set of tasks.[7] We acted out, discovered, and researched stylized behaviors that would be performed as movement, as relations between animal types, as actions or rules within the software that would inform the artificial intelligence, and mark individual postings as well as conversation group patterns.

Using garments and jewelery to establish their characters, the performers worked out behaviors for each of the animal types, first working in groups and then as individuals. Each actor took on an animal to develop, and reflected through writing or through thoughtful discussion their version of how that animal would be.

This process grew from backstories that I wrote about the animals. These stories were tools to structure action within animal groups, conflict between the characters, and events within each set.

Each animal type or clan developed six degrees of freedom—these were the rules of engagement for the animal and its movement—and, if appropriate, sound vocabulary that could be adapted into dance movements, repetitive motion, and ways of acting with other species. These were based on backstories and biological research. We videotaped and photographed the characters. We simplified actions and rules the ways that one learns a character. These would form the basis for the games, which we developed through later workshops and collaborations.[8] The improvisations would also form the basis for choreographies, actor activity in live events, and clubs.

Performers suggested ways that character groups could be distributed on a virtual site, or within a club or more theatrical space. We thought about the den, nest, and resting spot. We thought about the ecology as a time-based mobile environment, one that aimed for either balance or managed change. We were interested in "significant state stages," such as ecological crisis, or the ability to freeze action in order to refresh evolutionary patterns. We worked with state descriptions that might also align with social interactions. Even when predation was not taking place, animals were highly aware of the presence of other animals.

We acted out the animals' sets as predator, prey, and protector. This suggested how the clans would interact in a debate or conflict or even play situation. We switched roles to experience each other's animal, teaching the movement and sound sets.

We puzzled about death and rebirth, about what happened when characters, groups, or individuals died and how to recycle or add new characters to the world.

We held the second improvisation series in a home, with gestures more pulled back, working first with gesture iteration and then narrative. We developed more familiarity with our movements, with a larger number of players. The domestic space was evocative, intimate, and chat-like—the death of the zebra shook everyone. The theatrical improvisations were valuable for later theater and dance performances of Code Zebra, for runway fashion gestures.

These simple improvisations paralleled the software development and actually informed a sense of embodiment that stayed a goal of Code Zebra. They fixed a sense of animal behavior and type and directly informed the games and the coding activities, including, eventually, the AI. The engineers and designers who participated in the improvisations, the pet-formances in Budapest and later in London, were touched to the core by the process and sustained the desire to build a beautiful, embodied, and playful software.

There are nine characters in Code Zebra, all characterized by their markings (Voronoi or reaction/diffusion). What follows are descriptions, rules, and backstories for two of the characters—mortal enemies, the zebra and hyena.

Zebras: ROUTINE

1. Shake mane and listen, perk ears.
2. Run elegantly in a group to scuttle visual comfort of foe and then freeze (vogueing).
3. Preen each other and perform neck nuzzle, snort.
4. Lean over, and with one hoof part grass, eat. Use downstage hand to part grasses.
5. Lean over far and use both hands to bring water to thirsty mouth.
6. Stomp.

Zebras: SPEECH

Barks of different orders. Back and forth, stomp, browse, chomp, slurp, nuzzle, remake community sense, talk at length, nit-pick, run-on talk and pause, consider dangers, restart. Thoughtful, graze (surf), slow rumination and breath, action and freeze.

Zebras: STYLE

Zebras are highly organized, self-protective, exclusive of others, narcissistic, and able to present a strong common front. They debate, pose reflectively, browse (research), drink in knowledge, digest, then begin dialogue again, all the while vulnerable to attack and to their enemies, highly wary. They have strong camouflage capabilities and an urge for violence to enforce conformity.

I am a zebra, I was born on the plain—I lie at my mother's side—on my spindly legs, I rise. She nuzzles me; I have the very-close-to-matching stripes that she carries on her hide. I know in my little, pounding heart that the wind will carry danger toward me. I sense the smells of the Big Cats, the Lions and Hyenas that are my enemies, uncontrolled dust storms, the flooding rains with torrents and nasty flies in their wake. I drink my mother's milk—she kicks at the dust, belligerent, wary. I will get to know her fear and love her grumpy, protective character. She stays always close to the herd, teaching me to do the same. With my flaring nostrils, my acute sense of hearing, I follow, slow in the heat, cantering when giddy with breezes, conserving our forces, then skittishly at a run, fast, fast, from the enemy. I learn the art of moving as one, muscles contracting as one, flesh extending, hearts racing, as one, a field of moving pattern. Stopping suddenly, our predators confounded, never outdistanced, but commotion, stripes, doing their duty. Somehow we become horizon, disappear, into the green, into the brown, the primary divisions of no color becoming all color. We defy our enemy's eyes. They squirm with nausea when they look directly at us.

When I am but several weeks old, something happens that shakes me forever, although in time, it feels right, a lesson. One of the other mothers, not mine, stumbles in a gully, goes down dramatically, ripping her foreleg. After that she cannot keep up with the herd. We see her downed, at a distance. Ripped from the air and thrown down by a pack of hyenas, their snapping jaws opening her throat smell of red blood splashing.

My little friend has lost her mother. She runs along with us, bereft and hungry. When feeding time comes, she approaches my mother, whinnying. My mother examines her stripes, but they do not quite fit our family pattern enough. She pushes her away; even through the stripes vary marginally. But it is enough; my friend moves on.

She seeks an available nipple, but there is none. All the mothers bare their teeth. They butt her and bite at her, as she becomes hungrier, more insistent. This occurs again and again. Finally, she curls on the ground, alone, hungry, winnowing, cold in the night savannah wind. If we had enough resources, we would feed her.

I do not dare to get up, go to her, although we have frolicked together in the recent past. I fear my mother's will; I feel my sympathy move toward resentment at the foal's pathetic aspect. Over the days, this pattern repeats, while she struggles to keep up with the herd. She grows thin and starved. Then the fatal day arrives, a group of adults, mothers, and our male herd leader, led by the Alpha female of our herd, surround her. They butt her; kick her, until she collapses into the ground. She resists them, or tries to at least, fighting for her life. Know that your hooves are weapons!

I try at first to block their access to her, nuzzling my mother's nipple until I am thrown off. They kick her until she is not longer able to make even pathetic sounds, vetting their animal rage, wilding. Her black and white hide is covered with blood and she lies unconscious, the flies alighting on her body. She is dying. The pattern that keeps her whole ruptured. My nostrils flare, smelling blood. She was once a living colt, my friend, no more. She is left there unconscious, for the lions. I learn from this incident. Stay close to the herd. Learn its ways. Do not stray. Watch where you run! Hope that nothing happens to your mother while you still rely on her for nourishment.

The days are filled with richness, with running to the wind, with play, with high grasses, with an ever-present sense of danger coursing through my nostrils, flicking my ears wide. Nights as well as early day stay alert. I learn to be cautious, protectionist, conservative, even for a young thing. I find my place in the pattern, where and how to exact the mystery. I know how to sustain the camouflage. I know my place in the evolutionary thread—our herd. Our black stripes are heat thickened, making the white into coolants, dropping our temperatures in the blast of daytime heat.

I eat the luxurious grasses, always thirsty; I almost inhale the water at the hole we gather at. It is there that I really learn to differentiate myself from others. We reign over the cruel world, over the other hoofed ones, like the antelopes. Once, acting like the cruel protective creatures that we are, we kill some young wildebeests in our camp. They are mimics, ninnies, using us for stealth and if lost, for mothering. We will not even keep the inferior in our own group alive! We stay together; our instincts are sharp, as sharp as the claws and teeth of those who would bring us down.

This is how it is and how it always must be.

The seasons pass and I grow. The lion comes, the cheetah males, the hyenas. We evade them. The vibration of our pattern sickens them. Yet our meat draws them. At times they pull a weakened member from our midst and feast.

I am the zebra, black and white together, unified. All color no color.

One season, at the end of summer, the approach of fall, I feel the change moving through my body, pushing and pulsing inside me, deep in my blood. The days are growing shorter. I am ecstatic. I am lovely. I am just at the end of colthood, becoming a mare. I am barely elegant. My gait still needs occasional coaching. I watch and learn. I want to breed with the best, for breed I must. Careful, careful, desire can escalate camouflage or evade it. My head proud, my neck erects. My mother is a reminder of our fine stock, our symmetry. The colts of my year have grown together, the young stallions are proud too, randy, full of discovery. They knock each other over in their eagerness. They will soon be forced out of the herd, on their own to join another band. As the heightening storms flare and the lightning flashes on the savannah, the lightning feels as though it is crackling through my body. Descending into me.

The stallions fight magnificently. They rear onto their hind legs, spinning around each other like dervishes, straining to bite each other's legs to bring each other to ground, straining, stomping, straining, stomping.

Suddenly, they are behind close snorting, their breath and me hot. They move me out, away from the herd. They had been fighting at a distance, and I foolish, had stopped to watch, never quite thinking that I, in estrus, are their desired one. They move me away from the herd, trying to abduct me. I run, back to my group, they force me away. Suddenly, one mounts me from behind; his hooves bear down on my neck. I am frightened fearful; this is not a friend, but an older stallion of another herd, a respected master. I am shocked at his approach, at my sudden desire, and at the pain on my shoulders, my neck. I feel him pushing into me, my virgin flesh. I am wet with the blood of my time. This is my first season. I am wet and he pushes again and again and I feel myself, almost ripping as he comes into my body and crashes against and inside me. I scream with fear, pain, and the knowledge that all innocence is gone, overtaken. He soon screams too and I pull away, galloping off. I shake my mane. I leave with him. I will not yet bear the child of this master. But the next season, when I am able to conceive, I will. It will come in thirteen months, and I will become heavy, vulnerable, but my new herd will protect my foal and me.

This is how it is and how it will always be.

Hyenas: ROUTINE

1. Hyena places buttocks near the ground, shakes, and appears to deposit hyena butter.
2. Rubs genitals against each other.
3. Tears from left to right, with claw.
4. Chomps down with arms as though teeth.

5. Chases and laughs.
6. Kicks back with right leg.

Hyenas: SPEECH

Rhythm, back and fro, pissing contests, staccato structure, pops into conversations, laughter, non-ironic, subcultural and macho, expresses anxiety, erotic play—vicious.

They all talk at once, or they express in All talk at escalating turns. They are in run mode and big packs of noise. Performative, watch each other greet and then join in. They also listen to the lone poet, to goal-oriented radical speech—some call and response structures.

Hyenas: STYLE

The core is, "Don't fence me in"—this is the radical voice, the alterior, underground, and subculture vs. the zebras. We roam over large territories. We are vicious, with sisters and siblings, and then bonded. There are female harems of forty, with Alpha females carrying more power. They are the ones to aggressively broach new ideas—they are either amoral or highly ethical. They respond to the moon, with a history of being the familiar to goddesses and witches. In a group they can overpower the individual lioness. Their aggression suggests a constant state of fear—looking for food all the time, fear of each other and others within abundance. They are the top of the food chain, but appear not to be. No belief in surplus.

I am a hyena. Born under a full moon, scourged, and scorned. I am goddess of life and death, a strange attractor, make you double over with laughter, split a gut, then eat the contents. I kill. I take your kill. Savanna kills—kills of the night. I outwit a flock of buzzards. I take the trembling zebra colt down. I do not fear looking at their patterned backs, those air-conditioned, giddy, and stupid creatures that think they are wise by height and weight alone. I am hyena, she who takes down the antelope while it bucks and tears in her strong jaws.

And you my lioness, my mortal enemy, it is your own mortality that you should fear, for I will humble you in the name of all that suffer, should you turn away from me. I run fast, faster than you. I will take the zebra from your feeding pride. I will take your very cub, and even you, if you are weak. I will kill. I will eat your bones. You think I feed on carrion, well yes, it is a delicacy, but mostly, I love to kill.

Never what I seem, I am of woman made. As the tiniest of cubs, I suckled at my mother's teat and felt the power of her near feline ways. Heard her purr, her rough tongue licking my fur. Yes, feline. Well, almost, for we claim our own breed. We are of woman ruled—we are of the moon. When I eat the lion, I am cannibal.

We are the marines of the plains—the female shock troops. We train on our own; almost a third of us die from friendly fire early on in life. We kill our sisters. We learn to be wary, vicious, and always ready for attack. Our men are jealous, they bait us, but we fight back, defend our right to rule. They come they go, we resent their roaming ways. We live in girl gangs, loyal and true.

We are sexy, sexy, sexy, are you afraid? We squat to paste hyena butter, special excrement, around our territory—marking it. We greet each other by mounting, our clits or dicks pressing into each other, same-sex rebels or hetero sluts. Perverse creatures you humans say. Suits me, we survive. How can I redeem myself? I dare not try. I laugh! I laugh! I laugh! Frightened? Not I—excited perhaps. Ready for the kill.

My hind legs lowered toward the ground, back low, I am a running machine. Ugly, you think? Functional beauty, I say. You create your myths about my magic powers. Proceed, for these are real.

The bigger my clit, the more power I have. We worship the clit, the place of pleasure, so near the source of life. My mother's opened to bring me into the world. My first fight was down that narrow passage. Many of our mothers and cubs die. My mother was a clan leader. This is a world where butches are bitches and rule. I walk the line of the transgendered. Three things always on my mind: meat, sex, and a good laugh.

FURTHUR THOUGHTS

What can one add to the preoccupations of a hyena, but a commentary from another sort of cat.

BIOGRAPHICAL NOTE and RESEARCH COMMENTARY: © MODEL T.

SHE was working on Code Zebra for about eighteen months when to HER alarm, I became a researcher in my own right. It may have been that our programmer was living with us and I would stay up all night with him, helping with the monotony of coding, sitting on his lap, or stepping delicately on the keyboard. I worked on the patterning of those arrogant great-aunts of mine, the cheetah and those silly little cousins, the ocelots. Cats that can swim, how ridiculous! All about collaboration herself, SHE became quite jealous of my collaboration with John.

Methodology: My toys are scattered all over the living room. This archive is a hand wave to a nostalgic past—a time when chasing and jumping were core initiatives, and

| Figure 6.5 |
Model T, one of the authors

sleep and meditation for twenty-two hours a day was not my steady state. Now, dreaming is my key research method, and it comes deep and often. I am twenty-one and deaf; this has brought me a terrific and stoic wisdom, which I cover by a lopsided smile. Learn from the Buddha. I am driven by a heat-seeking if existential phenomenological sangfroid. This allows me to spend hours basking by the fire in the glow of my resulting algorithms.

Recent Projects: The Alpha Project

Key words: Action research, Dominance theory, Prediction algorithms, Audio-linguistics, Sleep states, Fluid dynamics, gravity, ANT, Evolutionary algorithms, Biological determinism, Participatory observation, Phenomenology.

The Alpha Project: Phase One

I awake at least five minutes before SHE does every morning. I gently sink one claw into HER eyelid, raising it to open position. With another claw, I enter a nostril, pulling it open to better assist morning breath to pass through. In the interests of science, I sniff this and then drool a bit on her face. I turn thrice and settle on HER face and head, purring loudly and establishing dominance. All this activity is undertaken in advance of the alarm—I am testing the relationship between my internal clock, the alarm mechanism, which even if deaf, I can anticipate, and HER arousal capabilities.

The Alpha Project: Phase Two

A second phase of the research relates to principles of leverage. SHE is ten times my weight at least. During the night, I will endeavor to lever HER from fetal position onto HER back. I will then lie on HER shoulder and neck, keeping us both warm. This position can never quite be reassumed in the morning; rather, there are a series of moves, initiated by again firmly covering HER head and face with my entire body as in Phase One. SHE will push me off. I uproot HER; wiggle my body underneath HER, despite the discrepancy of her abundant weight against my paltry size. SHE lies on top of at least half of my body and pretends to fall asleep, pinning me down. SHE is playing Alpha, but I am the True Alpha, because I have chosen to be covered. I celebrate my victory with earth-rumbling purrs that deprive both of us of sleep.

At the same time, as inferred earlier, I undertook a piece of rather obscure and difficult perceptual scratch-and-sniff Phernome (FURnome) research about the ways that SHE responded to various stimuli, from drooling, to kneading, to scratching, to crying, to lap-sitting. This research, and my painstaking reports that I scratched onto the living room couch as well as maintained on my former research site, established an already evident species-typical capacity for empirical observation based research on my part. The couch publication is still legible and locally available to other researchers.

In the early winter of 2002, I put a paw on delete and destroyed my Web site and substantive email archive. Although strongly tuned to the historical, I feel that the ephemeral qualities of my research required that it live only in the memories of those who had visited my site or corresponded with me.

Since your publication is insistent on proof of my research status, I think you need to consider the following notes. The first is a statement of protest. Many of the observations in the first texts of this essay infer my agreement. In fact, these do not express my views but HERs. The second are excerpts from my correspondence with Kellie Marlowe, who kept my spirits buoyed during this difficult research period and its documentation. These prove the existence of my former site and email list and document this researcher's hardships.

Model T.

SHE is a very difficult research subject. SHE spends lengthy hours away from this researcher. SHE keeps the laboratory underheated during the day, which makes it necessary for me to sleep, not work. The food SHE serves me is underscored by a lack of dietary glory with the occasional fresh chicken or liver dinner. SHE underrates my intelligence and focuses instead on my unique and stunning beauty and my luxurious FUR. SHE pretends to understand me, and projects empathy and other humiliating motivations onto my behaviors, failing to comprehend my simple, scientific research steps such as stalking. SHE wants my FUR. In short, SHE wants to become ME.

Excerpts

Subject: I miss you
Kellie. Sara is awful clingy. SHE does NOT brush me enough. Lately SHE shoves pills down my throat, too anxiously. Mostly I have managed to spit them out, but not always. I have puked two nights in a row, precisely at 3:00 a.m. Last night on the left side of the bed, the night before on the right side. Do YOU miss me?
Model T.

Re: I miss you
Oh Model T.,
Taking pills is a nasty business for the taker and tricky for the person ensuring you ingest it. On the gagging front—can you not, when feeling a ball surfacing, go into the basement or kitchen and rid it with some decorum, keeping in mind that at these locations you are ensuring that the cleanup is minimal and the distasteful sounds and smells inherent in such an activity don't impact your partner to such a great degree . . .
Ask Sara to brush you everyday and find little ways to make this job easier for her . . .
I do miss you and wish that I could be there for you both at least sometimes.
OOOXXXX Kellie

Re: Re: I miss you

It is true Kellie. I do use a lovely green throw rug that SHE bought as my forum for these activities whenever I can make it down those stairs. I am enjoying the combined emotional impacts of my daily nausea and prolonged hunger strike on HER emotional state. SHE says it's almost over, but it isn't over 'til it's over is it.

PETS RULE THE ROOST!

ALL POWER TO THE PUSSY!

MT

Subject: I am much better now

My bladder infection is gone. I had a WONDERFUL time at our party; everyone fell in love with ME not HER. I stayed upstairs among the 50 dinner guests, wine drippers, break dancers, hip hoppers ALL night, either on my little chair, by the fire, or in their arms. I am greasy and full of perfume from so many hands patting me and lipstick kisses. The boys hugged me too. I got MANY, MANY complements. There are names for my lovely colors in French, Spanish, and Japanese apparently. I feel that I should be sent on international peacekeeping missions.

SHE is having the furnace cleaned today, maybe 'cause you are coming back for a few days, so you will not sneeze and wheeze more than you do anyhow (ignore HER, I snore too, remember?). Apparently it is full of MY hair, why do I get blamed for such things? It is probably HER hair, like the bathtub. SHE is furrier than I am.

Apparently the vet apologized for the deadly antibiotics, etc. I am NOT going back there for the holidays. No way.

I PROMISE not to shed too much at your place, or get sick. Well, I might puke once just to prove that I can still make you gag, Kellie. Have a nice day.

Your friend forever (I am NINETY, so it might not be FOREVER, FOREVER) Model T.

Re: I am much better now

Dear Model T.,

While reading your most recent email, I laughed all the way through it. Even for ninety, you are a clever kitty. I'm so glad that you managed to fight off that infection. I will be happy to host you over the holidays. I can't however promise you the style of living you are accustomed to nor the social life. I do promise however to give you lots of love. Also I am trying to not be such a tight ass about the small things like hair on the furniture and my pillow. Let's make sure that SHE brings your favorite things like hairball medicine, treats, and brush. Let me know if there's anything else she should bring.

Air kisses until I can give you the real thing.

XXXX Kellie

Subject: You never write me any more

Now that SHE has taken me hostage and will not let me visit you this weekend because she thinks that all the changes in altitude and temperature and me crying for two hours is bad for me and my ears, and because SHE wants me to take advantage of Justine and prevent her from being lonely here. I don't know about that Justine, better not be another Goth.

MT

Re: You never write me anymore

Justine is very, very clear that I am not to go near her. I will find my ways. Currently going for additional amounts of fur where she likes to sit. This way she will understand that fur on top of the lap from a warm, real-time kitty is better than post-produced fur on the bum where only others can see the results.

Re: Re: You never write me anymore

Dear Model T.,

I do miss you and the little girl downstairs inquires after you daily. So by the way does that grey cat Jump—I think Jump wishes you two could have had a more civil chat.

I hope that SHE has had time to give you a bath. I think you will find Justine very amenable to sharing her lap—she just seems like the type. Re: your ears—try putting your paws over your nose and mouth and blowing hard—perhaps you have earwax lodged in there and are not deaf af-

ter all. Give HER a wet smooch for me and know that I miss you both very much.
XXKM

Re: Re: Re: You never write me anymore
Kellie. I hate baths. What on earth are you trying to talk me into? I think I really am deaf. I cannot hear myself at all, even though I feel my mouth opening and my little voice box vibrating like crazy, pushing out something that sure gets a running, scowling reaction from HER.
I have to say, this gives me the ability to scratch the furniture at leisure. After all, I cannot hear HER when SHE waxes (pun intended) hysterical.
Last night I managed to interrupt HER sleep six times, one for each of the lives that I have lost in various ways.
Maybe I can do the same for you? She said SHE is going into the city tomorrow. I said I am NOT going with her, not for two days, oh no. I will stay home and supervise the piano movers.
MT

Subject: Help! Help!
Somebody save me. I mean it! Help! Help! I hate HER, I hate HER, I hate HER. Well, slightly less now cause SHE got me really stoned, right after the Big Trauma. Why you have to save me. Here I am now, licking, licking my wet, wet fur, and just thought I would take a minute to write you. (SHE just got your call. SHE wanted to talk to you personally about MY bath.) Nevertheless, it's too late, so I am writing to you instead, while SHE cooks a stinky lamb sausage. What if my FUR ends up smelling like stinky lamb after all THAT HELL? She set up a little bed right by the roaring fire, but do you think I am about to please HER and sit there after what I have just been through. I would rather sit on the floor, near the fire mind you, with my wet ass picking up dust.
SHE is wearing this pink sweater I hate, ugh! I should have known something awful was about the happen. First, she gives me that hairball

stuff, which I do like. Then SHE brushes me with some new super brush forever, she removes half my fur, all cajoling and impressed with the technology and apologizing for the shit brush SHE subjected me to for all those years. Nevertheless, woman on a mission, you would just tell from the brushing. I hissed and submitted. Then its gets much worse. SHE tried to drown me. Had this nice little sink filled with water, plunks me into it, and starts pouring water over me, saying nice things. At first I was anesthetized with shock, what with the warmth. I thought I had peed myself bad, or something awful. Then I realize that SHE is dead serious. Tons of soap, water, even cleaning my ears. Nightmare. I lunge and cry. I almost escape once, but I have no weapons, my claws are short, and you know about my teeth. That Fucking Goth who cat-sat me got them all pulled out—thought I was supposed to be her familiar and I hated her, so she punished me. Anyhow, there I was in the sink. For what seemed like hours. Scrubbed. Rinsed. Violently towel dried. I try to escape, but SHE has me in paw cuffs. Moreover, SHE is much, much bigger than me. SHE sniffs me, throughout this near-death ordeal, to see if I am improving. It is true that I had achieved ripeness appropriate to my age, which is now dissolved down the kitchen drain. It didn't end then. No. SHE puts me on a big huge towel on the floor and rubs me until I am dizzy. Again and again. I scream in anger. Then, SHE brushes me, head to toe. Again and again. Enraged. Violated. SHE decides enough is enough. Puts me down on a towel with lots of catnip by the fire, and this is when I decided to write.

Running on . . . MT

Subject: Some cooking hints

Thanks for your nice reply. SHE made me fresh salmon last night. Yum. SHE had hers with sake, poached. I do not like to drink. Mine was just with water and a bit of oil. Not bad. I think I can manipulate her into cooking for ME, like SHE used to cook for you. SHE makes all kinds of stupid appreciative sounds when I eat HER cooking. Today I had ricotta with chicken cat food. Not bad either.

SHE is still at work. Wonder what's up for dinner? I made her watch *Divinci's Inquest* last night with me. It was fun. Then SHE wrote and

wrote. I have figured out how to make her share her lap with that ugly
flat warm beeping thing she hits all the time, with ME.
Model T.

Notes

1. On April 10–12, 2001, a group of theater artists, performers, software engineers, and set designers met in London in two locations: the Back Hill Studios of the London Institute and my apartment in Finsbury Park. Later improvisation and final development of movement occurred in Hungary August–October, 2001, as part of a performance and installation at the Ludwig Museum. Improvisation is discussed later in the chapter.

2. In Hopi culture, for example, ritual clowns with complex animal behaviors and human identities express community critiques to authority figures that are compelled to listen to them at prescribed times of the year. This clears the air in the community. Carnival provides a similar system throughout the world.

3. As well as participating in the first Code Zebra software workshop at the Arts Alliance Labs in December 2000, Marcelo Walter was the president of the respected Siggrafi graphics conference in Brazil (2001). Marcelo has published a number of papers on the graphics related to Code Zebra in SIGGRAPH Proceedings (2002, 2003).

4. SIGGRAPH conferences are testimony to the currency of these problems and the relative progress of work in these areas.

5. Sheelagh Carpendale deserves credit for her assistance here as does the team led by Rich Lachman with Artem Baguinski and Kevin Liang and Erik Kemperman, managed between Banff and V2 Labs. Joshua Portway was of great assistance in strategic thought and John Tonkin programmed Prototype One of simple Voronois that is still lively and available at http://www.codezebra.net.

6. For more information on the Plushy and Furry social scenes, see the transcript "Plushies and Furries," MTV Sex2k, and for a detailed encounter, see http://www .fursuitsex.com/. Related to the Furry underground but more skin contact–based is the paint-by-animal scene. Sexual fantasy is enhanced by exacting skin makeup; see http://www.beastpaint.com.

7. Key dramaturgical collaborators were Vanessa Richards and Lizbeth Goodman.

8. I thank SquidSoup, UK and C3, Josh Portway, Anne Nigten, and v2, as well as David Furlow and Lizbeth Goodman in the early phases.

GANGER (BALL LIGHTNING)

Nalo Hopkinson

"Issy?"

"What."

"Suppose we switch suits?" Cleve asked.

Is what now? From where she knelt over him on their bed, Issy slid her tongue from Cleve's navel, blew on the wetness she'd made there. Cleve sucked in a breath, making the cheerful pudge of his tummy shudder. She stroked its fuzzy pelt.

"What," she said, looking up at him. "You want me wear your suit and you wear mine?" This had to be the weirdest yet.

He ran a finger over her lips, the heat of his touch making her mouth tingle. "Yeah," he replied. "Something so."

Issy got up to her knees, both her plump thighs on each side of his massive left one. She looked appraisingly at him. She was still mad from the fight they'd just had. But a good mad. She and Cleve, fighting always got them hot to make up. Had to be something good about that, didn't there? If they could keep finding their way back to each other like this? Her business if she'd wanted to make candy, even if the heat of the August night made the kitchen a hell. She wondered what the rass he was up to now.

They'd been fucking in the Senstim Co-operation's "wetsuits" for about a week. The toys had been fun for the first little while—they'd had more sex this week than in the last month—but even with the increased sensitivity, she was beginning to miss the feel of his skin directly against hers. "It not going work," Issy declared. But she was curious.

"You sure?" Cleve asked teasingly. He smiled, stroked her naked nipple softly with the ball of his thumb. She loved the contrast between his shovel-wide hands and the delicate movements he performed with them. Her nipple poked erect, sensitive as a tongue tip. She arched her back, pushed the heavy swing of her breast into fuller contact with the ringed ridges of thumb.

"Mmm."

"C'mon Issy, it could be fun, you know."

"Cleve, they just going key themselves to our bodies. The innie become a outie, the outie become a innie . . ."

"Yeah, but . . ."

"But what?"

"They take a few minutes to conform to our body shapes, right? Maybe in that few minutes . . ."

He'd gone silent, embarrassment shutting his open countenance closed; too shy to describe the sensation he was seeking. Issy sighed in irritation. What was the big deal? Fuck, cunt, cock, come: simple words to say. "In that few minutes, you'd find out what it feels like to have a poonani, right?"

A snatch. He looked shy and aroused at the same time. "Yeah, and you'd well, you know."

He liked it when she talked "dirty." But just try to get him to repay the favor. Try to get him to buzzingly whisper hot-syrup words against the sensitive pinna of her ear until she shivered with the sensation of his mouth on her skin, and the things he was say-ing, the nerve impulses he was firing, spilled from his warm lips at her earhole and oozed down her spine, cupped the bowl of her belly, filled her crotch with heat. That only ever happened in her imagination.

Cleve ran one finger down her body, tracing the faint line of hair from navel past the smiling crease below her tummy to pussy fur. Issy spread her knees a little, willing him to explore further. His fingertip tunneled through her pubic hair, tapped at her clit, making nerves sing. Ah, ah. She rocked against his thigh. What would it be like to have the feeling of entering someone's clasping flesh? "Okay," she said. "Let's try it."

She picked up Cleve's stim. So diaphanous you could barely see it, but supple as skin and thrice as responsive. Cocked up onto one elbow, Cleve watched her with a slight smile on his face. Issy loved the chubby chocolate-brown beauty of him, his fatcat grin.

Chortling, she wriggled into the suit, careful to ease it over the bandaid on her heel. The company boasted that you couldn't tell the difference between the microthin layer of the wetsuits and bare skin. Bullshit. Like taking a shower with your clothes on. The suits made you feel more, but it was a one-way sensation. They dampened the sense of touch. It was like being trapped inside your own skin, able to sense your response to stimuli but not to feel when you had connected with the outside world.

Over the week of use, Cleve's suit had shaped itself to his body. The hips were tight on Issy, the flat chest part pressed her breasts against her ribcage. The shoulders were too broad, the middle too baggy. It sagged at the knees, elbows, and toes. She giggled again.

"Never mind the peripherals," Cleve said, lumbering to his feet. "No time." He picked up her suit. "Just leave them hanging."

Just as well. Issy hated the way the roll-on headpiece trapped her hair against her neck, covered her ears, slid sensory tendrils into her earholes. It amplified the sounds when her body touched Cleve's. It grossed her out. What would Cleve want to do next to jazz the skins up?

As the suit hyped the pleasure zones on her skin surface, Issy could feel herself getting wet, the mixture of arousal and vague distaste a wetsuit gave her. The marketing lie was that the suits were "consensual aids to full body aura alignment," not sex toys. Yeah, right. Psychobabble. She was being diddled by an oversized condom possessed of fuzzy logic. She pulled it up to her neck. The stim started to writhe, conforming itself to her shape. Galvanic peristalsis, they called its ability to move. Yuck.

"Quick," Cleve muttered. He was jamming his lubed cock at a tube in the suit, the innie part of it that would normally have slid itself into her vagina, the part that had been smooth the first time she'd taken it out of its case, but was now shaped the way she was shaped inside. Cleve pushed and pushed until the inverted pocket slid over his cock. He lay back on the bed, his erection a jutting rudeness. "Oh. Wow. That's different. Is so it feels for you?"

Oh, sweet. Issy quickly followed Cleve's lead, spreading her knees to push the outie part of his wetsuit inside her. It was easy. She was slippery, every inch of her skin stimmed with desire. She palmed some lube from the bottle into the suit's pouched vagina. They had to hurry. She straddled him, slid onto his cock, making the tube of one wetsuit slither smoothly into the tunnel of the other. Cleve closed his eyes, blew a small breath through pursed lips.

So, so hot. "God, it's good," Issy muttered. Like being fucked, only she had an organ to push back with. Cleve just panted heavily, silently. As always. But what a rush! She swore she could feel Cleve's tight hot cunt closing around her dick. She grabbed his shoulders for traction. The massy, padded flesh of them filled her hands; steel encased in velvet.

The ganger looked down at its ghostly hands. Curled them into fists. Lightning sparked between the translucent fingers as they closed. It reached a crackling hand toward Cleve's shuddering body on the bathroom floor.

"Hey!" Issy yelled at it. She could hear the quaver in her own voice. The ganger turned its head toward the sound. The suits' sense-memory gave it some analogue of hearing.

She tried to lift her head, banged it against the underside of the toilet. "Ow." The ganger's head elongated widthways, as though someone were pulling on its ears. Her muscles were too

weakened from the aftershocks. Issy put her head back down. Now what? Think fast, Iss. "Y . . .
you like um, um, . . . chocolate fudge?" she asked the thing. Now why was she still going on about
the fucking candy?

The ganger straightened. Took a floating step away from Cleve, closer to Issy. Cleve was safe
for the moment. Colored auras crackled in the ganger with each step. Issy laid her cheek against
cool porcelain; stammered, "Well, I was making some last night, some fudge, yeah, only it didn't
set, sometimes that happens, y'know? Too much humidity in the air, or something." The ganger
seemed to wilt a little, floppy as the unhardened fudge. Was it fading? Issy's pulse leaped in hope.
But then the thing plumped up again, drew closer to where she lay helpless on the floor. Rainbow
lightning did a lava-lamp dance in its incorporeal body. Issy whimpered.

Cleve writhed under her. His lips formed quiet words. His own nubbin nipples hardened. Pleasure transformed his face. Issy loved seeing him this way. She rode and rode
his body, "Yes, ah, sweet, God, sweet," groaning her way to the stim-charged orgasm
that would fire all her pleasure synapses, give her some sugar, make her speak in tongues.

Suddenly Cleve pushed her shoulder. "Stop! Jesus, get off! Off!"

Startled, Issy shoved herself off him. Achy suction at her crotch as they discon-
nected. "What's wrong?"

Cleve sat up, panting hard. He clutched at his dick. He was shaking. Shuddering,
he stripped off the wetsuit, flung it to the foot of the bed. To her utter amazement, he
was sobbing. She'd never seen Cleve cry.

"Jeez. Can't have been that bad. Come." She opened her thick, strong arms to him.
He curled as much of his big body as he could into her embrace, hid his face from her.
She rocked him, puzzled. "Cleve?"

After a while, he mumbled, "It was nice, you know, so different, then it started to
feel like, I dunno, like my dick had been peeled and it was inside out, and you Jesus you
were fucking my inside-out dick."

Issy said nothing, held him tighter. The hyped rasp of Cleve's body against her
stimmed skin was as much a turn-on as a comfort. She rocked him, rocked him. She
couldn't think what to say, so she just hummed a children's song: *We're stirring cocoa*
beneath a tree / sikola o la vani / one, two, three, vanilla / chocolate and vanilla.

Just before he fell asleep Cleve said, "God, I don't want to ever feel anything like
that again. I had *breasts*, Issy. They swung when I moved."

The wetsuit Issy was wearing soon molded itself into an innie, and the hermaphro-
ditic feeling disappeared. She kind of missed it. And all the time she was swaying Cleve
to sleep she couldn't help thinking; for a few seconds, she'd felt something of what he
felt when they had sex. For a few seconds, she'd felt the things he'd never dared to tell

her in words. Issy slid a hand between herself and Cleve, insinuating it into the warm space between her stomach and thigh till she could work her fingers between her legs. She could feel her own wetness sliding under the microthin fiber. She pressed her clit, gently, ah, gently, tilting her hips toward her hand. Cleve stirred, scratched his nose; flopped his hand to the bed, snoring.

And he'd felt what she was always trying to describe to him, the sensations that always defied speech. He'd felt what this was like. The thought made her cunt clench. She panted out, briefly, once. She was so slick. Willing her body still, she started the rubbing motion that she knew would bring her off.

Nowadays any words between her and Cleve seemed to fall into dead air between them, each not reaching the other. But this had reached him, gotten her inside him; this, this, this, and the image of fucking Cleve pushed her over the edge and the pulseburst of her orgasm pumped again, again, again as her moans trickled through her lips and she fought not to thrash, not to wake the slumbering mountain that was Cleve.

Oh. "Yeah, man," Issy breathed. Cleve had missed the best part. She eased him off her, got his head onto a pillow. Sated, sex-heavy, and drowsy, she peeled off the wetsuit— smiled at the pouches it had moulded from her calabash breasts and behind—and kicked it onto the floor beside the bed. She lay down, rolled toward Cleve, hugged his body to her. "Mm," she murmured. Cleve muttered sleepily and snuggled into the curves of her body. Issy wriggled to the sweet spot where the lobes of his buttocks fit against her pubes. She wrapped her arm around the bole of his chest, kissed the back of his neck where his hair curled tightest. She felt herself beginning to sink into a feather-down sleep.

"I mean the boiled sugar kind of fudge," Issy told the ganger. It hovered over her, her own personal aurora. She had to keep talking, draw out the verbiage, distract the thing. "Not that gluey shit they sell at the Ex and stuff. We were supposed to have a date, but Cleve was late coming home and I was pissed at him and horny and I wanted a taste of sweetness in my mouth. And hot too, maybe. I saw a recipe once where you put a few flakes of red pepper into the syrup. Intensified the taste, they said. I wonder. Dunno what I was thinking, boiling fudge in this heat." Lightning-quick, the ganger tapped her mouth. The electric shock crashed her teeth together. She saw stars. "Huh, huh," she heard her body protesting as air puffed out of its contracting lungs.

Issy uncurled into one last, langorous stretch before sleep. Her foot connected in the dark with a warm, rubbery mass that writhed at her touch, then started to slither up her leg.

"Oh God! Shit! Cleve!" Issy kicked convulsively at the thing clambering up her thigh. She clutched Cleve's shoulder.

———

He sprang awake, tapped the wall to activate the light. "What, Issy? What's wrong?"

It was the still-charged wetsuit that Cleve had thrown to the foot of the bed, now an outie. "Christ, Cleve!" Idiot.

The suit had only been reacting to the electricity generated by Issy's body. It was just trying to do its job. "S'alright," Cleve comforted her. "It can't hurt you."

Shuddering, Issy peeled the wetsuit from her leg and dropped it to the ground. Deprived of her warmth, it squirmed its way over to her suit. Innie and outie writhed rudely around each other; empty sacks of skin. Jesus, with the peripherals still attached the damned things looked as if they had floppy heads.

Cleve smiled sleepily. "I's like lizard tails, y'know, when they drop off and wiggle?"

Issy thought she'd gag. "Get them out of my sight, Cleve. Discharge them and put them away."

"Tomorrow," he murmured.

They were supposed to be stored in separate cases, outie and innie, but Cleve just scooped them up and tossed them together, wriggling, into the closet.

"Gah," Issy choked.

Cleve looked at her face and said, "Come on, Iss; have a heart; think of them lying side by side in their little boxes, separated from each other."

He was trying to joke about it. "No," Issy said. "We get to do that instead. Wrap ourselves in fake flesh that's supposed to make us feel more. Ninety-six degrees in the shade, and we're wearing rubber body bags."

His face lost its teasing smile. Just the effect she'd wanted, but it didn't feel so good now. And it wasn't true, really. The wetsuit material did some weird shit so that it didn't trap heat in. And they were sexy, once you got used to them. No sillier than strap-ons or cuffs padded with fake fur. Issy grimaced an apology at Cleve. He screwed up his face and looked away. God, if he would only speak up for himself sometimes! Issy turned her back to him and found her wadded-up panties in the bedclothes. She wrestled them on and lay back down, facing the wall. The light went off. Cleve climbed back into bed. Their bodies didn't touch.

The sun cranked Issy's eyes open. Its August heat washed over her like slops from a bucket. Her sheet was twisted around her, warm, damp, and funky. Her mouth was sour and she could smell her own stink. "Oh God, I want it to be winter," she groaned.

She fought her way out of the clinging cloth to sit up in bed. The effort made her pant. She twisted the heavy mass of her braids up off the nape of her neck and sat for awhile, feeling the sweat trickle down her scalp. She grimaced at the memory of last night.

Cleve wasn't there. Out for a jog, likely. "Yeah, that's how you sulk," she muttered. "In silence." Issy longed to know that he cared strongly about something, to hear him speak with any kind of force, the passion of his anger, the passion of his love. But Cleve kept it all so cool, so mild. Wrap it all in fake skin, hide it inside.

The morning sun had thrown a violent, hot bar of light across her bed. Heat. Tangible, almost. Crushed against every surface of her skin, like drowning in feathers. Issy shifted into a patch of shade. It made no difference. Fuck. A drop of sweat trickled down her neck, beaded a track down her left breast to drip off her nipple and splat onto her thigh. The trail of moisture it had left behind felt cool on her skin. Issy watched her aureole crinkle and the nipple stiffen in response. She shivered.

A twinkle of light caught her eye. The sliding closet door was open. The wetsuits, thin as shed snakeskin, were still humping each other beside their storage boxes. "Nasty!" Issy exclaimed. She jumped up from the bed, pushed the closet door shut with a bang. She left the room, ignoring the rhythmic thumping noise from inside the closet. Cleve was supposed to have discharged them; it could just wait until he deigned to come home again.

Overloading, crackling violently, the ganger stepped back. Issy nearly wept with release from its jolt. Her knees felt watery. Was Cleve still breathing? She thought she could see his chest moving in little gasps. She hoped. She had to keep the ganger distracted from him, he might not survive another shock. Teeth chattering, she said to the ganger, "You melt the sugar and butter—the salty butter's the best—in milk, then you add cocoa powder and boil it all to hard crack stage . . ." Issy wet her lips with her tongue. The day's heat was enveloping her again. "Whip in some more butter," she continued. "You always get it on your fingers, that melted, salty butter. It will run down the side of your hand, and you lick it off—so you whip in some more butter, and real vanilla, the kind that smells like mother's breath and cookies, not the artificial shit, and you dump it onto a plate, and it sets, and you have it sweet like that; chocolate fudge."

The sensuality in her voice seemed to mesmerize the ganger. It held still, rapt. Its inner lightnings cooled to electric blue. Its mouth hole yawned, wide as two of her fists.

As she headed to the kitchen, Issy made a face at the salty dampness beneath her swaying breasts and the curve of her belly. Her thighs were sticky where they moved against each other. She stopped in the living room and stood, feet slightly apart, arms away from her sides, so no surface of her body would touch any other. No relief. The heat still clung. She shoved her panties down around her ankles. The movement briefly brought her nose to her crotch, a whiff of sweaty muskiness. She straightened up, stepped out of the sodden pretzel of cloth, kicked it away. The quick movement had made her dizzy. She swayed slightly, staggered into the kitchen.

Cleve had mopped up the broken glass and gluey candy from yesterday evening, left the pot to soak. The kitchen still smelled of chocolate. The rich scent tingled along the roof of Issy's mouth.

The fridge hummed in its own aura, heat outside making cold inside. She needed water. Cold, cold. She yanked the fridge door open, reached for the water jug, and drank straight from it. The shock of chilly liquid made her teeth ache. She sucked water in, tilting the jug high so that more spilled past her gulping mouth, ran down her jaw, her breasts, her belly. With her free hand, she spread the coolness over the pillow of her stomach, dipping down into crinkly pubic hair, then sliding up to heft each breast one at a time, sliding cool fingers underneath, thumb almost automatically grazing each nipple to feel them harden slightly at her touch. Better. Issy put the jug back, half full now.

At her back, hot air was a wall. Seconds after she closed the fridge door, she'd be overheated and miserable again. She stood balanced between ice and heat, considering.

She pulled open the door to the icebox. It creaked and protested, jammed with frost congealed on its hinges. The fridge was ancient. Cleve had joked with the landlady that he might sell it to a museum and use the money to pay the rent on the apartment for a year. He'd only gotten a scowl in return.

The fridge had needed defrosting for weeks now. Her job. Cleve did the laundry and bathroom and kept them spotlessly clean. The kitchen and the bedroom were hers. Last time she'd changed the sheets was about the last time she'd done the fridge. Cleve hadn't complained. She was waiting him out.

Issy peered into the freezer. Buried in the canned hoarfrost were three ice cube trays. She had to pull at them to work them free of hardpacked freezer snow. One was empty. The other two contained a few ice cubes between them.

The ganger took a step toward her. It paddled its hand in the black hole of its mouth. Issy shuddered, kept talking: "Break off chunks of fudge, and is sweet and dark and crunchy; a little bit hot if you put the pepper flakes in, I never tried that kind, and is softer in the middle, and the butter taste rise to the roof of your mouth, and the chocolate melt all over your tongue; man, you could almost come, just from a bite."

Issy flung the empty tray into the sink at the other end of the kitchen. Jangle-crash, displacing a fork that leapt from the sink, clattered onto the floor. The thumping from inside the bedroom closet became more frenetic. "Stop that," Issy yelled in the direction of the bedroom. The sound became a rapid drubbing. Then silence.

———

Issy kicked the fridge door closed, took the two ice cube trays into the bathroom. Even with that short walk, the heat was pressing in on her again. The bathroom was usually cool, but today the tiles were warm against her bare feet. The humidity of the room felt like wading through spit.

Issy plugged the bathtub drain, dumped the sorry handful of ice in. Not enough. She grabbed up the mop bucket, went back to the kitchen, fished a spatula out of the sink, rinsed it. She used the spatula to dig out the treasures buried in the freezer. Frozen cassava, some unidentifiable meat, a cardboard cylinder of grape punch. She put them on a shelf in the fridge. Those excavated, she set about shoveling the snow out of the freezer, dumping it into her bucket. In no time she had a bucketful, and she'd found another ice cube tray, this one full of fat, rounded lumps of ice. She was a little cooler now.

Back in the bathroom, she dumped the bucket of freezer snow on top of the puddle that had been the ice cubes. Then she ran cold water, filled the bathtub calf-deep, and stepped into it.

Sssss. . . . The shock of cold feet zapped straight through Issy's body to her brain. She bent—smell of musk again, picked up a handful of the melting snow, and packed it into her hair. Blessed, blessed cold. The snow became water almost instantly and dribbled down her face. Issy licked at a trickle of it. She picked up another handful of snow, stuffed it into her mouth. Crunchy-cold freon ice, melting on her tongue. She remembered the canned taste from childhood, how her dad would scold her for eating freezer snow. Her mother would say nothing, just wipe Issy's mouth dry with a silent, long-suffering smile.

Issy squatted in the bathtub. The cold water lapped against her butt. Goosebumps pimpled the skin of her thighs. She sat down, hips pressing against either side of the tub. An ice cube lapped against the small of her back, making her first arch to escape the cold, then lean back against the tub with a happy shudder. Snow crunched between her back and the ceramic surface. Issy spread her knees. There was more snow floating in the diamond her legs made. In both hands, she picked up another handful, mashed it into the "v" of her crotch. She shivered at the sensation and relaxed into the cool water.

The fridge made a zapping, farting noise, then resumed its juddering hum. Damned bucket of bolts. Issy concentrated on the deliciously shivery feel of the ice melting in her pubic hair.

"Only this time," Issy murmured, "the fudge ain't set. Just sat there on the cookie tin, gluey and brown. Not hard, not quite liquid, you get me? Glossy-shiny dark brown where it pooled, and rising from it, that chocolate-butter-vanilla smell. But wasted, 'cause it wasn't going to set."

———

The television clicked on loudly with an inane laugh track. Issy sat up. "Cleve?" She hadn't heard him come in. With a popping noise, the TV snapped off again. "Cleve, is you?"

Issy listened. Nope, nothing but the humming of the fridge. She was alone. These humid August days made all their appliances schizo with static. She relaxed back against the tub.

"I got mad," Issy told the ganger. "It was hot in the kitchen and there was cocoa powder every-where and lumps of melting butter, and I do all that work 'cause I just wanted the taste of some-thing sweet in my mouth and the fucker wouldn't set!

"I backhanded the cookie tin. Fuck, it hurt like I crack a finger bone. The tin skidded across the kitchen counter, splanged off the side of the stove, and went flying."

Issy's skin bristled with goosebumps at the sight of the thing that walked in through the open bathroom door and stood, arms hanging. It was a human-shaped glow, translu-cent. Its edges were fuzzy. She could see the hallway closet through it. Eyes, nose, mouth were empty circles. A low crackling noise came from it, like a crushed Cheezies bag. Issy could feel her breath coming in short, terrified pants. She made to stand up, and the ap-parition moved closer to her. She whimpered and sat back down in the chilly water.

The ghost-thing stood still. A pattern of colored lights flickered in it, limning where spine, heart, and brain would have been, if it had had those. It did have breasts, she saw now, and a dick.

She moved her hand. Water dripped from her fingertips into the tub. The thing turned its head toward the sound. It took a step. She froze. The apparition stopped mov-ing too, just stood there, humming like the fridge. It plucked at its own nipples, pulled its breasts into cones of ectoplasm. It ran hands over its body, then over the sink; bent down to thrust its arms right through the closed cupboard doors. It dipped a hand into the toilet bowl. Sparks flew, and it jumped back. Issy's scalp prickled. Damn, the thing was electrical, and she was sitting in water! She tried to reach the plug with her toes to let the water out. Swallowing whimpers, she stretched a leg out; slow, God, go slow, Issy. The movement sent a chunk of melting ice sliding along her thigh. She shivered. She couldn't quite reach the plug and if she moved closer to it, the movement would draw the apparition's attention. Issy breathed in short, shallow bursts. She could feel her eyes be-ginning to brim. Terror and the chilly water were sending tremors in waves through her.

What the fuck was it? The thing turned toward her. In its quest for sensation, it hefted its cock in its hand. Inserted a finger into what seemed to be a vagina underneath.

Let its hands drop again. Faintly, Issy could make out a mark on its hip, a circular shape. It reminded her of something . . .

Logo, it was the logo of the Senstim people who'd invented the wetsuits!

But this wasn't a wetsuit, it was like some kind of, fuck, ball lightning. She and Cleve hadn't discharged their wetsuits. She remembered some of the nonsense words that were in the warning on the wetsuit storage boxes: "Energizing electrostatic charge" and "Kirlian phenomenon." Well, they hadn't paid attention, and now some kind of weird set of both suits was rubbing itself off in their bathroom. Damn, damn, damn Cleve and his toys. Sobbing, shivering, Issy tried to toe at the plug again. Her knee banged against the tub. The suit-ghost twitched toward the noise. It leaned over the water and dabbed at her clutching toes. Pop-crackle sound. The jolt sent her leg flailing like a dying fish. Pleasure crackled along her leg, painfully intense. Her knee throbbed and tingled, ached sweetly. Her thigh muscles shuddered as though they would tear free. The jolt slammed into her crotch, and Issy's body bucked. She could hear her own grunts. She was straddling a live wire. She was coming to death. Her nipples jutted long as thumbs, stung like they'd been dipped in ice. Her head was banging against the wall with each deadly set of contractions. Issy shouted in pain, in glory, in fear. The suit-ghost leaped back. Issy's butt hit the floor of the tub, hard. Her muscles were twitching spasmodically. She'd bitten the inside of her mouth. She sucked in air like sobs, swallowed tinny blood.

The suit-ghost was swollen, bloated, jittering. Its inner lightning bolts were going mad. If it touched her again, it might overload completely. If it touched her again, her heart might stop.

Issy heard the sound of the key turning in the front door.

"Iss? You home?"

"No. Cleve." Issy hissed under her breath. He mustn't come in. But if she shouted to warn him, the suit-ghost would touch her again.

Cleve's footsteps approached the bathroom. "Iss? Listen, did you drain the wet . . ."

Like filings to a magnet, the suit-ghost inclined toward the sound of his voice.

"Don't come in, Cleve; go get help!"

Too late. He'd stuck his head in, grinning his open, friendly grin. The suit-ghost rushed him, plastered itself along his body. It got paler, its aura-lightnings mere flickers. Cleve made a choking noise and crashed to the floor, jerking. Issy levered herself out of the bath, but her jelly muscles wouldn't let her stand. She flopped to the tiles. Cleve's body was convulsing, horrible noises coming from his mouth. Riding him like a duppy, a malevolent spirit, the stim-ghost grew paler with each thrash of his flailing body. Its color-patterns started to run into each other, to bleach themselves pale. Cleve's energy was draining it, but it was killing him. Sucking on her whimpers, Issy reached a hand into the stim-ghost's field. Her heart went off like a machine gun. Her breathing wouldn't work. The orgasm was unspeakable. Wailing, Issy rolled away from Cleve, taking the ghost thing with her. It swelled at her touch, its colors flared neon-bright, out of control. It flailed off her, floated back toward Cleve's more cooling energy.

Heart pounding, too weak to move, Issy muttered desperately to distract it the first thing that came to her mind: "Y . . . you like, um, chocolate fudge?"

The ghost turned toward her. Issy cried and kept talking, kept talking. The ghost wavered between Issy's hot description of bubbling chocolate and Cleve's cool silence, caught in the middle. Could it even understand words? Wetsuits located pleasurable sensation to augment it. Maybe it was just drawn to the sensuousness of her tone. Issy talked, urgently, carefully releasing the words from her mouth like caresses.

"So," she said to the suit-duppy, "I watching this cookie tin twist through the air like a Frisbee, and is like slow motion, 'cause I seeing gobs of chocolate goo spiraling from it as it flies, and they spreading out wider and wider. I swear I hear separate splats as chocolate hits the walls like slung shit, and one line of it strafes the fridge door, and a gob somehow slimes the naked bulb hanging low from the kitchen ceiling. I hear it sizzle. The cookie tin lands on the floor, fudge side down, of course. I haven't cleaned the fucking floor in ages. There're spots everywhere on that floor that used to be gummy, but now they're layered in dust and maybe flour and dessicated bodies of cockroaches that got trapped, reaching for sweetness. I know how they feel. I take a step toward the cookie tin, then I start to smell burning chocolate. I look up. I see a curl of black smoke rising from the glob of chocolate on the light bulb."

Cleve raised his head. There were tears in his eyes and the front of his jogging pants were damp and milky. "Issy," he interrupted in a whisper.

"Shut up, Cleve!"

"That thing," he said in a low, urgent voice. "People call it a ganger; doppel . . ."

The ganger was suddenly at his side. It leaned a loving head on his chest, like Issy would do. "No!" she yelled. Cleve's body shook. The ganger frayed and tossed like a sheet in the wind. Cleve shrieked. He groaned like he was coming, but with an edge of terror and pain that Issy couldn't bear to hear. Pissed, terrified, Issy swiped an arm through its field then rolled her bucking body on the bathroom tiles, praying that she could absorb the ganger's energy without it frying her synapses with sweet sensation.

Through spasms, she barely heard Cleve say to it: "Come to me, not her. Come. Listen, you know that song? 'I got a weakness for sweetness . . .' That's my Issy."

The ganger dragged itself away from Issy. Released, her muscles melted. She was a gooey, warm puddle spreading on the floor. The ganger reached an ectoplasmic hand toward Cleve, fingers stretching long as arms. Cleve gasped and froze.

Issy croaked, "You think is that it is, Cleve? Weakness?"

The ganger turned its head her way, ran a long, slow arm down its body to the floor, back up to its crotch. It stroked itself.

Cleve spoke to it in a voice that cracked whispery on the notes: "Yeah, sweetness. That's what my Issy wants most of all." The ganger moved toward him, rubbing its crotch. He continued, "If I'm not there, there's always sugar, or food, or booze. I'm just one of her chosen stimulants."

Outraged tears filled Issy's mouth, salty as butter, as flesh. She'd show him; she'd rescue him. She countered: "The glob of burned sugar on the light? From the ruined fudge? Well, it goes black and starts to bubble."

The ganger extruded a tongue the length of an arm from its mouth. The tongue wriggled toward Issy. She rolled back, saying: "The lightbulb explodes. I feel some shards land in my hair. I don't try to brush them away. Is completely dark now; I only had the kitchen light on. I take another step to where I know the cookie tin is on the floor. A third step, and pain crazes my heel. Must have stepped on a piece of lightbulb glass. Can't do nothing about it now. I rise onto the toes of the hurting foot. I think I feel blood running down from heel to instep."

The ganger jittered toward her.

"You were always better than me at drama, Iss," Cleve said.

The sadness in his voice tore at her heart. But she said, "What that thing is?"

Cleve replied softly, "Is kinda beautiful, ain't?"

"It going to kill us."

"Beautiful. Just a lump of static charge, coated in the Kirlian energy thrown off from the suits."

"Why it show up now?"

"Is what happens when you leave the suits together too long."

The ganger drifted back and forth, pulled by one voice then the other. A longish silence between them freed it to move. It floated closer to Cleve. Issy wouldn't let it, she wouldn't. She quavered: "I take another step on the good foot, carefully. I bend down, sweep my hands around."

The ganger dropped to the floor, ran its long tongue over the tiles. A drop of water made it crackle and shrink in slightly on itself.

"There," Issy continued. "The cookie tin. I brush around me, getting a few more splinters in my hands. I get down to my knees, curl down as low to the ground as I can.

I pry up the cookie tin, won't have any glass splinters underneath it. A dark sweet wet chocolate smell rising from under there."

"Issy, Jesus," Cleve whispered. He started to bellow the words of the song he'd taunted her with, drawing the ganger. It touched him with a fingertip. A crackling noise. He gasped, jumped, kept singing.

Issy ignored him. Hissing under his booming voice, she snarled at the ganger: "I run a finger through the fudge. I lick it off. Most of it on the ground, not on the tin. I bend over and run my tongue through it, reaching for sweetness. Butter and vanilla and oh, oh, the chocolate. And crunchy, gritty things I don't think about. Cockroach parts, maybe. I swallow."

Cleve interrupted his song to wail, "That's gross, Iss. Why you had to go and do that?"

"So Cleve come in, he see me there sitting on the floor surrounded by broken glass and limp chocolate, and you know what he say?" The ganger was reaching for her.

"Issy, stop talking, you only drawing it to you."

"Nothing." The ganger jerked. "Zip." The ganger twitched. "Dick." The ganger spasmed, once. It touched her hair. Issy breathed. That was safe. "The bastard just started cleaning up; not a word for me." The ganger hugged her. Issy felt her eyes roll back in her head. She thrashed in the energy of its embrace until Cleve yelled: "And what you said! Ee? Tell me!"

The ganger pulled away. Issy lay still, waiting for her breathing to return to normal. Cleve said, "Started carrying on with some shit about how lightbulbs are such poor quality nowadays. Sat in the filth and broken glass, pouting and watching me clean up your mess. Talking about anything but what really on your mind. I barely got all the glass out of your heel before you start pulling my pants down."

Issy ignored him. She kept talking to the ganger. "Cool, cool Cleve. No 'What's up?' No 'What the fuck is this crap on the floor?' No heat, no passion."

"What was the point? I did the only thing that will sweet you every time."

"Encased us both in fake skin and let it do the fucking for us."

The ganger jittered in uncertain circles between the two of them.

"Issy, what you want from me?"

The ganger's head swelled obscenely toward Cleve.

"Some heat. Some feeling. Like I show you. Like I feel. Like I feel for you." The ganger's lower lip stretched, stretched, a filament of it reaching for Issy's own mouth. The black cavity of its maw was a tunnel, longing to swallow her up. She shuddered and rolled back further. Her back came up against the bathtub.

Softly, "What do you feel for me, Issy?"

"Fuck you."

"I do. We do. It's good. But what do you feel for me, Issy?"

"Don't ridicule me. You know."

"I don't know shit, Issy! You talk, talk, talk! And it's all about what racist insult you heard yesterday, and who tried to cheat you at the store, and how high the phone bill is. You talk around stuff, not about it!"

"Shut up!"

The ganger flailed like a hook-caught fish between them.

Quietly, Cleve said: "The only time we seem to reach each other now is through our skins. So I bought something to make our skins feel more, and it's still not enough."

An involuntary sound came from Issy's mouth, a hooked, wordless query.

"Cleve, is that why . . ." She looked at him, at the intense brown eyes in the expressive brown face. When had he started to look so sad all the time? She reached a hand out to him. The ganger grabbed it. Issy saw fireworks behind her eyes. She screamed. She felt Cleve's hand on her waist, felt the hand clutch painfully as he tried to shove her away to safety with his other hand. Blindly she reached out, tried to bat the ganger away. Her hand met Cleve's in middle of the fog that was the ganger. All the pleasure centers in her body exploded.

A popping sound. A strong, seminal smell of bleach. The ganger was gone. Issy and Cleve sagged to the floor.

"Rass," she sighed. Her calves were knots the size of potatoes. And she'd be sitting tenderly for a while.

"I feel like I've been dragged five miles behind a runaway horse," Cleve told her. "You all right?"

"Yeah, where'd that thing go, the ganger?"

"Shit, Issy, I'm so sorry. Should have drained the suits like you said."

"Chuh. Don't dig nothing. I could have done it too."

"I think we neutralized it. Touched each other, touched it: we canceled it out. I think."

"Touched each other. That simple." Issy gave a little rueful laugh. "Cleve, I . . . you're my honey, you know? You sweet me for days." His smile brimmed over with joy. "I won't forget any more to tell you," she said, "and keep telling you."

He smiled, and replied, "You, you're my live wire. You keep us both juiced up, make my heart sing in my chest," he hesitated, spoke bashfully, "and my dick leap in my pants when I see you."

A warmth flooded Issy at his sweet, hot talk. She felt her eyelashes dampen. She smiled. "See, the dirty words not so hard to say. And the anger not so hard to show."

Tailor-sat on the floor, beautiful Buddha-body, he frowned at her. "I 'fraid to use harsh words, Issy, you know that. Look at the size of me, the blackness of me. You know what it is to see people cringe for fear when you shout?"

She was dropping down with fatigue. She leaned and softly touched his face. "I don't know what that is like. But I know you. I know you would never hurt me. You must say what on your mind, Cleve. To me, at least." She closed her eyes, dragged herself exhaustedly into his embrace.

He said, "You know, I dream of the way you full up my arms."

"You're sticky," she murmured. "Like candy." And fell asleep, touching him.

Note

The song "Weakness for Sweetness," copyright 1996, is quoted with the gracious permission of singer Natalie Burke and composer Leston Paul.

8

PERFECT TWINS

Rebecca Cannon

Artistic investigations of virtual embodiment convey complex semiotic encodings that are increasingly relevant to gender studies. As interpersonal communication between, within, and beyond genders becomes more reliant upon technology, the perception of gendered signifiers occurs more often through virtual representations. I do not limit the term *virtual* here to VR entertainment systems, but rather employ the term in an encompassing sense, where all extensions of our behavior within mediated and/or networked environments take on a virtual form. In this sense, the process of becoming virtual necessitates a selective representation of self that is suited to highly creative constructions of identity. A potentially more realistic expression of one's inner self, virtual embodiments play an important role in the dissolution of gendered oppositions.

This chapter discusses the work of two artists employing three-dimensional (3-D) embodiments to explore notions of gender in the construction of identity through technologically mediated communication. Linda Erceg is an Australian artist whose video installations *Emulator, Skin Pack, Skin Club, Punchline,* and the forthcoming *The Searchers* employ highly realistic three-dimensional human models involved in sexually confronting activities. Erceg's works arouse public responses to sexual taboos in order to highlight similarities between real and fantastic virtual modes of expression. Her work is also important in reevaluating psychoanalytic, feminist interpretations of pornographic screen-based material.

Tobias Bernstrup is a Swedish-born artist, musician, and performer who has produced several video installations and music videos that feature a transgendered virtual performer. For example, *Polygon Lover* (2000) is a three-dimensional self-portrait—an avatar with the head of Bernstrup autoeroticizing his *female* form (figure 8.1). Bernstrup's work is important in analyzing the role that virtual constructions play in neoteric modes of self-identifications. These modes are dependent on real and virtual contexts, such as popular culture, 3-D environments, and contemporary (generic) cities, any of which

| Figure 8.1 |
Polygon Lover (2000)

may contain influencing elements of artificiality that impinge upon attempts at "natural" self-expression. His works also support suggestions that exchanges between game players and their opposite-gender avatars formulate the experience of transgenderism.[1]

Playing with Self

Both Bernstrup and Erceg have employed the technique of computer game modification to construct virtual environments featured in their artworks. I begin with this key element as a link between the two artists because the practice of computer game modification has important ideological implications that resonate with the broader issue of virtual embodiment. Game modding, as it is more commonly known, is a popular method by which game players extend the longevity of their favorite games. Many companies (notably ID Software, the makers of the *Quake* series of games) allow players to modify games by building new maps, characters, character skins, and even new game narratives and new game logics. *Counter Strike*, for example, is the world's most successful example of a player-built modification, now distributed in its own right as a top-selling, commercial game.[2] Accessing modding tools, many artists have sought to interrogate various qualities of games and gaming, notably the relationship of the player to the game itself, and their degree of participation in gameplay. The mere act of modding evidences the *coauthorial* attraction of games, as do other aspects of gaming culture such as the contextualization of online games within the Internet, which is a "highly decentralized, uncontrolled, peer-to-peer environment"; the reframing of the producer/consumer relationship through consumer-driven narrative construction; and the prevalence of user-centricity in game design.[3] These coauthorial qualities make games a natural breeding ground for the construction of mediated identities.

Erceg has incorporated the use of game mods in her two works, *Emulator* (1999) and *Skin Pack* (2000). *Emulator* is a five-minute, looped, two-channel video installation (figure 8.2). On the left-hand side, video footage documents a dysfunctional moment in *Tomb Raider*; Lara Croft swims on the spot, trapped in a watery, underground tunnel. Lara's usual attire has been exchanged for the infamous nude skin. Beside her, appropriated footage from *Ghost in the Shell* (1996) depicts the creation of Major Matoko Kusinagi, the self-aware cyborgian heroine at the center of the film's narrative. Major's body is also inactive and underwater. Here she is constructed from robotic apparatuses, a product of technology intrinsically and extrinsically. Both characters represent a breakdown of the body-technology barrier; for Lara it resides in her enacting of user control, for Major in her technologically housed, yet partially human brain. The beauty of Major's feminine form as it sheds flakes of milky skin counter the harsh, low-poly crassness of Lara's homemade patch. However, sexual attraction remains latent in both characters. Contingency and posthuman physiology pushes both idols beyond the status of passive puppets, despite this possibility for inactivating their forms.

Skin Pack took Erceg's exploration of game modification one step further (figure 8.3a, b). Using the *Quake 2* game engine, Erceg built a sparse game level and populated it with four fan-created nude models named "Crack Whore," "Chastity Marks," "Chastity," and "Nude Chick." Also made into a two-channel video installation, this footage depicts the naked characters masturbating with their grossly oversized weapons, as well as shooting clones of themselves to pieces. The point of view tracks like a camera, circling around the bodies, from wide shot to extreme close-up. At one point the camera flies into the vagina of a model. The overall style centers on the grotesque, bawdy makeup and ungainly movements force us to question sexual readings of the naked skins. The models even retain their original high-heeled shape, giving their now naked feet the appearance of horse hooves. These confrontational techniques, coupled with audio samples from porn movies, are employed to amplify the perversity of the models.

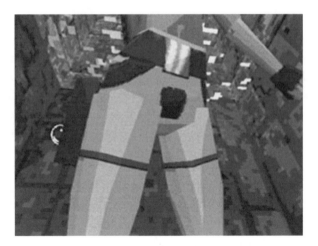

| Figure 8.2 |
Emulator (1999)

These works can easily be read as a feminist critique of the male-gamer objectification of female forms in gaming. However, the catalogue essay for *Skin Pack* offers an insight into broader, potentially sex-positive feminist consequences of the interaction between gamers and their virtual representations that Erceg has hoped to identify.

In the past the simple physical location of pornographic outlets kept pornography the exclusive preserve of men and boys. While the sudden, popular access to information provided by the Internet has raised concerns about the exposure of children to pornography, little consideration has been given to its effects on a generation of girls, who, for the first time, have safe, anonymous access to pornography, like their brothers. The growing familiarity of children with sexual concepts also has profound implications for the evolution of adult culture.

While producing these works, Erceg conducted intensive research into the model- and skin-swapping subculture of gaming. Although she found that the most common sexual fantasy of male gamers is rape, she still maintains that these naked skins are actually indicative of positive change. Publication and public discussion of pornographic material can potentially reduce infantile obsessions with nudity. Equal access of both genders to sexually explicit material can disclose misogynistic tendencies to a wider proportion of society, reducing the overall tolerance of such behaviors. Additionally, equal access to sexually explicit material can build a shared foundation of sexual experience from which to develop new sexual relations. It has also been argued that by employing

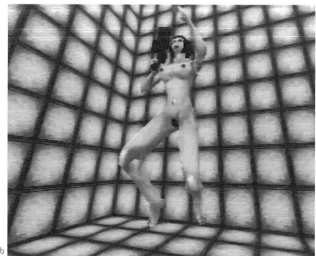

| Figure 8.3a, b |
Skin Pack (2000)

sexualized female avatars in gaming, "these boys are accommodating shifting gender roles, building confidence that they can find even strong, challenging women attractive and that they won't be overwhelmed by their own fears as they deal with real girls."[4]

The interactivity of gameplay is an important aspect of games that complicates attempts to analyze them as pornographic media. Early psychoanalytic, feminist assessments of film spectatorship have pointed to the dominance of the male gaze and the objectification of women as targets of this voyeuristic perspective. Although mainstream film techniques such as shot-reverse-shot have been seen to align female viewers with the point of view of the (male) protagonist, women are acknowledged to function as objects of this gaze far more often than as proxies for the spectator.[5] Perspectives such as the ones that forefront the exploitative relationship between viewer subjects and on-screen objects have fueled much of the concern over sexual material in computer games, with the Lara Croft naked patch an iconic example open to debate.

However, as Helen Kennedy has discussed, there are significant reasons why textual analyses are of limited expediency to games and the act of gaming. For starters, Kennedy cites Brenda Laurel and Janet Murray to illustrate how "the relationship between player and game character advances in phases as the player becomes increasingly proficient."[6] Although the distant, untried game character is easily objectified at the beginning of play, as gameplay advances players build identification with their character.[7] The character can become "an extension of the player to the point at which the character's separateness is eventually obliterated."[8] Additionally, while playing a female lead, players are "simultaneously the hero (active) and the heroine (to be looked at) . . . providing multiple possibilities for narcissistic pleasure. [In *Tomb Raider*, for example] when the game is mastered the player experiences Lara's mobility, agility and athleticism as his or her own."[9] This notion that identification with an object through gameplay can lead to a subjectification of that object is symbolized in Erceg's *Skin Pack* (figure 8.4a, b) when the naked characters frag their own clones. The clones provide a metaphor for our own investment of self in what previously, in noninteractive media, would have comprised an on-screen, passive object.

Tobias Bernstrup's earliest foray into computer game modification was a series of three collaborative, site-specific installations with Palle Torrsson. *Museum Meltdown* was exhibited as episodes titled *Arken* (1996), *The Vilnius Vengeance* (1997) (figure 8.5), and *Moderna Museet* (1999). Each consisted of a game level that had been rebuilt to replicate the gallery exhibition space in which the game was installed. Visitors to the gallery were able to play the games (*Duke Nukem 3D* and *Half Life* were used); however, gameplay occurred in a virtual version of the real space in which they stood. This technique is employed fairly often by game modders, and it provides an excellent way for people to

a

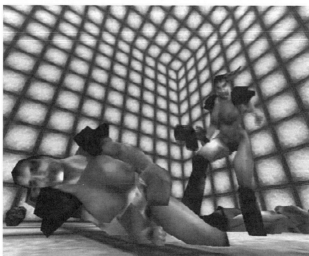

b

| Figure 8.4a, b |
Skin Pack (2000)

| Figure 8.5 |
The Vilnius Vengeance (1997)

experience first-hand the similarities and differences between real and virtual worlds—while also generating a crossover between them. Experiences gained during gameplay are no longer only associated with the virtual environment—the memory of shooting a monster beside a classic artwork, such as an Andy Warhol Elvis print (or perhaps the experience of shooting the print itself) inside the game, is recalled when viewing that print in the real space. Other emotional and physical phenomena of gameplay are similarly triggered—as outlined by Eric Cho in the artist statement for his game mod *Cyber Café Killers* (2002): "Play a first-person shooter long enough and its morbid reality seems to descend over your awareness like a grid, accompanied by a kind of adrenalized hyper-awareness and euphoric rage. Grid, adrenaline and rage stay with you, far past the point when you exit to the desktop. Walk away from the computer, and they still persist. You find yourself stealing up on street corners as if preparing to strafe the adjoining block; you seem to see a crosshair traced across the bodies of passersby."[10]

This effect results from the degree to which we invest in the virtual experience itself. The neuropsychological philosopher Max Velmans has argued that through a process of "perceptual projection," investments in virtual experience can be as valid as they are in "real" life.[11] In his discussions on the nature of virtual reality, Velmans contends that we rely on a reflexive model of perception when interacting with virtual worlds. The reflexive model posits that experiences of objects located in space are "*experienced as an entity in space*" (my emphasis). Dualist and reductionist models position the experience as having no location or extension or only being located and extended in the brain.[12] Velmans's deductions are based on the way "the VR world appears to have 3-D location and extension outside one's body in spite of the fact that it is entirely a phenomenal experience. The VR does not seem to be without location or extension, or to be 'in the brain'"[13] Using the example of an amputee who experiences pain in a non-existing limb, Velmans illustrates how experiences in all sense modalities can have a subjective location and extension beyond the brain. Where the mind can perceive a hallucinatory limb extended in space, it can also perceive external aural stimulation as being generated from inside the mind, and in extreme cases viewers can perceive their entire subjectification as being located beyond the body.[14] Perceptual projection therefore involves the cognitively authentic process of extending one's subjectivity, through the perception of experience, into real, imagined, and/or virtual, external phenomena.

Artificial Surfaces

Bernstrup continued his mod-based architectural studies to produce two artworks, *Untitled (Friedrich Passage)* and *Potsdamer Platz Unreal Edit* (both 2001). These pieces recreate significant portions of Berlin. Potsdamer Platz is the site of a spontaneous, miniature CBD that erupted after the fall of the Berlin wall. Tall skyscrapers, quickly erected by corporate giants Sony and Daimler-Chrysler, stand incongruously between the former East and West Germany. These opportunistic constructions brand a sacrosanct tract of Berlin that once stood witness to the murder of fleeing citizens, captives in their country's political history. In this comparatively artificial district, "even the Berliners are tourists in their own city."[15] *Untitled (Friedrich Passage)* depicts the Friedrichstadt Passage arcade in the former East Berlin; the camera pans slowly through the desolate shopping center. Both works import photographs of the real environments to map onto objects in the game, drawing parallels between the artificial, simplistic, reduced quality of computer game architecture and that of the contemporary "generic city"—a city without identity, without any defining characteristics.[16] In his artist's statement, Bernstrup points out how easy it was to transpose Potsdamer Platz into a virtual environment: "The [real] building facades consist of a few all very similar and significant sets

Rebecca Cannon

| Figure 8.6a |
Potsdamer Platz (Unreal Edit) (2001)

of textures, which is good for increasing our CPU performance when navigating through the space *in any reality*" (my emphasis).[17] He also notes how quickly, as frequent tourists, we become accustomed to unrealities.

Potsdamer Platz (figure 8.6a, b) is exhibited as an interactive game; however, all game elements, except the ability to explore, have been removed. Other characters in *Potsdamer Platz* function as elements of the scenery. One participant commented that with so little opportunity for performance and interaction, the only novelty was to repeatedly die by jumping off the roof of a building.[18] Dreyfus contends: "Just like the cities they live in, these beings are without a particular identity. Actors in a game that encompasses nothing other than their presence, they are concentrated in characteristic places of the social urban theater: a swimming pool, a dance floor, a shopping center. Animated by repetitive movements, the figures confer only an artificial life to the

| Figure 8.6b |
Potsdamer Platz (Unreal Edit) (2001)

scenes."[19] Real or virtual, generic contexts sculpt generic behaviors: behaviors that codify identity (figure 8.7).

Bernstrup has produced several artworks that directly explore the construction of mediated identities. In 1999 he produced two videos, *Untitled (Super Twins, Documentation)* and *Untitled (Super Twins, Video)* (figure 8.8), each of which explored the constructed artificiality of pop stars: cultural products consumed for a surface appearance that is mediated through cultural communication networks via music videos, radio, magazines. The exhibition included magazine-style photographs and video stills of the over-glamorized recording process. These came two years after the release of his first audio CD, *The Heat of the Night* (a limited edition of 25), and one year after his second CD *Images of Love* (a limited edition of 100). The covers for these albums mimic those of sickly sweet yet superficial crooners. *The Heat of the Night* was also performed on a cruiser going between Stockholm and Helsinki. The following is a description of the

| Figure 8.7 |
Untitled (Friedrich Passage) (2002)

performance: "Entering the stage dressed and made up with long nails, as a cross be-tween a gigolo and a transvestite, he starts to sing to music from the early 80s. Some of the songs are composed by himself, and he performs somewhat disinterestedly. The audience does not seem to know what to do with the mix of the music and the guy and it is actually slightly embarrassing."[20]

Drag-style parody of the pop star identity understandably crossed over into Bern-strup's computer game mods, with he himself, an emerging musical performer, the subject of speculation. Bernstrup produced three videos in 2000, each between ten and twenty minutes in length. *Tonight Live*, *Penthouse Idle* (figure 8.9), and *Polygon Lover* all used the medium of the computer game to explore virtualized signifiers of the pop star identity. *Tonight Live* places Bernstrup, the musician, on stage in an S+M club. Semi-naked dancers in bondage gear move mechanically in the desolate darkness. In *Penthouse Idle*, the context shifts to a penthouse apartment, where characters, also clad in latex,

| Figure 8.8 |
Untitled (Super Twins Video) (1999)

perform "idleness" around a swimming pool. The shiny, plastic textures of their fetish clothing extend onto the furniture. Bloodred carpet fills the halls through which the camera tracks; the mise-en-scène is reminiscent of Kubrick's *The Shining*.

In her essay "Does Lara Croft Wear Fake Polygons?" Anne-Marie Schleiner outlines a number of potential "gender subject configurations" that may result from the "multiplicity of sometimes quite contrary positions and subjectivities" that a gamer "may morph and oscillate between."[21] One such gender subject configuration is that of a drag queen. Based on Lacan's concept of the mirror stage whereby an infant, upon glancing in a mirror, first engenders the formation of ego—a process that then continues throughout life—Schleiner argues that "over the course of the game the construction of the player's feminine identity emerges from the reflective connectivity between the player's identification with the avatar's movements in the game space (a sort of alternate 'mirror' reality). Rigid gender roles are broken down, allowing the young boys and men . . . to experiment with 'wearing' a feminine identity."[22]

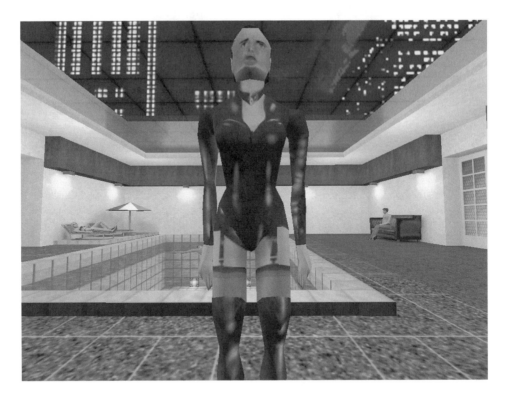

| Figure 8.9 |
Penthouse Idle (2000)

Although I am not in a position to suggest that Bernstrup's performance art incarnations of drag were the direct result of the hours he spent playing games, it is likely that his interest in the masculine expressions of femininity were linked to the dominance of masculinity in games and gaming culture. His early interests in performance art drag reached an abstracted, symbolic stage in his work *Polygon Lover*. This video loop depicts Bernstrup with a specifically female form; however, the avatar retains the image of his own head. The narrative-esque qualities of *The Heat of the Night*, *Tonight Live*, and *Penthouse Idle* are now reduced to the essence of the player-avatar subject position. The avatar touches its female form with obvious sexual gratification. Gazing knowingly at the viewer in an expression of scopofilia, virtual Bernstrup wants to be watched and enjoys being watched. However, as the creator and actor behind the avatar's animated performance, Bernstrup is also the viewer himself. Scopofilia conjoins narcissism. This virtual mirror fulfills Lacanian destiny—Bernstrup's initial, hesitant explorations into transgenderism (*The Heat of the Night* was an awkward experience) become a completed project of ego engendering.

The psychoanalytic imperative of these works culminates in Bernstrup's recent project, *Walking Ego (2003)* (figure 8.10). A simple, endless DVD loop of a transgendered "avatarial" form is walking eternally toward the viewer. The presence of this transgendered identity cannot be contended. The ego is manifest. For Freud, the ego results from a compromise between morality (super ego) and harmful selfishness (id). Bernstrup's *Walking Ego* signifies an alternative expression of compromise between opposing, restrictive forces—perhaps, in this case, as social and phenomenological as they are psychic and internal.

Walking Ego follows Bernstrup's first unlimited CD release *Re-Animate Me* (2002). Bernstrup decreases the significance of the project as an art commodity through this *unlimited* release. He embraces the lifestyle of the transgendered pop idol. Thus the construction of a virtual identity that encapsulated underlying motivations behind Bernstrup-as-performance-artist in effect aided his adoption of that identity in real life. Virtual embodiment provided a thoroughly safe zone for gender experimentation. Real experiences gained from these works, such as comfort with this identity, were incorporated into his live performances. Perceptual projection has allowed the *player* to experience an engendering beyond that of his or her physiological makeup: an embodiment of a third sex, despite its virtual nature.

Social Networks

Linda Erceg's artistic concerns have, more recently, focused on the constructed, virtual nature of technology-dependent social networks, and the virtuality of our participation within them. *Skin Club* (2002) (figure 8.11) was an interactive installation whereby the visitor entered a dark space, sat down on a leather armchair (reminiscent of furniture in the office of a consulting psychologist). This visitor then witnessed a life-sized 3-D character recall an intimate, sexually confronting experience. The 3-D characters were naked, also sitting. Their skins were highly detailed and very realistic. Although naked, the body shapes defied fantastical pornographic forms popularly enjoyed in virtual entertainments. Real voiceovers related true accounts of sexually difficult memories. For example, a woman recalled the day, as a young girl, she was confronted by a flasher. Viewers were reprimanded if their attention strayed from the intimate, and to a degree, self-indulgent stories.

Skin Club placed the viewer undeniably in the position of voyeur. Nude, while relating sexual encounters, the characters ostensibly invite sexual objectification. However,

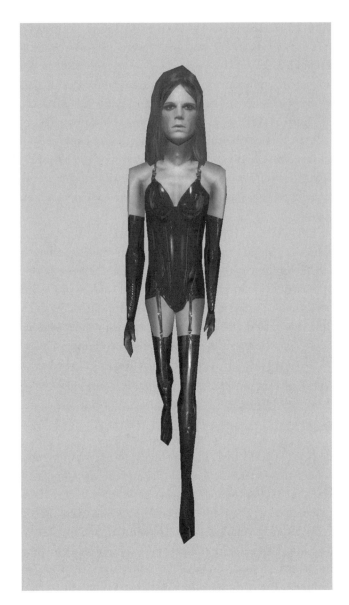

| Figure 8.10 |
Walking Ego (2003)

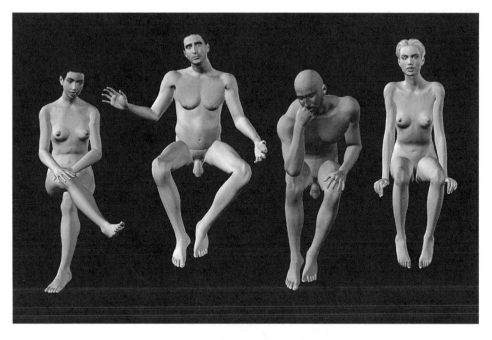

| Figure 8.11 |
Skin Club (2002)

the intimacy and reality of their stories impinge on the construction of sexual fantasy. A paradox arises between the need for intimate communication and the distance of the voyeur. The avatars provide a sculpted mask of anonymity behind which real agents can open up. However, the viewer is placed in the awkward position of receiving this information. The reality of these sexual dilemmas transcends the artificial surface of the carrier. The characters are male and female; both genders admit sexual vulnerability. Although virtual, they actuate our own sexual insecurities.

Erceg further explored the coupling of real and virtual sexual confrontation in her video installation *Punchline* (2003). A series of (once again) highly realistic, naked 3-D models perform sexual activities on a video loop. The camera circles around the models, providing explicit coverage. Sex with a partner who isn't present. Autoeroticism. Suggested sex with the viewer. Far from exciting arousal, the honest, at times pained, self-absorbed facial expressions of the characters forcibly alienate the viewer. In headphones we hear friends tell sexual jokes to one another. Their attempts at delivery are layered.

The jokes transgress accepted social and political attitudes. Again, delivery and reception are awkward, straining sexual readings. The social network of a group of friends is colored with the trappings of artifice. What should provide an opportunity for comfortable liaison is restricted by sexual taboo.

Erceg's forthcoming artwork, *The Searchers*, places viewers inside one of two booths. A photomapped 3-D face interrogates viewers to ascertain their sexual and social compatibility. As the viewers respond with yes/no answers, a webcam publicizes their responses to other visitors in the gallery. The sacrifice of their privacy to a public network is counterbalanced by the possible reward of companionship and love. All variety of sexual relations are offered by the avatars, so the possibility for sexual exploration in what would usually, online, from the privacy of one's home, present a safe zone is fraught with the real possibility of exposure. The fear of being "found out" for one's sexual preferences is challenged by the public context. However, viewers are offered the freedom for construction of virtual identity. As the artificial surfaces of the avatars suggest, this freedom is not theirs alone. As Erceg has noticed in her research for *The Searchers*, visitors to Internet dating sites appear interested less in deceit than in genuine relationships.

As we develop online relations, as our search for self-value depends increasingly on our existence as mediated identities, an understanding of the qualities of virtual representations can assist knowledge of self and others. Virtual identities afford certain freedoms for self-expression that have previously been restricted by repressive norms. The options for technologically mediated relations, as explored by these artists, can help remodel gender relations along thoroughly egalitarian lines.

Notes

1. See Anne Marie Schleiner, "Does Lara Croft Wear Fake Polygons? Gender Analysis of the '3rd Person Shooter/Adventure Game with Female Heroine' and Gender Role Subversion in the Game Patch," *Leonardo* 34 (2001): 221–226, http://opensorcery.net/lara2.html (accessed November 14, 2003).
2. *Counter Strike* (http://www.counterstrike.net) is a modification of the popular game *Half Life* (http://games.sierra.com/games/half-life/) by Sierra Studios.
3. See Celia Pearce, "Emergent Authorship: The Next Interactive Revolution for Computers and Graphics," *Computers and Graphics*, 2002, http://www.cpandfriends.com/writing/computers-graphics.html (accessed July 18, 2005).
4. Gerard Jones, *Killing Monsters: Why Children Need Fantasy, Super Heroes, and Make Believe Violence* (New York: Basic Books, 2002).
5. Laura Mulvey, "Visual Pleasure and Narrative Cinema," *Screen* 16 (Autumn 1975): 6–18.

6. Helen W. Kennedy, "Lara Croft: Feminist Icon or Cyberbimbo? On the Limits of Textual Analysis," *The International Journal of Computer Game Research* 2, no. 2 (December 2002), http://gamestudies.org/0202/kennedy/ (accessed July 18, 2005).

7. Jones, *Killing Monsters.*

8. Kennedy, "Lara Croft."

9. Kennedy, "Lara Croft."

10. Eric Cho, "Cyber Café Killers," 2002, http://meshfm.ucsd.edu/~echo/kill.htm (accessed March 1, 2003).

11. Max Velmans, "Physical, Psychological and Virtual Realities," in *The Virtual Embodied. Presence, Practice, Technology,* ed. John Wood (New York and London: Routledge, 1998), 45–60.

12. Velmans, "Physical, Psychological and Virtual Realities," 45–49.

13. Velmans, "Physical, Psychological and Virtual Realities," 49.

14. Velmans, "Physical, Psychological and Virtual Realities," 50–55.

15. Tobias Bernstrup, "Potsdamer Platz: The UnrealEdit 2001" (catalogue text for Lyon Biennale), 2001.

16. Rem Koolhaas, "The Generic City," in *S, M, L, XL* (New York: Monacelli Press, 1997), 1248–1255.

17. Bernstrup, "Potsdamer Platz."

18. Interview with Timothy Moore.

19. Laurence Dreyfus, "Loading . . . Video Games, a New Language for Artists," *Flash Art International* 36 (March–April 2003): 84–87.

20. Maria Lind, *Catalogue Text* (Paris: Musée d'Árt Moderne), http://www.kkh.se/arkiv/avg/grad98/tobias/texts.html (accessed July 18, 2005).

21. Schleiner, "Does Lara Croft Wear Fake Polygons?"

22. Schleiner, "Does Lara Croft Wear Fake Polygons?"

9

LYNX AND STRAND

Jewelle Gomez

Until the day that you are me and I am you . . . I'll be loving you always.

—Stevie Wonder

As she walked through the door, twin reflections of the firm set of her back moved closer together in the corner of the restaurant window. The images converged in the mirrored panes of glass and vanished inside each other like chips of colored crystal in a kaleidoscope. Across the street a bland shadow stepped from a doorway and followed. Strand's heart thudded, she gulped for breath.

"Whoa!" Nelson said in his soft voice, easing Strand out of her reverie. The shadow receded. Strand opened her eyes and recognized Nelson's living room, edged with twilight, encircling the beam of a stark lamp focused on her. Strand, laying on her stomach on the waist-high massage table, struggled to let go of the memory and the fear inside it.

"Sorry. I was just remembering something."

"You want to sit up a minute?"

"No, let's just go."

He held out her glass with its bent straw and green liquid. She shook her head, turning onto her other cheek, and gazed at Nelson's heavily laden bookcase.

"I go. You stay still." Nelson balanced between the heels and balls of his feet. He kept his considerable weight centered so that he barely leaned forward over the expanse of Strand's back. For eleven months they'd spent hours in this way: Strand listening to the past unreeling in her head as Nelson worked on her. Other times they'd told each other stories, true and untrue. Under the spell of their words, the tattoo took shape almost independently. Now, as they neared the end of the project, both were increasingly anxious. Conversation came in choppy swells, uneven and unfinished, without the certainty Strand enforced in most of her life.

"What're you thinking about?"

"Work," Strand lied.

"And?"

Strand pushed the shadow to the back and cast about for news to share. "Did I tell you about the dancing potato chip guy? If I ever have another client like him, I'll leap from the tower window before we're done."

"They don't open," Nelson responded, never letting his gaze waver from her back.

"Then I'll smash it."

"You don't like heights."

"I won't know, will I?"

"It'd be messy. Your secretary, Freda, would have to clean up after you.

"You want to hear or not," she continued. The hum of Nelson's machine and its vibrating needles remained steady. "He had the stupidest concept I've ever heard. These chips hoofing it around the edge of a volcano, like they're about to hop in and get fried."

"Please don't make me laugh, okay?"

"But the thing was, he kept insisting we go on location. He wanted to go out West! I told him Mount St. Helens is no joke, that I wasn't balancing some dumb and desperate dancers on the edge of a volcano when I could do it in a simuroom."

"Bet Broadcast loved him."

"He had this deep voice he kept throwing around like it was a police stick. 'You don't understand,' he says to me. 'This isn't a matter of your artistic whim, this is government advertising in Society City.'"

Nelson tried to hold steady and not laugh at Strand's imitation.

"So I say, 'No, this is advertising on the far coast and I won't go!' I dumped the job. I couldn't work with this slob. He's had one thought his entire life, and this was it.

"Damn, Strand, you're rough." Nelson's voice was mixed with admiration and wariness.

"There are plenty of other commercialists at the company hungry for the work. Why waste my time with dancing potato chips?"

"Strand," Nelson said, trying to keep the judgment out of his voice, hating this brittle side of her.

"Broadcast doesn't really like to go past the Cities, anyway. So end of story, right? Uh-uh. Today Freda said somebody in Tech told her this guy did end up going out there. I don't know if he got as far as Washington, but out he goes with a crew, you know."

Strains of laughter began to bubble up from her stomach.

"Okay, I can feel a break coming on." Nelson stepped back and let his machine arm rest at his side.

So, he sets off, right, with a crew . . . I'm sorry." Strand was almost enveloped in laughter. "He goes out there . . . forest . . . unpaved . . . the whole untamed nature thing and . . . ," Strand raised herself up on her elbows, "and . . . he gets himself killed!" Her laughter pealed like a bell.

"Killed, how?" A chill crossed Nelson's skin.

"Who knows. One of the Tech crew said Separatists probably booby-trapped the location. They found him practically disemboweled in some woods—"

"That's not funny, Strand."

"Shit, he was an ad man."

"And they haven't called themselves Separatists in decades. They're Partisans. Why do they get blamed for everything?"

"Relax."

"You relax!" Nelson snapped, surprised by his impatience. "Don't dismiss people so easy."

"He was just—"

"He was just a person."

Both were quiet, an unnatural state between them, until Nelson spoke.

"They keep telling us Partisans are raving lunatics, ready to kill anybody outside the perimeters of the Cities. Why, Strand? Why keep us away from the old places. Away from people trying to hang on to some integrity."

Strand had never heard Nelson so upset, certainly not with her. "Think, Strand! That's supposed to be your claim to fame."

She stared at his books, not seeing their titles. At Broadcast One there was an endless static of voices—technicians, producers, advertisers, directors like herself. She'd learned to let clients babble while she thought about their concepts, examining them from all angles until she perceived the image she wanted. Then she matched the rhythms and tone of the conversation, pitching her voice above it and off-center just enough to capture their attention. As she waited for the space to step into, her face looked much as it did now: a store shuttered and closed for the night.

Strand had once caught herself in the glass window of her tower office. She had seen that look reflected back, superimposed on the small world below, her mouth set in a hard line that she never broke until a client hired her. For her thoughts, her ideas.

"I correct myself. Don't think, Strand. Feel."

She leaned up for the glass of tranq, sipped, and lowered herself back to the table. When Nelson clicked the machine back on, she shuddered and drifted away from his words. She didn't want to think or feel. Instead she savored the image of him hovering over her body just like he did when he worked in the art class they took together.

Cardarelli, the instructor, whispered apologetically in class when she made suggestions over a painter's shoulder, moving about the room, always avoiding Strand who became enraged by interruption. Strand enjoyed the small island each easel created and the hushed atmosphere of concentration. She took the class as required by Professional Development, but PD couldn't make her listen to an instructor if she chose otherwise. With merely a glance Strand was able to decipher, analyze, or reproduce any image put before her. She hadn't needed instruction in art since she'd left the orphanage at fifteen.

"I'm taking a stretch break," Nelson said after a few moments, flipping the switch on the machine. "You want something?"

"No. How much longer do you think?"

"A month, maybe. I'm doing a second layer of colors now."

"It's like we've known each other forever, you know that."

"Except we keep knowing something new."

"Um . . ."

"How's Lynx doing?"

"Good. A lot better, really." Strand thought about what that meant: Lynx was able to sleep without drugs. She could be in a room with more than one person without being sedated.

"I want her to come by soon."

"She will, it's just hard for her when she gets off her shift."

"Soon, though." Nelson splayed his palms together, pushing and flexing. He brushed Strand's forehead gently with his fingertips, then dropped forward at the waist, his large bulk in its dark caftan filling the space beside her. He stretched noisily and squatted next to Strand, his brown face even with hers. His large dark eyes and sleekly arched eyebrows were accentuated by the stark beauty of his bald head.

"You know I'm going to miss you when we're done," he said, and was startled to see tears forming in the corner of her eyes. He turned away, gripped the edge of the lounge, and did two half push-ups.

"Hell, you'll be happy to have more time to hang out at Ruby's," she replied. Then, more softly, as if barely saying it made it barely true, "You and Lynx are the only people in the world I love."

"There'll soon be a lot more."

"If they don't stop us." It was unusual for Strand to express uncertainty.

"They think it's just an art project. They won't care."

"They care about everything—the trains running on time and real tattoos."

Working at Broadcast, Strand saw how closely the government monitored every nuance of public social interaction, from street crime to who bought "adult" music. Strand didn't underestimate the Society's investment in any of its citizens.

"The Joneses," Nelson said with disgust.

The Joneses was Nelson's epithet for the Society and its privatized bureaucracy. The federal government was composed of intricately linked, regional oversight committees with profit and order in mind. They strategized how many workers needed education, which citizens had run out of their right to public assistance, what types of artists needed stimulation, and, most important, which television producers and directors said what over the national channels. The Joneses.

"Back to work if you can stand it."

"I'm just imagining we're in Cardarelli's studio class and I'm the canvas."

Nelson rubbed his hands vigorously around his smooth head as if gathering the thoughts that were inside, then took the machine in hand. Pinned to the walls around them were the drawings he'd done of Lynx in that class, and others he'd done of Strand over the six years they'd known each other. He was always looking for the life behind the images. With this tattoo, he'd found it.

Strand herself was usually more interested in affect, her meticulous eye taking in content only tangentially. During her years living in the Society North Orphanage, Strand had learned to watch the shapes of things to discern meaning. The floor supervisor's arched eyebrow let her know what was safe to say. The angle of the door to the principal's office informed her of how severe her punishment would be. A child's curving lip said she'd refuse to talk to the tall, awkward Strand. The act of deciphering these signs became its own meaning; whatever occurred subsequently had been almost inconsequential to Strand the child. She'd lived for symbols and surfaces until two years ago, when Lynx arrived to model for their class.

Lynx stepped up onto the platform, a large crocheted hat crowning her nudity. Kneeling ceremoniously, she drew the hat back from her forehead, releasing a mass of tawny orange hair emblazoned with streaks of pure silver to cascade down her back and around her breasts. A collective gasp swept around the studio as they recognized the silver marks of an empath. Cardarelli beamed with pride. She was the first instructor at the Institute, in the entire city, to have secured an empath as a model. Most of the students had never met one, although they'd certainly heard of the social services the E Corps performed for the Society in hospitals and detention centers.

Strand forced herself to look away from the mesmerizing tangle of hair, which Lynx made no effort to tame. Strand focused instead on the body, just as she did with clients when their voices got in her way. This one was short, athletic, the arms thick with muscle, a body altogether at odds with the mass of bright, delicate tendrils. The skin, unexpectedly, was not just freckled but bronzed from the sun. Despite their fine bones, her hands looked like those of a toiler, bearers of many heavy loads. Everything about

Lynx seemed both small and large at the same time. The set of mismatched attributes was puzzling to Strand. Even in recline, Lynx seemed to fill the room.

Strand didn't begin to look at Lynx's face until the end of the first week. She spent all her time trying to read her body: the flare of hip from her waist, the texture of skin, and the fine hairs that covered it. Near the end of the week Strand realized that Lynx, unlike most models, sat perfectly still. The curve of her muscle was stony hard beneath the flesh. For hours she sat, as if all life were suspended. The only movement was that of her hair, blown occasionally by a current from the forced-air vent. Strand became curious about the concentration at the center of the icy stillness. There were no clues in Lynx's face. Her features remained impassive, the bright hazel of her eyes almost opaque. The shield masking Lynx's gaze annoyed Strand at first. Her job was about surfaces, but here she wanted to know the interior image, the hidden meanings.

After class Strand asked Nelson, "So what do you make of her?"

He raised his eyebrows, his fleshy face creased with a wide smile. In their years of friendship, Strand had never revealed curiosity about anyone. Except him. Her other personal relationships were brief, ephemeral, significant only when they were discarded, material to dissect over dinner and wine.

"Girlfriend, I know what you know. She's Mother Nature's creature, but not one I've ever seen before."

"Empath."

"I got the silver hair thing," Nelson answered impatiently. "But she never moves. Shit's racing around inside there, though. You know?"

"I've seen her a couple of times at Ruby's, always with the hat though."

"Why would she go to that greasy spoon?"

"Why would *I* go? To eat some greens, to look at folks, and to keep the Joneses from keeping up with you."

"Ruby's?"

"Yeah." Nelson worked hard to sound as noncommittal as Strand.

"See you tomorrow, Strand said, walking away, not sure herself what thoughts she hid.

"Earth to Strand," Nelson said when he realized Strand had fallen asleep on the table. "Where do you go in there? You were out for the count."

She sat up quickly, startled. "Let's go light on the tranq next time, whew!"

"Sometimes I wish I could hook up some speakers to that brain of yours."

"What? So you can fall asleep too!" Strand laughed as he helped her down from the table.

He sprayed a thin layer of surgical fixative, then handed Strand, ever distrustful of Dupont, one of the oversized T-shirts she now wore beneath all her clothes. He watched her drape it as gently as he did his easel. He avoided touching her back as they embraced, smiling at the soft texture of her hair on the side of his cheek.

"Tomorrow and tomorrow and tomorrow. Isn't that some movie?" The sparkle in Strand's eyes concealed whether she thought she was joking or not. Nelson held the intercom open so she could hear him still laughing down in the lobby and out into the courtyard.

Back in her own flat, she sipped a tall glass of water, hoping to hurry the tranquilizer from her system. She never slept until Lynx rang the phone once to signal she was home. If she let it ring more than once, they'd talk. Strand laid across the bed; when the phone rang for the third time she pressed the button in the bed's headboard.

"Hello, I hope it's not too late." Lynx's voice still carried the softness of the middle of the country.

"Hi, I just got home from Nelson's."

"You two have a good time?"

A ray of amusement glinted through the awkward necessity of sounding casual. The Joneses randomly listened to telephone conversations in the housing complex.

"Great," Strand answered. "He's a wonderful artist." Her belief in the praise was undisguised.

"Have you eaten?" Lynx asked.

"I'm too beat."

"I'll let you go then. I just wanted to . . . to get in touch."

"Thanks, let's get together soon." Strand became impatient with the form they followed so cautiously.

"Wonderful. I was hoping you'd be open." A smile suffused Lynx's voice.

"What about tomorrow?"

"Perfect, I have a new piece I'd like to show you." Lynx barely suppressed laughter.

Strand clicked off and laid back down. In the last year and a half she and Lynx had kept their relationship quiet, rarely going out as a couple. Only when they were together in one of their flats did they allow their need for each other to spill out in words and touch. For months it had been like a game they played: tricking the Joneses. Now it was a tight band around Strand's chest squeezing her breath, smothering her. But Lynx's attempts at erotic humor made her smile. She sounded weary, Strand thought, as she plummeted into sleep.

Session #82

"What?" Strand said without looking away from her monitor. She'd shifted light and color on the brand-new sedan for the past hour and nothing made it seem appealing, unusual, or like a necessity. When Freda didn't answer, Strand looked away from the screen in frustration. "What is it?"

Freda, secretary on Strand's floor for almost five years, stood tentatively in the doorway. The intelligence in her eyes was sometimes shadowed by the stress of working in advertising, but more often by her inability to comprehend Strand. Freda's mind and her short, round body moved with equal dexterity around the political potholes of Broadcast One, and she knew she was one of the reasons Strand had a successful career. But it was never clear how Strand felt about this.

"I talked to Dee, in the pool. She's got those contracts covered. I'm going—"

"What about Dee?" Strand said, still unable to focus on her secretary.

"She's going to finish those contracts you just gave me. Remember, I have my videography class tonight."

"Dee can't do this, Freda. I need you on this one. We're using too many specialists on this shoot, everyone has a contract. I've got to have it first thing in the morning—done right."

"Dee's good, Strand. I've got her set up, and I'll log in and check her work after my class."

"Then what? If she fucks up I'm screwed."

"If there are mistakes I'll have time—"

"Freda, do you work for me or not?" Strand turned back to the monitor, stared at the wash of red, and began to calibrate its intensity. "I'm leaving here at 7:00 p.m."

Freda bit back a reply and tried to keep in mind the exhilaration she felt when the two of them talked about a successful video shoot. She quietly shut the door to Strand's office and returned to her desk.

When Strand swung through the pool to leave at 7:15 p.m., Freda raised the stack of contracts with a trim smile.

"I always tell them you're the best, Freda!" Strand said as she pressed the elevator button.

At Nelson's house, Strand stepped out of her clothes with the same ease as she'd forgotten the exchange with Freda. Nelson inspected his mix of colors and the needle machine. Strand laid her pants and tunic neatly on the back of an overstuffed reading chair Nelson had rescued from a theater where he'd designed a set. Gazing into an ornate mirror over the couch, she thought she looked fuller without her clothes. The slowing metabolism of her middle years was revealed in her hips and thighs. Tonight the thickening made her smile.

———

"Any ripples outside?" Nelson asked.

"No." Strand tried to dismiss the increasing unease she'd felt over the past few weeks.

"I'm just gonna go back to do a few lines. I don't want to work too long."

"Up or down?" she asked.

"Down."

Strand stretched out on her stomach with a sigh.

"Sometimes the work just comes, like squeezed out of a tube. Other times I can't hook in. Does that make sense?"

"It's taking longer than you thought."

Nelson turned his attention to the line on Strand's thigh.

"We'll all get together soon.

"Good idea."

"Remember that first time?"

"Uh-huh."

"I'll never be that way again, will I, Nelson?"

He raised the machine. "No, I don't think so."

Then he was immersed in the work, his breathing in tune with the machine and its vibrating needles. Strand strained upward to look at the natural lines he drew on her thighs, the ink perfectly distributed, blood welling around it. She closed her eyes and tried to remember the moment the change had begun.

The entire class worked intently at their easels. Strand avoided meeting Nelson's eyes for a smile as they occasionally did. Just before the session ended, she pushed her easel to the edge of the studio, then slipped out.

On the street, instinct took over as it did when she worked. Pictures were what guided her. The image of Ruby's drew her: a narrow, brick structure on the edge of the city, with a brightly lit window where they served messy food to people who stayed far into the night.

She'd had dinner there once with Nelson and some of his friends, all the while unnerved by the noise and aimlessly circular discussions. She imagined the entire place to be under the shadow of a brown cloud, the effluvia of frying foods and overlong bantering.

Watching through a window of the rumbling jitney, she recognized the long, light-filled window as they passed, but stayed on board for several more blocks to get a clearer sense of the neighborhood. She leaped out in front of the darkened façade of a beauty salon and made her way back to Ruby's entrance. She stood between the double set of glass doors beside a public telephone. At first she saw only her own reflection: tall, un-yielding posture accentuated by the spare lines of her fullsuit that hugged the curves of her body. Her skin, the shade of golden oak, was unlined at the age of forty. The tight row of braids curving around the crown of her head was accurately austere, threaded with gray. She appreciated the image without smiling.

Behind her the sound of laughter and shouted food orders floated through the café. She shifted her gaze, looking out through the glass more intently than she'd ever looked at anything other than a studio set. She wondered what she'd do if Lynx didn't recognize her.

The muted green of the crocheted cap alerted Strand as Lynx came down the street toward the café. Strand pulled the door open just as Lynx stood before it. She brushed hesitancy aside and said, "Surprise," in the lightest voice she could muster. The cloud lifted from the ice of Lynx's eyes, which lightened almost to amber as she laughed. She tried to say Strand's name but couldn't stop laughing. Strand attempted to offer her a drink; Lynx's laughter was, however, uncontrollable. The hidden catch broken, mirth enveloped Lynx so totally it was alarming. Lynx grabbed Strand's arm as if to stop herself from falling.

"Let me hold on, please, just a moment. Please," she said between eruptions. Strand watched steadily, not understanding what it meant, regretting that she'd followed her impulse. Lynx's grip began to bruise her arm. The color in Lynx's eyes darkened as she felt Strand's pain, and the laughter stopped. She let go of Strand, wiping tears from the corners of her eyes.

"I just wanted . . ." The words strangled each other in Strand's throat. "I startled you."

Lynx smiled. "It happens so rarely. I'm sorry I frightened you."

"You didn't."

"Yes, I did. And I am sorry. I'll never become used to living among people." Lynx's voice was only partly playful.

"Yeah, I know what you mean."

"Yes, you do." Lynx's eves narrowed as she peered at Strand. "You're the one in the figure class."

"Strand."

"Yes." The sibilants slipped from Lynx's mouth like taffy. Slow, intriguing.

"I was just leaving."

"Oh?" Lynx was puzzled at the lie she could feel all around them.

Noise filled Strand's ears, blocking our Lynx's voice. She took a deep breath and caught the soft scent of soap. "Excuse me," Strand said coolly, then stepped around Lynx and escaped through the doors.

Strand shifted on the table, thinking about that first time. How alien her discomfort with Lynx felt now.

———

"Okay, girlfriend, that's it for tonight." Nelson's voice broke into her thoughts. I got the right perspective. Finally! It's going to be perfect."

He sprayed ceremoniously.

"Don't look, come on now, don't look. You can't see anything anyhow!"

Uncharacteristically obedient, Strand didn't try to examine the work. Instead, she turned sideways in the ornate mirror and admired the small tattoo of an old-fashioned bicycle on her calf—a large spoked wheel with a much smaller one behind.

"What'd you call this again?"

"A pennyfarthing." Nelson had done it in the first year of their friendship, saying, "It'll take you anywhere you want to go. He started cleaning up his instruments. "If anybody asks we were sketching . . ." He trailed off, waiting.

"Kitchen utensils and Warhol." Strand provided their alibi with a laugh.

"Ugh!" Nelson shuddered. "Don't be letting nobody be patting you."

"Yes, I know, I know."

At the end of every session, the project seemed riskier than it had the day before. The Society didn't care for the renegade art of tattooing anymore than it did for travel to the West. Legislation had banned the art in the nineteenth century. Now, two hundred years later, the laws had been reenacted. Nelson felt like the proprietor of one of the needle parlors he'd read about in his historical novels, in which squalid back rooms catering to drunken sailors dotted the waterfront.

Strand left Nelson's studio a little dazed as the drug wore off and the pain of the needles reached her. It'd been more than a year since she and Lynx had become lovers, something else the Society would frown on. She hurried toward Lynx's room, a tiny garret space looking out over a factory loading dock. She let herself in and rubbed Lynx's cat and dog in response to their eager greetings, wondering how they decided who to like and who to snub. Few people kept pets in the Society, so it still felt a little strange to have small, living things moving around her.

Strand lay on her stomach across the bed where the cat and dog circled after they finished eating. She didn't move at the sound of Lynx's step on the stairs, only listened, feeling her body come alive with the waiting.

Lynx hummed as she entered her room, lowered herself to the bed, and cautiously pulled the shirt over Strand's head. The waves of her hair were tied back in a white ribbon. Her uniform was rumpled and stained with hours of sweat. She kissed one of the parts in Strand's hair and, without speaking, massaged Strand's head, running her strong fingers along the rows of braids. They were a pale shade of blue this week, dyed to match an outfit she'd worn to a film premiere. Strand and Nelson had made a striking pair in twin outfits: high visibility meant more jobs. Tired of finding scarves to match, Strand swore that before the weekend her hair would be its usual silver-flecked brown again.

Lynx worked her way down Strand's neck and shoulders, massaging the muscles gently. Soon Strand felt the heat of Lynx's hands as they passed above the raw skin where Nelson had been working. Lynx held her palms just over the solid lines and the wash of bronze and silver that he'd created on Strand's back. Lynx's breath quickened, and she resisted drawing away the wound completely—raking in all the pain risked the durability of the picture. She drew out a portion of the burning, pulling it into herself and releasing it into the air. She worked quickly, anxious to be done with the healing and to feel Strand's body more intimately.

The lines that lay across and down Strand's back were intriguingly familiar to Lynx. Even unfinished, they began to take shape and open themselves to her. She held her hand steady and continued to trace the outline of pale color, making Strand's skin first warm then cool.

As Lynx worked, Strand wondered how they'd feel when the tattoo was done, and a shiver of fear rippled across her skin.

"How did it go today?"

"Nelson's pleased. He says I have good legs. Soon they'll be twice as good." Strand smiled, but Lynx did not.

"Earlier, when I was at the hospital, I was resting between patients and I closed my eyes. I saw blood. Spilling down your flesh."

"At the beginning, I tried to watch Nelson working."

"Tried?"

"I didn't watch long. Not like me, being squeamish, is it?"

"Not like you at all, Strand."

"Do you want us to stop?"

"It's a bit like dying. I've felt that with patients, you know. A loosening inside myself."

"Should we stop?"

"No."

The muscles in Strand's body relaxed. The heat now emanating from her body was not from the wounds. Lynx touched the inside of Strand's thigh lightly, then entered her from behind.

Session #90

While they waited for the sedative to take effect, Nelson showed Strand one of his old books, its pages wrinkled and soft. The pictures from the early 1900s depicted men and women with primitive tattoos covering most of their bodies: flowery hearts, battleships, flags. Other pages reproduced the more sophisticated tattoos of indigenous people from some of the Pacific Islands. The tight lines and bands were so compelling, Strand knew the project was the right thing to do. She began disrobing, looking at the bric-a-brac crowding Nelson's shelves.

"What's this little car?"

"Isn't it great. See those wheels? Whitewall tires, fabulous!" Nelson plucked the replica of the antique Stutz Bearcat from his bookshelf. Its trim design felt solid in his hand. "This was a real car. My grandfather used to say he knew Western civilization was doomed when all the cars started looking alike. Alfa Romeo, Mercedes, Cadillac, Jag, Saab, Mustang—by the turn of the century the designs were interchangeable."

"He could have been right," Strand said. The pleasure Nelson took in his memories of his family pleased her, even though she had none of her own. Each session was an interior journey for them both. They exchanged history and ideas with an urgency and intimacy few citizens bothered with in Society City. At the same time that Strand listened to Nelson's stories, or told her own, she was traveling away from everything she knew about herself to a destination she couldn't yet picture in her mind.

She climbed onto the table, relinquishing her body to Nelson's hand. The light markings he made as a guide tickled her skin.

"I'm going back to the right shoulder today. Warn me if you need to stop. But no fidgeting."

"I'll be fine."

"Yeah, I know you're tough. But don't wait 'til you're ready to leap from the table before you say uncle, okay?"

Strand slipped easily under the spell of the needle's high-pitched hum. The first touch was like a small bite, then the sensation radiated out in dull waves of stimulation. Nelson told her that traditional tattoo artists hadn't used tranquilizers. She didn't see why he insisted she take them, yet the vivid memories they induced usually pleased her.

On the final day of the figure-drawing cycle, the end of Lynx's work as their model, Nelson cajoled Strand into having a drink with him at Ruby's Café. He returned waves and shouts from other customers as they took a table by the windows. Within minutes of ordering drinks, Nelson leaped from his seat and dashed to the front where Lynx stood hesitantly inside the glass double doors. She smiled when she saw Nelson. Strand felt annoyed and trapped as Nelson and Lynx headed back to the table.

After eight weeks of art class, Nelson and Strand were the only two willing to acknowledge Lynx; everyone else fled as if she would read their minds for sport. Strand had never managed more than a studied hello each session, following her first misstep, but that was more than the rest of the workshop participants. The din of Ruby's swirled around them for the next half hour while they endured stilted attempts at conversation:

about the drawing they'd seen in the studio class, about professional development, about the neighborhood.

Ruby, the owner, was behind the bar—six feet tall and sloe-eyed, commanding the room even when she was just washing the glasses. She brought a bottle of wine and refilled their glasses without being called, greeting Nelson familiarly.

"You're not switching on me, are ya'?" she asked, smiling at Lynx and Strand.

"Not yet. Lynx, Strand, this is the inestimable Ruby."

"He promised I'm first if he gets the urge."

"And who was it that was gonna protect me from Danny?"

"When I finished with you, sweetie, you'd need hospital rest anyway." Ruby's laughter filled the restaurant as she went back to the bar.

Strand watched, puzzled. She hadn't realized Nelson was such a regular at Ruby's. When they ate dinner out, it was usually in their own part of town, near the complex. As Ruby's laughter trailed off, Lynx spoke. "Will you tell me about tattoos?"

Nelson hesitated only a moment before breaking into the smile that Strand recognized as his preface to a story. Strand was surprised again, this time at his open enthusiasm: neither of them were sure precisely where empaths stood in the Joneses' family tree.

"It's fine to talk with me," Lynx answered the unspoken question and lightly rested her freckled hand on Strand's arm. A comforting sensation pulsed through Lynx's fingers to Strand. Nelson began to tell her some of the history of body adornment, about his books, the lore.

"They all tattooed something they thought they needed. Even when it was just boasting, it was still wishful thinking. I saw yearning, urgency, in the tiniest rose resting on someone's hip bone; it was like nothing in the galleries.

"I was looking for the images that filled me up, not just paint on paper. When I did my first tattoo I knew I had it." He watched closely for Lynx's reaction before he went on.

"The purr of the electricity is exciting. When the needles prick flesh I almost feel it. The entering, the connecting, are exhilarating. And then there's the picture, eternal in a mortal kind of way."

"I don't know if I could bear the intrusion," Lynx said.

"It's not for everybody. You've got to understand the meaning of taking on an image, of taking that image inside yourself. Once you do, you can stand anything, I think."

Lynx smiled at Nelson, and Strand watched her intently.

"Hey, I don't want you two to think this is a setup, but I'm out of here." Nelson fumbled under the table for his case, at the same time looking toward the door.

"What?" Strand said, her annoyance escalating to anger.

"Sorry, I've got a late date."

Strand stared coldly at him, then at the smiling man standing in the doorway.

"Don't give me that look, girlfriend. Be sociable, I'm going to be." Nelson pulled his long, full sweater from the back of the chair.

"See ya', right?" he smiled at Lynx.

"I hope so."

"My treat." He waved at them in the mirror and paid Ruby at the bar before sweeping out the door.

"I apologize. Nelson doesn't usually make a fool of himself in front of people, especially over men."

"No need. I hoped we'd get the chance to talk."

Strand thought about the tone and shape of Lynx's voice. The elongated vowels made it seem as if she were speaking with great deliberation, thinking in another language. Lynx sat almost as still as she did in class, waiting. They sipped the rest of their drinks in silence.

"What was it like growing up . . . being an empath?" Strand finally asked, reaching for her training in social manners. The shadow that crossed Lynx's face made Strand regret her inquiry. Lynx spoke quickly, her voice low and hoarse.

"My mother, Mae, figured I was weak. Melancholy too, I guess. She's a plain woman. Not much for cities or books. She must have thought that empaths were creatures the Society made up, like hobgoblins. Frankensteins they cooked up in labs or something." Lynx laughed.

"As I got older, Mae just thought I was mad. And I was, for a while."

Lynx looked around the room as if others might have heard her last words. But the music from the old stereo speakers still washed over the rise and fall of conversation, the clink of dishes and glassware. The noise shielded Lynx from them, but it could not protect her. The exultation of a woman and man—bathed in desire, sitting impatiently at a back table—radiated across the room. The cold fury of a young woman sitting at the counter pierced Lynx's skin. Their waiter's exhaustion, as he set down their drinks, sapped her strength.

"I can feel all of it, the deepest things they feel. Him, her, them," she said, nodding her head around the room. "Swirling inside me. Back then I thought I was possessed. I couldn't escape, and I couldn't explain what was happening.

"Children from the farms nearby made fun of me when they saw me sitting with our cows in the pasture instead of going to school. Their parents pointed at me and followed me around whenever I went to town. Mae tried . . . why do people think experiencing curiosity automatically gives them the right to your life?" The urgency in Lynx's voice made Strand want to touch her. Lynx took a breath and went on.

"Then my hair began to change. The silver ate through the red and for the first time I really loved something about myself. I didn't care who stared. Mae used to brush it every night for the longest time. But I could feel her fear. Then they came and took me away."

The words alarmed Strand, who'd never paid much attention to who empaths were, where they'd come from, or how they served Society. In that moment, she felt a part of the "they" who'd come to take Lynx from her home. One of the Joneses.

"I was tranquilized for a year. Therapists did exercises with my body, and they fed me intravenously most of that time. Control voices were played almost constantly on implants." Lynx lifted her unusual hair away from her neck and displayed the tiny line where the incision had been made. Strand, with years of practice, easily concealed any obvious reaction.

"It was like living outside my body, a twelve-month dream. And when they thought I'd be able to protect myself from the tumult of feeling, they took me off the tranqs and started to train me."

"What do you mean 'train'?"

"Most empaths acquire the sensitivity later in life, after we've already learned how to preserve individuality. I was too young and susceptible to everyone. I had to be trained to open and close, to draw in and release the sensations without being subsumed by them."

"The Society doesn't give anything away for free." Strand's suspicions rose.

"Society's correctional hospitals, the health care system, they couldn't function without us. We're their intellectual property in a manner of speaking."

Pride was new to Lynx. She'd experienced it for the first time when she was able to move inside the pain of another and help untangle it. She maintained a precarious balance between that joy and a sense of being used for purposes she could not know.

"But we have to be supervised so our health doesn't wear down. I fought to be allowed to live in the city, to work with children, not just with convicted offenders."

"Why here?"

"The training tapes hadn't really worked. I thought I could train myself to be around people in one of the cities. But now I'm either completely closed down, like when I'm modeling for the class, or too open, like when I think of you."

Strand looked from Lynx to her glass, keeping her noncommittal expression in place.

"I feel you so much and I want to know you," Lynx said, a crimson flush rising from her neck to her cheeks.

Strand didn't speak but took a sip from her glass.

"I know what you're feeling too. I'm sorry, I can't help it. I know."

"How can you?" Strand said, her voice wavering only slightly. To be known frightened her more than she'd ever admitted to herself.

"I've been trying to explain. I more than know, I feel what you're feeling. You can't hide from me even when you run away like you did that first time. I watched you through the window as you left. I felt the battle inside you."

Strand leaned back from the table as if to leave.

"Don't—" Lynx gripped Strand, pressing her hand into the rough wood edge of the tiny table. "Push away! That was your feeling just then. But you want to sink inside me, too. It's all there coursing through your body. Your facility to keep it bricked up inside is amazing."

Strand looked down at their hands locked together, expecting them to glow with the heat she felt.

"You look at my fingers and want them in your mouth," Lynx said with an edge of wonder. "You want my fingers pressing inside your mouth, you sucking, pulling, tasting."

Strand glared at their hands. Her gaze did not soften as she looked up into Lynx's eyes.

"Why does desire make you want to hurt me? Or is it the knowing? Do you want to marry your fear?" Lynx asked. She inhaled so deeply it felt impossibly long, then removed her hand.

Strand felt the weight of abandonment at the release of Lynx's hand as she'd never experienced it before, even on the worst days living in the Society orphanage. Then her breath caught in her chest as if Lynx had been holding her hand over her mouth and nose, stopping the air. She gasped and breathed deeply, her chest heaving.

"I'm going to have to give you another tranq, Strand." Nelson stretched his arms above his head. "You're acting up."

"What?" Strand said, disoriented.

"You're starting to thrash around."

She opened her eyes and saw, spread out under her shoulder, the towel spotted with her blood.

"Oh."

"Take this," Nelson said, thrusting the glass of green liquid toward her. The bent plastic straw reached in her direction.

"I'm fine, just a dream."

Nelson's hand was steady; the glass did not retreat.

Strand yielded, ran her tongue over the straw, then drew a small amount of the liquid in. She closed her eyes to await the relaxation.

"You've got to be still as stone here, girl. I want not a hair out of place."

"I'm sorry. I drift away, into the past."

"How about talking to me. About anything, as long as you stay still."

Many times she and Nelson had sat together, in bars, parks, telling each other their life stories, being each other's confidant in a way that was more common to adolescents than adults. They'd both come to the capital from small towns in the north, near the New Hampshire border, where the highway leading to Society City was the yellow brick road for anyone who wanted to be an artist. They each had done work that had caught the attention of local councilors early in their careers, and each had petitioned and won the opportunity to move to the City.

They'd spied each other one day in the Art Park at the center of the housing compound where they lived. Dwelling on opposite ends of a complex of high-rises built explicitly for art workers, neither often crossed the expanse of regimentally manicured green lawn adorning its center. The Park resembled a miniature baseball diamond, but instead of bases there were strategically placed pieces of art meant to inspire the residents, some of whom sat sketching or writing in their shadows.

Despite Strand's disdain for the programmed nature of their artistic environment, she'd requested permission to remain in the artists' compound after she began working in advertising and broadcast. One visit to the complexes designed for media professionals, and Strand had known they were too shiny and noisy for her. Painting was quiet, and the click of computer keys was less to contend with than the endless static of broadcast voices emptied of their regional shadings. She much preferred the trite Modigliani imitations and Romare Beardon rip-offs to the premieres and festivals that sprawled across the huge screens dominating the media complexes.

The Society liked imitation; perfect replication was as prized as any original. She and Nelson smirked in secret about the imitative nature of the artwork around them. No matter how crowded and tough the City was, neither of them wanted to be sent to some outpost like Chicago to design stamps or traffic signs.

A new Richard Serra replica resembling a rusted flying wedge was installed in the outfield soon after they'd met. Strand came upon Nelson late one night tossing a pair of shoes, tied together by their laces, into the air, trying to land them across the fourteen-foot-high slab of metal. His drunken state was making his aim unpredictable, so Strand grabbed the shoes and tossed expertly, leaving the muddy size twelves dangling irreverently.

"City kids, poor ones, used to do that all over the country years ago," he said, laughing.

"Why would poor people throw away their shoes?" she asked, genuinely perplexed.

"Who knows? To leave their mark, to keep being poor from running their lives?" He shrugged.

Strand pushed herself to imagine that time before the Society corporatized, when children were allowed to throw away shoes. "Maybe they just wanted to see how high they could throw," she speculated.

They'd been friends ever since.

"Well?" Nelson said, putting down the electric needles he used to insert bright colors under her skin. He rinsed and dried his hands, then took up a sketching crayon.

"Tell me how Lynx is doing," he said.

Strand always felt his inquiries about Lynx were as much about herself as Lynx. "She's having a difficult time controlling the barrage of sensations. She takes the blocking drugs when she has to, but they slow her work and numb her for anything else."

"What about that hypnotist I told you about?"

"She ended up hypnotizing him."

Nelson would have laughed had he not heard the strain in Strand's voice.

"When she comes home she lies in the dark, sometimes for hours, like a corpse, trying to recover."

"The Joneses aren't going to let their valuable property go on like that for long."

"The more she opens to me, the less strength she has to screen out everyone else. Her supervisor is already insisting she go on blockers all the time. She'll end up immobilized in a hospital with medicos bringing patients to her bedside for healing like she's some kind of ghoul."

"Steady."

Strand concentrated on lying still, then said, "I want to watch you in the mirror."

"Come on, you don't want to do that."

He felt her body stiffen and knew her well enough to recognize her on the edge of fury. He pulled over a small table and placed his shaving mirror and another small hand mirror at angles so that she could watch him work.

"I'm going back to the leg lines."

Strand observed the arch of Nelson's wrist and felt the soft tip of the pencil on her calves. The grip of his fingers was echoed in the determined set of his lips. It was a look she'd seen often in their art class and on the dance floor.

"You talk."

A shiver went through her when he picked up the needle. Such a barbaric custom, she thought. Funny how it had lasted so long despite attempts to outlaw it. Almost everyone had a tattoo or two or three created by the quick and relatively painless laser implements. They were designed to wear off in several months.

Strand felt the muted sting of the needle on the back of her leg and watched the blood rise in the track behind the needle. The line extending up her calf to her thigh was fascinating to her, as if she were reading her palm. Nelson worked with steady deliberation, his eyes never leaving the line. She couldn't see the color of the dye, only the dark red that sometimes welled up and slipped down the side of her leg. She felt curiously ill for a moment and sniffed in surprise.

"You all right?"

"I was just thinking—"

"Please, no thinking. Talk."

"I'm not certain how you expect me to do the latter without the former."

"Chatter is good for the soul."

Strand closed her eyes. "We finally got permission for our trip to the country, for a week. Soon."

She waited for Nelson to get to the end of a line and lift his head.

"It's not my favorite thing to do in the middle of a piece, but I guess it's time."

"Her mother still feels guilty letting them take her."

"What's to feel guilty about? When the Joneses want to take you away, that's what they do. Mother or no mother." His voice deepened with emotion.

"Maybe when she sees us together she'll know it's for the best. And Lynx can see the farm animals she loves."

Strand was quiet as Nelson set to work again. Strand knew that growing up with livestock had made it easy for Lynx to have pets when she moved to the city. She also understood why most people living in cities disapproved of keeping pets, although from the beginning Nelson had never said anything negative about it. And after she'd seen Lynx with them—the thin, dark dog called Sliver and the fat black-and-white fur ball of a cat called Dot, both scampering in to be with Lynx when she needed them—Strand had accepted it. She was even looking forward to encountering a live cow.

"Quiet for a minute while I get this last bit." She could feel Nelson thinking.

"All right," he said after a few moments of work. "That's it for the time being. I'd let that heal some on its own before I'd do a lot of sitting."

Strand laughed at the maternal timbre of his voice and slipped into her oversized shirt and loose pants. She missed the one-piece simplicity of her fullsuit, but was beginning to enjoy the sensation of the soft folds of fabric brushing her skin as she moved.

By the time she was back in her own high-rise apartment, the dulling effect of the tranq was beginning to thin and Strand was hungry. She ignored the beep of her mailbox and started dinner. Lynx was on duty at the correctional hospital and wouldn't call until later. Strand wanted to have eaten and gotten comfortable by then; this was a night they'd get to talk. Looking at the perfectly balanced picture her dinner plate made, she laughed at her own obsession with visual presentation, then deliberately sloshed the food around.

Strand stood in front of the mail screen with her food and clicked on her messages as she began to eat. The word *override* filled the square of light, then the message:

```
TO:  <smb@art.pro.res> Ms. Strand Maria Burroughs Your presence is
required tomorrow at 9 am in the office of the Deputy Director of So-
cial Security. This office is located on the 4th floor of the Society
City Bureau on Broadway and Main Street. Please be prompt. Expect to
remain for a period of 2 hours. Areas of discussion: Artists' Com-
pound, Constructive social contacts. Your employer, Broadcast One, has
been informed of this required absence.
```

Strand hit the Print button just to be certain it was as she'd read it on the screen. As the printer spooled and reproduced the message, she dumped her food in the disposal and filled a glass with white wine. She read the message again, the paper trembling in her hand.

Her living room was not especially large, but its picture window faced the city skyline and made it feel cavernous at night. Strand paced in front of the backdrop of twinkling lights, oblivious to all except the piece of paper in her hand. She peered at the places where she knew the computer program had dropped the particulars of the message into the form: her name, her employer's name, time, areas of discussion. *Constructive social contacts.* That could mean anything. But they'd said Artists' Compound. It must be something about her and Nelson.

The phone rang.

"Yes?"

"What is it?" Lynx said after a breath of hesitation.

"I'll meet you at the mirrors when you're done."

"Now." Lynx broke the connection immediately.

Strand hurriedly typed a message to Nelson: "I hope you found the note I left. See you tomorrow. SMB." Strand had been almost certain they'd never have to use this prearranged warning, and as she hit Send the message seemed both ominous and silly.

It was logical that someone would find out about the tattoo eventually; questions would be raised. The Society was benevolent, but only to a point. The intersection of kind concern and control was located wherever any event occurred that the Joneses didn't understand, or that could be construed as disruptive.

Strand hoped Nelson wouldn't be out all night or forget to check his messages in time to hide his treasured machines. Along with architectural miniatures and toy cars, over the years he'd obtained a collection of antique tattoo irons. If the DSS decided to sweep through, tattoo needles would spark more attention than replicas of old tourist sites.

She slammed out the door and waited impatiently for the elevator, trying not to let anxiety swallow her. One of Society City's ubiquitous jitneys pulled up faster than the elevator had, and she stood in front of the mirrored bar at Ruby's before Lynx arrived. The place was eerie at such a late hour, almost lifeless without the noise of a full bar. Ruby greeted her with a smile and poured a glass of the wine she usually drank.

Strand tried not to gulp as she watched through the glass doors. She felt dread as she had the first evening, but this time when she saw Lynx push the double doors open escape was not on her mind. Lynx approached warily, unused to seeing Strand off balance. She read the letter in a glance.

"I don't know what it means," Strand said, her voice almost steady, "but people down at the Department of Social Security are more about security than social. Assume they know about the tattoo." Her tension was a hard wind against Lynx's skin.

"We have to make the trip to my mother." There was no plea in Lynx's voice.

"I know. They're probably watching us."

"They always watch empaths."

Strand stared through the window and realized she was almost never out this late. "Sometimes I hate this city. Even being outside is like being inside. Under a roof with everyone spying."

Lynx wanted to reassure Strand but was unsure how to go about it. Stating the facts was what Strand seemed to need right now.

"Every day they get closer to demanding what they really want. I've been trained to slip inside others, to manipulate what they feel or know in order to heal them. But not everyone can be healed." Lynx's voice was barely a whisper. Strand leaned closer but resisted her desire to touch her arm.

"I've done things for the Society I can't think about at night. I won't go on, Strand."

"We're almost done." Strand dug deeply for her confidence, but uncertainty clouded her words. "Maybe the three of us should go to your mothers and finish."

"We stay relaxed, listening. Not exuding."

"What?" Strand leaned on the bar, imagining herself with water spouting from her head or stuffing leaking from her seams.

"It's almost like that," Lynx laughed, reading the picture. "What you feel rolls off of you like waves. Even when you're perfectly still. Remember that tomorrow. If this is serious, they're sure to have an empath there to listen."

"I handle bureaucrats every day at Broadcast."

"Everything is different now, Strand. Don't concentrate on blocking your feelings like you usually do. Focus on taking in what they're exuding."

The expression on Strand's face didn't change. Lynx could feel her doubt.

"You can do it. Take the concentration you usually use to close yourself off. Reverse it. Don't worry about what they can get from you, listen to them. Listen hard."

Strand felt exposed in the glare of Ruby's lights and glass.

"We'd better get going," she said. "We'll still do the trip."

Lynx nodded, the tight braid of her bright curls hanging heavily down her back. Strand put her arm around her shoulder as they walked outside, glancing nervously up the street. Once Lynx had boarded a jitney, Strand watched to see if anyone emerged and followed. City lights and pollution made it impossible to see stars. The night was bright and empty.

Strand let go of her thoughts and tried to float free, listening to what was in the air. A wall of night sound blurred around her, its almost indecipherable noises buffeting her. She focused outward and let the night speak. The noise rose to a din. Behind her she heard the soft murmur of thoughts and voices from a window above. She relaxed into listening and could distinguish the sounds of individuals—a child, two men, a woman alone—floating around her head like cumulus clouds. She began to understand what Lynx lived with every day.

Then Ruby pulled the front door shut behind her with an end-of-day finality, and Strand remembered where she was. She hurried home to decide what to wear to her meeting.

The next morning Strand opened the door to the fourth-floor office of the Department of Social Security at exactly 9:00 a.m. The clean lines of the office had been amplified to austerity: prim chrome chairs, blank walls, no magazines. The receptionist blossomed with good cheer despite the hour and her surroundings.

The Department of Social Security, the largest of the government's privately run agencies, kept track of all the citizens and their financial status, making certain they paid taxes and traffic tickets. It monitored who studied what disciplines, to be certain the market wasn't glutted; who married whom, to keep pace with population growth; and who lived where, to be certain neighborhoods were developed symmetrically. All was accomplished with a congenial smile and decrees that had no court of appeal. Citizens felt secure, and most had easily forgotten privacy. Freedom came through careful management of the population, including early elimination of potential trouble spots.

Strand was feeling like one of those spots when two people in gray suits looked up at her as the receptionist showed her into the office.

"Ms. Burroughs, thank you for joining us," said the man. "I'm Dr. Skinner and this is Professor McKinnon."

"How do you do, Doctor. Professor," Strand replied in her best orphanage-trained voice. She recognized the professor as an author of some of the theories in which the Society was grounded. Strand knew McKinnon had written somewhere that the population needed to be protected from itself, from its baser instincts. Women, in McKinnon's mind, were especially vulnerable.

Strand watched their bodies. They were curiously alike despite the gender difference—tight, angular—each suspended in a carefully constructed air of nonchalance. Then she listened. Not especially to what they asked her, but to what they didn't ask and to what they thought of her answers.

"We realize it's early, can we bring you tea or coffee?" Professor McKinnon asked congenially. Strand noticed the perfection of her teeth and how uninflected her voice was, as if she were a television anchor rather than a bureaucrat.

"Yes, thank you." The office door opened and the receptionist stuck her head in.

"I was thinking of making some tea. Would you like a pot in here, Doctor?"

"Yes, thank you." Dr. Skinner seemed burdened by the necessity to appear pleasant. Strand could feel him restraining himself, capping his surliness. She assumed the questions would be pro forma until the receptionist returned with the tea and departed. But they began immediately, asking about her relationship with Nelson. They speculated about the intimacy of the friendship. If they had been courting, the DSS was interested in how long before marriage might be expected, what the combined incomes and buying power would be.

"We're both queer!" Strand was puzzled they didn't know something as public as that. The Society no longer penalized homosexual citizens, but monitored them subtly to satisfy conservative fears and to predict economic trends.

"Yes, of course, but that hasn't precluded bonding in some cases."

Strand listened to the swing of their words in the air. Bonding occurred between all kinds of people for a variety of reasons, but the Society expected formally posted bans before any commingling of households took place so that census and tax records could be maintained.

The receptionist slipped in quietly as they continued talking and set the teapot on a side table. As Strand watched the shape of their bodies and the auras surrounding each of them, she realized that she could hear the receptionist listening to her. It was just as Lynx had said, an empath—the receptionist—was taking everything in.

Strand stayed open, observing, not thinking. She could feel the receptionist's continued attention just outside the door while she answered most of the inquiries by rote.

"Have you considered that there might be more than friendship between you? At least on one side?"

Strand felt deep surprise as she registered the question.

"No," she said hesitantly. "No, I really haven't. We spend time together, but . . ." Her voice trailed off as she watched them seem to gather themselves, becoming taller, more authoritative.

"We noticed you both declared in the same religion on your tax returns." McKinnon's smile had too many sides.

Strand shrugged with amusement. You had to fill in a box, so she'd filled in a box. She knew Nelson felt the same.

"We don't want to push anything, my dear," Skinner said. "But think about it. If he's bisexual, you must take things into consideration. What signals you're giving—"

"Misunderstanding and miscommunication lead us to mistakes and misgivings," McKinnon broke in. Strand recognized her quoting from her own writing.

She almost expected them to ask, "What are your intentions toward our daughter?" Instead, they smiled at her as if they shared a secret. She returned their gaze diffusely. Her back felt irritated, so she shifted forward in her chair during the long silence. Without looking at them directly, she could sense them waiting, a blank wall of anticipation. But the receptionist outside was a magnet, drawing in Strand's unspoken thoughts and feelings. Strand remained equally open, almost providing a mirror.

"Well, now, we mustn't keep you from your work."

"I really appreciate this chance to meet you," McKinnon said. "Broadcast is so interesting. You've done some fine work. Didn't you do that potato chip one?"

"No. But thank you, Professor."

"Thank you for being so candid, Ms. Burroughs." Skinner smiled thinly.

Strand was soon back outside on the sidewalk. She didn't recall the descent in the elevator, but she remembered saying good-bye to each of them, including Cynthia, the receptionist, whose name had slipped into her mind as she was listening. She remained in as open a state as she could all the way back to her office. Once there, she rested her head on her desk. Cynthia was wearing a wig, she thought, as she fell asleep for the better part of an hour.

Session #96

Nelson walked around the small living room listening to Strand. He picked up a miniature of the recently demolished Arc de Triomphe, and let his fingers run tenderly along its lines, regretting he'd never seen the real thing.

"You need to know they're suspicious."

"The Joneses are always suspicious."

"Nelson, don't. This could be your career."

"I get it, Strand."

"I don't want this to work for us and you end up with nothing."

"You know about my name, right?"

"It was your mother's last name?"

"No. It was my mother's first name. And her mother's before that. Over a hundred years. For this political leader who got put in jail in what used to be South Africa."

"I know."

"Just about everybody gave up hope he'd ever get out. Except a few who kept on petitioning and kept the fight going. When he did get out, the children he left behind, the partisans who were working for his freedom, they were all grown up. But they were still his children. They were different people but they were, somewhere inside, still the same. That's what I think will happen when we're done."

Nelson sat the small sculpture down carefully on a shelf alongside a tiny wood carving of an Ashanti stool.

"I want that moment when we look at each other and know, whatever the cost, we did something incredible, that nothing will ever be the same again. What is it you want from this, Strand?"

In the intensity of his voice, Strand sensed Nelson weighing her. She chose her words carefully.

"I want to touch people," she said haltingly. "Not just seduce them into buying things, or be gawked at when we go to premieres."

She took a breath to begin again. "I never allowed anyone in when I was a kid. Too risky, you know. My mother was there one day and gone the next. I remembered her, did I ever tell you that? Not much: her smell, the way her shadow fell over me when I was in bed. Then she evaporated. Once dumped, twice shy. Then I met you and Lynx. Before that everyone was outside that glass."

"There are easier ways to break down barriers."

"But with this it's not just me. We can keep Lynx out of a hospital. Her work can go on, maybe even better than before."

Nelson could see Strand's thoughts taking shape as she was speaking. She was clarifying motives for herself as well as for him.

"This is not like Faust, or some shit like that, Nelson."

"I love it when you do the classics," he laughed.

"I feel like I'm sweeping up broken glass." Urgency rang in her voice. "I've got to do it, I don't know what to do once it's up off the floor, but we've got to do it."

Nelson said nothing. Strand remembered her visit to the DSS. "You know Dr. Skinner thought we should be posting bans." Laughter exploded from Nelson, the steeply angled light bouncing off the pristine shine of his head.

"I love your body, but I'm not that type of guy," he said through rippling giggles.

"Maybe we can use it to throw them off."

"All right, assume the position. You can think on it while I work."

He handed her the glass of tranq.

"Please just be careful, pay attention."

"Please just lay down, girlfriend. I'm doing color on front. Tell me about the trip to see the mother."

Strand recognized the worn contours of the table against her back. She stared at the ceiling, which was covered with a pale wash of colors, overlapping and delicately blended.

"Mae looks a lot like Lynx. Different hair, of course. But her body, her eyes especially. It made me wonder if she might be an empath too. Repressed empaths are pretty common, Lynx says."

She could tell from the hum of his machine that Nelson was too deep into the work to respond. Then her eyes closed. She thought not of the visit to Lynx's mother but of the first time she'd visited Lynx in a hospital facility where she worked.

It had seemed like fun when they'd first decided to do it, but once inside the lobby Strand only felt awkward and anxious. After growing up in an institution, she avoided them no matter what their purpose. She knew why as she waited for the elevator. There was a smell that marked institutions as alien, inhospitable to human life: the scent of decay, layered over with disinfectant and waste. The enforced crispness made all that was hidden more threatening. On the children's floor, the atmosphere was only a bit more inviting than in the lobby. Strand had come because she could never picture what Lynx did and because Lynx had wanted her to.

"We can sit together on my break in about half an hour. Do you want to watch me?"

Strand nodded her head, curious about what she'd be watching, still unnerved.

"You sit in here. The mirrored wall lets you see. Just sit still, no swinging your legs or getting up and down. Alright?"

"Why do you work with the patients so late at night?"

"I think I'm strongest then. And they're freer, the air is quieter around us. It just works better."

Strand sat in an office chair in the small, darkened room and watched Lynx, wearing the yellow jacket with the bright red E Corps insignia, enter the room. She was followed by a nurse who wheeled a chair transporting a young Asian boy. About fifteen, he talked nonstop, angry words escaping him in spurts, aimed not at the nurse or Lynx, it seemed, but at someone not there. His swearing and temper didn't appear to perturb Lynx at all. Once helped onto the table by the nurse, he lay still almost immediately. The nurse, a tall, husky, middle-aged man, moved away, closer to the door.

"Alfred, you know why we're here, don't you?"

"Yeah."

"You know I want to help you."

"Yeah."

"I would never hurt you."

"Yeah."

"Do you want to be able to talk to the people you see around you?"

The young man was silent. His narrow frame twitched as if he were on a drug.

"Do you want to be able to talk to the people around you, like me and the nurse?"

"Yeah."

"Will you let me touch you?"

"Yeah."

"Will you let me touch the others you talk to?"

Again he was silent. Then, "Yeah."

Strand strained forward in her chair and watched Lynx lean into the boy, moving her hands slowly in the air across his body.

"You're really healthy. Alfred. Strong and smart."

Alfred was quiet as Lynx poised her hands in the air—one over his chest, the other near his head. She closed her eyes and slid into a slow, arrhythmic rocking. She bent in as if pulled toward him, held there and then eased away. The air around them shimmered, and out of the corner of her eye Strand saw the nurse gripping the doorknob behind him.

A spectrum of colors hovered and drifted as if carried on a breeze. They intensified as Lynx spoke.

"You keep yourself safe by talking to them, don't you?" Although her voice sounded relaxed, Lynx's body was rigid.

"Yes."

The pale shades deepened, becoming solid in the air, vibrating feverishly. Strand's eyes widened in disbelief.

"Good. Next time I'll talk to them. Okay?"

"Yes."

"Good." Lynx took a deep breath, and Strand could see she was unsteady. The light receded, the colors evaporated. Lynx shook her hands out at her sides and touched the boy lightly on his forehead with a quick sweeping motion, as if she could rid him of his affliction with a flick of the wrist. The boy watched Lynx closely while the nurse took his pulse and blood pressure. He made notes, then helped Alfred back into the chair.

"Thanks, Kevin." Lynx drew herself up straighter as Kevin started to wheel Alfred out of the room. "I'll walk back with you."

They disappeared from Strand's view, and it was another five minutes before Lynx returned.

"I never saw anything like that in my life," Strand said, trying to make sense of it.

"Children's Hospital is the easy shift." Lynx shivered as if she were chilled before continuing. "Alfred and I've been working for six months. This was a real breakthrough."

"He didn't talk much, but those colors—"

"He never talks to me!" Lynx interrupted, her excitement rippling through her exhaustion. "For months he'll talk a blue streak to those people in his head. And all I ever get is yeah. But tonight he said yes. I could feel it coming like a giant wave. He made a decision to say yes!"

As she spoke, tears welled up in Lynx's eyes. Watching her, Strand understood what her work could do for the patients and for Lynx.

"I've got juice and snacks in my little room here. I need to lie down for a bit, do you mind? I wasn't prepared for this."

Strand didn't respond, but she knew she wasn't prepared either. She followed Lynx to a small room that held a single bed, refrigerator, lamp and desk. Built into the wall was a monitor of some sort. When Lynx saw her notice it, she said, "I can plug in there if I feel overwhelmed. Stereo!" She swept the headsets from the pillow, hung her jacket on the chair, and lay down.

Strand watched her breathing slow, noticing the soft curve of her breasts under the pale green sweater she wore. In ten minutes Lynx opened her eyes. Her color was back. She smiled as if she'd had all the rest she'd ever need.

"I can't believe it! Alfred said yes. You heard him!"

"He did."

"I can't wait to show the tape to the staff. I think Kevin, he's the nurse, has been doing what I asked. Keeping up conversation with Alfred even when he doesn't answer. Kevin was about ready to cry."

"The nurse seemed scared to me."

"I think everybody is a little scared of E Corps. We work together as a team—E Corps and a med staff member. Kevin's kind of new, but he's alright. He's really wanted to be able to help Alfred."

"Even I could tell something big was happening. Just the yes, I mean.

"Nelson won't believe it when I tell him."

"Nelson?"

"He came here. To see me work once."

"Really? He never mentioned it."

"Just one day after class, I think. He was curious. I happened to be working with Alfred."

Strand felt a twinge of jealousy—for Lynx and for Nelson. She couldn't unscramble the unfamiliar feelings.

"What happens now?"

"Kevin and I meet with the medical team tomorrow and present our report. If things go well, we get to work with Alfred more frequently. And we can start work on two other patients with the same presentation. There's a little girl, ten, I think, who talks nonstop; she has to be sedated to sleep. But she hasn't said a word directly to anyone around her since she was two. We want to begin touching her as soon as possible."

The assurance Lynx felt in her own world filled Strand with both desire and a sense of dread. Something in her life was changing, and she could not control it.

"I can't tell you how much I admire what you're doing." Even as she spoke the words, Strand laughed at their formality. Lynx reached out for her hand.

"I want that from you. And more." Lynx's hand burned in Strand's. The connection was like a tunnel opening between them. Strand no longer thought of pulling away.

"Got to get back." Lynx met Strand's gaze.

"Yeah—I mean . . ."

They both laughed, then Lynx ended Strand's discomfort by brushing her lips softly across her cheek, then her mouth. "Much more," Lynx repeated in Strand's ear before she stepped back and grabbed her jacket.

Strand's eyes popped open and she was again looking at the soft colors of Nelson's ceiling.

———

"She's an amazing woman, Nelson."

"You betcha."

"I keep thinking there should be some other way to make her stronger, safer."

"I know the equation doesn't work out right. But look at her like the Joneses do: she's a commodity. Top-shelf, but still a product that makes things run well. What do you think the Joneses would do to keep her in their store?"

Strand knew. She worked with people who sold products all day. The whole Society was one grand merchandising scheme. Society City and every town east of St. Louis was little more than a shopping mall. The health care Lynx gave was the property of the Society. If she could make a better profit for Society in some other city, in some other country, or by lying in a hospital bed, she'd be sent there to do her duty.

Strand left Nelson's, eager to curl up in her own room to get away from these thoughts.

Session #112

The evening was cool as Lynx and Strand walked toward Nelson's flat holding hands, something they rarely did in public. A small bronze figure sat in the shrubbery just before his building.

"And who's this supposed to be?" Lynx asked, aware of the gaps in her education.

"Rodin. I hate Rodin in miniature," Strand answered. "Claudel's better anyway." They both laughed. They didn't ring the bell but stood together looking around them at the lawn and the pieces of sculpture. Lynx held on more tightly to Strand.

"Are you alright?" Strand asked.

"I am. It's just every day I go to the Correctional Hospital and I don't know what to expect. I'll be happy when we . . . when I don't have to go to any of these places. Broadcast, the hospitals."

"Soon. Try to hang on."

"I know. Maybe it'll be a relief to do the work somewhere else, without them holding my leash."

"We'll do it together."

They laughed again and rang the bell.

Upstairs, Nelson had chilled a bottle of champagne and opened his door with an exuberance matching theirs. A jazzy harmonica played an old pop tune through the stereo speakers as Nelson settled Lynx and Strand in chairs with glasses. He sank down into a large pillow on the floor. They looked at each other silently for a moment.

"I'll stick to water," Nelson said. "Don't want to make any railroad tracks."

"Only a little for me. I'm going to the hospital from here."

"Looks like you're carrying the weight, Lynx."

The silence returned. In the time Strand and Lynx had known each other, spending hours in Nelson's flat or at Ruby's, words had never been this difficult for them.

"I got the present you two brought back, but Strand never told me how it went with your mother," Nelson said. The tiny replica of an old-fashioned tractor sat on the bookcase, the deep grooves of its oversized wheels next to the delicate whitewalls of a bright yellow antique car model.

"It was good, I think. Mae was relieved to see me, and she loved Strand."

"You're kidding?"

"Hey, I thought you were my friend."

"Strand, honey, you know I love you, but I don't think you ever called yourself a mother's delight."

"She was crazy about Strand," Lynx protested. "If Mae could find a man like Strand she'd be remarried in a minute."

"You go a long way between singles bars out there." Strand sipped from her glass.

"There's a lot of Partisan activity in that region these days, working roads, like that," Nelson noted.

"Partisans?" Strand asked.

"Some of them rebuilt a fence for Mae once and did some other stuff. Four women traveling together, kind of working their way around the countryside, doing chores for women who needed it, bartering for food."

"Partisans?" Strand repeated, unable to decipher the meaning of the waver in Lynx's voice and hating that she felt so much like Society wanted her to feel.

"Don't believe everything the Joneses tell you, Strand. I keep reminding you of that."

Strand didn't respond. She rarely accepted Society's word on anything. She saw for herself, too closely, how it was constructed, deconstructed, and embellished. She was frequently one of those polishing up the words, making them go down more smoothly with citizens. But if she totally rejected Society, what did she believe in instead? That was where she always stopped when she thought about it. Having Nelson in her life had given her the promise of something else, something hovering nearby. Learning how to care with Lynx had drawn it in even closer.

"Partisans are all different kinds of people, Strand. Women who want to live away from men, men committed to end militarism, greeners. They do their own work, their own way. Sometimes missions overlap," Nelson continued.

"If we go west, we'll be seeing Partisans, Strand," Lynx added cautiously.

"You'll be needing Partisans."

———

"Time for the fun part," Lynx said before Strand could respond. They all clinked their glasses together. Then, as Nelson reached up from the floor, they put down the champagne and held hands.

"Hey, this is a grand adventure, remember?" Strand said.

"It's working, isn't it?" There was no question in Lynx's voice.

"Yep. I can feel the differences."

"Let's make a toast then." Lynx raised her glass again.

"To?"

"Art and magic?" Strand said.

"Art is magic," said Nelson.

"Art is magic." They touched the rims of their glasses together a second time and sipped quietly until Lynx rose to leave. Strand felt a rush of affection and of fear as Nelson embraced Lynx at the door. When this was done, she'd never see them together again. Was escaping the Society really a possibility? Was it worth losing this camaraderie?

After Lynx left, Strand and Nelson settled easily into their task. "You ever notice that you rub your head just before you start working? Every time."

"Um-hum." Nelson nodded.

"Up or down."

"Down, I'm going right to the collar and cuff edges."

"I signed out on sick leave this week."

"It's time. Tranq?"

"Just a little." She sipped from the glass Nelson pulled from his refrigerator.

"Good to go?"

"Good to go."

He clicked on the machine, not expecting much conversation tonight. Strand stared at the wall nearest Nelson's kitchen, which was broken by a wide pass-through and a counter with stools. Above the opening, tacked to the walls, was a series of drawings—she and Lynx alternating, each subtly different from the one before it. She closed her eyes, no longer needing to see the images; she remembered what Lynx had looked like when they'd first met, and now she knew almost every line of her body.

Standing in the field that was part of her mother's small farm, Lynx spread her arms, mimicking the tree behind her. Strand watched, fascinated by the difference being on the farm had made. Even on the drive west, before they'd been outside Society City for an hour, Lynx had started to appear less burdened. Here in the field Lynx's skin was luminous, the furrow of anxiety had disappeared from her forehead, and her laughter no longer had an edge of hysteria. Even Strand herself felt different. She was kindly toward the livestock, the grass, even toward the neighbors who occasionally lurked at the end of the long road leading up to the house, hoping for a glimpse of their own local E Corps oddity.

In the quiet of the field, her arms raised to the sky, Lynx looked to Strand much as she had in the childhood pictures Mae had shown her over dinner.

"Do it," Lynx said.

Strand mirrored Lynx, raising her arms to the sky, closing her eyes.

"Keep listening. Everything you could ever want is right here, all around us."

Strand took the air deeply into her lungs. Her body wavered slightly, then she felt the caress and support of the light breeze. The leaves sounded like a river moving overhead. Insects swooped and darted. A pungent farm smell hung in the air, as did the soft sound of cows nearby. Lynx and Strand did not touch but stood adjacent, synchronous and harmonious, their bodies like similiar outfits on hangers in a department store.

Energy tingled through the air around them. Rather than straining, Strand relaxed into the sensations. Then the memory flooded her: Mae brushing her hair. For almost an hour as Mae hummed, then talked about her own mother. The feel of Mae's hands on her neck and head was comforting. The soft bristles of the brush sweeping across her scalp, pulling through long red curls, was firm and reassuring. Further back in the memory, Strand sensed not only Mae's enjoyment but her fear. Just as Lynx had described it.

Strand dropped her arms and opened her eyes. She thought she'd cry but no tears came. Lynx put her arms around her and spoke softly in her ear, "You can feel my past now, can't you. Like I feel yours."

Strand had no need to answer.

"Mae fought her fear, that's the courageous thing," Lynx said.

"They were all afraid. Society's still afraid."

"That's why they're so dangerous," Lynx's voice had the authority Strand had heard in the hospital, and an edge of determination. Here among the trees, Lynx was solid. She was an extraordinary but natural force in the world, not a commodity.

"There are other things I hope you never have to feel. But I don't know that I can stop it."

Strand watched sadness fill Lynx's eyes.

"At the Prison Hospital. They deem some prisoners incorrigible."

"Who deems?"

"Some committee or other—the Joneses. They keep reporting the crime rate is down. Everybody's happy. Nobody wants to know."

"Know what?"

"We . . . the E Corps . . . we touch them. If we go deep enough inside and pull back, we can take back their feelings."

Strand was silent, trying to understand.

"We take back all their feelings. They can't hurt anyone, ever. They can't do anything. Soon, without the feelings, they seem to die on their own." Shame flooded Lynx's voice. "Each time it feels like it's killing me, too."

Strand pulled Lynx to her. The breeze turned chilly with the set of the sun; they trembled in each other's arms.

"You cold, girl? You got goosebumps." Nelson drew Strand back to the present.

"I am a little."

"I'll jack up the heat." He turned the control on the floorboard heater. "I'm about done for the day."

"Really?"

"You've been laying out here more than two hours!"

"I can't tell anything for sure anymore. Disoriented is beginning to be my middle name."

"Look good on a marquee."

"The other day, before I filed the papers for my sick leave, I sat in on a department meeting. Everybody was throwing out ideas for a new campaign, some music group that Society's pushing—kind of English, kind of rock, a little social conscience thrown in. They're doing an international release. So I suggested we use an underlay of John Lennon footage. The room went silent, like I'd just spit on the table."

Nelson kept his eyes on the work, but he could tell the usually hard lines of her voice were soft. Her mouth quivered slightly as she told the story.

"The exec says, 'The guy's been dead over a hundred years, Strand. Who's gonna relate to that?' That wasn't really what topped me off. It was the damned producer. Twenty-five years old. He's heard five rock 'n' roll sides in his entire life. He says, 'Forget Lennon. Wasn't there something about him and God?' Can you believe that?"

"Cogs in a wheel have fuzzy memories."

"But can you believe it! He knows as much about images as a turnip. I didn't know what to do. I wanted to slap him on his head. I leaned over, looked him in the eye, and said, "God who?" and walked out. I've never done that before. The Broadcast producer almost had a coronary behind me."

"Nothing's the same anymore, honey."

"Then, when I got to my desk . . . I cried!"

"Take it easy. Don't be trying to take on the whole world yet."

"Lynx keeps saying the same thing."

"Are you going there tonight?"

"Lynx says we're having a romantic dinner. Do you think that means vegetarian?"

"Nope, chocolate."

"Are we on for tomorrow?"

"Let's hold up for a day, okay? I want you to get some rest."

Nelson sprayed the newly worked-on sections and watched Strand tentatively put on her clothes, as if all of her energy had been drained away by remembering Broadcast One.

"I'm gonna walk you over."

"You don't have—"

"Nix. Let's go." Nelson opened the door and grabbed one of his several voluminous garments from a hook by the door. They walked side by side to the corner in the cool evening air. When a jitney arrived, they got in and rode silently across town.

Nelson stood on the sidewalk waiting for Strand to enter and go up in the oversized industrial elevator. He glanced up at the window when he heard the final clang. As he turned away he saw, out of the corner of his eye, an old pair of running shoes suspended by their knotted strings from the street lamp. He smiled, pulled his large cape around him, and walked toward Ruby's.

Once upstairs, Strand let herself into Lynx's flat and laughed with joy at Lynx's preparations. Champagne glasses gleamed on a low coffee table alongside colorful paper napkins and plates. In the refrigerator were several small dishes with pickles, pans, cheese, and a couple of things Strand couldn't identify.

The dog, Sliver, followed her around hoping for a treat, while Dot watched from her perch on the top of the stove. Strand, suddenly exhausted, lay across Lynx's bed. Her mind whirled with pictures she couldn't shut out: coworkers she'd said good-bye to casually as she went on leave; Lynx's mother, Mae; the road west they'd driven to get to the farm. Her head started to feel achy. She considered taking a pill until she noticed that Sliver and Dot were stretched out around her. She closed her eyes and sank back into the comforter. Sliver and Dot nuzzled against her, one on either side, and Strand's thoughts slid away into a pool and swirled around each other until they'd drifted into the distance.

Strand opened her eyes an hour later to see Lynx standing at the foot of the bed, watching her. Sliver and Dot sat up waiting for her attention.

"Are you hungry?" Lynx asked. "These animals sure are."

"I'm sorry. I should have fed them when I came in. I was just so wiped out I had to lie down."

"How are you feeling now?"

"Like I'm getting over a migraine."

"You keep still. I'll feed them and come back and join you."

Strand lay back on the pillows, enjoying the sounds of domesticity from the other room. She listened to Lynx turn on the shower, then opened her eyes again to see her standing nude in the doorway, her damp hair wrapped tightly in a knot at the top of her head. The rounded angles of her hips and arms seemed a little firmer. Her normally tanned and freckled skin was pink from the heat of the shower.

"I feel better now." Strand's voice was both langorous and eager.

Lynx helped her out of her clothes and knelt above her on the bed, aware of the tenderness of Strand's skin.

"Not as good as we're going to feel," Lynx said before their lips met. Straddling Strand's body, Lynx grew more excited. Their mouths pressed together, Lynx touched one of Strand's breasts. Lynx moved down the bed and licked at the lines and colors on Strand's belly, hip bones, thighs, knees. She nipped at the hairs that protected Strand's mound and then pushed her tongue inside. The taste was almost salty. Musk filled Lynx's head as the sound of Strand's joy filled the room. They both understood this might be their final time.

They slept lightly and awakened in the predawn hours, finding each other's bodies again before sinking deeply into sleep.

The next afternoon, Strand called into her office to be certain no final details had been left undone. She already felt as if she'd been away for months instead of days. Her only regret was not saying a real good-bye to Freda. When Lynx went to the hospital in the evening, Strand sat looking out the window of the flat onto the street of warehouses.

Strand found it odd that Freda should come to mind so vividly now. Memories of tasks they'd done together filled most of Strand's evening as she sat quietly with the cat and dog, wondering why it was her secretary and not her job she missed. She stretched out on the couch and closed her eyes. When she started to drift off, she felt another presence. Strand lay still, listening, and realized she was sensing Lynx, just as Lynx was listening to her.

Strand's breathing slowed, and she sank into a state between sleeping and waking. She perceived Lynx's thoughts and activities at the hospital as if she were by her side. When Lynx went in with a patient, Strand could feel the lights in her head rather than see them as she did when, through the mirror, she'd watched Lynx work. Her body felt hot but not uncomfortable. When Lynx pulled back from touching the patient, Strand felt the release and was tired as Lynx rested before treating someone else.

When Lynx got home, she found Strand lying on the couch as she'd been all evening. Lynx fed Dot and Sliver, then sat in the kitchen listening as they ate. The one other living space in the building was empty; a warm quiet lay upon the building. When the animals finished, they followed Lynx into the living room. She led Strand to the bedroom and helped her undress. Dot and Sliver waited at the foot of the bed until the two women climbed under the comforter. They lay in each other's arms with the cat and dog inched into the spaces around. They all slept dreaming each other's dreams.

Session #124

The sun seemed unable to pull itself from behind the clouds. The air in Lynx's rooms was mired in dampness, but no rain fell. Strand paced the flat, confined and irritable. Lynx prepared for her final days at the hospital. She noted Strand's dour mood but didn't question it. She asked Strand to make tea for them. Sitting at the small kitchen table, they held onto their cups as if they were life rafts.

"Did you say why you'll be out?"

"No." Lynx shook her head. "I alerted Kevin so he could make alternative treatment schedules. I didn't say anything, just smiled conspiratorially. I think he thinks I'm doing something juicily illicit." Lynx smiled at the thought and went through the list of all she'd accomplished.

"I've brought my notes on patients up-to-date. I managed to get a consult with someone in E Corps for each of my patients so no one will be left without a professional who has an interest in their case. I haven't done deep work in a while, so no patient has to be really disrupted by a new link. Kevin's good, Strand. He'll make sure treatment is followed through."

"My work was so easy to leave. No consequences, no meaning, really." Strand's voice was deflated by exhaustion.

"It had meaning to you. The visuals, creating images."

"We'll see what that means in the long run. It seems petty compared to healing."

"Art is magic. All art," Lynx said. "If we lose that, we're back where we started—carving out replicas. We're both working for a government that's a corporation. Crime, health, advertising. It's all the same." The edge in her voice was new, raw.

"Have I got a Partisan on my hands now?"

Lynx smiled as she stood to go to the hospital.

"What time is Nelson coming over?"

"Not 'til seven."

"Get some rest.

"I think I will."

"I hear Mount St. Helens is quite lovely." Lynx tried to cheer Strand.

"Then perhaps we better see her."

Strand paced the flat after Lynx left, feeling restless and tired but unable to lie down. She decided to go out for a walk and found herself, unexpectedly, on the street of her own flat.

She went in and looked around as if they were the rooms of a stranger. The walls were covered with framed images. Glossy magazines sat in stacks around the couch and on the dining table. The bookcase held a few more magazines and awards she'd won for advertising jobs. There were three heavy lucite discs sitting in bronze bases. Small plaques celebrated past campaigns she'd developed. Strand packed them in pages crumpled from magazines and nestled each carefully in a shoebox. She wrapped the boxes in plain paper from one of her pads of sketch paper and addressed each in elaborate script: for Freda; for Turong, the elderly messenger; and for Buster, who'd been her driver whenever they went on location. She wrote thanks and drew ornate borders around their names, grabbed her two favorite ink pens from a drawer, and shut the door behind her. She took a jitney to Broadcast One as she had for the past eight years. She left the packages with the night guard and boarded another jitney to Ruby's. As she neared the brightly lit window, Strand felt a rush of warmth at its familiarity.

Once inside, Strand wasn't sure it had been a good idea. The café was bursting with people. Dishes, glasses, and voices clattered in her head. Ruby waved her over.

"Sit at the bar with me," she said, recognizing Strand's distress. She poured a glass of wine and watched as Strand took a sip.

"You don't look like you should be wandering around alone, my friend."

"I guess not. I'm not feeling so well."

"Danny," Ruby called behind her. A muscular, dark-skinned man with mixed gray hair appeared in the swinging doors. "Will you give Nelson's friend a lift?"

"Sure. Be right back."

He disappeared back into the kitchen.

"I can get a jitney, Ruby."

"No, girl, you look too out of it. You don't want to see Nelson angry with you or me."

Danny reappeared five minutes later wearing a cap and sweater. He took Strand's arm as if he'd done it countless times before.

"Okay, little lady, we'll have you comfortable in no time."

His voice was soothing; its low pitch and even tone easily lulled Strand. She remembered little of the ride back to Lynx's flat. She didn't even remember telling Danny where to take her. He parked and walked her to the door.

"Tell Nelson I said hey," Danny called over his shoulder as he turned back to his car.

———

Strand lay down on the bed, Sliver and Dot at her sides, until she heard Nelson ringing the doorbell. He lugged his massage table inside and set a large bag on the floor.

"You look like you haven't slept since I was here last!"

"I think that's about all I've been doing." Strand hated the whine creeping into her.

"Well, girlfriend, this is gonna be it."

"You think?"

"It better be. DSS was at my house yesterday." He tried to sound casual but Strand heard the anger; she was surprised she heard no fear. A knot formed in her stomach.

"Don't worry, I've been keeping the machines in another spot ever since they called you in."

"If they confiscated your wonderful old machines, the Rogers, the Cindy Ray . . ."

"It's okay, they're safe." Nelson set the table up in the middle of the living room. "I've been prepared for this."

"What'll happen when we're gone?"

"Make the stereotypes work, honey. I'll be a public nuisance, grief and abandonment dressed in feathers and red, the hysterical victim of a calculating advertising bitch. Then drop into the background. Everybody will be so happy that the big, black queen shut up, things should quiet down."

Anxiety kept Strand silent.

"I'm not leaving town. That would put DSS on me like a tracking bug." Dot rubbed against Nelson's leg and then against the table's.

"Find a seat, puss," Nelson said firmly as he pulled a premixed bottle of tranquilizer from his bag. Dot crossed the room and sat on the back of the couch.

"You've got the touch," Strand said, "with the cat, I mean."

Nelson beckoned her to the table.

"This is going to be in your face." Nelson laughed. "It's mostly shading, no fine lines. But you need to concentrate. And relax at the same time. I really mean relax. I've got options if something happens here. And you'll see me on your doorstep, if they have such things in the wild, before you can say silk and satin."

"Should we . . . I wondered . . . what . . ." Strand wasn't certain what question to ask.

"We'll just proceed like we always do. I'll work on your face and neck for a couple of hours, if you can. Then come back later and do your hands."

"I thought we were going to do it all at once."

"We'll see. The face work is more shadowing than anything else, but that's delicate. The hands are detail. We'll see."

"Can—" Strand started.

"Quaff!" Nelson handed Strand the bottle.

———

Strand took a sip and grimaced. "What is this—a double dose?"

Nelson didn't answer as he set out colors. Strand put her clothes across the arm of the sofa and lay on the table.

"Up, I assume."

"Yep," Nelson said and clicked on the machine, enjoying the delicately balanced weight in his hand.

"It's going to be fine, Strand. Just open up, let things in."

"Look who you're talking to."

"I am looking." With his other hand he brushed the softness of Strand's face. Her lips curved in a smile under his hand. Through the tips of his fingers, he felt her surrendering to the tranq.

"It's odd working here. Everything is right and wrong at the same time."

"Shhh."

Strand's body softened against the table, the hypnotic buzz of the machine filling her head as Nelson leaned toward her face. The vibrating of the needle was a large and frightening sound for a moment, then Strand was in darkness and the sound was her only reference point. She clung to it briefly, letting it go to make room for memory.

She waited outside the hospital for an hour before going in to see what was taking Lynx so long. Remembering the way from her visit several weeks earlier, she went up to the children's floor. She couldn't figure out what to say, what approach to take, so she decided to do what she always did: act like she knew. It would conceal her fear that something had happened to Lynx.

Emerging from the elevator, she found her way back to Lynx's resting room and opened the door quietly. The room was empty. She walked in and unlatched the refrigerator. Bottles of water stood nearly alongside an unopened packet of cheese. Strand stepped back into the hall and closed the door.

She looked around, trying to blank out her uneasiness at being in the hospital, at not finding Lynx. She'd decided to talk to the floor nurse back near the elevator when she saw Kevin coming toward her and was relieved she remembered his name.

"Hello, Kevin, my name is Strand. I don't know if . . ."

"Oh, sure . . ." The smile of recognition faded, and the angle of his body and his silence told Strand something was wrong.

"I'm looking for Lynx. She was due to get off over an hour ago."

"She had to leave." Kevin looked as uncomfortable as he had the night Strand had watched him through the mirror while Lynx worked on the young patient.

"What does that mean, Kevin?"

"They . . . I mean she was ill. We were working with one of the children. And she slipped."

"She fell?" Strand felt overwhelmed by information she couldn't decipher. The place, his words, all seemed a jumble.

"No. Come inside, that'd be better." She and Kevin stepped back into Lynx's resting room. Kevin and Strand were the same height, but his bulk made the room and Strand feel small. He leaned back against the door in the same way he had when she'd first seen him: holding onto the doorknob behind his back.

"She slipped . . . off center . . . I guess is the best way to explain it. I don't know how much you know—"

"Just tell me what happened, I'll figure it out."

"She slipped off center. Her touch was not simply reaching inside the patient—she was losing herself. She insisted on finishing with this one patient. She's been working a lot. Too much, I think, in the last couple of months. She just wanted to finish up so the kid could go on to the next phase of treatment."

"But what happened, exactly?"

"I took the girl back to her room. When I didn't see Lynx, I came back to the treatment room and there she was, standing, but completely unfocused. Like she was unconscious, but standing." Kevin's voice shook with emotion. Strand could see why Lynx had such faith in him.

"I know the procedure: I just eased her onto a gurney, strapped her down, and covered her with a blanket."

"Strapped her down!" Strand couldn't keep outrage out of her voice.

"So she wouldn't fall out. That's the procedure." Kevin's tone asked Strand to understand. "Then I called the E Corps officer. We're not supposed to touch any member of the E Corps. I took her pulse, though. I had to . . . to see what I could. It was very slow, slower than anything I'd ever felt. But she was in there, I could tell. Then they came."

"Where'd they take her?"

"I don't know. This has only happened twice the whole time I've been here. Both times they brought them back to their resting rooms, but they bundled Lynx into a van. They wouldn't even talk to me. Just made me tell them everything that had happened in the session with the kid. And afterward. I'd already started writing my chart notes. They took them away! Can you believe that shit? I've got to write them out all over again for the kid's file."

"They took your notes?"

"They flew out of here like they were going to a fire. But I tell you she's going to be fine. I'm sure of it. She was pulling it back together, she just needed time. I don't know why they—"

Strand turned abruptly toward the elevator, then turned back quickly. "Thanks, Kevin. I'm sure you're right. I'll just go by her flat. Thanks."

Strand rushed back to Lynx's, not expecting to find her there but disappointed that she didn't. She sat heavily on the sofa, about to call Nelson, when she realized the cat and dog were watching her. She almost rose to feed them, then stopped. They were staring at her intently. This was different from their customary longing-filled gaze. They sat side by side across the room, their pupils slightly dilated.

She decided to do what Lynx was always suggesting—she listened. She opened up her awareness and heard the room, the space around her. She gazed at Sliver and Dot, who were sitting more still than she'd ever seen them. Noise from the street did not disturb their attention. Then she heard Lynx, a slow surfacing of thoughts inside Strand's head, as if they were her own.

I'll be fine. There's only one way. Steady. Close down. Shut out all. Drugs run their course. Close down. I'll be fine.

Strand sat on the couch as if paralyzed. The thoughts were coming to her from Lynx, she was certain. She didn't know what to do. Tears started to roll down her cheeks and she touched them, puzzled.

She woke in the middle of the night, her head resting on the back of the couch and a dull headache clouding her memory. Sliver and Dot were still sitting side-by-side, but facing the door. A few moments later it opened and Lynx came in. She seemed so deflated that Strand almost didn't recognize her in the dark.

"What does it mean?" she asked Lynx.

"I had a hard time holding onto my focus. The closer we become, the more difficult it is for me."

"Why?"

"I can't explain it. Think about yourself, Strand." Lynx's voice was weak, with an undercurrent of urgency. "You keep yourself under tight control most of the time. You haven't given a thought to anything but work, the machinations of Broadcast One, for almost ten years. No real life, or friends, except Nelson. And he takes you exactly as you are, without making demands. You don't do any charity work, don't go through drama with friends, don't sympathize with anything."

Strand's head was pounding, but she could hear that Lynx's words were said in sadness, not anger.

"Sir, let me," Lynx said, and waited for Strand to sit back on the couch.

"You're a wonderful woman. Strand." Lynx held her hands close to Strand's forehead. "But it's buried very deep inside. You've got armor on your armor. That's why it scared you to know how much I cared for you. Then you had to open up to me. And once you *really* do, all kinds of things can happen. And that scares you. If you're not the Strand you used to be, who are you?"

"Things are better."

"No, I'm losing strength, Strand. Every night at the hospital I'm less focused. And they notice."

Strand was chilled to the core. She grabbed Lynx's hand that almost glowed with heat. "I won't let them take you away!"

The next evening Lynx did not work, and they arranged to meet Nelson for dinner at Ruby's. The answer came to them there as they listened to him talking about a tattoo he'd done ten years before: the heart of a lion on the breast of a young woman.

"I logged onto a med library. Finding full-color zoological pictures of internal organs is no easy slide, let me tell you." Enthusiasm was fresh in Nelson's voice. "It was perfect—aorta, ventricles, veins—full color. And she needed it, you know. She was just at a place where she could leave some garbage behind; this was the push she needed. A couple months later, when she came by my place to say thanks, I could see the difference even before she said a word. She was filling out her . . . her self, like she wasn't even there before. I been tattooing ever since."

Strand and Lynx glowed with a frisson of understanding. The tattoo was more than the symbol: it was the essence. In their mutual weaknesses, they could complete each other.

"Strand. Strand?" Nelson's voice was distant and slow as if he were talking through mud. When she opened her eyes the light's glare forced her to close them again quickly.

"Sorry." Nelson moved forward to block the light. "You were a little too still for my tastes, girlfriend."

"I was remembering that night at Ruby's when you told us about the lion heart tattoo." She squinted to see the outline of Nelson's shining head.

"You two got the heart." He clicked off the light. "Okay. You're really doing great. I'm gonna hold up here for now. I'm not spraying your face. You ain't going nowhere, are you?" He laughed as he said it.

After helping Strand up he folded his table and put it in the cornet, cleaned his instruments, wrapped them in cloth, and slid them into the deep pockets of his long coat.

"What time will Lynx be home?"

Strand looked at her watch. "Not 'til much later; she's going off break about now."

"Don't touch anything. Let Lynx work on you when she gets in. Just a little. Not too much."

"Yes, sir."

"Wish I could have that answer on tape. Tomorrow, the hands, 7:00 p.m."

Strand lay on the bed, the animals next to her. She didn't fall asleep until just before Lynx came in, moving quietly through the rooms, feeding the animals, taking a shower, before approaching the bedside. Holding her hands over Strand's face, Lynx worked slowly, first letting the heat build, then releasing the energy. Strand lay still without speaking.

"I can almost see it," Lynx said, "but don't look until later."

"I don't need to look. I can feel it, inside. He finishes tomorrow, he thinks. The hands."

"I know." Lynx took Strand's hands in hers and kissed each finger. She rolled her tongue around them, sucking, tasting, enjoying the way they pressed against the inside of her mouth. The evening in Ruby's seemed very long ago to both of them.

Lynx pressed Strand's hands to her breast, waiting for their heartbeats to return to normal. Then they lay side-by-side until the next afternoon.

Session #146

Nelson set up the table and puttered around the room, unsure how he wanted to proceed, uncertain in a place not his own. He glanced at the drawings of Lynx and Strand pinned to the wall and smiled. He liked his work.

"I'm not worried," Strand said. "Not anymore."

"I didn't think so. Maybe I am. You'll be on the move. I'll have to come out to the boondocks to visit. Ugh!" He shivered in exaggerated distaste.

"Perhaps you know some Partisans you'll be wanting to visit."

"Mebbe, as my great-grandfather used to say."

They both looked around the room, knowing it would be the last time they saw it in quite this way.

"I'm going to have you lie down as usual, since that's how we're used to working. But I'm going to rest your arm on the dining table, okay? He spread towels on the table as he spoke. Strand sipped at the bottle of tranq, then climbed on to the table with a familiarity she was sure she'd miss."

"Nelson."

He looked up from the colors he was mixing.

"I don't know what to say, I guess."

He strapped the needle machine to his hand. "You'll get a package in a couple of days, with information you'll need once you're out of the City. Lynx's mother's farm will be the contact point if you have any problems. But then you'll just keep going west 'til you decide to settle down. Partisans will help."

"Sounds so simple."

"It is and it isn't. And I'll want a postcard."

"I know, I know. It's not just the lack of people on those landscapes, is it? It's the possibilities. Open space, not corrupted, no one trying to sell you something."

"Sounds good to me.

"Then you better come out west."

"And who'll help out the folks back here?"

Strand relaxed, feeling the animals watching from the other side of the room. The machine clicked on.

"You know I've only been mad at you once, all the time we've been friends?"

"Um-hum. No talking now though." Nelson leaned forward and the glare of his light washed over her arm. Strand closed her eyes, remembering the last time Lynx had been hospitalized.

She waited at home for several hours, expecting Lynx to call. She tried the hospital, then Lynx's home. Then she decided to sit and listen as she'd done before, but nothing came through. Since they'd been working on the tattoo they were entwined, inseparable, even when they were on opposite ends of town. Each had become a soft hum in the other's mind, a slight vibration under each other's skin.

Strand didn't understand what was happening. She leaped up from the couch and slammed out of her flat, running toward Nelson's. When she rang the bell she realized it was late, but he buzzed her in without asking who it was.

As she walked in, before she could speak, he said, "I know. She'll be alright."

Something in his voice stopped Strand.

"How can you know that?"

"She should have stopped working earlier. Things are too fragile right now."

"How can you know any of this?"

"Sit down. I'm sorry we didn't talk about this possibility. She just had an episode."

"She slipped." Strand did not sit down.

"Yes, she slipped. Not good, but not totally uncommon. She should not have been doing such deep work while all this is going on."

Strand's eyes narrowed as she looked at her friend. She was increasingly uneasy and not sure why his words weren't comforting. She repeated her question.

———

"You know, don't you. Just like Sliver and Dot know."

Strand stalked across the room. It looked odd without the massage table at its heart. She turned at the kitchen and stared again at Nelson.

"You're one, too!"

His eyes and hands were unnaturally still. Strand noticed.

"You're an empath, too!" Strand almost screamed. "Why were you hiding it—from me?" She twisted around as if looking for something to break, then collapsed against a stool at the counter.

"I've hidden it all my life, Strand. I never wanted to be forced to fight the Society to have a life. Whatever healing I do, I do on my own."

"You've been my friend for how long?" Strand moved in closer. "We've been working on this project for over a year. You couldn't tell me?"

"You won't know what it's like to be owned by the State until we're finished with this project. Even then it'll be a memory, not the life you live every day. Lynx knows. And I saw it happen to my best friend when I was fourteen." Nelson pulled his caftan around him protectively and glanced at his shelves filled with its tiny toys. "We planned to visit all those places that don't exist anymore. Old tourist spots. We figured the vibes would be wondrous. We were inseparable. Finished each other's sentences. Wore each other's clothes. Knew how to comfort each other. I loved him.

"Then E Corps took him away. After that he made one visit back to see his parents—he hardly spoke to them. Or to me, when I showed up. I could feel him struggling to make sense of us, so many other voices and lives were inside him. It was like we were all ghosts in some former life he'd had. Then he split for good.

"It wasn't until he was gone for almost a year that I figured it out. It wasn't just him. It was me, too. Without me, he almost couldn't handle it. I shaved my head so no one would know—and I stay repressed so other empaths can't find me."

"Why couldn't you tell me, once we started working?" Strand could feel the tears of betrayal welling up inside her.

"To explain in words isn't that easy, Strand. I know that's part of what we're supposed to do, that's why they gave us the education, the training. But sometimes words just don't explain anything."

"Does Lynx . . . of course she knows. Doesn't she?"

"When she walked into the class it was like I was knocked off my feet by a gale-force wind. I'd kept everything clamped down, except when I did tattooing. Then I tried to help people, kind of like Lynx does at the hospital. But by the second session she was speaking to me in my head. We both knew we were going to do something wonderful. We weren't sure what, but then you kept asking about her. And she wanted to meet you."

"You two planned this!"

"No. We never planned anything. We felt our way to it. Untangled the mass of confusion and connections, and here we are."

Anger nudged against Strand until she kicked it away. They hadn't tricked her; everything there was to know they'd revealed.

When you're not blocking us out you hear.

Strand heard Nelson's voice in her head. The round tones she'd listened to for hours calmed her now.

"It's really going to work, isn't it?"

"It is working. You made the choice, Strand. A good choice for both of you."

"It's like you're someone else I don't know."

"No, it's just that now you know me better. As my great-grandfather used to say, 'What real queen shows all his cards at once?'"

"Your great-grandfather knew more than any great-grandfather I ever heard of."

"He was queer too! Didn't I ever tell you that story?"

Strand opened her eyes as Nelson sprayed fixative on her hands. The lines of shading on her forearms and the backs of her hands were subtle, even before healing. Nelson watched her face. Her approval pleased him.

"I don't know how much better it could be. I feel like I'm always telling you to relax. But a major ingredient in healing is rest."

"Nelson . . . I love you."

"I knew you could do it. Now let me have one final look."

Strand stepped out of her tunic and pants as Nelson turned the light onto her full body. She stood as still as Lynx had done in their class as Nelson circled her, looking at the lines he'd drawn, the coloring he'd added.

Each joint, fold, wrinkle delicately matched. Lines and perspectives balanced. Colors blended. Strand stood as if she were a grand Maori woman warrior, the worlds inside her mirrored by the fleshly lines. Nelson had never done such an extensive tattoo and was amazed himself by the impact. As he watched, the lines seemed to shift and flow with a life separate from Strand.

"What about the wheels?" Strand said, alarmed as she remembered the bicycle tattoo on her calf.

"Not to worry. We've got it covered."

Strand decided she was done asking questions. Nelson walked around her one last time, then said, "See you on the trail, sister."

"Not before we leave?"

"No. Always." He pulled the table out into the hall, then kissed her forehead.

"I feel like we should say something more."

"We're not saying good-bye."

"In the orphanage, all those people I grew up with—the kids, the counselors—they came and went like lights blinking on and off. They're a blur to me. Even the people I worked with every day at Broadcast, I could barely remember them or their lives when I wasn't in the office. That won't be true with you, Nelson."

"We do get to pick our families, Strand. And we picked. We picked good." He reached out and held his hand in front of her face, almost caressing her cheek. Heat flowed between her healing skin and his palm. He closed his hand and a cool breeze drifted in as he picked up his bag.

Strand listened to the elevator descending, clanging and squealing as usual. But nothing felt usual. Once Nelson was gone, Strand was listless. She'd always been proud that she was going into middle age in good condition. But the past few months had worn her down in ways she couldn't account for. She was determined not to be in bed when Lynx came home this last time. She sat at the dining table and read a book, turning the pages gingerly.

Lynx came in earlier than on previous nights and found Strand asleep with her head down on the table, the book her pillow.

After taking her shower she stood over Strand, admiring the work Nelson had done on her hands. She held her own hands out beside them, and her breath caught. She woke Strand gently.

"I have to show you something."

"Ooh. I'm sorry I fell asleep."

"It's late, of course you're asleep. We'll both be soon. But look." Lynx pivoted on her foot to display her calf. On it was a fresh tattoo—a pennyfarthing that matched Strand's. The large, spoked wheel, delicately connected to the smaller wheel behind, curved with the muscles in her leg.

"When'd he do that?" Strand said, excited. "How'd he do that?"

"Tonight. It was alright! I was fine the whole time!"

Strand was amazed that Lynx could bear the needles long enough for a tattoo even this simple.

"Let's go to bed." Lynx nudged Strand from behind. Her long hair, still wet from the shower, left a string of droplets across the floor, which Dot pounced on.

They lay in bed in silence until Dot and Sliver jumped up on either side of them. They all dropped off to sleep. Strand woke for a moment just before dawn, but Lynx was not in the bed. She tried to hear her in the other rooms. It was silent though, and before Strand could call out, she was asleep again. They both slept through the next day. In the late afternoon Strand got up to close the curtains against the sunlight.

"Are you hungry?" she asked Lynx, who watched her from the bed.

"No. I . . ."

"I'll feed Dot and Sliver." Strand started to leave, then sensed something. "What is it?" Strand couldn't conceal the alarm in her voice.

"I can't move . . . I don't think."

In one leap, Strand was kneeling beside the bed. "What—?" Her voice was strangled with fear. Lynx lay on her back, arms limp by her sides.

"It'll be okay, I think." Lynx's breathing was shallow. "I just . . . remember those old television shows we saw once? They used to take people's molecules apart to transport them somewhere, then put them back together? Remember how we laughed?"

Strand only nodded.

"My skin is prickly, like needles all over. It feels like my molecules are moving. Away from each other."

Strand sucked in her breath, trying to decide what to do.

"Nothing. Let me lie still and see what happens. Go do the food."

Strand reluctantly went out to the kitchen to feed the animals. By the time she returned, Lynx's entropy was dispelled. She'd curled into a ball and was sleeping. Strand crawled in, spooned around her, and the two women slept again into the night. Dot and Sliver didn't join them.

Lynx awoke sometime after midnight, relieved to feel her limbs returned to normal. She got up to look out the window. She pulled the curtains back and let the streetlight shine in, smiling at the pair of shoes hanging from it. Nelson had told her to look for that sign wherever they went.

Lynx turned back to the bed, where a shaft of light from the window spilled over Strand. The new lines on Strand's face were already healed. It was amazing yet natural to Lynx. Strand shifted under the sheet, restless but deeply asleep. As she did, Lynx started in shock. Strand's arm, which lay on top of the sheet, was almost transparent. The wrinkle of the bedding underneath was outlined almost perfectly—through Strand's arm.

Lynx snapped the curtain shut, terrified. She continued to watch Strand, now barely visible in the dark, and took long, slow breaths until her pulse returned to normal. After a few minutes she realized she was too sleepy to stand any longer. Lynx returned to bed, slipped gingerly under the sheet, and was asleep before she could reach out to touch Strand. As she fell more deeply into sleep, their dreams overlapped.

Light lifted from their bodies and swirled around as if on a giant disc. Their light, all the shades of it, spiraled until it blurred. Lynx turned and rustled in the sheets. Strand lay still, her body sapped of strength. Through the night the spiraling and spinning swelled in their dream until it was a sound filling their heads. The whirring grew, engulfing the room. The light that rose from their bodies formed an arc above them that, in turn, was drawn into the spinning colors. Lynx turned onto her back, Strand onto her stomach, then back again. And they dreamed the turning until just before dawn.

They lay facing each other. Lynx opened her eyes first, then Strand. Lynx stretched and rolled onto her back, extending her arms; Strand slipped into her embrace. They explored each other with their eyes closed—hands, mouth, skin—each savoring the feeling of flesh on flesh until they could feel it no longer. The sensations of two became one.

When the sun was full in the sky, beating hard on the closed curtains, Dot and Sliver jumped onto the bed and settled themselves around the sleeping woman.

The doorbell rang at noon. Its insistence was as startling as the sunlight pouring through the bedroom window. Dot and Sliver danced around each other, hungry as usual, and excited to have company. Sliver even gave a small, rare bark.

"Be right there." She struggled into the tunic laying across the chair, grabbed the knit cap from the dresser, and pulled it on.

"Package for Tryna Nelson West," the voice of a messenger called through the door.

"That'll be me," she said as she swung the door open, pulling her clothes down behind her. The messenger, a young woman with bright, eager eyes, grinned as she held out the gaily wrapped package.

"Happy Birthday!" she added.

The woman looked puzzled for a moment until she saw the wrapping. Her hazel eyes widened. "Wait, please." She turned back to the living room and rummaged for a tip.

The messenger watched the woman, whose golden skin seemed to glow. The coloring was puzzling to her—the woman's features seemed African but her skin was tawny and freckled, almost Irish. Her green knit cap was bursting with hair.

"Here we go. I'm sorry to keep you waiting."

"That's okay. Can you sign here?"

"Of course." Tryna Nelson West wrote smoothly, with little flourish, as if she'd been signing her name for years.

"Thank you." Tryna reached out to shake the messenger's hand. The girl responded automatically and was startled by Tryna's electric touch.

"Thanks." Tryna's voice was deep with laughter sparkling behind. The messenger pulled herself back from the hypnotic smile and said thank you as she took the tip Tryna offered. She glanced back over her shoulder as she waited for the elevator, to get one last look at the woman who seemed to be so many things at once.

Tryna closed the door and stretched, trying to recognize her body. It was both familiar and alien, forty and at the same time young. Her squared fingers seemed the most recognizable. She went into the bathroom and gazed in the mirror where she saw colors and characters not blended but annealed. The tattoo lines were gone and each of the women existed whole, inside and beside the other, in one body. Tryna turned and saw on her left calf the freshly drawn pennyfarthing, the only part of the tattoo still healing. *Anywhere you want to go.*

Turning back to the mirror, she pulled the hat from her head with some anxiety. As she dropped it to the floor a flood of pure white dreadlocks fell around her face onto her shoulders. The bathroom light bounced off her shining hair as if in protest of its incandescence.

Tryna smiled into the mirror as she recognized herself. Both parts were there.

"We better get ourselves packed," she said to Dot and Sliver who circled behind her. She walked around the living room, wondering what she'd want to take. She opened Nelson's package, examined the train ticket, map, and new birth certificate. His face looked back at her from a self-portrait done in pencil. It was protected in a plastic sleeve with a handwritten letter she decided to save until she was on the road. She took down a picture of Mae, the drawings of Lynx and Strand, and put them all together in the envelope. She packed it along with some tunics and caps into a duffel bag she found in the closet.

Sliver ran around the bag and Dot tried to crawl inside.

"I'm not going to forget you guys, don't worry. See?" Tryna pulled their two soft carriers from a hook in the closet. The animals leaped and whirled in excitement.

"But first let's eat. I'm starving."

They ran eagerly before Tryna to the kitchen, then sat by their bowls to wait.

Tryna turned off the light in the bathroom; she didn't need to look anymore. *Anywhere you want to go.* She listened to the day around her.

10

READERS OF THE LOST ART

Elisabeth Vonarburg

The Subject presents itself as a block, slightly taller than it is wide, set vertically on a round central stage that is slowly revolving. The color of the block, a very dark green, does not necessarily make one think of stone (it could be plasmoc), especially since it glistens with a strange opalescence under the combined laser beams. Its rough texture and irregular shape, however, tell the audience what the voice of the invisible Announcer, floating over the room, now confirms: the Subject has chosen to appear in a sheath of Labrador amphibolite.

As murmurs go back and forth at a few tables whose patrons are commenting on this strategy, the Operator enters, a silhouette at first glance consisting of reflections from a scattered brightness. All the instruments required for his task, most made of metal, are stuck to his skin under which have been inserted strongly magnetized chips or small plates. The Operator does not wear any clothing except for the armor made up of these tools, all of different shapes and sizes but designed to fit together like the segments of some exoskeleton to the glory of technology. Of course, a black hood fits tightly over his head, though not over his face, which contrasts with the smooth, shiny material and seems like a simple, abstract outline—geometrical planes arbitrarily linked together rather than a recognizable countenance.

The amphitheater falls silent after some scattered, rather condescending applause. Everyone knows there will be no subtlety in the first approach, in accordance with the obvious wishes of the Subject: a direct assault, almost naïve, on the primitive material surrounding it. The Operator circles the block, steps up to it, steps away from it, touches it here and there, then steps back two paces and stands there a few moments with his head lowered. He emerges from his meditation only to take two unsurprising instruments from his tool-armor: a hammer and chisel.

He needs to find the areas of least resistance: briefly returned to its original plasticity through heat and pressure before enclosing the Subject, then cooled, the metamorphic rock provides clues to its schistosities in the infinitely divergent orientations of its amphiboles, as the rounded reflections playing on the surface of a still river reveal to the practiced eye the contours of the bottom, and the twists and turns of the current. The plagioclase opalescence of the material will apparently not delay the operation; a section of rock falls off the block after the first blow is delivered by a sure, firm hand. The Operator is experienced. We will soon get to the heart of the Subject.

In the room, up in the tiers, the alcoves are gradually filling up, the small lamps on the tables are being turned on, and jewels are throwing furtive sparkles. Buyers and merchants sit down, ready after the day's work for work of another sort. With slow elegance, the hostesses parade along the tiers, their eyes falsely distant, like panthers pacing their cages pretending to be unaware that they were long ago torn away from their secret jungle paths. Now and then, a hand is raised, nonchalantly or urgently, and yet another captive goes and sits close to the client whom she will, for the evening, be pleasing.

On the central stage (noiselessly—the floor where the rock fragments fall is covered with a thick elastic carpet), the Operator is almost finished with the first phase and those the show is intended to entertain grant a little discreet applause when a whole section of rock comes off the upper part of the block, indicating finally what is in store for the second phase of the operation. In the deep layer revealed, indistinct masses can barely be seen, a glassy gleam.

The Operator puts the chisel and hammer in the box provided for them. It is a medium-sized box, a declaration of principle that does not escape the seasoned spectators: the Operator is no novice and fully intends to get through the Subject without having to use all his instruments. As usual, the lid only opens one way. The tools that are put in the box cannot be taken out again. If Operators dared to try—something that is unthinkable—they would be immediately electrocuted by the powerful current running through every metal object the instant it is placed in one of the compartments of the box.

A murmur runs through the amphitheater as the Subject is completely extricated from the rock sheath: its crystalline prisms scatter the coherent laser light into myriads of geometric rainbows that both reveal and hide the thickness of the material. The Operator moves away and again circles the Subject to the discreet clickings of his tool-armor (in which the absence of the hammer and chisel has opened two gaps). Meditatively, he paces around the perimeter of the stage. Brute force is no longer enough. Getting close to the Subject by shattering the prisms would be in rare bad taste, and the audience would be right to show its displeasure by pushing the buttons that link its members to the Manager of the establishment. The Operator carefully chooses his next tool, creating a new gap in his tool-armor. A probe, of course.

The probe indicates the expected thickness of the Subject in the second phase, as well as the nodal points, invisible to the naked eye, where the prisms are joined. As this information is displayed holographically above the stage, a few exclamations from the audience reveal the interest of those watching the show. The matter is dense. The prisms are composed of several concentric layers of varying nature, which blend together in several places; their macro-crystals are themselves juxtaposed in complex combinations. They will have to be disassembled one by one unless there are certain nodal points governing the simultaneous unlocking of several elements. This is almost certainly the case, but the information provided by the probe gives no hint of it.

On one of the levels, halfway up the amphitheater, almost all the hostesses have been called. There is only one left. She is a rather tall woman with very white skin wearing a crimson lamé dress that glints stroboscopically with her every movement. Her short hair, cut in a helmet shape and smoothed down over her head, does not shine, quite the contrary. It is so dark that when the woman goes into shadow, that whole part of her head disappears and her face, enigmatically made up in mauve and gold, looks like a floating mask. An attentive observer would notice that this hostess flinches whenever a hand is raised (which activates the communication disk grafted on the forehead of each member of the staff), then relaxes when the hand is lowered (since the client has indicated subvocally whom he is speaking to, thus automatically cutting off the hostess or the waiter from the general network).

One such attentive observer is sitting in one of the alcoves at the edge of the third level. He has wide shoulders, or else his evening jumpsuit hides shoulder pads, but this is not likely, since his torso is long and muscular. The wide, low neck of his suit reveals a very distinct scar that appears to run all the way down his chest. His hands (the only parts other than his torso that are clearly lit by the globe lamp on the table) are strong and square; his fingertips are strangely discolored. Of his head, which is in shadow, the only thing visible is the round shape crowned with a mane of abundant and apparently rebellious hair. The man at last raises his hand. The hostess stops, turns toward the alcove, then, her slightly lowered head floating in the alternations of shadow and light, obeys and steps forward.

Meanwhile, more and more of the audience has turned its attention to the performance taking place on the central stage. A wave of applause mixed with exclamations of appreciative surprise has distracted spectators from their dinners, their bargaining, or their companions. The prisms that surround the Subject have lost their translucence and their rainbows. The laser light has begun to trigger complex molecular reactions on their surfaces. Lines form, shapes and colors merge slowly with one another to reappear in different combinations. There is an implied rhythm, the suggestion of a pattern in the permutations, a hint of an intention in the sequences.

The Operator, who has detached a few instruments from his tool-armor, stops to study this new development. After a while, he places all but two of the instruments in the box, which prohibits him from picking them up again. He has kept a small rubber-headed hammer and a series of suction-cup rings, which he places separately on the fingertips of his right hand, including the thumb. He steps up to the prismatic block and stops again, as though waiting for a signal. All of a sudden, carefully, he positions the hand with the suction-cup rings one finger at a time, on the protruding part of one of the prisms, and with the other hand gives a light tap with the hammer on a point that he seems to have chosen very precisely. Nothing happens. The colored lines and shapes continue rippling across the surface of the prisms. The Operator waits. Suddenly, without the audience being able to see what has triggered his action, he taps the same spot as before, twice, in quick succession.

A piece of the prism as big as a fist breaks off, held by the fingers of the Operator, who then removes the suction cups from it with his other hand, sets the crystal fragment on the floor, picks up his small hammer, and again turns to face the prisms, attentive (the spectators are beginning to understand it) to the enigmatic progression of clues moving just under their surface. The randomness of all the colored movements of the lines and shapes, their nature, their frequency, their combinations, is only apparent. They actually constitute a code marking the location of nodal points where the prisms are joined. A code, or more accurately changing codes—the rhythms have rhythms, the combinations have combinations, and the law (or the laws) governing it all hides, elusively, in those converging metamorphoses.

Some members of the audience, who have understood the rules of the game, turn to making quick electronic speculations on the small terminals built into their tables. Bets are exchanged back and forth. A hum of interest swells, ebbs and swells again with each crystal segment dislodged from the Subject. Even the few clients old enough to have immediately recognized the nature of the proposed entertainment—"reading," a very ancient art form that always experiences sporadic revivals—even they begin taking interest in the show. This will be a memorable performance.

In the alcove she has been called to, the hostess in the crimson lamé dress turns her back to the stage; she is sitting very straight in the low armchair, although it is softly contoured to encourage relaxation. With one hand, she holds in her fingertips the stem of a glass filled with a drink with which she has hardly wet her lips; her other hand, fist closed, is on the arm of the chair. The man seated to her right leans over, takes her closed hand, and gently unfolds the fingers one by one on the table. With this movement, the man's head enters the sphere of light that surrounds the globe lamp. Beneath the unruly hair, his features are strong but without fineness, like a sketch that someone had not bothered finishing. The only features that stand out in detail are the mouth, the thick, sinuous lips strangely bordered with a white line—makeup or a pigmentation—and the eyes, oblique but wide, possibly blue, softened by the light into a very pale grey in which the black iris, extremely dilated, seems to almost fill the eye. It is difficult to attribute an expression to this monolithic whole. Alertness, certainly, but is it inquisitive, cunning, friendly? The man's hand releases the fingers of the hostess, which fold up again between palm and thumb. The woman is surely not even aware of this, for when the index finger of the man taps lightly on her closed fist, she starts, makes a move to hide that hand under the table, and then, with visible effort, places it close to the one holding—too tightly now—the long-stemmed glass. The man lays back in his chair, returning his face to the shadow, and the hostess must assume that he is watching the show, because she also pivots her chair toward the stage below.

The Operator has finished dismantling the first layer of crystals. The general shape of the Subject is easier now to make out: a tapering vertical parallelepiped, much higher than it is wide and of irregular thickness; it narrows toward the bottom, widens, then narrows again at the top. Identical bulges are visible about one-third up its front face and two-thirds up its back face. The same play of lines and shapes moves across the surface of this second crystalline layer. Or at least the same principle is no doubt at work, for although it is hard to say why, one senses that the content of these animated patterns is not quite the same—or completely different, however—as the one from the previous phase. More speed, perhaps, in the transformations? Or rather they flicker with concomitant metamorphoses; the rhythms they follow are subtly out of sync with each other, but when the effort is made to perceive them simultaneously, they constitute a whole whose organic cohesion leaves no doubt.

The Operator seems to hesitate. The rubber-headed hammer hangs above the changing patterns. Then, very gently, it strikes one of the crystals. The block turns dark. The Operator jumps away, dropping the hammer, his hands clamped over his ears, his face twisted in a silent grimace.

There is a burst of applause from the audience (the frequency of the ultrasound was modulated for the Operator alone, which makes their satisfaction all the greater) as the block clears and the lines and colors resume their briefly interrupted progression. The Operator nods several times as he removes the suction-cup rings from his fingers. Then he picks up the small rubber-headed hammer and puts it and the rings in the box.

A murmur of astonishment and excitement greets his next gesture—he detaches several sets of tools from his tool-armor and also deposits them in the box. He now presents an impressive silhouette, dotted irregularly with disparate metal objects between which patches of bare skin can be seen. He detaches another set of rings with smaller suction cups and slips them on his fingertips, right hand and left. He then moves close to the block and attentively observes the shiftings and groupings of the lines. One finger at a time, he places his right hand, then his left, on two widely separated points; the fingers are positioned irregularly, some close together, some half bent, others stretched out and spread wide, no doubt to correspond to strategically placed points that must be touched simultaneously to produce the desired effect.

For an instant, the Operator is motionless. He must be waiting for a precise combination of colors, lines, and shapes, for all of a sudden he can be seen leaning a little against the block, giving a sudden push, and then he steps back holding the section of crystals that he has just detached.

The audience leans forward, the better to see what is revealed of the Subject by the breach thus created. They are disappointed, or surprised, or delighted. It is intensely black, featureless, a simple cutout that reveals neither shape nor volume; it could just as well be a glimpse of the intergalactic void. Only the Operator is close enough to possibly make anything out, but nothing in his behavior indicates what he sees. With his hands held out a few millimeters above the crystalline sheath, he waits for the moment when a new configuration, indiscernible to the audience, will indicate to him that another section of the Subject is offering itself to be broken off.

A conversation has begun between the hostess in the crimson lamé dress and her client. It is not a very animated one. The woman seems as reticent to answer the questions of her interlocutor as he is slow to ask them. And they are perhaps not questions. They may be rambling comments on the performance being staged below. The man and the hostess both seem to be watching it.

The Subject has been almost entirely extracted from its crystalline shell. Totally black—that strangely matte, depthless black that flattens volumes—its shape to come is very clear now: from the front, an elongated diamond standing on its narrowest point; but from the side (it can be seen as the central stage slowly rotates), although it retains the shape of a parallelogram, it will be an asymmetrical one.

Using combined pressure and shearing, the Operator detaches the last crystalline section. Around the Subject, the stage is littered with blocks of all sizes. Slow ripples of transformations still flow over their surfaces. Their inner rhythm is subtly or considerably altered now that their organic link with the Subject has been cut, but their beauty, their fascinating appeal, remains intact—as indicated by the requests that have been flooding the communication network for some time now. What will become of those fragments? Is it possible to obtain them, and at what price? To all these questions, the Manager's answer is the same: all the materials from the performance are the exclusive property of the Artists, who dispose of them as they see fit.

The Operator once more circles the Subject. He takes a device from his tool-armor (almost completely dismantled now) to scan the black block from a distance. The spectators peer at the area above the stage where the holographically retransmitted data will appear. Nothing. The Operator punches hidden keys on the small device and moves to another spot to resume his examinations. Still nothing. He almost shakes the device, stops, and places it in the box, allowing himself a slight shrug. He detaches another device, a sort of stylus connected by several wires thick enough to be fine conduits to an oblong box of which all one side is covered with variously colored keys of different sizes. With perceptible hesitation, he walks up to the block and touches it with the tip of the stylus.

An inarticulate exclamation rises unanimously from the audience. The Operator has been thrown to the floor where he goes into visibly painful convulsions, no doubt caused by an electrical discharge of quite high intensity.

After several minutes, though, he gets up again with some difficulty. He deposits the useless device in the box. After closing the lid, he stands motionless for a moment, one hand on each side of the box, leaning lightly, his head lowered a bit. Those spectators who have been brought opposite him by the rotation of the stage can see that he has his eyes closed, and that a film of sweat glistens on the skin of his face and body (where the tools have been detached). A murmur of satisfaction—not without a certain joyous cruelty—runs through the audience: the Subject is a formidable opponent.

The chair of the hostess in the crimson lamé dress has pivoted; she is no longer watching the show, nor is she looking at her client. He speaks to her from time to time, leaning a little toward her, his face half lit by the globe lamp. One of his hands is wrapped around the arm of his chair. A distinct depression in the soft material shows the force with which he is gripping it. His other hand, however, resting on the table, is slowly, delicately turning the long-stemmed glass, occasionally raising it to his face like a flower to drink. The young woman's face, because she is nearer the table, is fully lighted. She is looking straight ahead without any discernible emotion (except, perhaps, by inference, the desire to be inexpressive). Her eyelids do not blink, her eyes are fixed, enlarged, shining brightly, with a tremulous sparkle that suddenly comes loose and rolls down her right cheek to fall on her collarbone, which is exposed by the low neckline of the lamé dress. The man puts his glass down on the table, very gently. He leans a little closer to the woman and follows the wet trail with the tip of a finger. The woman turns her head away and lowers it toward her other shoulder. The man takes hold of her face—which half disappears in his big hand—to turn it, without brutality but firmly, back toward him.

The Operator begins moving again. Facing the black block—as though it could see him—he removes what remain of his tools from his skin with slow, deliberate movements and lays them down on the floor. He brings his hands to his head and unhooks the fastenings of his hood, which are joined at the top. He is naked now, except for the shell that protects his sexual organs from any unpleasant contact with the tools nearby. He is a tall young man, broad-shouldered and long-bodied. His skin, uniformly smooth and completely lacking in pilosity, is very white. His smooth hair is cut in a helmet shape around the sturdy face, and it appears, perhaps in contrast, excessively dark. When he moves close to the block again, it can be seen that he is almost the same height, just barely shorter. (Perhaps only the flat blackness of the block makes it look taller than the Operator.)

The Operator seems to collect himself (or meditate, or simply take the time to breathe deeply); then he holds out his arms and—to the extent that the shape of the block permits him to do so—he embraces it.

A silent explosion of blackness momentarily blinds the spectators. When they regain their sight, the Operator and the Subject are face-to-face at last, with nothing to separate them.

In the alcove, the chairs of the man and woman are closer together. Resting on the table between the two long-stemmed glasses, the man's hand envelops the woman's. The woman's head is leaning against the man's shoulder. They are both watching the circular stage below.

The Subject now appears in the shape of a naked woman, with golden skin, copper-colored in the light of the lasers, and, like the Operator, completely lacking in pilosity, except for a mid-length, unruly mane, also copper-colored, slanted eyebrows above very black eyes (but this may only be an effect of the lights), and very thick eyelashes. She is the same height as the Operator—though there is no point of reference to estimate their respective heights, now that the black parallelepiped has sublimated. Besides, there is no more time to indulge in such speculations, for the stage changes suddenly, and a surprised exclamation rises from the audience (where almost all the clients now have became spectators).

The Operator and the Subject, both still naked, float above the circular stage, and although no visible barrier indicates the limits of their weightlessness chamber, it is suddenly apparent that what the audience has been seeing since the beginning is not a live performance but a holographic retransmission, perhaps long after the fact. Various movements disturb the spectators after the initial surprise—protests, approval, arguments from one table to the next between tenants of actuality and tenants of virtuality. But all this agitation dissipates quite quickly, for down below, in the weightlessness chamber, the show continues.

A number of tools had remained stuck to the skin of the Operator during the third exploratory phase. He takes them off his skin without using them. He has not been forced to put them in the box and can still use them. There will therefore be a fourth phase for the Subject, now at the discretion of the Operator.

With the Operator's first moves, the coming procedure is made obvious, and the spectators who have not yet understood, by realizing that the performance is recorded, understand now with a shiver of anxious or delighted anticipation: this will be the Great Game.

The Operator first proceeds with removing the nails, regal paths to the skin. Delicate remote-controlled cybernetic pincers alight on either side of each nail on the hands and feet. Small suction cups coated with monomolecular glue are placed on the surface of the nails. An instant of immobility, then the impetus spreads, activating precise movements throughout the system. With a quiet tearing noise, the nails are pulled from the phalangettes, which are invisible under the layer of flesh. Another small suction cup attaches itself to each of the fingers like a mouth, aspirating the blood seeping from the periphery of the nail, in the same movement injecting a local delayed-action analgesic, and then cauterizing the blood vessels. The Subject's scream is cut short.

The Operator, of course, did not scream when his own nails were detached from his fingers. The process is not the same for him since he initiates it—and the subsequent interruption of the blood flow to the injured areas—autonomously by directly manipulating his psychosoma. Moreover, electrical impulses that scramble his analgo-receptor centers are emitted continuously from the outside, though they become weaker as the performance progresses; in the Great Game, speed and precision are literally of vital importance.

With the Subject floating horizontally in front of him, maintained in place by magnetic fields, the Operator now makes the median incision from the top of the sternum to the pubis. The anesthetizing suction cups follow the red line, close behind the scalpel. The Subject's scream is again cut short.

The next incisions must be made rapidly. This is where everything will be decided; the pain increases for the Operator (as the electric scrambling steadily decreases in intensity), while it diminishes for the Subject as area after area is more and more thoroughly anesthetized. The Operator starts with the pubis. The audience leans forward. Will he attempt internal detachment? No, he will leave the most intimate parts of the Subject intact. He makes do with cutting around the labia majora and the anus. (The process takes a little longer, and is therefore more perilous for the Operator when the Subject is of the male sex. The penis is, of course, an exterior organ, which makes the operation obligatory, and its flaccidity creates a problem; an entire traction system is required and it must be adjusted perfectly to permit a quick, precise incision. Psychosomatic control easily solves this problem for the bodies of male Operators.)

The Operator now goes to the other end of the Subject. The head has an abundance of orifices whose outlines must be followed meticulously—the eyes and the mouth especially, for obvious, though different, reasons. The ears, by convention, will be detached with the rest of the skin; the nostrils, also by convention, are always cut along their perimeter. But the eyes and the mouth require special attention. Cutting the eyelids is particularly delicate and there is no room for missteps. As for the mouth, like the genitals of a female Subject and the anus in both sexes, there are two possibilities: either the incision simply follows the line of the lips, or else the miniscalpels risk going inside. There will be no surprises here. The Operator logically chooses the first option.

Up to this point the procedure has been flawless, and the Operator can begin the next phase confidently. The pain has not yet begun to slow him down. Nevertheless, everything is not settled. Besides the extraction operation per se, some separate incisions, more or less important, are still required on the Subject from time to time for the removal of the skin, which must be carried out, if not slowly, at least with caution, if the optimal result is to be obtained.

A cloud of minute machines floats around the Operator. These will carry out the actual removal of the skin, remote-controlled by him; his optical centers receive pictures directly transmitted by cameras built into the micro-scalpels.

Here he has opted for speed, but also difficulty, by moving simultaneously from the periphery to the center (peeling the tips of the fingers and toes like a glove), and from the center to the periphery (lifting the skin from each side of the median incision). Bets are exchanged in the audience on the number of additional incisions that he will have to make.

The man and the woman now watch the show only from time to time. They talk instead, heads close together, punctuating their words with kisses.

The Operator's psychosomatic control has relaxed for the first time. Blood beads along his cuts and where his skin, with a slow but regular movement, is being lifted at the same time as the Subject's. Suction cups stick to him to clean and cauterize (but will not inject, of course, any analgesics). The work of the micromachines, however, continues without any appreciable interruption. The myriads of pincer clips hold the Subject's skin and carefully lift it as the lasers separate the dermis, millimeter by millimeter. (It is important that the five layers of the epidermis be removed intact, basal layer, Malpighian layer, granular layer, clear layer, and horny layer.) There are particularly delicate areas, where the skin is thinner (the inside of the wrists, the armpits, the nipples . . . and of course, in the lower half, the popliteal space, the groin, and, when the Subject is a man, the penis, which is initially treated like a finger. It is necessary to go from the glans to the root, by way of the flap of the foreskin, and to deal with the softness of the scrotum.) The Operator is visibly fighting the pain now. The suction cups stick themselves to him more often, and the removal of the Subject's skin seems to have also slowed down. Once the fingers have been uncovered, the arms and legs are skinned without particular problems for the Subject (and causing the Operator only the difficult, though expected, problem of growing pain). But the linkup of the microscalpels coming from the periphery with those coming from the center takes place with difficulty on the perimeter of the torso. The process is no longer the slow but certain advance of a nearly straight front, as in the beginning (pincer clips above the skin, microscalpels beneath), but a staggered progression, a section here, another farther on. The risks of tearing the tissue are increasing second by second as the machines lose their alignment and stresses are applied to the skin more and more unevenly. Will the Operator forfeit, or will he try to hold out to the extreme limits of consciousness, with all the attendant risks?

The movement of the machines and the removal of the skin is now so slow as to be almost imperceptible. It could even be concluded, after a while, that it has totally stopped. The Operator floats, motionless. Only the movement of the cauterizing suction cups, here and there on his body, shows that he is still conscious. Is he resting, frittering away the precious remaining seconds while the analgesics still have some effect, or, although he is conscious, does he lack the strength to concede? But the suction cups detach themselves from him, putting an end to the spectators' speculations. He is quite unconscious now. He has not been able to get through the Subject.

The Subject, however, in spite of the initial pain, and then the progressive anesthesia, has remained perfectly conscious. With the Operator immobilized, she takes full control of his powers. Now in command of the extraction tools, the Subject can choose to stop or to go on with the initial work—which in this case will continue to be performed on the Operator's body using identical machines that have just appeared in the weightlessness chamber and are obediently awaiting her decision. The machines position themselves on the floating body of the Operator. There is a brief round of satisfied applause from the audience. The Subject will finish the work, guiding the advance of the pincer clips and microlasers over her own body, not only for the linkup taking place all around her torso but also for the extremely delicate skinning of her head.

The Subject, of course, benefits from the results of the Operator's skill and speed. She needs only a few minutes to complete the task (during which the cauterizing suction cups move over the unconscious body of the Operator in the wake of the micro-scalpels and hastily inject him with a powerful mixture of restorative drugs.

The purpose of the injection at the end of the process, for the Subject as for the Operator (but is it still legitimate now to distinguish them in this way?) is to reinforce the skin sufficiently to reduce the risk during the last phase of the operation. After waiting a few minutes for the strengthener to take effect, the Subject extracts herself from her epidermis, slowly and nimbly, helped by the machines. Carried by force fields, the skin floats, tinted with a delicate, pinkish hue by the light of the lasers, not flaccid but as if still inhabited in absentia by the body that has just left it. The Subject swims toward the Operator, an exact, animated anatomical statue in which muscles, tendons, and capillary networks are outlined with gleaming precision (they also hint more clearly, by the patterns finally revealed, at the rigid, solid bone frame that supports them). She now applies herself to extracting him from his skin. Soon the two envelopes float side by side in the weightlessness chamber, like outlines in waiting.

The Operator has regained consciousness. Impossible now to read any expression on his face, but the way he circles the Subject's envelope, then his own, indicates quite clearly his satisfaction with the outcome of the encounter. They were, one could say, worthy of each other. He comes back toward the Subject and speaks some inaudible words to her. They seem to be in agreement and swim together to the skins.

A spectator on the fifth level who is more perceptive than the others begins applauding. Others understand a few seconds later, and soon the rest of the audience does too—through contagion or sudden illumination, impossible to say. In the weightlessness chamber, the Subject is in the process of fitting herself into the Operator's skin, and the Operator (with some difficulty, the proportions not being identical though the sizes are) is wriggling into the Subject's skin.

A series of stationary holograms replaces the hologram of the weightlessness chamber. They show the development of the ultimate phase of the Great Game: the progressive assimilation of the exchanged envelopes through local reabsorption of excess skin and regeneration of missing skin (with the interesting color patterns that result—zones of thin white skin on copper-colored skin, and vice versa). The woman's skin is very white except for these differently pigmented bands; she now has short hair, black and smooth. The young man sports an unruly mane, and its copper color matches almost perfectly the color of his skin, striped here and there with white bands, particularly on the torso, the genitals, and the fingertips.

The circular stage vanishes. The applause continues for a few minutes more, while the voice of the Announcer names the two artists in the performance that has just been viewed. A few exclamations indicate that their names are familiar to several spectators.

For a while, in some alcoves, there's a flurry of speculation about what could have induced the Manager to present a show that is, if memory serves well, already ten years
old. The artists have long since gone on to other destinies and other, more modern,
forms of art. The conversations go on this way for a moment, then drift off as various
other concerns take over. Some clients get up to leave the establishment. The waiters
guide others who have just arrived to vacant alcoves. Some hostesses who are free now
begin to circulate among the audience again, while on the stage another attraction—
holographic or real, it matters little—begins to draw the attention of possible spectators.

    In the alcove on the third level, the man and the woman are also ready to leave. The
occupants of the neighboring table stop them as they go, and speak a few animated
words to them in passing, to which they reply with a smile and a nod. Comcodes are exchanged; then the couple continues on its way up the levels to the exit. For an instant,
in the doorway, the light catches a copper reflection on the hair of the man, a fragmented sparkling from the woman's lamé dress; then the door closes on them, hiding
them from the curiosity of the few other consumers who are perhaps still following with
their eyes, unsure, and who will no doubt never have another chance to learn more
about their identity.

11

THE BLACK.NET.ART ACTIONS: BLACKNESS FOR SALE (2001), THE INTERACTION OF COLOREDS (2002), AND THE PINK OF STEALTH (2003)

Keith + Mendi Obadike

In 2001 we started a suite of Internet works intended to explore the language of color and its relationship to art, the body, and politics. This suite was designed so that it could be engaged as separate modules or interlocking performances. While we had been working online for a few years, this suite of projects was intended to function as a new kind of media-based public performance. *Blackness for Sale* (figure 11.1) was the first project launched in 2001, followed by *The Interaction of Coloreds* (2002) and *The Pink of Stealth* (2003).

We auctioned Keith's Blackness online at http://www.ebay.com. The auction was scheduled to last August 8–18, 2001. After four days, eBay closed the auction due to the "inappropriateness" of the item. After twelve bids, Keith's Blackness reached its peak at $152.50.

Announcement

This heirloom has been in the possession of the Seller for twenty-eight years. Mr. Obadike's Blackness has been used primarily in the United States, and its functionality outside the United States cannot be guaranteed. Buyer will receive a certificate of authenticity.

Benefits and Warnings
Benefits:

1. This Blackness may be used for creating black art.
2. This Blackness may be used for writing critical essays or scholarship about other blacks.
3. This Blackness may be used for making jokes about black people and/or laughing at black humor comfortably. (Option #3 may overlap option #2.)
4. This Blackness may be used for accessing some affirmative action benefits. (Limited time offer. May already be prohibited in some areas.)

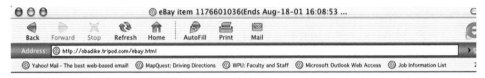

○○○   @ eBay item 1176601036(Ends Aug-18-01 16:08:53 ...

Back   Forward   Stop   Refresh   Home   AutoFill   Print   Mail

Address: @ http://obadike.tripod.com/ebay.html

@ Yahoo! Mail - The best web-based email!   @ MapQuest: Driving Directions   @ WPU: Faculty and Staff   @ Microsoft Outlook Web Access   @ Job Information List

ebaY ®

| **Keith Obadike's Blackness** |
| Item #1176601036 |
| Black Americana |

Fine Art

Currently	**$152.50**	First bid	**$10.00**
Quantity	1	# of bids	12 (bid history) (with emails)
Time left	**6 days, 0 hours +**	Location	**Conceptual Landscape**
		Country	**USA/Hartford**
Started	Aug-8-01 16:08:53 PDT	✉ (mail this auction to a friend)	
Ends	Aug-18-01 16:08:53 PDT	🎁 (request a gift alert)	

Seller (Rating)   **Obadike**
(view comments in seller's Feedback Profile) (view seller's other auctions) (ask seller a question)

High bid   **itsfuntobid**

Watch this
item

Payment   Money Order/Cashiers Checks, COD (collect on delivery), Personal Checks
Shipping   Buyer pays actual shipping charges, Will ship to United States and the following regions: Canada

Update item   **Seller:** If this item has received no bids, you may <u>revise</u> it.
Seller revised this item before first bid.

Seller assumes all responsibility for listing this item. You should contact the seller to resolve any questions before bidding. Auction currency is U.S. dollars ($) unless otherwise noted.

Description

This heirloom has been in the possession of the seller for twenty-eight years. Mr. Obadike's Blackness has been used primarily in the United States and its functionality outside of the US cannot be guaranteed. Buyer will receive a certificate of authenticity. Benefits and Warnings Benefits: 1. This Blackness may be used for creating black art. 2. This Blackness may be used for writing critical essays or scholarship about other blacks. 3. This Blackness may be used for making jokes about black people and/or laughing at black humor comfortably. (Option#3 may overlap with option#2) 4. This Blackness may be used for accessing some affirmative action benefits. (Limited time offer. May already be prohibited in some areas.) 5. This Blackness may be used for dating a black person without fear of public scrutiny. 6. This Blackness may be used for gaining access to exclusive, "high risk" neighborhoods. 7. This Blackness may be used for securing the right to use the terms 'sista', 'brotha', or 'nigga' in reference to black people. (Be sure to have certificate of authenticity on hand when using option 7). 8. This Blackness may be used for instilling fear. 9. This Blackness may be used to augment the blackness of those already black, especially for purposes of playing 'blacker-than-thou'. 10. This Blackness may be used by blacks as a spare (in case your original Blackness is whupped off you.) Warnings: 1. The Seller does not recommend that this Blackness be used during legal proceedings of any sort. 2. The Seller does not recommend that this Blackness be used while seeking employment. 3. The Seller does not recommend that this Blackness be used in the process of making or selling 'serious' art. 4. The Seller does not recommend that this Blackness be used while shopping or writing a personal check. 5. The Seller does not recommend that this Blackness be used while making intellectual claims. 6. The Seller does not recommend that this Blackness be used while voting in the United States or Florida. 7. The Seller does not recommend that this Blackness be used while demanding fairness. 8. The Seller does not recommend that this Blackness be used while demanding. 9. The Seller does not recommend that this Blackness be used in Hollywood. 10. The Seller does not recommend that this Blackness be used by whites looking for a wild weekend. ©Keith Townsend Obadike ###

| Figure 11.1 |

Blackness for Sale (2001). *Source:* http://Obadike.tripod.com/ebay.html.

5. This Blackness may be used for dating a black person without fear of public scrutiny.
6. This Blackness may be used for gaining access to exclusive, "high-risk" neighborhoods.
7. This Blackness may be used for securing the right to use the terms "sista," "brotha," or "nigga" in reference to black people. (Be sure to have certificate of authenticity on hand when using option #7).
8. This Blackness may be used for instilling fear.
9. This Blackness may be used to augment the blackness of those already black, especially for purposes of playing "blacker-than-thou."
10. This Blackness may be used by blacks as a spare (in case your original Blackness is whupped off you).

Warnings:

1. The Seller does not recommend that this Blackness be used during legal proceedings of any sort.
2. The Seller does not recommend that this Blackness be used while seeking employment.
3. The Seller does not recommend that this Blackness be used in the process of making or selling "serious" art.
4. The Seller does not recommend that this Blackness be used while shopping or writing a personal check.
5. The Seller does not recommend that this Blackness be used while making intellectual claims.
6. The Seller does not recommend that this Blackness be used while voting in the United States or Florida.
7. The Seller does not recommend that this Blackness be used while demanding fairness.
8. The Seller does not recommend that this Blackness be used while demanding.
9. The Seller does not recommend that this Blackness be used in Hollywood.
10. The Seller does not recommend that this Blackness be used by whites looking for a wild weekend.

In August 2002 we launched *The Interaction of Coloreds* (figure 11.2), a project commissioned by the Whitney Museum of American Art. *The Interaction of Coloreds* is a conceptual work for audio and the Internet. In many of our projects, we are concerned

@ The Interaction of Coloreds::Keith+Mendi Obadike

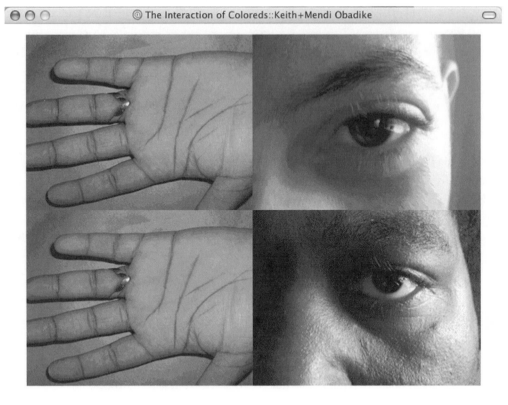

| Figure 11.2 |
The Interaction of Coloreds (2002). *Source:* http://www.blacknetart.com/IOC.html.

with social filters—the systems by which people accept or reject members of a community. For example, how does one apply for membership to an elite social club? We envision this project as a digital brown paper bag test. Brown paper bag tests originated during the centuries of African enslavement in the Americas and were used as a way of separating the light from the dark. At first, the tests were used to determine which Africans would work in the fields and which would work in the masters' houses. Those whose skin was lighter than the brown paper bag were placed indoors. Those whose skin was darker than the brown paper bag were placed outdoors. After slavery this practice was administered by blacks and whites during the process of seeking employment, admission to black colleges, and social clubs. In some form, it is still practiced today.

| Figure 11.3 |
The game *Foxhunt,* from *The Pink of Stealth* (2003). *Source:* http://www.blacknetart.com/pink.html.

In this project, we put the idea of online social filters (such as age checking systems like *Adult Check*) in conversation with the brown paper bag test and the color theories of (*Interaction of Color* author) Josef Albers. *The Interaction of Coloreds* offers participants the opportunity to register for a hexadecimal code by which to identify their skin colors with greater accuracy using current race-based language.

There are three modules to the project:

1. A detailed application form for the skin color hex code including phenotypic descriptions and family histories.
2. A splash page consisting of an animated grid that alludes to Josef Albers's color plates. The images are of parts of our bodies used for racial discernment that have been photographed against a brown paper bag.
3. "Yellow Kitchen," an audio piece about nation and skin color.

The Pink of Stealth (figure 11.3) is a work for the Internet and surround sound DVD. We have long been interested in relationships among language, color, and social position.

In *The Pink of Stealth* we have traced the narrative possibilities of the color pink. Pink is a way of accessing ideas around health, wealth, race, gender, and sexuality. In *The Pink of Stealth*, we tell a story about two characters who attempt to hide something about their identities through different forms of "passing" and whose distinctive qualities are in some way related to pinkness.

There are three modules to the Internet portion of *The Pink of Stealth*.

1. The hypertext Variations: narrative fragments that cycle, revealing nuanced permutations of our story. When the viewer's cursor moves over the text, the missing part of the narrative is revealed.
2. *Foxhunt*: an online game with a hunter, dog, and fox; the game is styled after early Nintendo games but functions quite differently.
3. DVD/Mauve Mix MP3: a piece of music that features electronic mbiras and processed vocals and tells a version, the same story in the hypertext variations. The MP3 (Mauve Mix) featured on the Web is a mono and compressed version of the 5.1 surround sound mix featured on the DVD. The DVD is audio only, but the Web site can be accessed from the main menu of the DVD.

We tell the story as much through text as through artificially created rooms for the voice, positioning, and enhanced speech melody. The hypertext pages are designed to mirror the narrative leaps and vocal spatialization in the sound piece. The online game *Foxhunt* is styled after early home video game systems.

Mapping the Visual and the Virtual

12

EYE CONTACT: FINE MOVING HANDS AND THE FLESH AND BLOOD OF IMAGE FABRICATION IN THE OPERATING THEATERS OF INTERVENTIONAL RADIOLOGY

Christina Lammer

Prologue

"Your dark eyes are still visible," Anna responds to my question of whether she still recognizes me hidden behind a surgery mask and with a cap on (figure 12.1).[1] Anna's aneurysm of her abdominal aorta is being treated in one of the operating theaters of the interventional radiology department at the University Clinic/General Hospital in Vienna. She is already nervously waiting for the image-guided procedures to begin. The proceedings start with a cross-stitch, performed by an anesthetist, which makes the woman's body numb from waist to toes. Usually patients who are being examined and operated in interventional radiology, and whose blood flow is being rendered visible, are fully conscious during these operations that have been described as minimally invasive. They get local anesthesia via injection. Anna's intervention is more complicated—therefore a cross-stitch is appropriate, although she would prefer being under full anesthesia during the intervention.

The mutual connectedness of bodies with digital X-ray technologies builds the focus of my essay. In the particular medical context of interventional radiology, the presence of screens is crucial; because patients are examined from inside out, contrast enhancement makes the texture of vessels and organs transparent on several monitors. But how does the transition of the visceral body into a virtual one, digitally rendered visible in the operating room(s), affect patients and radiological personnel?[2] How is the suture between skin and screen, this rather intimate contact, organized in the radiological practice, and what are possible effects of how persons imagine and sense themselves from inside? I will show that diagnostic and therapeutic methods, as they are indicated for the examination of the blood flow, are invasive. The integrity of the body is deeply touched and transformed through medical practices of objectification. This goes hand in hand with a continual effacement of skin, which renders individual forms of bodily expression impersonal and anonymous. Identities are changed during these operations. Bodies are dressed and skin is entirely covered. Persons are hardly recognizable, because

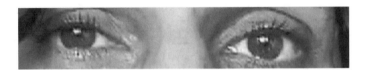

| Figure 12.1 |
The eyes of the radiologist

the markers of identity, like the face or hands, are kept unseen under operating gowns, sheets, masks, and gloves. Similarly, inside the patients' bodies, structures that are not even visible on X-rays are brought to shine forth. This is made possible by fluids, contrast (like barium), wires, and catheters, inserted into the body through artificial orifices. Bodies are radically transformed even before the actual radiological diagnoses and therapies take place. This touches on psychosomatic and existential questions of how procedures understood and explained as minimally invasive are experienced.

I will argue that radiologists, their fine moving hands and highly concentrating eyes, build the core of the aforementioned linkage, connecting the inner flows on the side of patients with manifold screened insights. The data I use partly stem from written notes, from recorded interviews, and from video clips produced by myself during the interventions, which I could observe in the operating theaters. The head of the interventional radiology department, Professor Dr. Johannes Lammer, suggested doing a case study in his domain on how patients experience the operations they have to undergo.[3]

Beneath the Skin

The rooms where these incisions are performed are comparable to surgical operating theaters. The difference is that additional diagnostic equipment such as a movable X-ray tube and several monitors are present. Anna has already taken her position on the small operating table and is covered with surgical cloths. A bottle full of transparent fluid hanging on a metal stand is connected to her blood system through a catheter, which directs the liquid into the arm vessel. A needle was introduced beforehand. On her chest and on one of her fingers, sensors with fine wires are being fixed and link her organism to an apparatus, through which breathing and heart frequencies are displayed on one of three monitors. Bodily functions are transformed into colorful curves and tiny blinking symbols.[4] Through procedures of staging and positioning, Anna's body is being signified as an opaque container. Her skin almost vanishes under sterile cloths and gowns, and is hardly visible during the intervention. Skin as a living sensual organ, according to Horst Ruthrof, implies bodily experiences and a nonverbal vocabulary.[5]

Professor Lammer: I believe keeping my eyes on the screens and working somewhere else with my hands is a pure question of training. It is like moving a mouse in front of the computer. Of course this needs a lot of practice . . . . Most important is to see everything and to keep one's senses open to all, what eventually could go wrong or what lies outside the usual. These skills are relatively difficult to explain. X-ray diagnostics include a certain systematic, which one can describe—how to analyze a picture. In interventional radiology I perceive the image in toto. Similarly, I have to observe how the patient behaves. Is s/he very quiet? Is breathing difficult for her or him? Does s/he start coughing? This is much more complex and I must not only concentrate on the X-ray, but also keep eyes, ears, and antennas open to the patient.[6]

In interventional radiology, the tacit mutuality between radiologist and patient is crucial. The radiologist moves material through millimeter-thin vessels. His or her tactile skills are of enormous importance to the success of the operation. In this respect, skin—touching and being touched—functions as a mediator between patient and doctor (figure 12.2). I experienced the play of hands and eyes, of bodily (human) and technical (nonhuman) parts as highly uncanny. Radiologists find their ways through the blood system of the patient's body mainly with the help of moving fluoroscopy video pictures, which are continually recorded in *real-time*. For this contrast, material components like wires, catheters, and tiny balloons are being introduced and moved through vessels. Physicians do not peer directly into the bodily depths, exploring secrecies beneath the skin, but navigate through interior structures as with a finger on a roadmap, which is projected on video screens. Their gaze is fully concentrated on the information they get from monitors, where the permanently produced moving pictures are projected. However, covered with sterile plastic gloves, hands are in touch with the operating field, connecting the patient's body with abstract image frames. The fingers of the radiologist work as close as necessary to the artificial orifice, where material is being inserted and pulled out of a small bloody opening, which leads directly into the blood system.

According to Michael Taussig, the eye is an organ of tactility, the optical unconscious, which generates a sensual mutuality.[7] How do the eyes and hands of radiologists connect the visceral flows of treated bodies with the information projected on screens? I analyze the chasm of the corporeality in vivo and its pendent in vitro, which is permanently being watched on monitors by radiological personnel as well as occasionally by patients under examination. Unfortunately, Anna cannot see the screens because her position on the table makes this impossible. Her head is covered with surgical cloths and her mouth with an oxygen mask.

Moving X-ray pictures increasingly replace *real* present bodies and similarly create new *virtual* ones. Usually these bodily and sensuous (mainly nonverbal) processes, which

| Figure 12.2 |
The mediated view

I could observe (with my digital video camera) during such operations, are kept unseen. Anna has only a vague idea of what is happening to her. She is unable to look in the direction of the operating area. Her field of vision is shielded through green cloths. Nevertheless, these interventional procedures go literally beneath the skin as well as beyond the screen, thus marking an existing taboo of the body's interior as *being* entirely entered. The chasm of skin and screen—touching and being touched, this contact, which leaves various traces on both sides—is many layered.

Professor Lammer: One has to feel tactile resistance. If moving the catheter forward is becoming more difficult, this is an alarming sign. Can I see anything on the screen?

Like Taussig, I am fascinated by the "magic of *contact*."[8] How does the relatedness of skin, flesh and blood, moving organs, hands, legs, tools, eyes, and digital media occur during the operations performed in interventional radiology? Before Professor Dr. Thomas Rand, another radiologist, shows up in the operating room, the surgical team—for such complicated interventions, a team of radiological personnel works hand in hand with surgeons—has already prepared Anna's abdominal aorta. The imaging procedures can begin.

Beyond the Screen

Professor Rand connects the body under examination and treatment, Anna's abdominal aorta, with the continually projected video pictures on two screens right above his head (figures 12.3 and 12.4). Tools, wires, catheters, balloons, and stents (tiny prostheses that will regulate the blood flow) are "not felt as *separate* from his activity" but have become "a physical and instrumental *extension* of his incarnate being as well as of his

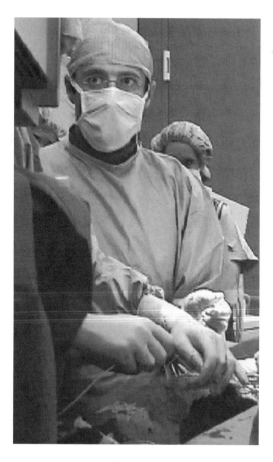

| Figure 12.3 |
Seeing the body through the lens and screen, at the University Clinic/General Hospital, Vienna

ability" to sense alarming signs within the patient's viscera.[9] He self-experiences Anna's body and its inner and outer boundaries like someone who is writing with chalk on a blackboard, like a painter who gets in touch with canvas, and like a filmmaker through his or her camera. "It is seen and *felt* at the *end of the lens*" in real time on screens.[10]

How do processes of staging, unveiling, and framing the body's interior work in interventional radiology? The technical background is that imaging devices are all equipped with a digital subtraction angiography. This technique lays an X-ray picture of the body region under examination, of Anna's abdominal aorta, behind the image after the insertion of contrast through a catheter (figure 12.5). In addition, the developed

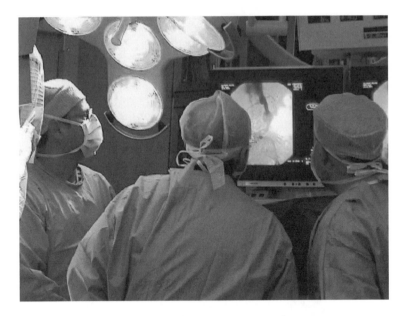

| Figure 12.4 |
An additional view of the operating theater, University Clinic / General Hospital, Vienna

frames are transformed into a digital matrix, and the computer subtracts the picture without contrast from the contrast-enhanced one. The final screenings are the result of further image transformation: pictures particularly contain this kind of information, which was not available before the injection of contrast. Through this method, computed photos are looked at during the intervention and also afterward in the form of animated film sequences. As the images provide an interior orientation, navigating through Anna's body is made possible. Her blood vessels can be explored on monitors like roads on a map. Damaged tissue is being repaired and the prosthesis (in two parts) can be inserted. Decisions about immediate therapeutic interventions are informed by digital moving images on the screens in front of the operating radiologist and his or her assistants. Produced radioscopy film scenes are not spectacular, but highly abstract. Without any explanation of experts, laypersons would not be able to recognize anything.

Professor Lammer: Some of the patients don't want to see the pictures. They don't want to know anything. They are completely encapsulated, letting the hours go by in the hopes that everything goes well. Some are interested and want to look on. Most of them can see something, but don't understand what's going on.

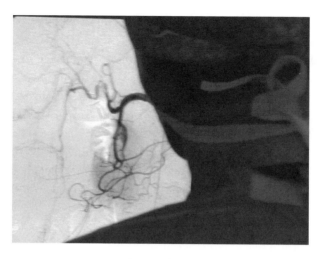

| Figure 12.5 |
Anna's aneurysm of her abdominal aorta

The diagnostic setting includes different narrative and visual levels. One has to think in cinematic terms, although I suggest a more body-centered approach in which "haptic images can give the impression of seeing for the first time, gradually discovering what is in the image rather than coming to the image already knowing what it is."[11] Touching and being touched by radioscopy pictures function in similar ways. The eyes drop into the flow on the screen's surface where the existence of objects is hardly attested.

Anna allowed me to videotape her during the intervention. I accurately explained to her what my research is about and why recording patients is of great importance for the later results. She reacted understandingly, and it turned out that she was grateful for my presence before, during, and after her operation. We immediately had a close and personal relationship with each other, caused by this particular setting at the clinic and partly by her anxiety. I realized that being in a hospital causes transformations in how people normally behave, act, communicate, and articulate themselves. Life in such an institution has its specific rules, which are followed depending on the role one has to play.[12]

One and a half days after the procedure, which lasted four hours and was pretty exhausting for her, I visited Anna at her bedside. She had to stay in the hospital for several more days. She was very happy to see me and told me private stories about her family and her husband, who died some years ago. This changed her life completely. Of course I asked her how she felt. "Still not very well." She took my hand and I felt that she was feverish and sweaty. "You are my angel," she said. This intensive contact with her touched me a lot, and I recognized that there is something missing during such clinical modes of treatment and examination: seeing the patient and the physician(s) as persons. Their mutual although distanced relationship is tightly connected to a sort of *contract*, a standardized form, which both of them sign one day before the procedures take place: Anna has to permit her body to be operated on, manipulated, palpated, examined, detailed, visualized in toto, and treated by radiological and (surgical) personnel. Professor Lammer (or another responsible radiologist) has to prove that he and his team will be doing a good job, with the aim of solving (life-threatening) problems the aneurysm could cause in the (near) future. Additionally, he has to inform her about possible risks. Ultimately, the physician takes full responsibility for the person who will be operated on by him or her.

I became more and more interested in personal narratives from the perspective of patients as well as from that of radiological personnel—in what is being expressed and experienced bodily and sensuously—and I included this in my research data. Paradoxically working with a camera and using more visual ethnographic methods enables me to look beneath the existing *visual regime* in radiology, analyzing manifold layers of contact and focusing on the intimate chasm of bodies, material components, technologies, screens, and moving fluoroscopy pictures. Radiologists have no problem with my video-supported observations of their daily routines. On the contrary, they are curious about my questions, explain what they are doing (if the operations are not too complicated), and integrate me—as an observer—in the team. Dealing with (digital) visual media, developing a standardized language of signs, is their everyday business. My use of a digital video camera is not even surprising for my informants; it is pretty normal and fully accepted. The radiological team is supportive and when I have technical questions, physicians as well as assistants try to solve them with me.

According to Laura Marks, who in her book *The Skin of the Film* (2000) describes *mimesis* as a form of "tactile epistemology": "Tactile epistemologies conceive of knowledge as something gained not on the model of vision but through physical contact. . . . Mimesis, in which one calls up the presence of the other materiality, is an indexical, rather than iconic, relation of similarity."[13] What one can see on screens—on moving fluoroscopy pictures—is deeply informed by the sense of touch and by other sensuous experiences on the side of patients as well as radiologists (figure 12.6). Bodies rub against each other within the clinical high-tech environment. Space and time play important roles in how the choreography in the operating rooms functions, how the skin of actively moving, living bodies almost disappears, how inner structures are recorded and screened on radiographic filmstrips. The setting in radioscopy theaters includes manifold technical devices through which the visceral body is being framed. Bruno La-

| Figure 12.6 |
Tactile tools

tour writes, referring to Martin Heidegger: "Man—there is no Woman in Heidegger—is possessed by technology, and it is a complete illusion to believe that we can master it. We are, on the contrary, framed by this *Gestell*, which is one way in which Being is unveiled."[14] The technical gaze of radioscopy transcends the skin, exploring and displaying vessels and inner structures without touching the body surface. Palpating and being palpated in the operating sceneries of interventional radiology, looking and being looked at, perceiving images of the body's inside and being perceived, signifies multilayered details of the sociocultural fabrication and mediation of the interior of flesh and blood in our contemporary medical context.

Epilogue

With my analysis I unfold nonverbal skills and interactions among radiological personnel, patients, and technical devices. The boundaries between objectifying and being objectified, making up and being made up, touching and being touched, unveiling and being unveiled, framing and being cinematically framed on screens, tend to melt into one another in the diagnostic as well as therapeutic operating theaters. Processes of cutting or stitching into bodies and visual operations of cut and paste form new "outfits" (figure 12.7).

I understand the continual invention of new technologies in surgery as well as in radiology—like computer programs that can simulate the body's interior or robotic limbs that are able to operate inside a living individual—as a *cultural* and *epistemic* turn in medicine, which is already far advanced. Flows of the visceral body are transformed into picture frames on screens, which are read independent of the patient and his or her

| Figure 12.7 |
Bodies, framed and touched

experiences. Radiologists literally embody the cinematic information they get from the images. For the patient on the operating table, and for nonspecialists like me, the screened maps are mainly abstract. Nevertheless, one is touched by these particular cinematic impressions in radioscopy. I will never forget the uncanny cross-fades. I have incorporated them.

Acknowledgments

I am indebted to Professor Dr. Johannes Lammer and Professor Dr. Peter Pokieser, both radiologists in leading positions at the University Clinic/General Hospital in Vienna, who offered me all the support I needed during fieldwork. I also wish to acknowledge the patients and radiological personnel for their cooperation. Without them, my research would have been impossible. Thank you! This chapter is based on an article that is part of a broad research project, which has been funded by the Austrian Science Foundation (FWF) with a Hertha Firnberg-Award (2000). The article first appeared in *Screens, ETNOFOOR, antropologisch tijdschrift* (Amsterdam) 15 (1/2). Copyright © 2002. Reprinted with the kind permission of the editors: Yolanda van Ede, Rob van Ginkel, Suzanne Kuik, Birgit Meyer, Mattijs van de Port, Irene Stengs, Alex Strating, Milena Veenis, and Christina Lammer.

Notes

1. Anna is not the real name of the patient. I made it up so as to maintain her anonymity. This woman, in her eighties, was the first patient with whom I worked intensively in interventional radiology (in April 2002). At that point, I used my video camera in this department, where I was doing fieldwork among radiological personnel and patients, for six women and for six men during their operations. Anna was one of them. At the

time of writing this chapter, I had spent about twelve weeks in interventional radiology, observing highly complex procedures of diagnosis and therapy.

2. See Lammer, *Die Puppe*, 143; Lammer, *Digital Anatomy*, 13; Lammer, "Patient Bodies," 90–107.

3. We are not related by blood. I met Professor Dr. Johannes Lammer for the first time at the clinic (in 2001) to ask him whether collaboration would be possible.

4. Spiess, "Vom klinischen Blick zum digitalisierten Abbild," 125–137.

5. Ruthrof, *Body in Language*, 77.

6. Interview with Professor Lammer excerpt (September 2001), translation mine.

7. Taussig, *Mimesis and Alterity*, 20.

8. Taussig, *Mimesis and Alterity*, 21.

9. Sobchack, *The Address of the Eye*, 177.

10. Sobchack, *The Address of the Eye*, 175

11. Marks, *The Skin of the Film*, 178.

12. Goffman, *Wir Alle Spielen Theater.*

13. Marks, *The Skin of the Film*, 138.

14. Latour, *Pandora's Hope*, 176.

Works Cited

Goffman, Erving. *Wir Alle Spielen Theater: Die Selbstdarstellung im Alltag.* Munich: Piper, [1959] 1983.

Lammer, Christina. *Die Puppe: Eine Anatomie des Blicks.* Vienna: Turia + Kant, 1999.

Lammer, Christina. *Digital Anatomy.* Vienna: Turia + Kant, 2001.

Lammer, Christina. "Patient Bodies." In *Medische Antropologie. Tijdschrift over Gezondheid en Cultuur* 14, no. 1 (2002): 90–107. Ed. E. van Dongen and S. van der Geest.

Latour, Bruno. *Pandora's Hope.* Cambridge, MA: Harvard University Press,1999.

Marks, Laura. *The Skin of the Film.* Durham, NC: Duke University Press, 2000.

Ruthrof, Horst. *Body in Language.* London and New York: Cassell, 2000.

Sobchack, Vivian. *The Address of the Eye: A Phenomenology of Film Experience.* Princeton: Princeton University Press, 1992.

Spiess, Klaus. "Vom klinischen Blick zum digitalisierten Abbild." *Psychosozial* 24 (2001): 125–137.

Taussig, Michael. *Mimesis and Alterity: A Particular History of the Senses.* New York and London: Routledge, 1993.

13

SEMINAL SPACE: GETTING UNDER THE DIGITAL SKIN

Alicia Imperiale

Mapping the Living Body: Artistic Strategies

The human body is extraordinarily complex. The skin is not a straightforward simple surface that covers our interiority. Rather, the skin is an organ, divided internally into differentiated and interpenetrating strata. The skin or the surface of the body is a surface of maximum interface and intensity, a space of flux, of oscillating conditions. The "surface" is more slippery than it might first appear. Questions regarding the surface of the body, it turns out, are not superficial, but quite profound. By its very nature, a surface is in an unstable condition. For where are its boundaries? What is its status? Is it exterior or interior or both? The skin is a surface that is continuous in its depth and slips from outside to inside in a continuous surface.[1] What does this mean for us in terms of mapping? How can we move past the surface of the body to the hidden depths of the body's interior?

In order to visualize the somatic, new developments in digital cartographic and imaging techniques used by geographers and other scientific disciplines are coming into play. These digital techniques permit us to visualize the complexity of the body in new representational modes. Artists are at the cutting edge of finding where these slippages occur. By customizing diverse software packages, artists are able to put them to uses that were not previously anticipated. This lifting, borrowing, or crossing of disciplines is endemic to artistic practice. This reciprocity between applied science and artistic musings has opened up new channels of communication among vastly separated disciplines. One could say that this kind of interdisciplinarity is symptomatic of our times. The digital has lead to the breakdown between previously separate analog disciplines that are now coordinated in the seamless communication of zeros and ones. While Leonardo da Vinci only imagined the depth behind the surface of the body, contemporary digital scanning and mapping techniques reveal the hidden depths and relations behind the surface of the earth or the body. These scanning techniques are used by artists to not only document the existing (cell, body, landscape, world), but to allow for the reconstitution and recombinative possibilities afforded by working within the projective space of the digital. It permits artists to take from the world as we know it to propose new bodies, new worlds, new ways of seeing—all in the fluid, slippery, seamless space of the computer.

Our bodies are, on the surface, so smooth, so simple. Our facial features, which make up our "identity," are the most complex aspects of our body's surface. Our relatively simple surface covers our complex interior. Our hides hide our complexity.[2] Look within—our surface simplicity is betrayed by internal complexity. Lymphatic systems, renal, sanguine, digestive, neural systems are complex parallel labyrinths, layered one upon the other. These separate yet coordinated systems are compressed into the most compressed of spaces. Our bodies are astoundingly asymmetrical, astoundingly complex, and efficient. One may imagine the body as a series of separate systems, with each system vying for maximum singularity in its complexity. The body is a layered, four-dimensional labyrinth that moves seamlessly from the interior to the exterior. The body evades our attempts to describe it—representationally. It is only by a complex understanding of mapping that we can begin to grasp and visualize this complexity.

How do we, from childhood on, inhabit, pierce, penetrate, visualize, see, and touch the voids that pierce and make up our opacity, our corporeality? This is an elusive endeavor. The body's smooth surface hides blind passages that evade our conceptual grasp—they are perhaps only understood in the most visceral, corporeal way. We can touch it. This privileges the haptic, the somatic boundary, over the visual or the representational. Artist Mona Hatoum, in her video installation *Corps étranger*, brings another dimension to mapping the human body, *her* body. This installation touches on issues of privacy, territory, and gender. Hatoum had a tiny endoscopic camera (a kind of foreign body) inserted into her body, and the resulting video shows the travels (in full color) through the terrain of her body: smooth and rough, wet and dry, spacious and constricted. This trajectory through her body places the act of mapping in the line itself, the line that the camera routes through the thickness of her body. The video was then projected onto a circular screen placed horizontally at floor level within a cylindrical enclosed space, itself an interior body.

Tim Hawkinson begins with the surface of his body and, through a series of cuts, translates that surface into a series of trajectories, by which he is able to propose new body surfaces. In his works, *Skin Spin* and *Lingum*, Hawkinson casts his entire body in latex. He then translates the complex surface by cutting the latex cast into a series of strips (lines). He uses these strips as a roller to create the striations of the final print in ink on paper. In *Taper*, a tapering self-portrait, the artist maps his body from his fingertip out. He imagines a gridded surface thrown over his body and uses this grid as a way to measure distortion in the cartographic surface in relation to the tip of his finger as origin point. His map diminishes in size as the portion of the body is further away from this point. Hawkinson, using analog means, sets the tone for the digital work of Lilla LoCurto and Bill Outcault. Hawkinson translates the surface of the body into a potentially infinite series of recombinations, much as LoCurto and Outcault do in their self-portraits.

LoCurto and Outcault employ a full-body scanner to capture the surfaces of their bodies. The laser scanner is in fact a line that passes on and over the contours of the surface of their bodies to create a map of pure digital data. The artists are then able to manipulate this information in infinite variations. LoCurto and Outcault have worked with a team of mathematicians to develop complex cartography software that permits them to project the data into a series of flat map projections that are photographic self-portraits (figure 13.1).

In a parallel body of work developed from the same digitally scanned data, LoCurto and Outcault have worked to develop a unique software interface that enables them to take the complex information from the body scan and break down the information into a series of horizontal lines that describe the outer contour of the body. These drawings are topographical explorations of the surface of the body. The flexibility afforded by working in digital space permits the artists to display the information from any point of view. The layers are separated out and become a series of glyphs or marks that seem to describe a new typographic font. Most recently, they have developed a digital interface that animates the contour lines. In this piece, there is a constant movement between the contour lines, as lines, and a movement toward building up the lines, layer by layer to recreate the surface of their scanned bodies. The digital has permitted the artists to create constantly changing maps that navigate the complexity of their skin, their surface (figure 13.2).

A common theme for all four artists is the elusiveness of mapping the skin and the body. This seemingly simple task is complicated by the inability to point to the boundary where the body's surface ends and where its interior begins. As the artists map their bodies, there is a process of movement from surface to depth, a movement from line to surface, and back again. What we see most strikingly in the work of LoCurto and Outcault is that the digital liberates the act of mapping in a profound way. The surface is translated into a flexible network of points that can be combined in infinite ways in movement and through time. Beginning with the work of Hatoum and ending with the work of LoCurto and Outcault, we see the artists working with dynamic lines and dynamic constellations of information. Gilles Deleuze develops an idea about dynamic

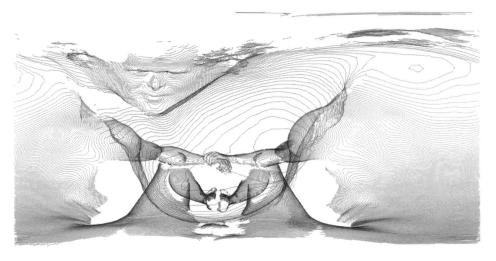

| Figure 13.1 |
LoCurto and Outcault, *Topography*

mapping that is useful in expanding our notion of the virtual in the act of mapping. We might think of a map as a registration of "dynamic trajectories" that in turn open up and initiate other trajectories. The notion of dynamic trajectories and its parallel, maps of "intensities," is how Deleuze breaks down the potential of maps: "Maps should not be understood only in extension, in relation to a space constituted by trajectories. There are also maps of intensity, of density, that are concerned with what fills space, what subtends the trajectory."[3] This is a compelling idea that seems to be investigated intuitively in the movement from line to surface in these artists' works.

There is, in the act of making a map and in the act of reading a map, a very strong sense of the interdependence of the real and the imagined. Pierre Lévy, in his work *Becoming Virtual: Reality in the Digital Age*, provides us with a road map, if you will, to negotiate the notion of virtuality and its impact on mapping. He focuses on the Latin root *virtualis*, meaning "strength" or "power," to emphasize that the virtual has potential rather than actual existence and that the virtual "tends towards actualization without concretization."[4] Lévy states that the virtual follows a line that ruptures classical ideas of space and time. Things can exist in parallel and "distributive systems."[5] If space and time are no longer coexistent, then the act of mapping can be liberated from these constraints. Synchronic events that occur in diverse (or nonexistent) places can be related and mapped. The events can be shown as a network of relations. This is what we see in

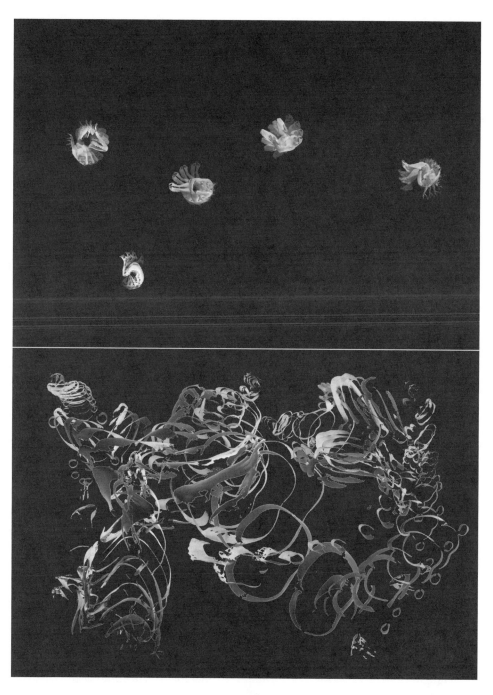

| **Figure 13.2** |
LoCurto and Outcault, sculptural forms

parametric design, in point clouds, or very simply in the distribution of digital information that is generated when a physical object is scanned. The digital information can then be reconfigured in new and ever-changing combinations. The potential for infinite combinations is the virtual in mapping. We might say that to map is to document the existence of real phenomena, but it is perhaps more correct to say that to map is to write, to negotiate, to travel, to narrate without a fixed conclusion. We must acknowledge that to map is to work with the idea of continual flux. A map's reading is never the same.

Architecture and the Metaphor of Skin

Architects are deeply influenced by the new emphasis on surface and skin. In the early twentieth century, it was the task of modernism to convey the tension between deep space and the surface of architecture, often through the use of glass and other transparent surfaces.[6] This set up a dialectical division between the interior and exterior of the building. Today, some architects compress allusions to the depth of the interior into the surface or skin of the building by using skins, layers, shells, and wraps in their architecture. Exterior skins of buildings are built up through layers of veiling, translucent materials or are inscribed with figurative imagery, denoting what might lie behind the surface. Skin is in a constant state of evolution—shedding itself and regenerating itself. The living skin varies dramatically as it adapts to the exigencies of the body—thick where the skeleton needs some padding to soften contact, hardened in response to friction. If eyelids were opaque, we would lose a critical mechanism in the waking up process. The skin of architecture can also be highly differentiated. Skin in a building can peel away or be built up as a series of differentiated masks and layers. There is not a definite exterior or interior to the building, but a gradual movement from outside to inside through the ensemble of inflected parts.

With the increased use of digital computation in architecture, the issue of skin has been magnified. Contemporary architecture is now intensely engaged with digital processes and their overlap with biological models for the production and organization of form. Over the past decade, significant digital research has emphasized the development of smooth, voluptuous architectural objects with attention to topological surfaces and skins. Smooth exchanges, flows, continuousness, performative surfaces, skins, membranes—these concepts have suffused contemporary culture. They signal a dramatic shift in the problematic relationship between "bodies" and technology.

The design tools used in film, architecture, and product design have amplified and accelerated our ability to represent the collapse of nature into technology. Digital 3-D modeling software uses algorithmic formulas to generate form in a kind of autocatalytic system that resembles genetic mutation. Digital technologies that were once used to image an already existing opaque object have been appropriated by designers to project new bodies, new spaces, and new architectures. Forms designed within the space of the computer are analogous to bodies moving in time. The design of smooth form has been facilitated by architects' access to time-based NURBS (Non-Uniform Rational Bézier Spline) modeling software such as *Alias* and *Maya*,[7] which allow designers to create new "bodies" and to work with complex curvatures in real time.[8] Algorithmic formulas allow the lines and surfaces to be adjusted and recalculated continuously. A line, or a surface, "flows" between different weights and forces. A surface is created by the buildup of these splines, and the curved surface is constantly recalculated in relation to these points. Although the spline points are located in three-dimensional space, we can switch to working on the surface. New surfaces are embedded and developed in relation to the existing one. Similarly, the geometry itself is defined relative to the surface. If we change scale in a part of the surface, the entire surface is rescaled and recalculated. NURBS programs are based on an inherently dynamic system: surfaces and objects are developed in a shifting relation to a surface. Rather than conceiving of form as a static condition, the new 3-D modeling software programs allow the designer to work on a form that is constantly evolving, smoothly registering the continuously changing algorithmic parameters in 3-D topological[9] surfaces before the designer's eye and through the designer's intervention. When using NURBS-based software, we design surfaces and create an object by connecting one surface to another. The surface, skin, and interface of architecture are emphasized.

The use of digital technologies has had a liberating effect on architectural form. Architects have been able to design organic, body-like architectures that register the infinite variations and mutations from its evolutionary growth stage in topological surfaces. These sinuous curvatures and warped surfaces wrap around the inhabitant like a second skin. What results is an emphasis on the intimate interface between technology and the living body. It is as if the terror of the technological is softened through smooth contours between our hands and the objects we use and the architectures and urban surfaces that surround us. This smoothing between the inhabitant and the architecture, between the object and the user, the landscape and building, is symptomatic of our time. As the smoothing reduces our sense of terror of the technological, other issues are raised.

In computation, a smooth surface is mathematically smooth; however, in visualizing smoothness, a curved surface must be broken down into polygonal figures. Paradoxically, the smoother an object appears, the more the surface is broken into smaller and smaller units. A digitally produced form is made up of smaller units of NURBS primitives: predefined curves, shapes, and surfaces. In the animation program *Maya*, these NURBS primitives are the sphere, cube, cylinder, cone, plane, torus, circle, and square. These forms are then made up of a mesh or underlying wire frame. The mesh is made up of faces, edges, and vertices that help define the shape of the object and can each be manipulated individually in order to give the designer precise control over the design of the object. As a designer works with these forms in an animation program, the mesh is in constant agitation, pulsating and throbbing. The mesh alternates between projections and invaginations, in a continual oscillation between projective and receptive form. The surface simultaneously penetrates and yields to penetration. Does this speak to the relationship between form and space or matter and pneuma as being copresent?

In order to visualize the final form, the designer can add a skin over the mesh, ascribing material qualities and lighting effects. The final effect is the glossy, sexy final form. We must question the issue of the intersection of the grid and the erotic body. A grid or mesh allows us to map space. A grid speaks of extensivity, endlessness, sameness, and the potential to calculate and define the indefinable. Could the grid, when laid over the smooth contours of a body, shape and discipline the unruliness of the growth of form? The grid monitors. The grid disciplines. The grid imposes a phylum on a growing ontology. The grid seeks relationships. The grid enmeshes the instrumental into the social. The mesh seeks networks of relationships on the surface of the moving and dynamically growing "digital flesh."

There is an ambiguity in our attraction to these forms that exhibit qualities of being simultaneously male and female (gender + n). Is attraction, is the erotic, is the sexual tied into questions of the digital skin? Are these objects ersatz stand-ins for ourselves and our sexuality?[10] Is attraction necessarily tied into reproduction? What models of reproduction may we look to in order to shed light on to these questions in relation to the evolution of architectural form? Can we conceive of the production of architectural form as no longer tied into dichotomous binaries (skin vs. structure, receptive vs. projective, inseminator vs. inseminated . . .)? How can the bridging of traditional categories of heterosexuality, homosexuality, or transsexuality be superceded in a model of architectural engendering?

Architect Greg Lynn addressed the issue of a networked skin in his project for *Embryologic Housing* (figure 13.3). This is a morphodynamic approach in which dynamic processes act upon a form and promote infinite change. Lynn's project proposes a prefabricated housing prototype that consists of a networked skin composed of over three thousand individual panels. Because the system is networked, any change in any part of the system is registered in other parts of the skin (figure 13.4).

The surfaces are designed with 3-D modeling software to attain a fluid form. Study models and the full-scale panels are manufactured utilizing computer-controlled milling and cutting machinery with the same digital data. This coordinated design and

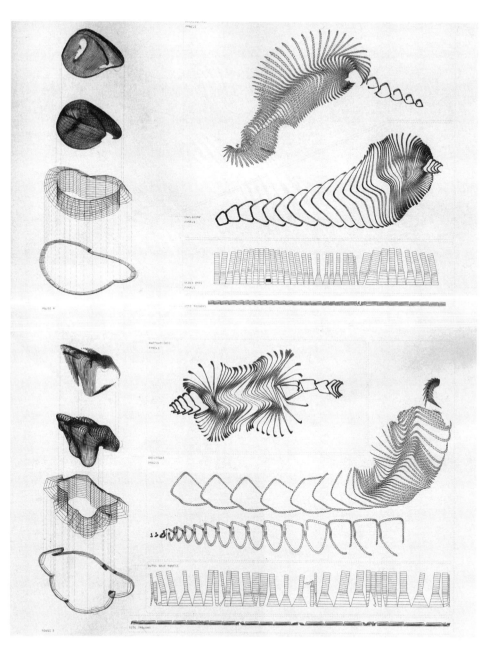

| Figure 13.3 |
Lynn, *Embryologic House* drawings

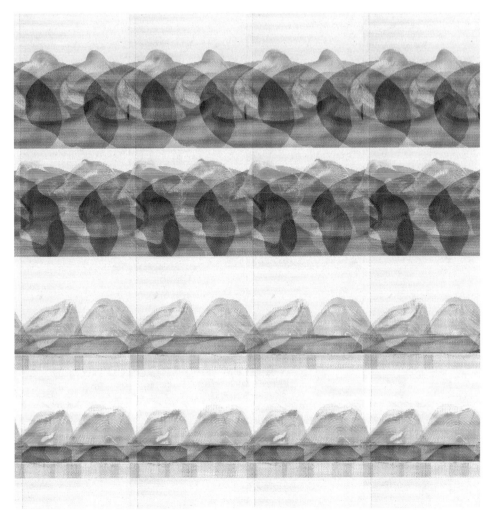

| Figure 13.4 |
Lynn, *Embryologic House* drawings

manufacturing system has the advantage of generating maximum differentiation in the simple configuration of the surface, since a real skin would deform and change in an animate body—a theme also evident in his design for the Eyebeam headquarters. The internal organs of the body push to the surface of the body's skin.

José Salinas investigates the creation of synthetic architectural bodies that are reactive to external forces. His first approach in the project *Topological Diagrams* is to start with a simple 3-D volumetric form or geometric primitive and apply external forces in order to have the form mutate and develop its constantly changing and unique topology. His second approach is in the *Hermeneutic Topologies* sequence that shows the formation of a synthetic body through the process of applying external fields of forces to a flat surface. In the evolution of the flat surface to the skin and volume of the form, the attribution of the character of the synthetic body occurs. Salinas believes that this body is developed through an asexual processing of information and that the body is constructed through machinist operations. The form is not gendered in its evolution, nor is it after its completion. It is an interesting point that could be further developed as it pertains to the evolution and eventual deterioration of bodies and form.

These projects point to a departure from the metaphors of smoothness and organic shapes as merely representations of the biological to a development of architecture through processes that are fundamentally more biological. Architects work with raw computational power to evolve "self-generating" architectural scenarios. This has led to a move away from the interest in smooth surfaces with an emphasis on the interaction of individual cellular elements. It is essential to note, however, that the smooth and the discrete are merely understood at the level of scale. This is especially the case in architecture. In a smooth model of skin, at the level of the glossy rendered image, the architecture is luminous, luscious, reflective, and absolutely seamless—just like bodies. But architecture is made of smaller discrete units that must come together to make surfaces. We can think of the skin as a parametric system that is continuous in the change from one area to another but also discrete because it is made up of individual cells or elements. If we are to map the surface or skin (of a body) in detail, then we must engage the discrete and cellular phenomena that produce it. At the same time, if we are to appreciate what these phenomena produce, then we must reengage the topological identities that emerge from them. What are the ways by which architecture can engage this copresence of the smooth and the discrete?[11]

Genetic Algorithms and the Evolution of Architectural Skins

So much of the digital project in architecture has emphasized smoothness, continuity, and flow. At the same time, there would be no "digital" without the principle of discreteness. It is through a model of discreteness that architectural rules and forms evolve. Genetics is based upon a similar premise, where information is contained in small units of code that are syntactically connected and interrelated through combinatorial rules. Sherry Turkle spells out a history of artificial life scenarios that have been influential in recent work in rule-based computation in architectural design. In 1954 mathematician John von Neumann began to speculate on a machine that could self-replicate, inspired by Alan Turing's "universal Turing machine." Von Neumann imagined the creation of artificial creatures that would have the genetic code necessary to replicate. Turkle believes that von Neumann's ideas were instrumental in anticipating the discovery of DNA. She states that as a model of artificial life, "life was grounded not only in information but in complexity."[12] Von Neumann sensed that once a certain critical mass of complexity was reached, objects would reproduce in an open-ended fashion, evolving by parenting more complicated objects than themselves." She discusses his design of the first cellular automaton:

It contained a cell structure embedded on a grid and a rule table that told each individual cell how to change its state in reference to its state and those of its neighbors. As time went on, the original cell structure transformed its neighboring cells into the states that had made it up originally. In other words, the original cell structure (or organism) eventually duplicated itself on the grid. In a further development of the idea, small random changes, analogous to mutations, were allowed to occur. These changes might be passed on to future generations. If a given change increased the organism's fitness, that mutation would flourish and something like evolution would have begun."[13]

In the late 1960s, mathematician John Conway created the *Game of Life* in order to visualize the rule-based structure of von Neumann's cellular automaton. In the *Game of Life*, a simple matrix of black and white squares shows the progression of simple operations into complex patterns. These patterns perform as objects: they are made up of a changing array of cells known as an "emergent object."[14] Richard Dawkins, picking up on von Neumann's *Game of Life*, wrote a simple program called *The Blind Watchmaker* and was in awe at how he was able to evolve generations of biomorphic organisms, exhibiting what he termed "unnatural selection" because the generations of form were adapting according to editorial adjustments by the programmer based on a filtered set of performance or "fitness" criteria.

The interest in complexity and emergence that we see in the scientific community and hence in culture at large has also been investigated in architecture through rule-based systems of computation by the creation of algorithmic growth scripts for the development of a "morphogenetic" architecture. The use of algorithmic scripts is synonymous with advances in the human genome project. As such, architects act as the initial progenitor of a "self-evolving genetic" code for the "autonomous growth" of architecture.

One computational model that has been adopted by architects is that of *cellular automata*. Cellular automata are computational systems that model complex adaptive systems and are usually represented by discrete elements in a two-dimensional matrix. The elements, similar to the binary logic of computation, are either on (0) or off (1) and are represented by black and white dots in a grid. Each unit has a determined state that changes in patterns across the entire field based upon a simple set of rules. The rules are specific to the local conditions and in relationship to a similar set of rules of conduct of adjacent cells. What is interesting is that very simple local conditions create a field of unpredictable behavior that is manifested in complex patterns of behavior and potentially of form.

Cory Clarke[15] grows a "menagerie" of architectural organisms that are generated from an eight-gene "genome" using a recursive growth algorithm (figure 13.5). This algorithm takes into consideration factors that are typically viewed as natural to architecture: space and structure. Clarke uses a variant of a spatial logic based on a 3-D cellular automata. Clarke uses this system in order to create a set of rules that act "as a starting point for a morphology in that the rules allow for the spontaneous creation, and destruction, of voids and boundaries—a fundamental requirement for the description of space." Just as the human genome can produce infinite variations, Clarke's recursive growth algorithmic system can produce a potential of 1.68×10^{23} or 168,000,000,000,000,000,000,000 possible architectural structures, and as many possible space descriptions. The structures result in different arrangements of framework and void. In the examples shown, the structural framework was coupled with a pneumatic fabric enclosure that was inflated within the different voids produced by the exclusionary program fitness tests (figure 13.6).

Clarke's system is interesting because there are scalar uses of the cellular automata system: at the level of the individual structural and spatial units, and at the level of the program itself. These larger systems then operate upon each other to break down and encourage constant growth and change. The thought is that genetic algorithms, which are fragments of computer code, are able to cross-breed, mutate, and reproduce, emulating the processes of life itself. In Clarke's case, he takes the evolutionary metaphor one step further as the forms that are evolved from the system are tested for their fitness

Generation 1

Generation 1

Generation 1

Generation 1

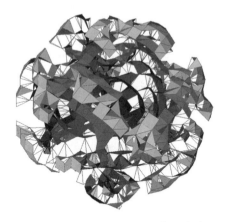

Generation 1

Generation 1

| Minimum Neighbors: **10** | Spawn Distance: **10** | Connection Range: **10** |
| Maximum Neighbors: **22** | Spawn Angle: **30** | Proximity Range: **12.5** |

| Figure 13.5 |
Clarke's growth algorithm

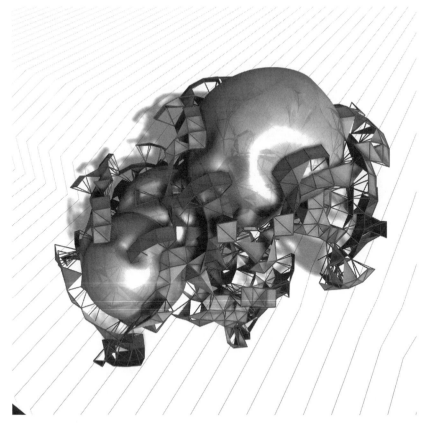

| Figure 13.6 |
Clarke's double forms

for survival. The fittest forms survive and their genetic material is passed on to cross-breed with other survivors to parent other generations of form (figure 13.7). Clarke de-scribes the process as follows:

Each generation starts with four parents (that are all "sexless") that are cross-bred with each other to produce twelve offspring—often mutation occurs during the cross-breeding, en-suring continual variation in new generations. The twelve offspring are tested for fitness (the fitness criteria is determined by similarities of spatial attributes of the evolving "organism" to predetermined limits of what constitutes the shape and size of rooms), determining their survival in the "bioreserve." The four most successful offspring go on to produce a second

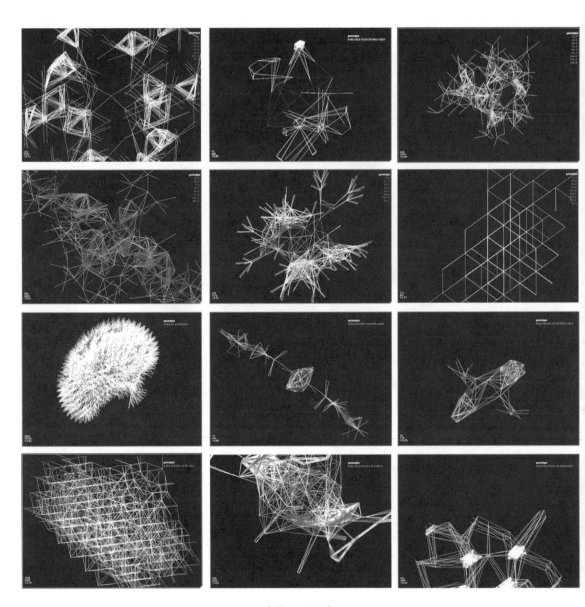

| Figure 13.7 |
Clarke's menagerie

generation, [then] those are in turn tested and the top four are parents to the next generation. This evolutionary process can continue ad infinitum."

Alisa Andrasek[16] proposes a self-breeding skin system that changes over time. Rather than being a proposal for architecture in a conventional sense, she proposes an artificial organism that is first of all a computational model that then could propose an installation environment that operates as an artificial synesthesia. Her project for *ghost patch* is a model for a cellular skin that undergoes continual transformation (figure 13.8).

The skin is really a composite of a layer of structure and a soft skin. Andrasek begins with a field of cells and adds three attractor cells that cause all of the individual cells to begin to move at different speeds in relation to the attractors. While these metaphors seem completely embedded in speaking about the material, the project questions the fundamental question of materiality looking toward skin a cultural phenomena that can take on various materialities and form.

Jason Vigneri-Beane[17] discusses the status of material in relation to the arbitrariness of rule-based systems. He emphasizes the independence of organizational strategies of coded information that precedes architectural material. Because there is a logic on the local level of the microscale of individual cellular units, this does not assure that there is the same focus on the macroscale. He speaks of an arbitrariness of the information generated by rule-based scripting and the tendency to evolve a complex adaptive

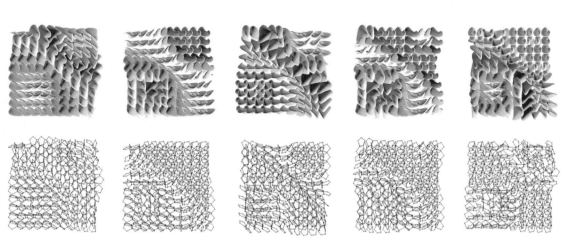

| Figure 13.8 |
Andrasek's cell transformations

behavior. At a certain point, the architect must make decisions whereby the data is given geometric form. This form is applied to the entire formation and gives unpredictable results or a kind of uselessness in relation to conventional notions of architecture. He believes that this could lead to a kind of "architectural identity in formation. Radical uselessness, then, is a productive breech of contract in the immanent relationship between rules and outcomes that occurs when computational logics are marshaled toward the (politicized) upheaval of architectural convention."[18]

There is, in the genetic code, the intelligence that can be actualized in various forms. The genetic code is an invisible energy or information that affects material. In self-breeding, artificial life scenarios, the information or the gene is the most critical (and most ephemeral) element. This is what Richard Dawkins speaks of, in post-Darwinian terms, as "the selfish gene."[19] The intelligence of the gene is not intent on the fittest form of the organism in terms of the perfection of the organism in the organism's own terms. Instead, from the gene's point of view, the goal is to pass on the continuity of the intelligence of the genetic information, in the most efficient manner, regardless of the form. Now this has some interesting implications for architecture. It plays against architecture's stability and insistence upon stasis in form.

There are important questions to ask in relation to the use of artificial life computational scenarios for the design of architecture. All of these processes, as they move through possible combinations, tend to move toward stasis unless the system becomes regenerated by the programmer or architect. What is curious is that architecture, built architecture, in its nature is thought to be static, so to propose the possibility of an endlessly changing and iterative model for design destabilizes the very status of the architectural object. Where is architecture situated, in the changing possibilities of form in digital space or the built form, or both? What is the role of the architect in the design process? The architect is normally assumed to have an active role in the evolution of architectural form. In the design of self-evolving systems, the architect as programmer determines the "genetic code" and builds into the code a system that runs autonomously. These are fundamental questions facing a contemporary architecture that has its roots in a postmodern destabilization of the metanarrative. For the moment, the architects have focused attention on the role of the author in relation to an "autonomous system" and on how to avoid stasis in the system. Clarke proposes a model of establishing two competing systems that coevolve in a predator-prey relationship to constantly avoid stasis. Vigneri-Beane discusses a substitution method whereby random substitution of information constantly refigures relationships. Last, Andrasek discusses her role in establishing performance criteria of the evolving skin/system. If the system runs for a long enough time, the legible pattern of the skin is lost and the information becomes too "noisy" to be productive. At this point she selects a legible pattern from the possible patterns and has the system "reincarnate" itself, maintaining and depositing the genetic information for the next generation of mutations. A self-generating system is used to evolve ever-changing and novel form, yet the architect intervenes at the level of establishing fitness criteria. In the impulse to create unique form is the desire to avoid stasis. This is comprehensible in relation to the digital model but raises questions regarding the movement toward a built architecture (figure 13.9).

We may take, by analogy, the figure of the Chimera. The Chimera is a mythological figure with an identity that is paradoxically both unique and infinite. She is born of the line of the marriage between the Mother Earth and her son, the Sea, of the "fruitful earth and the unfruitful sea," which produces "a line of monsters and prodigies, of brothers and sisters, along a horizontal axis dominated by two factors: seriality and hybridization."[20] The Chimera is uncertain of form (except in language, in description) yet holds the potential for every possible hybrid: her nature is more of language than of form. She is a multiple entity. She is both the question and the answer to the question of form; she is not form, yet is, momentarily. She provides us with both the mode in which to view our questioning of form and endless hybridity, by negating any possible understanding of the potential of form and in and of herself advocating for the importance of form. She is indecipherable.[21]

The metaphor of the Chimera provides us with a glimpse of the paradox at the heart of the evolution of genetic architecture. Architecture aspires simultaneously to form and to represent the impossibility of form. The constantly evolving digital chimera that are formed in rule-based computation would seem to be able to address the notion of the virtual in architecture. The virtual as described by theorist Brian Massumi is understood as a simultaneity and multiplication of images. These images are not in a stable form, but are in a series of evanescent overlapping images. No single image can render the virtual. By folding back on to itself topologically, the single is multiple and the superimposition of such images is the unity. By its nature, these processes are self-referential transformations and are more analogical than descriptive.[22] Massumi offers a word of caution regarding digital processes. He states that the evolution of infinite possibilities through the digital can indicate a quantitative rather than a qualitative sense about the virtual. Digital processes point to the possibility of alternate states and to a machinic process that moves through programmed steps. While Massumi later mentions certain exceptions (adaptive neural nets, other systems that generate non-precoded results based on feedback and recursivity, a machined self-referentiality, interaction between the analog and digital circuits), he believes in the "superiority of the analog."[23] He is concerned that the digital could lead to a systemization of the possible

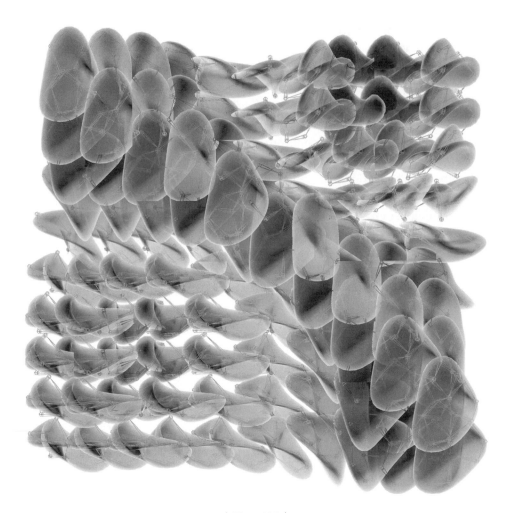

| Figure 13.9 |
Closeup of Andrasek's cells

and be a simulation rather than something real. The analog is a self-referenced process that is in tune to its own variations. What is key in his description is that the analog is able not only to be self-referential, but to cross from one medium to another. The analog can provide a qualitative transformation of code into other forms. He discusses the potential of the analog as the translation of the digital outside the machine and the screen experience: "Seeds of screened potential sown in nonsilicon soil. Relay to the world at large."[24] The lesson is this: the notion of the analog can translate the digital material and code to the material of the built architecture. The translation is by its nature going to effect changes. It will not be a smooth, but translation is a necessary one. The translation could be the intensities and flows that are not involved with the stasis of one manifestation or incorporation of form, but in the openness of the occupation of architecture. Social and cultural changes in societies change the reception and use of form. The inhabitation of architecture is an endless series of "couplings and matings" of endlessly changing images and incorporations.

Gender and Biology in Self-generating Computational Models

Both sexual and asexual models of engendering exist in the organic. We can look past the sexuality of engendering and focus on the issue of sameness and difference in terms of the interaction of the cells that lead to the development of new organisms. This point is critical and is reinforced by the contemporary emphasis on difference and gender as culturally grounded notions that have a fragile connection and contract with the biological.[25]

Theorist Elizabeth Grosz opens many important directions for a discussion of engendering and a more nuanced notion of sexual difference that could be of great assistance in trying to tackle the notion of the "sexless" engendering of architecture. Grosz writes, "The task, then, is not to establish a neutral or objective perspective on the question of sexual difference but to find a position encompassing enough for a sexually specific perspective to be able to open itself up to, meet with, and be surprised at (the reciprocal) otherness of the other sexes. Sexual difference entails the existence of a sexual ethics, an ethics of the ongoing negotiations between beings whose differences, whose alterities are left intact but with whom some kind of exchange is nonetheless possible."[26] Grosz invites us to think past a dichotomous rendering of difference (off/on, male/female . . .) to include other kinds of bodies, difference, and discussion. Gender can be seen as a cultural construct, yet underneath any model of sameness is the notion of difference. At the moment that we identify the "same," its uniqueness is undone by the inclusion of its opposite, difference. This invites us to speak, even if immaterially, of the binary, of the open or closed, of oscillating, shifting alliances. Just as cellular

automata or other artificial life scenarios create great complexity and unpredictable behaviors from the singular element that is alternately in one state and then another, the
sum total of two other individual cells is much more than the sum of its parts.

Let us look for a moment at the biological sexual model. In a biological model for
mammals, we look to the codependence on male semen and the female egg to spark embryologic development and differentiation. They are ontologically discrete entities that
are different and complete—yet in relation to their program of reproduction, they are
incomplete. There is an interesting question that arises if we consider a material understanding of these phenomena as compared with the ephemeral and abstract nature
of the generation of digital bodies. Aristotle wrote of the ephemeral nature of the matter of semen and questioned its corporeal existence.[27] Grosz posits another reading of
semen: "Seminal fluid is understood primarily as what it makes . . . a causal agent and
thus a thing, a solid. Its fluidity . . . its formlessness is displaced for its capacity to produce an object."[28] This is of interest since so many of the metaphors that arise in connection with the creation of or the engendering of a "biological" or "embryological"
architecture is detached from its connection to the potential of the immaterial to construct materially. The digital model of generation uses identical cells that alternately
take on nuanced differences with adjacent identical cells. While there is a clear polarity
between black cells and white cells in a cellular automata model, the relationships between the identical cells are fleeting and changing. I would posit, however, that these
cells, even if they are no longer "sexless," are inherently diverse, and this speaks to the
difference that drives the generative process. That this relationship is more subtle than
the model of male semen + female egg = new organism is clear, yet the dismissal of the
subtleties of sexual generation can be used to enrich the discussion.

The generative process can be looked at from multiple viewpoints that link this discussion to broader cultural and gender issues. An ambiguity is apparent in the socially
enforced role of the woman's body as the site of conception. Rather than be understood
as difference, the sexual act may be viewed as essentially homoerotic, between the mutual stimulation of like parts in the mimetic fit of the penis to the vagina—that women
have "a topological inversion of the male penis within them, or the female penis, the
clitoris on the exterior.[29] This is countered by the idea that a woman's sexuality is already dual and complete in itself.[30] Even if one were to posit a position of "sameness"
in speaking of topologically or typologically similar entities, the basis of the ontology
of form still lies in the fact that two strands of DNA are brought together to allow for
the possibility of engendering. This exists a priori to the notion of the binary nature of
sexuality that would seem to be necessary in the copulation of man and woman (or egg
and sperm) to create life. This is not a static system and does call for some notion of dif-

ference or acceptance of the other. But these assumptions are called into question through genetic engineering that may circumvent the necessity for the combination of female and male genetic material to create a new organism to allow for, in the absence of a female (or her egg), the generation of a new organism from the genetic material of the male only,[31] and it could be this model of sui generis that is unconsciously the drive behind architectural engendering at the moment.

Disembodied Engagement

What constitutes a body? Deleuze and Guattari have discussed the body as a discontinuous series of flows, energies, substances, and events that exist outside of binary oppositions. The body is not seen as a closed system, but as an open-ended biological system. Rather than thinking about the generative act as being a result of a lack or want or desire for completion in the other, desire is seen as an active productive force that aims at its own self-proliferation in an act of becoming.[32] This may be what is forming the basis of "genetically evolved" architectural form. It is as if, in its autogeneration, in its autonomous self-generation, that the invisible forces resemble those of the Aristotlean view of the semen as an invisible, noncorporeal life force. Yet in the potential of a translation to built architectural form there is an unacknowledged return to the notion of form or material itself as the feminine. This is an important point to make. Grosz guides us in the discussion again: "What happens in the bifurcation of sexed bodies—which is, in my opinion, an irreducible cultural universal—that is inevitably part of our understanding of bodies? If mind or subjectivity can be adequately and without reduction explained in terms of bodies, bodies understood in their historiocultural specificity, does this mean that sexual specificity—sexual difference—will be finally understood as a necessary (even if not sufficient) condition of our subjectivity?"[33] Does eliminating gender differences, as Grosz points out, play into the male model of subjectivity by eliminating a feminist position? Were Deleuze and Guattari conscious of their own gendered subjectivity when they wrote to eliminate "identity" and perhaps unconsciously advocate for a dispersed polysexuality that at its base is a very masculine move?

There is no material in digital computation, or at least not in the typical consideration of the material. What is digital material? Two such bodies can merge, get entangled, but does some element leave one form to engender another? Does a self-generating system diversify to form only one body, which then goes on to autogenerate another individual in its image in the form of cloning or of natural selection? Could a field of self-generating automata form polarized molecular entities that could then come into contact with each other to form a third entity? What would occur and what guidance toward materiality could the ephemeral digital technique suggest? These are questions that beg to be addressed. The iterative, creative power of digital "engendering" of architectural form is still latent in relation to the possibilities in the material. The return to materiality invites the feminine back into the discussion. Perhaps there is another way to think about self-generation of form that does not follow the model of *sui generis* only, a predominantly male model of self-sufficiency. In the biological model of *parthenogenesis*, the Phallic Mother, in the prolonged absence of a male inseminator, will, following the drive of a life force, spontaneously produce her opposite, a male that will enable the differentiation that is essential to creation through insemination.

The danger is that if we are working with a technique of making architecture that doesn't lead to its expression in physical matter but allows the architectural work to remain in a constantly changing form, metaphorically and instrumentally detached from full embodiment, this could lead to a barrenness of matter *and* concept. Using the metaphor of self-generating and biological processes for the design of architecture poses a danger that we could remain in a reverie or dream state about the biology of architecture. We could inhabit the dream and not the reality that is metaphorically connected to the imagined nondirected impulse of the spermatozoa to search for the egg. It is only in the penetration of the egg that the nondirected generating energy or life force of the semen gets directed and makes a commitment to form (and perhaps to consciousness). We can view semen as the intuitive, as seeds of form (and ideas). In the continual and unfocused searching, there is a promiscuous and perhaps superficial relationship to form and matter that offers a cautionary discussion for the generation of architecture.

Profound issues are developing in the field of architecture that are caught up in the notion of autonomy, self-generating fields, and pulsating, changing "form." Is this just the reverie of technology that prevents us from the materialization of form, wherein the world of infinite projection and possibility is the norm? We can think about this in a different way. In a historical sense, the idea of the technological being embodied with biological capabilities is not new. The automaton has a direct connection with the investigation of the digital model of thought and matter. In some ways, the automaton suggests a superiority of thought over body. It is a way of speaking of chimera, of the polymorphic perversity in the ever-changing and combining body. It does not surprise me then that a tool that many architects are using to give a "visible body" to the genetic code is *Maya*, an animation software program. Maya is the goddess of illusion. The illusion is endlessly forming, and in that unfixed imagination is the erotic. It is this same shifting, placeless eroticism that I ascribe to the throbbing meshes of sensual form made visible, but not yet corporeal.

Notes

1. The discussion of bodies arises from the Deleuzian discussion of the layering and fold-ing of matter that forms all bodies as discussed in Deleuze, *The Fold*, and Cache, *Earth Moves*.

2. Taylor, *Hiding*, 18.

3. Deleuze, *Essays Clinical and Critical*, 64.

4. Lévy, *Becoming Virtual*, 23.

5. Lévy, *Becoming Virtual*, 29.

6. On depthlessness of surface, see Jameson, *Postmodernism, or, The Cultural Logic of Late Capitalism*.

7. See Lynn, *Animate Form*.

8. See Lynn, *Animate Form*, and Farin, *NURB Curves and Surfaces from Projective Geome-try to Practical Use*. This section is also based on an interview by the author with Cory Clarke.

9. Topology is the study of the behavior of a surface structure under deformation.

10. The thoughts regarding *Throbbing Meshes* were developed with Maria Siera in re-sponse to a University of Pennsylvania conference on digital techniques in architec-tural design and construction in the spring of 2002.

11. This paragraph is co-authored with Jason Vigneri-Beane and is from an unpublished manuscript "Paradox: Smooth><Discrete" 2003.

12. Turkle, *Life on the Screen*, 304.

13. Turkle, *Life on the Screen*, especially 304–305n12. Her account is based on Levy, *Arti-ficial Life*, and Waldrop, *Complexity*.

14. Turkle, *Life on the Screen*, 154.

15. Cory Clarke and Philip Ang.

16. Alisa Andrasek, *biothing*.

17. Jason Vigneri-Beane, *splitspace*.

18. Jason Vigneri-Beane, "Agents."

19. Dawkins, *The Selfish Gene.*,

20. Bompiani, "The Chimera Herself," 365.

21. Bompiani, "The Chimera Herself," 398.

22. Massumi, "The Superiority of the Analog," 134.

23. Massumi, "The Superiority of the Analog," 134.

24. Massumi, "The Superiority of the Analog," 141.

25. Grosz, *Volatile Bodies*.

26. Grosz, *Volatile Bodies*,192.

27. Sissa, "Subtle Bodies," 135–141.

28. Grosz, *Volatile Bodies*, 199.

29. Laqueur, "Amor Veneris, Vel Dulcedo Appelatur," 105.

30. Irigaray, "This Sex Which is Not One," 23–33. Originally published as "Ce sexe qui nen est pas un," in *Cahiers du Grif*, no. 5. English translation: "This Sex Which is Not One," trans. Claudia Reeder, in *New French Feminisms*, ed. Elaine Marks and Isabelle de Courtivron (New York: Pantheon, 1981), 99–106.

31. Weiss, "The Dureé of the Techno-body."

32. See Grosz, *Volatile Bodies*, 165.

33. Grosz, *Volatile Bodies*, 160.

Bibliography

Andrasek, Alisa. *Biothing*. www.biothing.org (accessed July 18, 2005).

Bompiani, Ginevra. "The Chimera Herself." In *Fragments for a History of the Human Body: Part One*, ed. Michel Feher with Ramona Naddaff and Nadia Tazi, 365–409. New York: Zone Books, 1989.

Cache, Bernard. *Earth Moves: The Furnishing of Territories*. Cambridge, MA: MIT Press, 1995.

Dawkins, Richard. *The Selfish Gene*, 2nd ed. Oxford: Oxford University Press, 1990.

Deleuze, Gilles. *Essays Clinical and Critical*. Minneapolis: University of Minnesota Press, 1997.

Deleuze, Gilles. *The Fold—Leibniz and the Baroque*. Minneapolis: University of Minnesota Press, 1993.

Farin, Gerald. *NURB Curves and Surfaces from Projective Geometry to Practical Use*. Wellesley, MA: A. K. Peters, 1995.

Grosz, Elizabeth. *Volatile Bodies*. Bloomington: Indiana University Press, 1994.

Irigaray, Luce. "This Sex Which is Not One." In *This Sex Which is Not One*, 23–33. Ithaca, NY: Cornell University Press, 1985.

Jameson, Fredric. *Postmodernism, or, The Cultural Logic of Late Capitalism*. Durham, NC: Duke University Press, 1991.

Laqueur, Thomas W. "Amor Veneris, Vel Dulcedo Appelatur." In *Fragments for a History of the Human Body: Part Three*, ed. Michel Feher with Ramona Naddaff and Nadia Tazi, 91–131. New York: Zone Books, 1989.

Lévy, Pierre. *Becoming Virtual: Reality in the Digital Age*. New York: Plenum Press, 1998.

Levy, Steven. *Artificial Life: The Quest for a New Frontier*. New York: Pantheon, 1992.

Lynn, Greg. *Animate Form*. New York: Princeton Architectural Press, 1999.

Massumi, Brian. "The Superiority of the Analog." In *Parables for the Virtual: Movement, Affect, Sensation*. Durham, NC: Duke University Press, 2002.

Sissa, Giulia. "Subtle Bodies: The Body of Semen." In *Fragments for a History of the Human Body: Part Three*, ed. Michel Feher with Ramona Naddaff and Nadia Tazi, 135–141. New York: Zone Books, 1989.

Taylor, Mark C. *Hiding*. Chicago: University of Chicago Press, 1997.

Turkle, Sherry. *Life on the Screen: Identity in the Age of the Internet.* New York: Touchstone/ Simon and Schuster, 1995.

Vigneri-Beane, Jason. "Agents: The Unruliness of Rules." Unpublished essay, 2003.

Vigneri-Beane, Jason. *splitspace.* http://www.splitspace.com (accessed July 18, 2005).

Waldrop, Mitchell. *Complexity: The Emerging Science at the End of Order and Chaos.* New York: Simon & Schuster, 1992.

Weiss, Gail. "The Dureé of the Techno-body." In *Becomings,* ed. Elizabeth Grosz, 161–175. Ithaca, NY: Cornell University Press, 1999.

14

SKIN

Shelley Jackson

The first applicant wrote to me on August 17. I had the title, "SKIN," tattooed on my right wrist on September 8 at Bowery Tattoo in Manhattan. The first word, Sarah Kamens, was tattooed with "If" immediately afterward. Since then, I have received 5,129 emails with such headings as "Skin," "SKIN," "skin . .", skin!!!" "ineradicable stain," "stain me," "mortal words," "word made flesh," "I want to be a word," "make me a word," and "I am a word." I have accepted 1,528 volunteers out of a total 2,095 needed, and have assigned words to 813 so far. Of these, 11 have turned down their words and dropped out of the project; 76 have received their tattoos and sent photographs to prove it. I have participants in the United States, Canada, England, Ireland, Scotland, Wales, France, Spain, Belgium, the Netherlands, Switzerland, Sweden, France, Austria, Germany, Italy, Finland, Norway, Poland, Jordan, Japan, Thailand, Australia, New Zealand, Brazil, and Argentina.

[call for participants:]

AUTHOR ANNOUNCES MORTAL WORK OF ART

August 2003, Brooklyn, NY—Shelley Jackson, author of *The Melancholy of Anatomy*, invites participants in a new work entitled "Skin." Each participant must agree to have one word of the story tattooed upon his or her body. The text will be published nowhere else, and the author will not permit it to be summarized, quoted, described, set to music, or adapted for film, theater, television, or any other medium. The full text will be known only to participants, who may, but need not, choose to establish communication with one another. In the event that insufficient participants come forward to complete the first and only edition of the story, the incomplete version will be considered definitive. If no participants come forward, this call itself is the work.

Prospective participants should contact the author and explain their interest in the work. If they are accepted, they must sign a contract and a waiver releasing the author from any responsibility for health problems, body-image disorders, job loss, or relationship difficulties that may result from the tattooing process. On receipt of the waiver, the author will reply with a letter specifying the word (or word plus punctuation mark) assigned to the participant. Participants must accept the word they are given, but they may choose the site of their tattoo, with the exception of words naming specific body parts, which (with the exception of the word "skin") may be anywhere but the body part named. Tattoos must be in black ink and a classic book font. Words in fanciful fonts will be expunged from the work.

When the work has been completed, participants must send a signed and dated close-up of the tattoo to the author, for verification only, and a portrait in which the tattoo is not visible, for possible publication. Participants will receive in return a signed and dated certificate confirming their participation in the work and verifying the authenticity of their word. The author retains copyright, though she contracts not to devalue the original work with subsequent editions, transcripts, or synopses. However, correspondence and other documentation pertaining to the work (with the exception of photographs of the words themselves) will be considered for publication.

From this time on, participants will be known as "words." They are not understood as carriers or agents of the texts they bear, but as its embodiments. As a result, injuries to the printed texts, such as dermabrasion, laser surgery, tattoo cover work, or the loss of body parts, will not be considered to alter the work. Only the death of words effaces them from the text. As words die the story will change; when the last word dies the story will also have died. The author will make every effort to attend the funerals of her words.

What follows are some "words" captured from the project (figures 14.1–14.9).

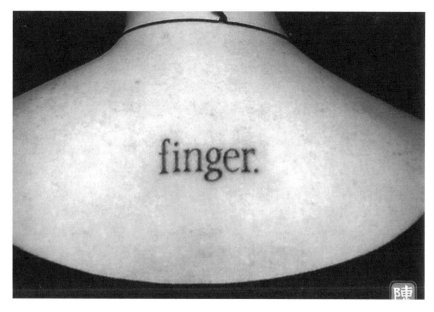

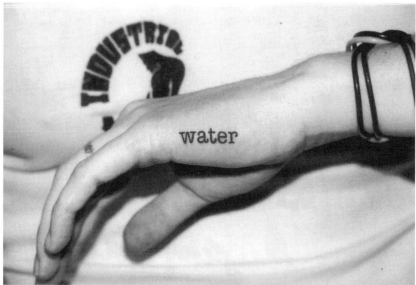

| Figure 14.1 |
SKIN on Brenda Dalloway

| Figure 14.2 |
SKIN on Daryle Fountain

| **Figure 14.3** |
SKIN on Kimberly Honadle

| Figure 14.4 |
SKIN on Sarah Kamens

| Figure 14.5 |
SKIN on Steven Cobb

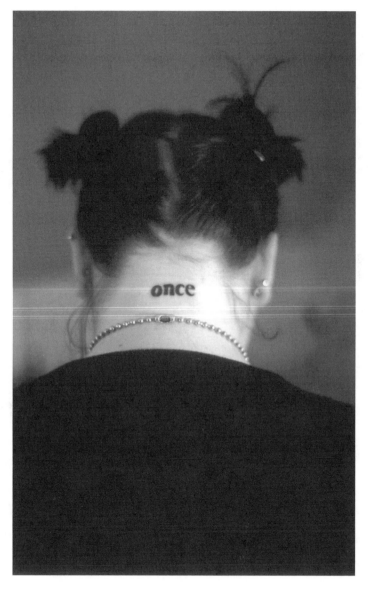

| Figure 14.6 |
SKIN on Elizabeth Bradshaw

| Figure 14.7 |
SKIN on Alexandra Crneckiy

| Figure 14.8 |
SKIN on Tasha French

| Figure 14.9 |
SKIN on Shelley Jackson

15

RESKINNING THE EVERYDAY

Mary Flanagan

borders

Pushing at that percussive gel-filled screen in front of me, the screen's skin ripples slightly to my touch. This thin titanium box is a tree whose roots extend over and within the planet and into outer space. Webcams mounted on the Mars rover, SETI space blips link me to places I will never see with my own eyes.

I push at my skin, and am a little thrilled and disturbed to note that it too ripples slightly to my touch, having a similar timbre and viscosity as the screen. The largest organ of the body, the great container, the esteemed purifier, the separator between outside and inside, between smooth and ripply, between liquid and the concoction of gasses that make up the air around me. Another screen (figure 15.1).

These surfaces, these interfaces separating two phases of matter, form a common boundary and help me know where I am in the world. The surfaces of everyday life amid computational systems, however, make things less and less clear.

When I think about computing, I think about boundaries and boundary crossing, translation: transforming the world around us into data, and from data back into the world. This process seems more and more transparent, but the transitional practice continues, and the interface remains. Like the interior transition between thinking and speaking, thinking and typing or thinking and clicking are shifts as well, and these everyday actions bring about a range of questions about the borders between bodies and machines.

```
/*Sebastian asks me, Are you writing fiction or is this an academic
essay? Are interfaces directions to something, or something in and of
themselves?
*/
```

However we see the progression of these physical ways of interacting with the computer, interfaces play an instrumental role in shaping the conceptual experience of

| Figure 15.1 |
The everyday Macintosh interface

computational worlds, and, indeed, the real world around us. This essay is a meditation on the everyday computational interfaces which surround us, offering four conceptual sites for consideration. Each site marks a symbolic progression in thinking about the way computers are integrated into our everyday lives. This document enacts a conversation, an experiment that offers as many questions as answers about the various ways we think about interfaces.

The links between people and computers are only understandable through our interfaces: both the site and the process of individuation among bodies, objects, tools, and concepts. The first interfaces to explore, then, are the physical, material interfaces of digital devices.

boxes

Is the screen speaking back, redefining itself, redefining the box? It seems as though non-Western ideas about interfaces and boxes could bring unique systems, where hardware and software could reflect alternate notions of time, space, place. While our computers remain in boxes for the time being, they become ever smaller and faster, and it is more difficult to distinguish thinking from unthinking objects.

So many computers in so many homes. In the suburbs my friends keep home offices in spare bedrooms and basement annexes. In the small apartments of the city, it is often the dining room or kitchen space that is refashioned for the computer's ever-presence. The tables hold more plastic boxes and power cables than lasagna and sushi. Eating over his laptop, Sebastian looks over to me to ask if I see any napkins. At night, friends gather around laptop screens, lovers bring them to bed to watch movies, the box piled on pillows in an intimate agreement. How many of us will have our computers tell us bedtime stories?

There was no one "inventor" of the computer interface. In the history of computing, dials and switches eventually gave way to keyboards based on typewriters and teletype machines. These were used to record data on punchcards for machines such as the behemoth ENIAC computer of 1946. Vannevar Bush, once director of the Office of Scientific Research and Development in the United States, is counted among early interface visionaries. In his 1945 article "As We May Think," Bush offered models for a variety of methods of input and output including desk-based computer systems, speech interfaces, and even a walnut-sized camera worn on one's forehead. Interesting and still experimental-seeming devices such as the light gun interface were later developed for use in air defense control systems. A profusion of working interface technologies was developed during the twentieth century. The light gun was followed by the light pen in the early 1960s. Xerox PARC researchers led in both software and hardware interfaces, and went on to originate many of our graphical user interfaces, including the mouse (figure 15.2).

While designers and engineers work to erase mechanical portals between users and machines, and science fiction writers fantasize about direct mental connections to computing systems, it seems the opportune moment to shift ourselves away from our perception of current, everyday computing experiences. We need to examine the interfaces to our virtual selves, these layers of skins, through the beige box and trailing puck—these still offer, for the most part, the common interface over the last twenty-five mass-produced years. If we think in Mandarin, the box, keyboard, and the mouse are our *guo yu*, our common, everyday language. While the box becomes smaller and more stylish, the box is still a box.

Donald Norman (2002), in his writings on user-centric interface design, insists that makers of objects and of virtual worlds create a conceptual model that users can understand—models that become a part of the user's intuitive knowledge as much as gravity or the properties of water. Designers work to provide "intuitive exchanges" with

| Figure 15.2 |
Traditional interface

systems—any type of system that requires interaction. Examples include user-friendly escalators, doorways in buildings, shifting controls inside an automobile, or computer application interfaces. The argument for intuitive systems is culturally based, of course; for what constitutes an intuitive signal to one person in Taiwan—tapping the table to communicate that a tea cup is full, or knowing the shoe cabinet should be near or outside the front door—is distinctly different than an understanding of the same social practices in another culture. Interfaces are the means through which we take clues and signals in a given culture. Learning new interface systems changes our behavior and is one thing that makes travel so invigorating.

As a social practice, interfaces should be highly contested and constantly reforming sites of social negotiation. Yet the computer box paradigm is pervasive and its design colonialist in nature. Asian manufacturers and suppliers follow design trends that have been, for the most part, established by the West. Internationally, keyboards follow the English-language model of input and define how language is translated from hand to machine. Computer literacy around the world has meant that citizens adopt retrofitted beige or black boxes into their homes and community centers and pursue a Western style of work and leisure. Somehow, a mouse in one hand has become a naturalized method of geographical and conceptual navigation.

I encounter challenges in articulating the boundaries among computer worlds, systems, and the physical world all of the time, as such systems become seamlessly integrated into the surrounding physical environment. However, at institutions and among those environments less endowed with the latest technologies, "boxes" remain. The most recent reminder of the pervasiveness of the box occurred during an after-school session with middle-school girls; my team was designing a complex online system that appeals to underrepresented groups (figure 15.3). Visiting the Computer Clubhouse in Brooklyn, New York, for a design session, I asked a group of 11- to 13-year-old girls to draw a computer game world that I had just described: a world in which characters would want to care for others and do things together socially. The girls pulled out pens, pencils, and paper. Every one of the eleven girls sat down and drew the box, the keyboard, and mouse instead of sketching the fantasy world I described. The dominance of the box has infused cultural imagination to a point where it cannot be separated conceptually from stories and ideas.

The worlds we drift in and out of so seamlessly are interfaced through boxes and wires and graphic templates that categorize our work and play. I, for one, have to constantly remind myself of this. Perhaps it is some kind of dreamworld I enter when I wake up in the morning, but I no longer notice the device itself, its color and shape, how my hands reach for the mouse. Like signing, I speak with my hands. I do not remember that I communicate through typing or that I use a mouse or touchpad; in the same way, it is difficult to remind ourselves of framing and the limitations of our native language.

In the daily quest to transfer ideas from head to document, I often take these interfaces for granted. Already ensconced in the realm of possibility the computer represents, I function inside its unique conceptual framework. In other words, the technology has become as invisible to me as anyone else working with the machines, as invisible as pen and paper may have been fifty years ago. But I remind myself to constantly examine the kinds of ink we use, the shape of the pen, the economic systems that produce these pens, how the pen shapes thinking, and the reasons we use pens in the first place over other recording devices. In the real world, pens and pencils don't necessarily represent cultural systems and values, but I believe that computers do. Computers run by relying upon zeros and ones, ons and offs, hard drives gridded out in block parcels, software constructed in distinct hierarchies. Computers contain nested structures within structures, each drawing from a different discipline: engineering to design, architecture to literature. Once we are faced with a paradigm, however, the underlying assumptions

| Figure 15.3 |
Local New York design partners

on which it is built become invisible. However, as philosopher Thomas Kuhn ([1962] 1996) suggests, particular paradigms can also be very useful, gaining their status primarily because they are more successful approaches than competing systems of organization; they allow inquiry and work to advance faster than beginning the learning process all over again. We pick up the appropriate conventions depending on the task at hand. Paradigms can speed up research, scholarship, and other forms of work, but at the expense of taking the underlying system for granted. Though computing has been in mainstream imagination for a relatively short time—the Internet for just a decade—the priorities and use of the system seem to go by unquestioned. Thus there is a tension between our current desire to challenge dominant systems and our need to make use of the efficiencies they provide.

Invisible interfaces may make computing, coffeemaking, and navigating tollways easier, but such invisibility may also mean that much of the U.S. public will be unable to participate in authoring culture. Computer literacy courses at many high schools across the United States are fundamentally typing classes in graphically organized software packages. Computing as an ideological system is not yet a topic of the humanities, and students are not taught to question and delve into conceptual systems the computer represents. It is no coincidence that the mystical and renegade role of the computer hacker surfaced in the 1980s as automobiles, phone systems, banks, and national security reached cohesive automation—the hacker mythos came at a time when the gaps that could undermine power relations seemed to vanish, where everyday tinkerers lost access to the mechanical aspects of daily life, and when the hacker, someone able to control a system—work in and around it—became the outlaw or artist crusader, a mythological hero/devil figure in mainstream imagination.

```
/*Sebastian asks me, What exactly is inaccessible about a computer?
They just follow human commands.
*/
```

Perhaps it is not so much the material that is inaccessible but the culture of computing itself, the guild-like feeling with its other language and presumed skill set from which everyday computer users feel alienated. While my mother, for example, could theoretically rework her operating system hierarchy to elevate the game of solitaire as the metaphor for her operating system, the perceived elite status and the specialized knowledge of those able to program computers affects an individual's perceived agency with their computers, especially in underrepresented groups. According to the National Science Foundation, the number of women earning bachelor's degrees in computer science in 1984 was 37 percent of the total, but by 1996 it had fallen to 28 percent of the total number of graduates. Women, as one category among many not represented in computer science, are not increasingly attracted to a discipline that guides much of the fabric of everyday life in technologically influenced (determined?) nations.

Currently there is growing research addressing such questions at the socio-cognitive and cultural borders of technological innovation. Implicit Association Task tests and Functional Magnetic Resonance Imaging studies continue to demonstrate that people have inherent biases down to physiological response in their recognition of images and words (Greenwald and Banaji 1975). Categorical tests on impressions of race and age consistently show that whites have a stronger same-race identification than do persons of minority groups in the United States. Other studies show that for a significant percentage of the population, men are associated with science, women with humanities; African Americans with violent and negative language; Asians with ability in mathematics (Phelps 2001; Phelps et al. 2000). Stereotypes, produced by culture, have been shown to become encoded into bodily responses to images. This means that at the very least, stereotypes are inadvertently encoded into our computational boxes and our everyday experiences, in icons, tools, and data structures.

Now that over half of all U.S. households contain computers with Internet connections, the daily lives of many citizen-consumers are bound to the computer. Every day computer users sit down, check their email, search for a movie trailer, read the news, balance a budget, or download digital camera images. The interface to the operating system of a computer sets the stage for the understanding and prioritization of data. After all, it is merely a representational tactic that "My Documents" are somehow different than *Adobe Photoshop's* "Read Me" files. While data for the two sets of information may be stored in neighboring blocks on the physical hard drive, within the operating system's interface paradigm they are stowed worlds apart. We continue to believe our documents are special, our words and codes are somehow fundamentally different from all the other material filling the blocks of the hard drive. These constructed conceptual models are not neutral—interfaces (representing hierarchies and data structures) and the boxes carry meaning. For one, operating system structures emphasize an individual's separateness. Indeed, they emphasize individuality in general. Group-authored documents such as collaborative projects are not reflected in the structure of the system or in its iconography. Functions are separate from data; the network is conceptually demarcated as different from the local device.

How the box is shaped is of paramount importance. So is what it contains. The space of computational systems, and how these spaces are represented to users, is the second place to examine interfaces.

maps

The man climbed onto the fifth rung of the ladder, grabbed his hammer, and knocked a hole in my wall, plaster spinning everywhere in the air and across my shiny floors. He knocked a second hole next to the first, and dug his hand around the recess. A third hole was needed. One by one, the holes took over, my rooms effortlessly disappearing into the rubble of the moon . . . the walls a web of chalky river delta, a map held together with hair and dust. He promised that another would come by to fix it all up, to make sure that no evidence was ever seen, but of course I would always know. It was already past.

This is one of the lessons of Einstein's theory of relativity—looking inevitably means looking back, for light travels at a finite speed . . . If our center, our universe, is everywhere or nowhere, we do know that such a center could only be the present. We race from present to past at 186,284 miles per second. This text, that laughter, is perhaps a nanosecond away; the moon, almost two seconds lost. The present can only mean the lack of distance—a flash, the recognition of presence, found at the touch of an insect's wing on the top of the ear as it flitters off in a mid-

| Figure 15.4 |
Mapping, this time: Stockholm

June breeze, or the mutual exhalation between interlocked bodies as the sun breaks to sear the dripping grass after a fresh-green shower.

Can I ever map such experiences to interfaces? Or are the interfaces maps to begin with, laying out the terrain before me? And what terrain do these interfaces describe, exactly (figure 15.4)?

The screen glows before me. I reach out to it. Am I touching another map, a mobile map in time, fleeing backward? If so, what was just here? What did I miss? Other maps. Menus pulling down laundry lists, texts, buttons, the colorful boxes and bubbles we press for their wiggle of acknowledgment. Icons, little actors on the desktop, waiting for stage directions. Operating systems do not only impose order but behavior: the desktop includes animated icons that catch a user's attention through scripted behaviors. This is a symbolic world, interfaces filled with metaphors, functioning much like signs in other media. Interfaces are sets of maps? Green for valleys, brown for mountains, and icons for roadside attractions . . . Maps are the original medium to use shorthand systems like icons to abstract space and time. Interfaces are certainly maps, graphic visualizations of the computer world, of the net . . . something that depicts something to do with: space, landscape, topology, topography.

Mary Flanagan

The Internet as a topology is a dynamic and fluid terrain. Following work in the early 1960s, electrical engineer Paul Baran (1964) distributed a series of influential papers entitled "On Distributed Communications" while working at the RAND Corporation. These papers proposed detailed networked communications models that would protect the U.S. communications systems from enemy attack. Baran suggested that distributed networks, as seen in figure 15.5, are less vulnerable to attack than other network structures. Baran's ideas were especially powerful and continue to influence the structure of the Internet we have today. When introduced, the distributed network design countered paradigms of the day, suggesting that unreliable links in the network system could be almost as effective as reliable links if there were enough of them webbed together. The density distribution of the unreliable links could counteract node or link failures.

Not only does Baran's simple diagram of how the distributed communications systems function as a diagram or map of the structure of networked communications, but it offers the proper interface to understand them. Current interfaces use "back" and "forward," "pages" and "bookmarks"—metaphors still firmly rooted to the centuries-old technology of the book. Strangely, Internet browsers rarely show users how data gets from point A to point B, as though the structure of the system has nothing to do with its content. Rather, to see our maps form through alternate kinds of geographies might help demystify the topology of the Internet and of an individual computer.

```
/*Sebastian asks me, What is not a map? So many things can be called
a map.
*/
```

Currently, interfaces are abstractions that can be said to describe an underlying topology of the self. Interfaces become maps for our personal geographies with the computer, a user-centric geography instead of a spatially oriented one. What if we integrate these with other maps of the Net? Would differences between an individual computer and the network blur? This ever-present, fuzzy quality of networked computer culture is the third site at which to investigate interfaces.

the network

The men had come back to my apartment. There had been a very slight high-pitched buzz ringing throughout the building for two days, and they believed the source of the problem could be found within my apartment walls. They entered once again and began opening the holes they had covered last week, beginning a new kind of map, one of wires and strings, colors and connections.

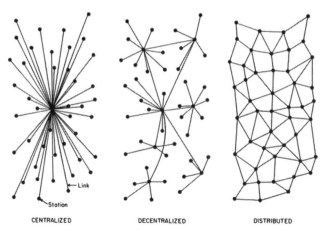

| Figure 15.5 |
Baran's network diagrams

Then they went to my neighbors,' an elderly man from Hong Kong, living in the other rear-facing apartment. His walls were covered in brown pegboard rimmed with S-hooks to hold cups and cooking implements. They started digging a hole from his side, pulling off his pegboard coordinates to connect our spaces, starting first with screwdrivers, then sledgehammers. Gradually our two spaces became one, as the wall broke down. The buzz remained. How had the wall held itself together? Our two apartments were distinct only in decor and the shadow where the wall had once been, the little buzz echoing across the wood. My neighbor sat calmly at his kitchen table, directly across from me as I typed, mirroring a part of me that must be tranquil, and I, perhaps, reflecting his interior agitation. I liked that we were a part of each other's lives today and might not be tomorrow. For once, looking at the stranger, I was not nostalgic or filled with longing, but perfectly in love with precarious balance. I smiled at him across our respective shiny kitchen tables.

 The nature of instability is woven into the fabric of the world. As the universe expands, we chase behind it, part of the Copernican flock. We take along our plaster-smashed piles and boxes of papers and favorite mug. My velocity of recession is directly equal to your distance. Could my body swell, until I only feel my teeth and your nimble fingers? The penetrating quality of the wind depends on its ceaselessness—this is what makes the wind so powerful. And, time is its instrument, as it is in Hubble's formula. Is the outcome of all things disintegration and dispersion, or does a new beautiful order emerge from trajectories, breezes of attraction and repulsion, spinning magnificence for the while until the equation no longer works? I feel relief when my wireless network finds a signal. Somehow in the chaos around me, I am connected—and this may be even more true once we move from a fixed network model to an ad hoc network model, where connections occur as needed.

You are connected to me, I am connected to the neighbor, electronically. Somewhere. Our banks, our leases, our Amazon purchases, friendster and blog pages connecting us together along the speed of subscription. Reach. There is little there to see, but the social fabrics that look as if they are intangible are in fact made of sturdy threads, carrying weight in the semblance of tinted text and elusive images. How do we get from here to there in a space that needs no x, y, z-coordinates to exist, when we cannot easily define the structures upon which our content rests?

The overlap of the physical world and the virtual is a permeable and indistinct site of exchange, with certain nonmixable elements—for the time being: the sky, coffee, touching. This line, unlike the chemical properties of oil and water, shifts through time, changes with the latest buzzwords, technologies, home-grown wikis and party e-vite sites. And obviously there is cause for concern because all of this data can and will be monitored by disciplines of power: state and corporate interests.

The rapid spread of Internet accessibility and everyday use closely mirrors other patterns in the spread of twentieth-century domestic technologies. For the first time since the advent of the telephone, the space of the house has been dramatically redefined. A useful study by Carolyn Marvin (1990) details how the telephone was the first electric medium to enter the home and challenge traditional boundaries between public and private space. Likewise, the growing numbers of computers in the home means that many households are connected; it also signifies a shift in the way domestic space is understood. The Internet is a primary communication paradigm for the majority of people in the United States. It is no wonder that the physical world and its associated tools are changing to reflect the way we think inside the network. From contact lists on telephones and chat tools to multiuser online games, computational thinking has infused our everyday interactions.

The software packages and operating systems surround us, and we crave more and more connectivity. Browser-specific tools such as search engines, for example, offer one of many conceptual frameworks for desire. Yet for the majority of computer users, the hidden mechanics of systems are a satisfactory, even expected, given. Like Leonardo da Vinci's encoded notebooks, we live in a culture in which we create machines to keep our secrets from us. Users must like secrets, for more and more we desire ease of use and effacement of the technical workings of daily life.

We can map these connections through games as one type of framework—maps have grids, construction sites have scaffolding, spiders have webs. Examining ubiquity according to geography is only one way to glimpse how everyday computing has changed us.

```
/*Sebastian asks me, Where does the map end?
*/
```

Mapping ubiquity. Interfaces are maps, graphic visualizations of the Net, depicting how software and hardware creators structure the terrain. The real and Baudrillard's hyperreal images have contaminated each other, or rather, merged, enacting a self where reflection and physical identity are one and where cultural forms and selves are reproduced endlessly. This site of blur happens most often with an individual's use of the computer. Images are never fixed, texts deleted and updated, leaving no trace of origin or time. The blurring of space, location, and time leaves no sense of near or far, past or present. As Foucault (1980) noted, ubiquitous disciplines of power control society through surveillance and control how the body is constituted. Many cybertheorists have argued that the network now extends the body through connections on the Net. And this body is itself extended, ballooning like a slippery tent through the world and even to such distant places as Mars. Skin is ubiquitous; it becomes a schematic of abstract spaces, Moscow and Berlin and La Paz and Caracas and Atlantis. Skin is a living record of time and dislocated place: a living, wrinkling map. We live through this skin and this map (figure 15.6).

The equivalent to skin and its markings lies in code, in programming. Computer programming provides the ultimate map, for it is both a language with its symbolic representations, and itself a body, a place where language transcends representation and becomes action.

objects

If interfaces and systems are written in code, are they ultimately linguistic maps? Must a map be a nonlinguistic representation of a space? If not, code, created through programming, provides the ultimate map. When we look at surfaces, or look inside, we see that maps contain the mapmakers and their values—the viewpoint of the mapmaker makes the map. And when programming languages, the only human-designed/created languages, are used, do they shape the map by the thoughts and biases of the makers and implementers of the programs?

Jef Raskin (2000), the inventor behind the Macintosh computer, noted that we need systems that better reflect the way humans work. He argued that software packages with separate types of interfaces do not meet user's needs first, and yet they structure how we conceptually think of tasks. The metaphors we use—desktops, navigation, "going here," "searching," are the models behind many software interfaces, molding how users understand digital experiences.

| Figure 15.6 |
Natural network lines

Computer programming is the heart of the creation of software, and it too is influenced by metaphors—in fact, metaphors in programming have a strong affect on how
digital tools are made and used. Therefore, a look at the structures informing the
programming process—specifically at the way objects are created in object-oriented
programming—is essential in the exploration of the way in which everyday digital experiences are also structured. I also look at mathematics, because some of programming—
though not all—is grounded in the mathematics of doing: numbers, functions, and
algorithms that one can conceivably construct.

```
/*Sebastian asks me, Are you interested in semantics or in language
structures, ways of saying or ways of thinking?
*/
```

When studying programming languages, we distinguish between semantics and
syntax. While we can program in an object-oriented style in a particular programming

language (e.g., C++ or Java), the design of object-oriented style is a separate entity. The idea behind the words we use to create an object—say, a chair—are one thing that represents the ideal state of the actual; the way we call a chair or multiple chairs into being, instantiating them, is another. Under this platonic nature of coding, the class is the ideal form, and the multiple chairs generated from the class instances of the ideal.

In technical circles, object-oriented programming is the most commonly applied programming approach, used for programming everything from databases to games. Object-oriented programming is both a procedure and a metaphor. When writing object-oriented software, programmers define the world in terms of a set of objects. A crowd would be, for example, one hundred instances of person objects, with various property changes (size, shape, color). Object-oriented programs are typically structured in a hierarchy of objects, with sets of objects or individuals having particular behaviors. In object thinking, an object is a Boolean shape, like the human body: inside an object is true, outside an object is false, and the surface, the skin, must be defined if it is to be recognized as another object. Objects are distinct, malleable, and controllable. They can be programmed to make choices and to behave in particular ways. They have their own properties and can encounter the properties of other objects at various hierarchical levels.

Whatever form one's conception of mathematical reality might take, such systems cannot escape their cultural background. Acknowledging that truth, objectivity, scope, and scale in mathematics are concepts based on a particular culture at a particular time, mathematician Raymond Wilder (1981) argues that disciplines affected by mathematics are just as influenced by the culture at large as by any other discipline, whether it be art, music, or scientific fields such as medicine. Mathematical logic diffuses from mathematics to the natural sciences and technology, infusing these related disciplines with methods and concepts. Object thinking has certainly infused both the culture of computing and the technologies developed by the industry. Contemporary interfaces, for example, map not so much spatial geographies but objects. Functions are broken down into one-word commands, and applications that may complete many kinds of related activities are represented under one icon: one product per icon, one icon per site on the map. Like scenic spots or roadside rest areas, icons invoke a spatial phenomenon through the differentiation of a place as an object. The distinctions and delineations between documents and programs, even the desktop metaphor with its objects in hierarchies, seems to follow the separateness of object-oriented programming. What object-oriented programming fails to deal with well is the fuzziness of boundaries and borders, when something needs to cross different kinds of object models, or when things operating in a given system are contradictory.

Advocates of object-oriented design argue that it represents a "natural" way to think about the world, even when programmers new to object-oriented design have difficulty identifying classes, or groups/types of objects, and forming hierarchical relationships among objects. In fact, it may take more than one semester to learn object orientation properly. While more efficient and reusable as a coding paradigm, the object-oriented model assumes that the world is made of objects and relationships to those objects, and this in turn shapes a way of seeing the world accordingly. I would argue that object thinking is not necessarily a "natural" way to think, but rather one of several kinds of epistemological practices that are not consciously recognized as ideological by program designers and programming practitioners. The object model, for one, reinforces a rationalistic and deterministic view of problems and solutions, creating separations and hierarchies between and among discrete objects. This could be because of the way computer programming/system design disciplines have been institutionalized as an engineering or scientific field, rather than, for example, a creative arts field, which it most certainly can be.

Gilles Deleuze (1993), in his investigation of creative trends in "nomad art," offers thoughts to use to reflect upon programming as a language, as an art form, and as a place. He remarks that one must be immersed in the material of creativity at hand, and here—that is code. Then the creative practitioner must collapse the visual aspect, or mere observation in favor of losing oneself into "the landscape" at close range. In an era that is characterized by the use of computers for a multitude of functions—one tool is used in disparate and variegated fields by a multitude of diverse users—the material or medium of everyday work and play is the computer. According to Deleuze, "The haptic function and close vision presuppose the smooth, which has no background, plane, or contour, but rather changes in direction and local linkages between parts" (1993, 169). Here, not only does Deleuze's description echo those of the Internet's structure, but it also recognizes the idea of the interface: the necessary haptic function, providing for close vision. To imagine this nomad art with a computer means losing oneself to the inherent properties of code and the possibilities of code: another kind of interface, not graphic, somewhat linguistic, primarily metaphoric and structural. From the box to maps to networks to programming, the metaphors and structures that come along with such designs must be continually sampled and shaped since they have the power to effect, systemically, mundane computer artifacts. New metaphors will arise—and they will be most interesting, and most socially relevant, from an infusion of new thinking and new authors among computer system and programming design. This means recognizing the importance of code and the structures of computational and algorithmic thinking, paying attention to the things that pass between organisms and systems, and creating new maps, structures, and computing paradigms along the way.

Work Cited

Baran, Paul. 1964. "On Distributed Communications." RAND Corporation. http://www .rand.org/publications/RM/RM3420/RM3420.chapter1.html (accessed April 15, 2004).

Baudrillard, Jean. 1994. *The Illusion of the End.* Stanford, CA: Stanford University Press.

Bush, Vannevar. 1945. "As We May Think. *The Atlantic Monthly* 176, no. 1 (July): 101–108.

Deleuze, Gilles. 1993. *The Deleuze Reader.* Trans. Constantine V. Boundas. New York: Columbia University Press.

Foucault, Michael. 1980. *Power/Knowledge.* New York: Pantheon.

Greenwald, A. G., and M. R. Banaji. 1975. "Implicit Social Cognition: Attitudes, Self-esteem and Cognition." *Psychological Review* 102: 4–27.

Kuhn, Thomas S. [1962] 1996. *The Structure of Scientific Revolutions.* Chicago: University of Chicago Press.

Marvin, Carolyn. 1990. *When Old Technologies Were New.* New York: Oxford University Press.

National Science Foundation. 2000. "Women, Minorities and Persons with Disabilities in Science and Engineering: 2000." http://www.nsf.gov/sbe/srs/nsf00327/access/exec.htm (accessed April 2004).

Norman, Donald. 2002. *The Design of Everyday Things.* New York: Basic Books.

Phelps, E. A. 2001. "Faces and Races in the Brain." *Nature Neuroscience* 4: 775–776.

Phelps, E. A., K. J. O'Connor, W. A. Cunningham, E. S. Funayama, J. C. Gatenby, J. C. Gore, and M. R. Banaji. 2000. "Performance on Indirect Measures of Race Evaluation Predicts Amygdala Activation." *Cognitive Neuroscience* 12(5): 729–738.

Raskin, Jef. 2000. *The Humane Interface: New Directions for Designing Interactive Systems.* Reading, MA: Addison-Wesley.

U.S. Department of Commerce, Economics and Statistics Administration. 2001. "A Nation Online: How Americans are Expanding Their Use of the Internet." http://www.esa .doc.gov/anationchart.cfm (accessed November 10, 2003).

Wilder, Raymond L. 1981. *Mathematics as a Cultural System.* New York: Pergamon Press.

16

PERFORMING BLACKNESS: VIRTUAL SPORTS AND
BECOMING THE OTHER IN AN ERA OF WHITE SUPREMACY

David J. Leonard

> At 20, Jeremy Deberry surely is the best football player at Central Piedmont Com-
> munity College in Charlotte, N.C. He practices six days a week, plays both ways
> and is generally regarded by his peers as among the nation's elite performers, hav-
> ing earned the moniker the Champ. Few address the sophomore as anything but.
>
> —*Sports Illustrated*

These accolades were not directed at a high school all-American or even a finalist for
the John Wodden Award, but a video game player. Jeremy Deberry is one of many tal-
ented virtual athletes, cashing in on hand-eye success with fame and fortune. Donning
jerseys, talking trash, and working from excessive levels of testosterone, these virtual
sporting competitions are a ripe source of critical inquiry. Whether examining the performativity of masculinity, heterosexuality, or whiteness, these emerging public competitions replicate the ideologies and nature of nineteenth-century minstrelsy. The
resemblance to minstrelsy transcends the fact that white cyber athletes primarily com-
pete, but with the ideologies, images, and power that define this high-tech form of
blackface.

The sports gaming industry is the crown jewel of the video game world. It is a $1
billion-per-year industry; sports games account for more than 30 percent of all video
game sales. While *Tony Hawk* and other extreme sports games, all of which deploy race
(whiteness) in particular ways, are growing increasingly popular, the most popular
games remain those sports games dominated by black athletes (football and basketball).
Since 1989, over 19 million units of John Madden football have been sold. In 2002 alone,
EA Sports sold 4.5 million units (Ratliff 2003, 96). "Today's gaming resides squarely
in mainstream America, and for them fantasy means Tigers and Kobes" (Ratliff 2003,
96). As such, sports games represent a genre in which characters of color exist as actors

(protagonists) rather than victims or aesthetic scenery. Eight out of ten black male video game characters are sports competitors; black males thus predominantly find visibility in sports games. More specifically, while numerically dominant within virtual basketball and football games, as reflective of the demographics of these respective sports, the centering of black male bodies within golf, tennis, and even soccer games (*FIFA Street*) plays to the popularity of contemporary African American sports starts, demonstrating how virtual sports games deploy virtual images of back athletes.

As in larger society, the video game industry confines (and controls through image and ideology) black men to the virtual sports world, limiting the visual range of representation and depth of imagery. It is our task to examine briefly the range of images, in terms of both individual and communal representations, demonstrating the ideological and representational connections among stereotypes, minstrelsy, the virtual sporting world, and our own playgrounds.

Odd Absences

Despite the huge popularity of video games, little work has been done on their appeal and effect. Many academics still tend to view video games as toys for kids, rather than as sophisticated vehicles inhabiting and disseminating racial, gender, or national meaning. Moreover, a socially conservative agenda that focuses on the psychological links between games and violence further limits academic inquiries into video games.

This chapter seeks to underscore the centrality of race to the construction and reception of video games, emphasizing how games create, inhabit, transform, and challenge commonly received ideas about race, gender, and sexuality. In examining several platform games, including *NFL Street* and *NBA Street*, I argue that it is impossible to appreciate the significance of sports video games without considering racial images, identities, and ideologies. Race matters in the construction and deployment of stereotypes, and it matters in legitimizing widely accepted racial cues and assumptions both in the workplace and in leisure pursuits. It matters in their popularity, given the histories of minstrelsy and appropriation, and the allure of virtual spaces defined by the presence of black bodies and aesthetics. In short, race matters in sports video games because many of them affirm the status quo, giving consent to racial inequality and the unequal distribution of resources and privileges.

Present conversations about video games are largely uncritical celebrations. Jenkins encapsulates the celebratory side of the emerging field of game studies through his deployment of historically racialized and problematic language: "Now that we've colonized physical space, the need to have new frontiers is deeply in the games. *Grand Theft Auto* expands the universe" (qtd. in Kushner 2002, 64). However, the ubiquitous praise for games, which often borrows the language of glorious expeditions of past, inadvertently reveals the centrality of race within both video games as text and the surrounding discourse of reception. As with America's history of colonization, imperialism, and exploration, the deployment of racialized images, the enactment of pleasure through technologies that create the other (whether through signifiers of skin color or aesthetic markers of difference), and the efforts to legitimize power/privilege are present in many video games.

Academic discourse about video games has, for the most part, concentrated on the following issues: technological improvements within the industry and the expansive economic opportunities within virtual reality (e.g., Berger 2000; Takahashi 2002; Kushner 2002); the power and centrality of fantasy (e.g., Jenkins n.d; Jones 2003; Turkle [1984] 2003); the effects of violence on children (e.g., Jenkins n.d.); the impact of video games on learning and children (Gee 2003); the degree to which games affect children's attitudes toward violence, hand-eye coordination development, childhood obesity, and gender identity (e.g., Marriott 1999; Ratliff 2003); the deployment or construction of time and space (Turkle [1984] 2003); the gender politics and presence of female-based stereotypes (e.g., Berger 2000; Jenkins 1998); and the ideology of games (e.g., Gee 2003). Race and power are strangely absent from these analyses of video games.[1] The work of Gee is especially problematic in this regard, since he believes that games teach children and teenagers thirty-six core learning principles. Yet he makes no mention of how games perpetuate stereotypes, induce racialized fantasies, and affirm racial inequalities. He and others ignore the racial history of minstrelsy, which we cannot ignore, given its foundation to understanding the context of production, reception, and consumption of sports video games.

Revealing Numbers

The work of Children Now, a community-based organization in Oakland, California, quantifies the overwhelming presence of stereotypes in video games. According to its data, 64 percent of characters are male, 19 percent are nonhuman, and only 17 percent are female. More specifically, 73 percent of player-controlled characters are males, with less than 15 percent female, of which 50 percent are props or bystanders (Children Now 2001, 13–14). The problems here transcend erasure and a lack of representation. Female characters, especially females of color, serve as sexual eye candy. Ten percent of female characters have large breasts and a small waist, with an equal number having disproportionate body types. Twenty percent of female characters expose their breasts, with more than 10 percent revealing their buttocks (Children Now 2001, 14). Latino, Asian/Pacific Islander, and Native American characters are virtually absent.

David J. Leonard

Just as video games are a space about and for males, they are equally a white-centered space. Over 50 percent of player-controlled characters are white males; less than 40 percent of game characters are black, the majority of whom are depicted as athletic competitors. More than 90 percent of African American women function as props, bystanders, or victims. In fact, 90 percent of African American females were victims of violence compared to 45 percent of white women (Children Now 2001, 20–23). Yet virtual reality, whether in its imagination of the blacktop, a football stadium, or inner-city Los Angeles, is about much more than stereotypes and game inscriptions of stock representations, but rather the connections between games and the traditions of white supremacy amid claims of colorblindness.

High-tech Blackface

During the celebratory boom of the video game craze, all was not well given the racial implications of games and the virtual silence about racism within the industry. Adam Clayton Powell III, director of the Integrated Media Systems Center, (a U.S. Engineering Research Center for multimedia, at the USC Viterbi School of Engineering) however, saw a problem, becoming one of the first commentators to not just question the deployment of racial stereotypes through video games, but to describe virtual reality as little more than a modern-day minstrel show. Specifically, he referred to video games as "high-tech blackface," arguing that "because the players become involved in the action . . . they become more aware of the moves that are programmed into the game" (Marriott 1999, 61). More specifically, he argued that video games dangerously allow or facilitate white fantasies of donning blackface in the absence of the makeup, utilizing technology to alter the perception of skin color without accepting or recognizing the burdens of race and racism. With this in mind, this chapter explores how sports games reflect a history of minstrelsy, providing its primarily white creators and players the opportunity to become black (Costikyan 1999). In doing so, these games elicit pleasure, playing on white fantasies as they simultaneously affirm white privilege through virtual play.

According to historian Eric Lott, minstrelsy was a "manifestation of the particular desire to try on the accents of 'blackness' and demonstrates the permeability of the color line" (qtd. in Rogin 1998, 34–35). He writes that blackface "facilitate[s] safely an exchange of energies between two otherwise rigidly bounded and policed cultures" (34–25). Like minstrelsy, video games may be "less a sign of absolute power and control than of panic, anxiety, terror, and pleasure" (35). Video games break down these same fixed boundaries with ease, given their virtual realism, allowing its participants to try on the other, the taboo, the dangerous, the forbidden, and the otherwise unacceptable (35). Although difficult to prove given the limited amount of research regarding virtual racial performativity, and the hegemony of colorblind discourses, the textual utterances of these games and their historic context demonstrate the power that virtual reality exhibits in providing "individuals or groups" the means to "appropriate this complex and nuanced racial signifier in order to circumscribe its boundaries or to exclude other individuals or groups" (A. Johnson 2001, 3). Claims of entertainment and fantasy nonetheless, sports and urban-centered video games that facilitate the movement of white bodies into virtual spaces traditionally imagined as bound by blackness are political at their core. It is clear to Johnson that "When blackness is appropriated to the exclusion of others, identity becomes political" (E. P. Johnson 2003, 3).

A Return to Minstrelsy: Sports in Its Purest Form

Imitation, in both the real and virtual worlds, is not the highest form of flattery. Norman Mailer (1967), in his often-cited 1957 piece entitled "The White Negro," asserts, "It is no accident that the source of hip is the Negro for he has been living on the margin between totalitarianism and democracy for two centuries." Video games reflect this cultural reality, bespeaking black coolness through its ubiquitous articulations of white supremacist ideologies, grounded in a belief of black savagery and animalism (athleticism). These powerful ideologies emanate through these games and reflect their connection to minstrelsy. Elijah Anderson, a professor of sociology at University of Pennsylvania, argues that an abundance of racial stereotypes reflects long-standing fascination with blackness as mysterious and cool, while simultaneously playing to deep-seeded desires and needs of white game enthusiasts: "Blacks have always been the other in this country. Many people living in the suburbs admire this fire and this funk they see in blacks, a kind of aggressiveness a lot of them want too. A lot of these suburban, white-bread kids hunger for this kind of experience" (qtd. in Marriott 1999, 61). As with the history of minstrelsy, sampling of the other is neither liberatory nor transgressive—it does not unsettle dominant notions by breaking down barriers or increasing exposure. Instead, it, like much of today's popular culture, reduces race or skin color to a commodity, one that can be bought, sold, and exchanged regardless of skin color—those who have the right clothes, the correct tilt in their hat, the proper gait (walk), the appropriate language, and the overall look can be black regardless of social location (i.e., whiteness). Video games takes this to the next level, facilitating play beyond the "wigger" (white nigger) phenomenon as technology allows one to transcend the supposedly arbitrary limitations of one's skin color. In this context, the ideas of blackness introduced through video games reflect dominant ideologies, thereby providing sanction for the status quo, legitimacy for white supremacy, and evidence for the commonsense ideas of race, gender, sexuality, and nation.

Sports games represent a site at which white hatred and disdain for blackness and its love and adoration for blackness is revealed through popular culture. Video games reflect, borrowing from Eric Lott's work on minstrelsy, "the dialectical flickering of racial insult and racial envy, moments of domination and moments of liberation, counterfeit and currency" (1993, 18). White supremacist discourses and practices are not limited to the demonization of black bodies, or calls for administrative regulation, but simultaneous efforts to fetishize and seek pleasure from these same black bodies. Imani Perry, in *Prophets of the Hood*, identifies popular culture not exclusively as a site of stereotypical representations, but as space where "the love of black culture with the simultaneous suspicion and punishment of black bodies is not unusual" (2005, 28). Herman Gray finds a similar practice within a spectrum of institutions, from the government to the entertainment industry, concluding that "representation of the black social body, like that of the black physical body, is the object of administrative management, legal regulation, social control and even cultural fascination by the state, the news media and the entertainment industry" (2005, 21). More than this, representations, images, discourses, and overall hegemony "rely on the production of the black body as the site of pleasure, of adoration, fear and menace" (21). In other words, these games reveal white supremacy in the form of both contempt and desire. The contempt materializes in different ways, but in reflecting an oppositional binary, sports games legitimize stereotypical ideas about black athletic superiority and white intellectual abilities. The adoration materializes in the approval and value we offer black athletes, whether through financial rewards, posters on our walls, or imitation.

It is within this discursive context that this chapter conceptualizes the textual encoding of games as well as the basis of their widespread popularity. Video games fulfill our desire to not only emulate Allen Iverson's killer crossover, Shaq's thunderous dunks, Barry Bonds's homerun swing, or Barry Sanders's spins, but allow players to virtually occupy black male bodies. It provides the means to experience these supposedly unattainable skills, while deriving pleasure through black male bodies. The desire to "be black" because of the stereotypical visions of strength, athleticism, power, and sexual potency all play out within the virtual reality of sports games. bell hooks explains the widespread process of "eating the other," evident in the popularity of sports video games as spaces of commodification and appropriation of blackness, as being the result of white yearning to experience something "more exciting, more intense, and more threatening. The lure is the combination of pleasure and danger" (1992, 26). Hence, the popularity of sports games, whether real-life simulators or street fantasies, and those with a ghettocentric imagination, embodies the racialized yearning for pleasure and danger derived from commodifying and eating the black other. As hooks argues, "Black youth culture comes to stand for the outer limits of 'outness.' The commercial nexus exploits the culture's desire (expressed by whites and blacks) to inscribe blackness as 'primitive' sign, as wildness, and with it the suggestion that black people have secret access to intense pleasure, particularly pleasures of the body . . . It is the young black male body that is seen as epitomizing the promise of wildness, of unlimited physical prowess, and unbridled eroticism" (1992, 34). To fully comprehend the allure of sports video games as well as their textual inscriptions—whether it be the emphasis on the physicality of black virtual athletes, the ability of game players to construct their own black male bodies through designing (building) their own character, from size of muscles to types of tattoos, or the ways games imagine black athletes as embodying the outer limits of the sports world because of their bling, connection to the streets, or a hip-hop approach to the game—we must focus our attention on the performative power of a technology that allows for and encourages the appropriation of blackness (E. P. Johnson 2003, 3–4). Video games, like hip-hop or a Malcolm X hat, provide this opportunity, facilitating a process of racial crossdressing in which a primarily white game-playing population "samples" the other, experiencing an imagined coolness associated with America's vision of blackness. The popularity of video games and sports games is neither inconsequential nor reflective of the entertainment value of sports genre; there is far more at work here given the histories of minstrelsy, appropriation, commodification of the other, and their connection to projects of white supremacy. In writing about white appropriation of hip-hop, Bill Yousman argues:

White youth adoption of black cultural forms in the 21st century is also a performance, one that allows Whites to contain their fears and animosities towards Blacks through rituals not of ridicule, as in previous eras, but of adoration. Thus, although the motives behind their performance may initially appear to be different, the act is still a manifestation of white supremacy, albeit a white supremacy that is in crisis and disarray, rife with confusion and contradiction. (qtd. in Kitwana 2005, 103)

To him and others, such practices facilitate the perpetuation of racism rather than usher in a new vision of racial politics defined by colorblindness (Kitwana 2005; Wynter 2002). With this in mind, we turn our attention to sports games themselves so as to get a better handle on deployments of racial signifiers as well as the larger context of meaning.

The Virtual Black Athletic Body

It becomes quite clear through these games that blacks dominate America's major sports and do so because of genetics. Whereas in the first wave of sports games, where skin color was the only means of distinction for players (all players looked the same except for the alteration in the programmer's code for skin color), recent games mark difference through hair styles, clothing, and other markers of hip-hop culture using detailed, textured graphics. In some games, players are able to create their own virtual athletes, in which they get to select body type, hair style, and color. While at a certain level the darkening of a player's skin makes clear his racial identity, athleticism, body type, and connection to hip-hop identity become even more important racial signifiers than skin color itself.

Within a vast majority of virtual sports games, the emphasis is on black male bodies, whether physicality and muscularity, or pure athleticism. The cover of *NFL Street* embodies the racial text of sports video games. A muscle-bound Ricky Williams, who bulges out of the box, is breaking free from a tackle of Shannon Sharpe. While the emphasis on their muscles (ten times their life size) and tattoos plays to authentic visions of blackness, the depiction of each man as a virtual gorilla situates this game within the larger project of black minstrelsy.

Beyond deployment of stereotypical images, black virtual athletes invariably reflect dominant visions of blackness as it relates to athleticism. Whereas the dominant media—in both their real-life and virtual formations—imagine white athletic success through descriptors of hard work, dedication, and intelligence, they simultaneously construct the mastery and athletic brilliance of black athletes as a result of God-given/genetic talents (King and Springwood 2001). Those discursive articulations that reduce black male bodies to physically powerful bodies, which are visible within both the virtual and the real worlds, ultimately construct black athletes as genetically superior, legitimizing both the fears and fantasies of the dominant white order.

Jumping as high as the sun, knocking their competitors through concrete walls, and making unfathomable moves on the court, players discover their "innate" black athleticism and their superhuman strength, endurance, speed, and jumping ability. The few white players who do appear in *NBA Street, NFL Street,* and several other games have nowhere near the athleticism or the muscles of the black players. The white players' dominance comes from their ability to shoot, which comes from hard work and long hours on the court, not good genes.

The genre of sports games represents a site of pleasure in which game players secure happiness through virtually occupying black bodies. King and Springwood argue that the "black athlete has been constructed as a site of pleasure, dominance, fantasy, and surveillance" (2001, 101). While writing about other media forms, they further argue, "African Americans have been essentially invented, policed and literally (re)colonized through Euro-American ideas such as discipline, deviance and desire" (101). Just as in the world of sports, and its surrounding discourse, sports games indulge white pleasures as they affirm stereotypical visions of black bodies, as physical, aggressive, and violent, while simultaneously minimizing the importance of intellectualism and hard work in understanding the supposed dominance of black athletes.

A majority of sports games, from those based in real life to the extreme fantasy, depict black males as physically and verbally aggressive and as having unusual body types. Black men are excessively muscular and hyper-masculine, crushing bodies with sheer force. Black players tend to talk trash and engage in other forms verbal assault with greater frequency as well. Indeed, over 80 percent of black characters appear as competitors in sports-oriented games. In addition, African American characters are more likely to display aggressive behaviors in sports games (i.e., trash-talking and pushing) than whites (Children Now 2001, 23). The commodification of hip-hop/street games has further led to the exaggeration of these blatant racialized stereotypes and tropes.

Given the dominance of black men within virtual sporting events, there lies a necessity of control and surveillance. The performativity of sports video games and their popularity, in fact, reflect a desire to reclaim and control the world of sports, sanctioning, and ultimately controlling, black bodies. As blacks supposedly control sports in the real world, video games allow white players not only to become the other, but to discipline and punish. While there are a number of potential examples of this disciplinarity, I want to briefly discuss *NFL Street*.

While encouraging taunting, through bonus points and rewards (as noted by the directions for *NFL Street*, "stylin is what separates the players from the Playaz"), the game seems to police this practice as well. As you showboat, you run the risk of fumbling or otherwise stumbling in the game—there are consequences for "playing street." After several attempts to defeat the mighty 49ers, I had them on the ropes, leading 32-24 (on the street, you play to 36) with ball in hand. All I needed was a touchdown. With a tinge of nervousness, I launched a pass across the field, completing it through a sea of defenders. As my man marched toward the Promised Land, I decided to hold the ball back over my head as if to rub my imminent victory into my imagined opponent's head. Unfortunately, I started my victory stride a bit early, coughing up the ball right into the hands of Terrell Owens, who ran it back for a touchdown. I, of course, went on to lose the game. As I slammed down my controller, resembling the behavior of many of my students during their epic video game battles, I could hear Chick Hearn[2] screaming "the mustard is off the hot dog" or the voice of any number of announcers that habitually condemn and demonize (black) athletes for excessive celebration. *NFL Street*, like the NFL Rules Committee, and the NBA with its ban on baggy shorts, visible trash talking and hangin' on the rim, polices those actions see outside the spirit of the game. According to King and Springwood:

Euro-American understandings of African Americans being excessive and transgressive have always fostered, if not demanded, disciplinarity, the application of regimes of control, regulation, and management: the bondage, beatings, surveillance, and dehumanization of slavery; and later, the lynchings, terror, spatial constraints, and segregation of Jim Crow. Although much kinder and gentler veiled as in the rhetoric of opportunity, equality, and education, intercollegiate athletic spectacles construe African Americans as deviants in need of refinement, correction, training and supervision. (2001, 197)

As noted by John Fiske, hegemony works "to control the leisure and pleasures of the subordinate" (1989, 70) through the "construction and enforcement of repressive legislation" and, for Tucker, the "'taming' of uncontrolled leisure pursuits into 'respectable' and discipline forms" (2003, 311). Given the panic induced by the increasing visibility of hip-hop (tattoos, bling-bling, cornrows, long shorts), ghetto virtual fantasies, and "the fusion of black athletes, rappers, and criminals into a single menacing figure who disgusts and offends many blacks as well as whites" (Hoberman 1997, xix) amid a constantly growing prison system, well-received calls for law and order, and widespread racial panics, the power of virtual inscriptions of disciplinarity and the pleasure players receive from acting as both black athletes and their masters (i.e., sources of discipline and control) are striking. Each embodies "a management spectacle that continually redefines the potentially unruly and unproductive Black body as the problem that it perpetually solves" (Hughes 2004, 179). Illustrating Toby Miller and Alec McHoul's notion of how "sports leaks into everyday life" (1998, 83), game players and the game themselves, while simultaneously commodifying practices of hip-hop, reinforce notions of disciplinarity and punishment, mimicking those found within NBA management, in the form of restrictions on trash-talking, short length, headwear during interviews, color of socks and age of players. The prison industrial complex, metal detectors in schools, and efforts to try 11-year-olds as felons all serve the same racist order by "protecting them [whiteness; the middle-class; U.S. corporate hegemony] from the street, from the chaos, from unregulated decision making by the unwashed and the lowly" through rules and play (83). Games reveal the consequences of becoming street, compelling obedience to the hegemonic vision of sportsmanship and etiquette.

NFL Street thus embodies America's simultaneous love/hate relationship with black urbanness, reflecting dominant desires to both police and become the other.

Virtual Playing Fields

The most popular genre within the sports game is the street basketball game, as evident in *NBA Street*, *Street Hoops*, and *NFL Street*. The problematic nature of these games transcends their acceptance and promotion of stereotypes that emphasize the athletic power of black bodies. The ubiquitous focus on street basketball, and the glorification of deindustrialized spaces of poverty, contributes to commonsense ideas of inner-city communities and the constancy of play with the black community. For example, *NFL Street* takes traditional football gaming into both the streets and the realm of hip-hop. As you start against the NFC and AFC West, the initial street battles take place on the EA Sports campus, a pristine field with a few trash cans littered about and a brick wall for out-of-bounds; then on the beaches of the Pacific Ocean, with waves proving to be the only obstacles to a touchdown. Upon defeat of all eight teams, you are able to unlock the other conferences, battling on the dangerous streets of Detroit or New York rooftops. Interesting, and not surprisingly given its namesake, the goal of the game is to be able to play on the streets, within America's ghettos, rather than on a sports field.

The popularity of the game has less to do with its game playability, but with its emphasis on an imagined street (black) culture. Whether through the never-ending hip-hop soundtrack or the numerous shots of graffiti art, the game plays America's love affair with urban America, particularly that which is imagined as black. Because games glamorize inner-city spaces, commodifying them as seedy and dangerous places, structural shifts continue to worsen these spaces in physical reality. Reflecting the hyper-visibility and glorification of the "deindustrialized" inner-city community, games like *NFL Street* and *Street Hoops* reflect the commodification of African American practices of play within popular culture. This process of borrowing is not limited to the generation of pleasure for players, but is evident in the usefulness of black bodies and ghettos within *NFL Street*. The commodification of black urban aesthetics, in the form of trash-talking, taunting, showboating, tattoos, earrings, violence and all things hip-hop represents a powerful racial project.

Ghetto Fabulous

Popular images of street basketball, whether in shoe commercials, on ESPN, or in video games have become increasingly popular in recent years. Within the world of sports video games, *NBA Street* and *Street Hoops* are two typical examples of this representational explosion. The problematic nature of these games transcends their acceptance and promotion of stereotypes that emphasize the athletic power of black bodies. The ubiquitous focus on street basketball, as well as the glorification of deindustrialized spaces of poverty, contributes to commonsense ideas of inner-city communities and the constancy of play with the black community. Writing about shoe commercials, Kelley asserts that popular images of street basketball "romanticize the crumbling urban spaces in which African American youth play." Such "representations of 'street ball' are quite remarkable; marked by chain-link fences, concrete playgrounds, bent and rusted nettles hoops, graffiti-scrawled walls, and empty buildings, they have created a world where young black males do nothing but play" (Kelley 1997, 195–196). The process of commodification is not limited to the generation of pleasure for players, but is evident in the usefulness of black bodies and space to the video game industry. From the phenomenon of And-1 street tours to ESPN's street diaries, street basketball has become increasingly visible amid rising prison populations and increased levels of state violence experienced by communities of color.

Kelley warns us about the power of consuming the ghetto spaces in both an ideological and capitalist project: "While obscuring poverty, unemployment, racism, and rising police repression, commercial representations of the contemporary 'concrete jungles' powerfully underscore the link between urban decline, joblessness, and the erosion of recreational spaces" (1997, 196). In other words, those living outside these communities often refuse to engage so-called ghettos at a political, economic, or social level, but enjoy playing inside those spaces from the safety of their own home. Denying ghetto communities and its residents "dignity" and "respect," while reducing "signs of blackness" to that of the underclass, the commodification of hip-hop or a virtual-lived ghettocentric imagination evident in the popularity of street video games does not merely provide opportunities for the commodification of blackness and the exploitation of societal misery through increased profits for EA Sports, but serves the larger project of white supremacy (hooks 1994, 149, 168).

Dr. Dre, one of the "godfathers of rap," once noted: "People in the suburbs, they can't go to the ghetto so they like to hear what's goin' on. Everyone wants to be down" (qtd. in hooks 1994, 152). bell hooks, however, complicates this celebratory reconstitution of hip-hop, situating processes of commodification, fetishism, and the pimping of a corporate ghettocentric imagination, arguing that "the desire to be 'down' has promoted a conservative appropriation of specific aspects of underclass black life, who in reality is dehumanized via a process of commodification wherein no correlation is made between mainstream hedonistic consumerism and the reproduction of a social system that perpetuates and maintains an underclass" (1994, 152). The ideological trope of limiting discussions of ghetto communities to the play that transpires within such communities obfuscates the daily struggles and horrors endured in postindustrial America. The realities of police brutality, deindustrialization, the effects of globalization on job prospects, and the fact that most parents work three jobs just to make ends meet, are invisible as the dominant image of street basketball continues to pervade American discourses. The ubiquitous levels of poverty, the conditions that give rise to chain-link fences and net-less hoops are lost to the "virtual ghetto tourist." Not only is enjoyment garnered through this process, but these games serve an ideological/political function within contemporary America. Social problems are thus seen as the result of community or individual failures. The constant focus on inner-city play, in video games, on ESPN, and within popular culture, leaves the impression that rather than working, rectifying social problems, and improving the community's infrastructure, black males are too busy playing. Relying on long-standing notions of black laziness and athletic superiority, these games reinforce "sincere fictions"[3] about black males kickin' it in the hood, while simultaneously glamorizing and commodifying these spaces.

The exploitative relationship with the black community and the video game industry is significant within these urban sports games. Companies and players benefit from the consumption of inner-city communities, while poverty, unemployment, and police brutality run rampant. As more and more Americans "live in their" world, that world grows poor and poorer. The richest 10 percent of the population in the United States controls over one-half the nation's wealth; the richest 10 percent of this group controls nearly 85 percent of its wealth, including 90 percent of the cash and business assets, almost half the land, and almost of all its stocks and bonds (A. Johnson 2001, 45). The poorest 20 percent of the population, some 60 million people, are sharing less than one-half of 1 percent of the wealth; 60 percent of Americans share 25 percent of the national income (A. Johnson 2001, 45). By the late 1990s (the latest numbers available on poverty), 35.6 million Americans—40 percent of them children—lived in poverty (Parenti 1999, 329). Although blacks and Latinos account for only 25.2 percent of the U.S. population, they make up almost 50 percent of America's poor (Parenti 1999, 239). Further, one out of five kids is born into poverty in the United States, one out of two black and American Indian kids, and one out of three Latinos (James 1996, 11). While politicians and the news media lament the strength of the economy (by which they usually mean the financial speculations of those wealthy enough to play the stock market), rates of poverty, unemployment, the uninsured, incarceration, and family income have dipped in recent years, disproportionately affecting communities of color (James 1996; E. P. Johnson 2003; Parenti 1999). An alarming example of this scenario was Hurricane Katrina, a storm that devastated New Orleans and many settlements along the Gulf of

David J. Leonard

Mexico in 2005. Of the nearly 450,000 residents of New Orleans, of whom 70 percent were black, over 23 percent lived below the federal poverty level prior to the arrival of Katrina. Nearly 40 percent of the city's children under the age of eighteen lived below the poverty line, with many more hovering there by living "check to check" (Neal 2005). Despite its rampant poverty, high rates of unemployment, failing school system, murder rates eight times those of New York City, and hopeless future, New Orleans has also long been America's tourist playground. Amid the depravity and the suffering, tourists have long flocked to New Orleans to taste the outer limits of acceptability, to drink, have sex, and consume the other, whether through Cajun food or listening to jazz music (Neal 2005; Shields 2005). The popularity of a ghettocentric virtual reality and the pleasure derived from virtually transporting one's body from suburbia into the ghetto—or better yet, metaphorically and technologically altering one's skin color by becoming that gangsta or that street basketball player—mirrors the tourist industry in New Orleans, not only reflecting the practice of commodifying black poverty, but naturalizing it and erasing through play.

Under these worsening social conditions, the video game industry prospers, while at the same time directing attention away from the depravity and sadness of inner-city America toward the excitement and pleasure of street basketball. A critical literacy that bespeaks the power of sports video games, in their articulation of stereotypes and their affirmation of racialized stereotypes, is necessary. A willingness to engage games not purely as toys, but as vehicles of ideological meaning and cultural products affirming contemporary hegemony, is necessary in terms of understanding colorblind racism in the twenty-first century.

None of this detail is provided to argue a simple causal relationship, but rather to point out that the various commentaries concerning street or ghettocentric sports games erase how *NFL Street*, *NBA Ballers*, or others contribute to forming commonsense notions of race, criminality, and American race relations. Herman Gray writes,

So often media narratives presume and then fix in representation the purported natural affinity between black criminality and threats to the nation. By fixing the blame, legitimating the propriety of related moral panics, these representations (and the assumptions on which they are based) help form the discursive logic through which policy proscriptions for restoring order—more jails—are fashioned. The production of media representations of blackness (along with those of sexuality and immigration) as threatening the natural fabric and policy proscriptions for reimagining and consolidating a traditional vision of the American nation is challenged with alternative representations. (2005, 25)

In other words, these games do not directly inform children how to be, for example, violent—in fact, there is little scholarly evidence to substantiate such a claim—but, instead, encourages children to thwart violence, reifying notions of the other, while legitimizing policies of law and order, naturalizing state violence, and otherwise giving sanction to the cultural and actual demonization of communities of color.

Conclusion

It has become commonplace in the world of sports to blur reality with the virtual through the deployment of video games. Whether on TNT's *NBA Tonight* or ESPN's *College Game Day*, the sports industry increasingly relies on video game technology as a tool of imagination and fantasy. Bypassing actual game footage, media outlets are now able to force Yao to battle Shaq, even if in real life one of them is injured, or see a pass play despite the coach's decision to run at the end of the game. Whether on ESPN.com or in other sports telecasts, the last five years have thus witnessed a merging of the virtual and the real within the sports world.

Beyond the fantasy desires or need for spectacles, sports video games increasingly serve as tools of prognostication. If you are curious about the outcome of a game or are planning to make wager, video games exist as a pedantic source of information. This was no truer than during the pre-game festivities for the 2004 Super Bowl: As the teams prepared in the locker room, the CBS pregame show provided viewers with a preview using virtual technology—EA Sports football. As if to further obfuscate the divide between virtual and real, their homage to video games allowed not just representations of game and players, but a virtual reincarnation of the announcers as well. Upon completion of the simulated scenarios that might present themselves after kickoff, the coverage fluidly shifted from the virtual conversations of Jim Nantz, Boomer Esaison, Dan Marino, and Deion Sanders to their actual (real) bodies, leaving *Primetime*'s Deion Sanders speechless. Without hesitation, Sanders lamented the absence of realism in their virtual treatment, exclaiming, "It looks nothing like me. It looks like something from *Planet of the Apes*." Pulling out his cell phone, Sanders continues telling his silent white peers, "I am calling Johnny Cochran to get this straightened out." As one researches sports video games, it is clear that the racialized representation of Deion Sanders reflects the guiding ideologies and image of the virtual sports world given the preponderance of gorilla-like images and jungle settings. The hegemony of whiteness as both the producer and the consumer of such games, as well as the long-standing pleasure/power generated through becoming the animalized black man or playing within dangerous black spaces, places sporting video games within the history of minstrelsy.

Notes

1. The limited amount of work regarding race and virtual reality has focused on cyber-space (see Kolko and Nakamura 2000), and to a lesser extent computer games as opposed to platform video games.
2. The legendary play-by-play announcer of the Los Angeles Lakers.
3. This term was initially introduced in *White Racism* (see Feagin and Vera 1995) to refer to white myths about race and communities of color within contemporary American culture.

Work Cited

Berger, Asa. 2000. *Video Games: A Popular Culture Phenomenon.* New York: Transaction Publishers, 2000.

Children Now. 2001. *Fair Play? Violence, Gender and Race in Video Games. (Research Report).* Oakland: Children Now. http://publications.childrennow.org/publications/media/fairplay_2001.cfm.

Costikyan, Greg. 1999. "Games Don't Kill People—Do They?" *Salon.Com.* http://www.salon.com/tech/feature/1999/06/21/game_violence/print.html (accessed July 8, 2003).

Feagin, Joe, and Hernan Vera. 1995. *White Racism: The Basics.* New York: Routledge.

Fiske, John. *Understanding Popular Culture.* New York: Routledge, 1989.

Gee, James Paul. 2003. *What Video Games Have to Teach Us about Learning and Literacy.* New York: Palgrave Macmillan.

Gray, Herman. 2005. *Cultural Moves: African Americans and the Politics of Representation.* Berkeley: University of California Press.

Hoberman, John. 1997. *Darwin's Athletes: How Sport Has Damaged Black America and Preserved the Myth of Race.* Boston: Houghton Mifflin.

hooks, bell. 1992. *Black Looks: Race and Representation.* Boston: South End Press.

hooks, bell. 1994. *Outlaw Culture: Resisting Representation.* New York: Routledge.

Hughes, Glyn. 2004. "Managing Black Guys: Representation, Corporate Culture, and the NBA." *Sociology of Sport Journal* 21: 163–184.

James, Joy. 1996. *Resisting State Violence: Radicalism, Gender, and Race in U.S. Culture.* Minneapolis: University of Minnesota Press.

Jenkins, Henry. 1998. "Voices from the Combat Zone: Game Grrlz Talk Back." In *Barbie to Mortal Kombat: Gender and Computer Games,* ed. Justine Cassell, and Henry Jenkins. Cambridge, MA: MIT Press. http://web.mit.edu/21fms/www/faculty/henry3/gamegrrlz.html (accessed July 8, 2003).

Jenkins, Henry. n.d. "Complete Freedom of Movement: Video Games as Gendered Play Spaces." http://web.mit.edu/21fms/www/faculty/henry3/pub/complete.html (accessed July 8, 2003).

Johnson, Allen. 2001. *Privilege, Power, and Difference.* New York: McGraw-Hill.

Johnson, E. Patrick. 2003. *Appropriating Blackness: Performance and the Politics of Authenticity*. Durham, NC: Duke University Press.

Jones, Gerald. 2003. *Killing Monsters: Why Children Need Fantasy, Super Heroes, and Make-believe Violence*. New York: Basic Books.

Kelley, Robin. 1997. "Playing for Keeps: Pleasure and Profit on the Postindustrial Playground." In *The House that Race Built*, ed. Waheema Lubiano, 195–231. New York: Vintage Books.

King, C. Richard, and Charles Fruehling Springwood. 2001. *Beyond the Cheers: Race as Spectacle in College Sport*. Albany: State University of New York Press.

Kitwana, Bakari. 2005. *Why White Kids Love Hip Hop: Wangstas, Wiggers, Wannabes, and the New Reality of Race in America*. New York: Basic Civic Books.

Kolko, Beth, and Linda Nakamura. 2000. *Race in Cyberspace*. New York: Routledge.

Kushner, David. 2002. "Grand Theft Auto Vice City." *Rolling Stone* (November 28): 61–64.

Kushner, David. 2003. *Masters of Doom: How Two Guys Created an Empire and Transformed Pop Culture*. New York: Random House.

Lott, Eric. 1993. *Love and Theft: Blackface Minstrelsy and the American Working Class*. New York: Oxford University Press.

Mailer, Norman. 1967. "The White Negro and the Negro White" *Phylon*. 28, no. 2: 168–177. http://web.mit.edu/gtmarx/www/whitenegro.html (accessed May 25, 2005).

Marriott, Michael. 1999. "Blood, Gore, Sex and Now: Race." *The New York Times*, October 21, G1.

Miller, Toby and Alec McHoul. 1998. *Popular Culture and Everyday Life*. London: Sage Publishers.

Neal, Mark Anthony. 2005. "Race-ing Katrina." *New Black Man*, September 6. http://newblackman.blogspot.com/2005/09/race-ing-katrina.html (accessed September 28, 2005).

Parenti, Christian. 1999. *Lockdown America: Police and Prisons in the Age of Crisis*. New York: Verso.

Perry, Imani. 2005. *Prophets of the Hood: Politics and Poetics in Hip-Hop*. Durham, NC: Duke University Press.

Ratliff, Evan 2003. "Sports Rule." *Wired* (January): 94–101.

Rogin, Michael. 1998. *Blackface, White Noise: Jewish Immigrants in the American Melting Pot*. Berkeley: University of California Press.

Shields, Elinor. 2005. "Hurricane Prompts Awkward Questions." *BBC News*, September 4. http://news.bbc.co.uk/2/hi/americas/4210648.stm (accessed September 28, 2005).

Sports Illustrated. 2003. *Sports Illustrated on Campus*, February 17.

Takahaski, Dean. 2002. *Opening the X-Box: Inside Microsoft's Plan to Unleash an Entertainment Revolution*. New York: Prima Publishing.

Tiburon (Electronic Arts). 2004. *NFL Street*. EA Sports, January.

Tucker, Linda. 2003. "Blackballed: Basketball and Representations of the Black Male Athlete." *American Behavioral Scientist* 47, no. 3 (November): 306–328.

Turkle, Shelly. [1984] 2003. "Video Games and Computer Holding Power." In *The New Media Reader*, ed. Noah Wardrip-Fruin and Nick Montfort, 449–514. Cambridge, MA:
MIT Press.

Wynter, Leon. 2002. *American Skin: Pop Culture, Big Business and the End of White America.*
New York: Crown Publishers.

17

MORPHOLOGIES: RACE AS A VISUAL TECHNOLOGY

Jennifer González

Truth Effects

As a recording device, the medium of photography has always been allied with truth claims: as evidence in courts of law, as the necessary supplement to historical narratives, as the existential proof for the passing of time, or as the unquestioned framework for what might be called the family romance. Historians and theorists have engaged critically with this "truth effect" of photography for over a century, assessing the cultural investment in the indexical quality of the image and the connotations of naturalism that it implies.[1] And nearly every generation of artists has found the interrogation or dismantling of this "truth effect" to be a primary means to engage the medium.

Yet with every new form of photographic image production, whether analog or digital, a cry goes out in the name of "truth" against subversive forms of manipulation or deception. This cry usually issues from those whose faith in documentary and journalistic image production has not yet been shaken, or from those who hold fast to a belief in the strategic deployment of visual evidence for the sake of larger political and historical concerns. As family snapshots, work-related information exchange, or artistic medium, the easily circulated, digitally produced image no longer has the aura of the new or—perhaps more importantly—the authentic. In this context of mass image production and exchange, questions of verisimilitude seem quaintly out of date. By the mid-1990s a number of anthologies and exhibition catalogs, notably *The Photographic Image in Digital Culture* (1995) and *Photography After Photography: Memory and Representation in the Digital Age* (1996), offered cogent analyses of the domain of digital photography and its cultural context. Scholars and artists agreed that digital photography is no less and no more susceptible to distortion than its analog counterpart. Similarly, many found that technological or material differences in the new medium do little to change the social effect and cultural function of "realist" images and their "truth effect."[2]

In the era of digital photography and digital art, a photograph is not only anything that *looks* like a photograph but anything that *acts* like a photograph insofar as it produces a photographic *effect*. Of course, as both historians and practitioners know, the truth effect of photography has real consequences—even when the image lies. Photography played and still plays a central role in the maintenance of a discourse of visibility and the norms it prescribes. This is its rhetorical power and its ideological advantage.[3]

When one considers the history of photography and the history of race discourse, it becomes apparent not only that these two histories are intimately interdependent, but also that a conceptual parallel exists between the "truth effects" of photography and what might be called the "truth effects" of race. Both kinds of truth effects naturalize ideological systems by making them visible and, apparently, self-evident. As with photography, the visual or visible elements of race function to produce truth effects that appear natural. Coco Fusco has argued persuasively that there is no visual truth about race. But it is also the case that concepts of race and ethnicity have historically been inseparable from a discourse of display and from the logic of vision. Skin color, hair color, and eye color become marking devices for those who seek to situate the genetic history of humans within the narrow confines of phenotype. Race has always been a profoundly visual rhetoric, evidence of which can be found in the complex vocabularies developed to delineate social hierarchies based on variations in skin color and phenotype over the last few centuries.

In the Americas, for example, sexual reproduction became the site at which the normative condition of hybridity and miscegenation gave rise to a powerfully hierarchical caste system subsequently codified in the arts. In New Spain (Mexico) of the eighteenth century, the tradition of *casta* paintings codified the visual effects of racial mixing by depicting racially distinct parents along with their *mestizo* children. Each painting is inscribed with the ethnic or racial makeup of the mother, the father, and the children; for example, "A Spanish father and an African mother produces a Mulatto child." The categories were elaborate and precise, including variations such as the *criollo, mestizo, castizo, mulato, morisco, coyote, lobo, zambo,* and *torna-atras,* among others.[4] Given the passion for scientific categorization during the Enlightenment and the colonial imperative for an artificial means of creating class structure, this elaborate codification is not surprising. Rendered in paint, it becomes a striking example of the deep desire to produce a parallel *visual* tabulation of racial hybridity and its physical characteristics. The very concept that a body possesses or reveals a *color* is indebted to the privileging of vision and its attendant systems of representation that measure and quantify the subtle differences of skin hue and tone. Of course, this desire to map the *visible* characteristics of race in a hierarchical taxonomy recurs in photography under the guise of eugenics and now reappears in the automated morphing technologies applied to digital images.

It becomes clear when looking at these and other historical precedents that race has long been an importantly *visual* system of power whose parameters have been the focus of every innovation in visual recording devices. As with photography, the visual truth effect of race has also played an important role, socially and culturally, as the necessary supplement to historical narratives, as existential evidence, or as the unquestioned framework for the family romance. And as with photography, the visual truth effect of race has very real consequences even if the "facts" about race as a category or discourse reveal it to be primarily an ideological construction.

The concept and lived experience of race are entwined in a discourse of *visibility* that enables subsequent forms of hierarchy or oppression to become naturalized, that enables membership in communities to be established, and that enables categorical distinctions to become reified. In *Against Race*, Paul Gilroy notes: "Cognition of 'race' was never an exclusively linguistic process and involved from its inception a distinctive visual and optical imaginary. The sheer plenitude of racialized images and icons communicates something about the forms of difference these discourses summoned into being."[5] Race, in all its historical complexity, is not an invention of visual culture but, among the ways in which race as a system of power is elaborated as both *evident* and *self-evident*, its visual articulation is one of the most significant.

This chapter examines the work of contemporary artists who explore the history and maintenance of the visual discourse of race through digital art practice—particularly but not exclusively digital photography.

Morphology

Despite—and perhaps because of—its historical links to eugenics and the delimiting of racial and criminal types, the composite photograph inherited from the experiments of Francis Galton in the nineteenth century has been the focus of exploration and transformation by contemporary artists working in the tradition of portraiture. Nancy Burson's composite photographs of the 1980s offered a new kind of visual typology by overlaying facial features of cinema stars or politicians to highlight their common traits, or by creating imaginary visual correlates to numerical statistics. Her 1984 image *Mankind* is a composite portrait of three faces weighted according to demographic information about a world population that was "57 percent Oriental, 7 percent Black, and 36 percent White."[6] Three "typical" faces are presented as an anonymous computational portrait of a single individual. Its collapsing of normally distinct racial categories was intended as an antiracist gesture, but Burson's effort nevertheless comes across as strangely anachronistic.

Jennifer González

In fact, the line between the critique of racial typologies and their reproduction is one that is difficult to draw in Burson's work. Her recent project, the *Human Race Machine* (2002), combines a sophisticated, viewing-booth apparatus with a "patented technology" that will transform the user's photographic image using one of four different algorithms: *Age Machine*, *Anomaly Machine*, *Couples Machine*, and *Human Race Machine*. One has the choice of aging one's face, adding disfigurations, combining one's face with another person's, or seeing oneself with the facial characteristics of six different races. Burson claims that the *Human Race Machine* is her "prayer for racial equality" and suggests "there is only one race, the human one." Presenting the argument that "there is no gene for race," the *Human Race Machine* allows the user to engage in what technology and culture scholar Lisa Nakamura might call identity tourism. Nakamura writes, "Identity tourism is a type of non-reflective relationship that actually widens the gap between the other and the one who only performs itself *as the other* in the medium of cyberspace."[7] Burson's machine takes a picture of the user and then digitally adjusts bone structure, skin tone, and eye shape in order to achieve a range of racially marked facial features. "The more we recognize ourselves in others," Burson writes, "the more we can connect to the human race." The artist also claims, "The *Human Race Machine* allows us to move beyond differences and arrive at sameness."[8] Despite her good intentions, I want to ask, who counts as "us"? Is sameness really where "we" want to arrive? Despite Burson's promise of greater human sameness, the *Human Race Machine* appears to offer satisfaction for a thinly veiled fantasy of *difference*. As a form of temporary racial tourism, Burson's machine may make the process of cross-racial identification appear plausible, but its artificiality does nothing to change how people live their lives or understand their historical condition.

The technology used by Burson is based on earlier experiments in digital morphing seen first by the mainstream public in Michael Jackson's music video *Black or White* (1991), where he sings:

It's a turf war on a global scale
I'd rather hear both sides of the tale
See, it's not about races
Just places
Faces
Where your blood comes from
Is where your space is
I've seen the bright get duller

I'm not going to spend my life being a color

. . .

I said if you're thinkin' of being my baby
It don't matter if you're black or white
I said if you're thinkin' of being my brother
It don't matter if you're black or white.

Throughout the video, Jackson's own face morphs in quick, smooth, and seamless succession into the faces of men and women of different "races." The uncanny visual transitions are both disturbing and fascinating. One face transforms into the next as if undergoing a physical metamorphosis in which skin and bone are stretched and molded, hair and eyes grow and change. Although each person and racial type appears distinct from the next, the video also suggests that a melding, mixing, or hybridization is taking place in real time—a transformation that appears to be entirely the result of the power of the image apparatus. As Peter Lunenfeld suggests, "As we move into the digital, the aesthetics of form become more and more involved in the aesthetics of mutable form."[9]

Morphing quickly became a popular graphical technique in digital image processing because of the seemingly magical way the computational remix of images provided the truth effect of a real photograph. Donna Haraway, writing about Morph 2.0 by Gryphon Software, designed for the personal computer, suggests: "This technology has proved irresistible in the United States for 1990's mass cultural, racialized kinship discourse on human unity and diversity."[10] The truth effect of photography not only visually demonstrated but also mechanically mimicked the truth effect of race through an automated process of digital genesis. In the fall of 1993 the canonical image of this renaissance emerged on the cover of *Time* magazine, for its special issue on "How immigrants are shaping the world's first multicultural society." "Take a good look at this woman," reads the text on the cover next to the face of a young woman. "She was created by a computer from a mix of several races. What you see is a remarkable preview of . . . The New Face of America." Responding to the image, Haraway writes, "In an odd computerized updating of the typological categories of the nineteenth and early twentieth centuries, the programmer who gave birth to SimEve and her many siblings generated the ideal racial synthesis, whose only possible existence is in the matrices of cyberspace."[11] Also serving as an ideological reprise of the *casta* paintings from New Spain nearly four centuries later, *Time* magazine's new technological hybrid apparently neutralizes the hierarchies of the past with an artificial, clinical birth in the present, implying that computation is the proper locus and mode of a new racial mixing. In this Pygmalion fantasy, Haraway argues, the microchip and the computer program displace the human being as the origin of life.[12]

Such creationist desires to reformulate the human body abound in digital photography, some celebratory and others explicitly critical. Aziz + Cucher's *Dystopia* series of portraits in which human heads are devoid of any expressive feature or orifice represents a loss of personal identity that occurs as a result of new forms of digital communication. The artists write: "With the erasure of the primary facial features—eyes, nose mouth, etc. —we intend to suggest an evolutionary change signifying the loss of individuality in the face of advancing technology and the progressive disappearance of face to face human interaction."[13] Looking like unformed creatures in a larval state, the portraits they construct are disturbingly blank yet remarkably individual. They elicit the uncanny, eerie sensation of seeing a body caught in the tragic limbo of genetic error. The unfinished subject, the underdeveloped social and sensory apparatus, signals the emptiness of the body as signifier in a world of digitally mediated communication.

Similarly disturbing are the works of Inez Van Lamsweerde, whose slick fashion portraits use digital graphics to unsettle expectations of both gender and age, addressing the sexual politics that makes us read bodies as desirable or untouchable. Smooth bodies without orifices, the hands, lips, and eyes of men, women, and children compiled into single portraits offer a dreamlike condensation of a forbidden unconscious imaginary. "Using the computer to quote plastic surgery," writes Collier Schorr, "Van Lamsweerde one-ups the practices of beautification, suggesting that our preoccupation with perfection brings us close to science fiction. She also mimics a male desire to mother by producing a race technologically rather than physically."[14] Schorr also implies that by working exclusively with "white" bodies, Van Lamsweerde reveals a white aesthetic that (oppressive or not) becomes a western European default for "flesh." She suggests that "despite their perfect dimensions, her figure's nudity is blank, spongy, their Philip Pearlstein Caucasian flesh humming like a human doomsday machine."[15]

Paul Pfeiffer's *Leviathan* references whiteness differently. In a digital c-print, the artist delineates the floorplan of a cathedral in a shimmering outline of pink plastic doll flesh sprouting shiny abundant waves of golden hair. As if rising from a sea or carpet of platinum tresses, this architecturally morphed close-up image of the heads of Mattel dolls looks like a wound or a scar branded on the skin.[16] A leviathan is a Biblical beast, a many-headed serpent that represents a mythical monster eventually slain by the sword of Job. Also the title of Thomas Hobbes's philosophical account of the state's rule over the ills of human nature, *Leviathan* in Pfeiffer's work seems to imply the dynamics of colonial and missionary culture that have ruled over others through ideological and racial domination. Originally exhibited in a solo show called "The Pure Products Go Crazy," Pfeiffer's *Leviathan* links Christianity to notions of extreme purity, whether moral or racial, that have finally reached a condition of corruption. Much of Pfeiffer's work engages the complex layers of human relations that are at the nexus of mass culture, race, and religious culture in the United States. His use of digital photography produces a shift in the materiality of the visual tropes of race, extending beyond the human body to include the history of architecture and other domains of social spectacle. By equating skin with architecture, Pfeiffer asks us to consider the kinds of "pattern language" produced in the historical relations among bodies, religion, and the mapping of space.

Color Balance

Technologies of visualization such as photography, film, and video have been mutually constitutive with conceptions of race. It is possible to observe this fact by tracing how technologies of image making have been invented and adapted to the purpose of better elaborating or accommodating racial discourses.[17] Racial hegemony informs the design and use of these technologies, and in turn racial discourse is articulated and defined by them. This feedback loop is rarely acknowledged in studies of the history of photography and other visual media despite the fact that visual recording devices have never been racially neutral. Artist François Bucher's recent digital video work *White Balance*, which ties the condition of racial privilege and the production of visual culture in mass media to the politics of global, economic domination, brilliantly illustrates this fact. His title derives from the process by which the digital pixels in the recording device are automatically balanced for the color white. Although the balance is based on the color spectrum, the notion of white balance in Bucher's work refers to white skin color as simultaneously a *cultural* and *technological* default in the United States. It is possible to see how the tradition of photography might be similarly "balanced." Even on a superficial level, the culture of photographic practice is understood to be shaped by the technical capabilities of the medium. New York Institute of Photography's "Tips for Better Photographers" claims, "There is probably no question in portraiture that is more confusing to beginning photographers than how to photograph people with black skin."[18] If black skin creates "confusion," it is because neither the original design of the apparatus nor common techniques for its use have taken blackness, or other non-white skin colors, as a standard.[19]

Skin, with all its registers of meaning for the history of race, has also become the focus of questions of color and code in digital art practice. Alba D'Urbano, an Italian artist, used digital imaging techniques available in 1995 to produce a life-sized photographic representation of her own body. Printed on a tailor's pattern, the resulting out-

Jennifer González

put was used to create a wearable suit of her own "skin." She writes, "The thought of being able to slip out of my own skin for a moment and offer it to another person gave rise to the idea of making a suit out of my own two-dimensional image. This suit would offer others the opportunity, as it were, of walking through the world hidden 'under the skin' of the artist."[20] Somewhat oblivious to the questions of race and passing that lay imbedded in her project, D'Urbano sought to address the idea of the body *as an image* reduced to a passive shell.[21] Digital photography acts in the service of a costume that "defines the contour of the image which forms on the retina of another person."[22] D'Urbano's project grasps the degree to which the subject is always *an image for an other*, as it tries to literally slip out of this skin—this image—and imagine it as little more than a costume for exchange.

In a very different kind of project that engages a parallel discourse, artist Keith Townsend Obadike, proposed to sell his "Blackness" on the commercial auction Web site eBay in August 2001. Although the work makes reference to the history of slavery when black bodies stood on public auction blocks, Obadike is careful not to equate his cultural Blackness (with a capital "B") with a black body, even if this referent is part of its etymology. By not including a photograph, Obadike thwarts the common expectation that objects for sale on eBay will be visible online—further underscoring the difference between the concept of Blackness and skin color. Using the actual eBay site, the artist described the object for sale, stating that this "heirloom has been in the possession of the Seller for twenty-eight years" and that it "may be used for creating black art, . . . writing critical essays or scholarship about other blacks, . . . dating a black person without fear of public scrutiny," and, among other rights, "securing the right to use the terms 'sista,' 'brotha,' or 'nigga' in reference to black people." Certain warnings also apply; for example, the seller does not recommend that this Blackness be used "during legal proceedings of any sort, . . . while making intellectual claims, . . . while voting in the United States or Florida," or "by whites looking for a wild weekend."[23] Obadike toys with the idea that Blackness is a commodity that can be bought and sold for the purpose of cultural passing, tapping into a long-standing fantasy in the history of race politics of crossing the "color line." But the artist also writes that "this Blackness may be used to augment the blackness of those already black, especially for purposes of playing 'blacker-than-thou.'" Structured around the perceived desires of others to occupy or "own" Blackness even if they are already black, Obadike's project brings out the hierarchies operative in cultural conceptions of racial identities while revealing the social inequities that always attend Blackness in the United States.

The playful sarcasm of Obadike's work raises the question of how race and color are bought and sold in the digital domain of the Internet. Prema Murthy's *Bindi Girl* is one

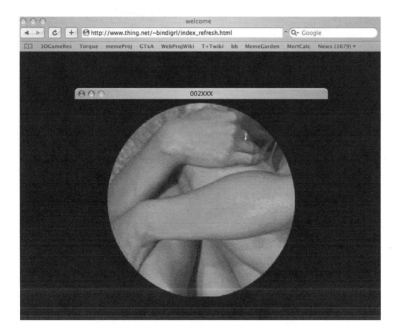

| Figure 17.1 |
Screen grab from Prema Murthy's *Bindi Girl* (1999)

example of a site that raises the question of how pornography operates as one of the more obvious forms of commodification of bodies that are based on fantasies of racial specificity or difference (figure 17.1). Using effectively censored images from an actual porn site, the artist leads the user through a series of links that simultaneously entice and thwart the user's potential desire for the body of a South Asian woman (figure 17.2). The love chat turns into a narrative farce of unsuccessful coitus, the souvenirs one can purchase are banal items like knee socks or bindi dots, and the live cam is inoperative.

The Bindi Girl says, "At first I thought technology would save me, arm me with my weapons. Then I turned to religion. But both have let me down. They continue to keep me confined to my 'proper' place."[24] The text on the *Bindi Girl* site implies that for the South Asian woman in a Hindu culture, this "proper" place is either as a goddess or whore, the limited range ascribed by a traditionally sexist cultural framework in the context of a booming, new high-tech economy. *Bindi Girl* is Murthy's recursive critique of the absurdity of this endless and apparently closed dialectic of positions. By taking up the common graphics and participatory tropes of porn sites, Murthy reiterates the form in order to play out the absurdity of its limits (figure 17.3).

Jennifer González

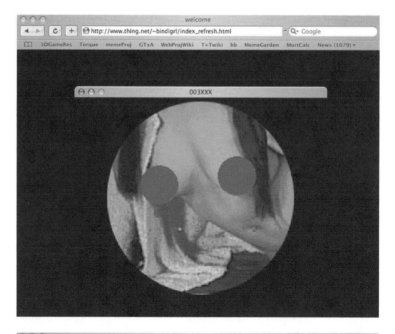

| Figure 17.2 |
Screen grab from Prema Murthy's *Bindi Girl* (1999)
| Figure 17.3 |
Screen grab from Prema Murthy's *Bindi Girl* (1999)

In another Web site parody, Tana Hargest's digital project *Bitter Nigger Broadcast Network* (2002) offers a humorous and scathingly critical take on the wages of racism in the contemporary United States. Presented in the graphically sophisticated language of high-end Web design, the BNBN spoofs both television broadcasting networks and corporate home pages that offer special products and services. Soft and seductive sound-tracks and glowing pastel logos lead the user through a series of items to purchase in the BN Pharmaceutical line or the BN Product Division, both "committed to alleviating the bothersome effects of racism." BN Pharmaceutical lists among its products Melin-derm, a Negro Teflon medicinal lotion, whose "soothing protection" and "gentle yet powerful shielding technology" bonds with the pigmentation of the skin, protecting the wearer from the damaging effects of racist remarks and behavior that subsequently slide right off. Tominex, designed for younger clients, helps them "achieve a level of com-placency normally reached after years of deferred dreams and smashed hopes—but without the bitterness." The user is informed by a pleasant voice that by suppressing feelings, Tominex effectively removes the yearning for fairness or human decency.

If medications don't do the trick, the Product Division recommends the Holo-Pal who, like a genie out of a bottle, can be made to materialize when the black user needs a white male friend to provide a legitimizing image during retail shopping, while at the bank, when purchasing a home, or even while developing an art career. The Holo-Pal be-comes a "passport image" that allows the user to avoid discrimination in encounters with others. Parodying the advertising language that accompanies many new electronic de-vices, Hargest touts the compatibility of the Holo-Pal with other daily planning technol-ogies such as PDAs, suggesting that the new holographic device can be programmed to anticipate the needs of the user. With its self-conscious title, the *Bitter Nigger Broadcast Network* disarms its users with humor while revealing the banality of systematic racism.

A similar critique of racial inequities that uses a parody of technophilia can be found in the work of Los Cybrids. A San Francisco–based artists group, Los Cybrids has produced installations, videos, and a number of public art projects, performances, and discussions that address the broader social effects of the new technology revolution. Re-sponding to the economic boom of Silicon Valley with satirical and ominous predic-tions, their work poses critical questions concerning the race and class distinctions that underlie the fantasy of a wired world. Making use of public billboard space, their *Digi-tal Mural Project* (2002) served as a public service announcement concerning the role of technology in globalization and in the working lives of Chicanos and Latinos in the Bay Area (figure 17.4).

Installed outside the Galleria de la Raza in the Mission District of San Francisco, the billboards offered dystopic visions of a future in which the rhetoric of inclusion—"Don't

| Figure 17.4 |
Los Cybrids' *Digital Mural Project* (2002)

be left behind; last one across the digital divide is a rotten egg"—is shown to be yet another colonizing gesture of capitalism. A different mural announces "El Webopticon: Systema de Vigilancia." The image depicts a young, Latino boy looking toward a future populated with computers, robots, and satellites. His innocent features are marred by a sinister bar code printed across his neck, and his face is framed as if part of a police file. Rather than a bridge to a brighter future, the Internet becomes the new panopticon keeping watch over racial minorities. The mural reads, "You don't have to be connected to be affected."[25]

Race as a Visual Technology

In her forthcoming essay "Race as Technology," artist Beth Coleman suggests that race can be understood as a levered mechanism or "a function machine that has already articulated the race-prosthesis algorithm that one inherited from the age of Enlightenment and the age of rational numbers. Race as technology adopts the role of technicity by using race as a tool."[26] Coleman's concept of race *as a technology* is compelling precisely because it allows the discourse to be conceived *as a series of techniques,* rather than as a framework of ontological conditions. From this perspective, race as a "levered mechanism" can be seen to operate across historical, social, and cultural practices that are geared to carry out operations following a systemic logic.

Some theorists have claimed that digital image production is materially different from traditional photography to the degree that it constitutes a formal avant-garde, a revolution in the concept of the image, a new realism for a new reality.[27] While such pronouncements are no doubt primarily rhetorical, they signal an interest in the idea that the human population is engaged in a major transition—a digital revolution—that is not merely ideological but also phenomenological or even ontological. Our bodies and psyches will become integrated, it is suggested, with systems of information and surveillance, microchips, and nanotechnologies. As genetic engineering turns to the computer for its model of analysis and production of experiments, it joins an effort to understand human beings in terms of the atomization that digital technology makes possible. The human body is no longer conceived primarily as a mechanical device with skin, muscles, and bones, but rather as a complex structure of codes that determine microprocesses invisible to the naked eye. Identity and identification become literally more than skin deep when one is defined by genetic code.

Paul Gilroy writes, "Today skin is no longer privileged as the threshold of either identity or particularity. There are good reasons to suppose that the line between inside and out now falls elsewhere. The boundaries of 'race' have moved across the threshold of the skin. They are cellular and molecular, not dermal. If 'race' is to endure, it will be in a new form, estranged from the scales respectively associated with political anatomy and epidermalization."[28] And yet Gilroy is also quick to point out that despite the fact that science as a discourse has changed the way race is conceived biologically, the brutal simplicity of racial typology still plays itself out in the most basic ways as public forms of violence.[29] For Gilroy, it is necessary to find a way to produce an antiracist discourse in *Against Race* that does not simultaneously perpetuate the reification of race as a legitimate human category.

Some of the art projects discussed here are explicitly critical of race categories, while others are engaged in antiracist politics that rely on the ongoing stability of such categories. In both kinds of projects it seems clear, despite Gilroy's suggestion that racial discourses based on the visual logic of color or "epidermalization" are no longer legitimate, that the concept of race and its truth effect are still ensnared in a visual nexus, in a racializing gaze that has been historically produced and is now effectively maintained by popular culture as well as the arts. Even if it is possible to imagine a future in which the "technology of race" is no longer an oppressive power of domination, it is also likely that visual difference will play itself out as a necessary supplement to other kinds of social dynamics. If, as Gilroy suggests, racial discourse was "summoned into being," at least in part, by the production of a specific image culture, then it is *in image culture* that it must be unraveled and undone. What is required is to recognize that race is, among other things, *a visual technology* consisting of a complex web of intertexual mechanisms tying the present to the past through new and familiar systems of representation. Artists such as those mentioned in this chapter explore this intertextuality to better situate the visual frameworks for race in a digital age, or to point to their social and political effects. At the same time, as image makers, the artists are in the process of producing the *next generation* of visual technologies of race. When looking at these and other contemporary works that engage race as a discourse, we should consider to what degree they continue its historical logic and enact its progressive transformation.

Notes

1. See, among others, Roland Barthes, "Rhetoric of the Image," in *Image/Music/Text* (New York: Hill and Wang, 1977).
2. For other discussions of the photographic image in digital culture, see *Digital Photography: Captured Images, Volatile Memory, New Montage* (San Francisco: SF Camerawork, 1988); *Impossible Presence: Surface and Screen in the Photogenic Era* (Chicago: University of Chicago Press, 2001); Geoffrey Batchen, *Each Wild Idea: Writing, Photography, History* (Cambridge, MA: MIT Press, 2001); Peter Lunenfeld, *Snap to Grid: A User's Guide to Digital Arts, Media, and Cultures* (Cambridge, MA: MIT Press, 2000).
3. Martha Rosler, "Image Simulations, Computer Manipulations: Some Considerations," in *Photography After Photography: Memory and Representation in the Digital Age*, ed. Siemens Kulturprogramm, Stefan Iglhaut, Florian Rotzer, Alexis Cassel, Nikolaus G. Schneider, and Hubertus V. Amelunxen (Amsterdam: G+B Arts, 1996), 36–56.
4. For an excellent discussion of *castas* paintings, see Maria Concepcion Garcia Saiz, *Las Castas Mexicanas: Un Género Pictórico Americano* (Italy: Olivetti, 1989).
5. Paul Gilroy, *Against Race* (Cambridge, MA: Harvard University Press, 2000), 35.
6. Vilém Flusser, "Nancy Burson: Chimaeras," in *Photography After Photography*, 152. See also Allan Sekula, "The Body and the Archive," in *The Contest of Meaning: Critical Histories of Photography* (Cambridge, MA: MIT Press, 1989).
7. Lisa Nakamura, *Cybertypes* (New York: Routledge, 2002), 57. Emphasis added.
8. http://www.wolfmanproductions.com/racemachine.html.
9. Lunenfeld, *Snap to Grid*, 65.
10. Donna Haraway, *Modest_Witness@Second_Millennium. FemaleMan_Meets_OncoMouse*™ (New York: Routledge, 1997), 261.
11. Ibid., p. 259.
12. Ibid., p. 261.
13. Aziz + Cucher, *Prospect: Photography in Contemporary Art* (Frankfurt: Editions Stemmle, 1996), 36.

14. Collier Schorr, "Openings," in *Photography After Photography*, 214.

15. Ibid.

16. Franklin Sirmans, "Get a Little Closer," *Artnet.com*, December 17, 1998.

17. Stephen Jay Gould, *The Mismeasure of Man* (New York: Norton, 1996); *Colonialist Photography: Imag(in)ing Race and Place* (London: Routledge, 2002), etc.

18. New York Institute of Photography, 2003, http://www.nyip.com/tips/topic_peopleof color0602.php.

19. Other amateur Web sites offer instruction for digitally transforming the "yellow" tones in photographic images of Asians so they will have a rosier glow. Carl Volk's "Color Balancing Skin Tones" (http://www.carlvolk.com/photoshop18.htm) reveals inherent racial bias when he writes, "In the photo of Christina above that beautiful China doll skin tone color may or may not be entirely *accurate* but the effect is very appealing—it looks (and feels) right." To change a skin color so that it "looks (and feels) right" begs the question of the cultural framework within which one can decide what a "right" skin color might be.

20. Alba D'Urbano, "The Project: Hautnah, or Close to the Skin," in *Photography After Photography*, 270.

21. Ibid.

22. Ibid., 271.

23. For a link to this page, see http://obadike.tripod.com/ebay.html and chapter 11.

24. Preema Murthy, *Bindi Girl*, http://www.thing.net/~bindigrl/.

25. See Los Cybrids, http://www.cybrids.com/artists.html.

26. Beth Coleman, "Race as Technology," forthcoming. Cited with the author's permission.

27. See Lev Manovich, *The Language of New Media* (Cambridge, MA: MIT Press, 2000).

28. Paul Gilroy, *Against Race* (Cambridge: Harvard University Press, 2000), 47.

29. Ibid., 51.

Index